WEBSTER'S
FAMILY
ENCYCLOPEDIA

W0009459

WEBSTER'S FAMILY ENCYCLOPEDIA

VOLUME 10

1995 Edition

This book is not published by the original publishers of **WEBSTER'S DICTIONARY**, or by their successors.

Exclusively distributed by
Archer Worldwide, Inc.
Great Neck, New York, USA

Copyright © 1981, 1983, 1986, 1987, 1988, 1989, 1990, 1991, 1992
1993, 1994 Market House Books Aylesbury

Worldwide distribution rights assigned to Archer Worldwide, Inc.
Great Neck, New York 11021

All rights reserved. No part of this publication may be reproduced
or transmitted, in any form or by any means, without permission.

Printed in the United States of America.

Abbreviations Used in Webster's Family Encyclopedia

AD	After Christ	ht	height	N.M.	New Mexico
Adm.	Admiral	i.e.	that is	NNE	north-northeast
Ala.	Alabama	in	inches	NNW	north-northwest
Apr	April	Ind.	Indiana	Nov	November
AR	Autonomous	Ill.	Illinois	NW	northwest
	Republic	Jan	January	N.Y.	New York
at no	atomic number	K	Kelvin	OAS	Organization of
at wt	atomic weight	Kans.	Kansas		American States
Aug	August	kg	kilograms	Oct	October
b.	born	km	kilometers	Okla.	Oklahoma
BC	Before Christ	kph	kilometers per	OPEC	Organization of
bp	boiling point		hour		Petroleum Ex-
C	Celsius, Centi-	kW	kilowatts		porting Countries
	grade	lb	pounds	Pa.	Pennsylvania
c.	circa	Lt.	Lieutenant	PLO	Palestine Libera-
Calif.	California	Lt. Gen.	Lieutenant		tion Organization
Capt.	Captain		General	Pres.	President
CIS	Commonwealth	m	meters	R.I.	Rhode Island
	of Independent	M. Sgt.	Master Sergeant	S	south, southern
	States	Mar	March	S.C.	South Carolina
cm	centimeters	Mass.	Massachusetts	SE	southeast
Co.	Company	Md.	Maryland	Sen.	Senator
Col.	Colonel	mi	miles	Sept	September
Conn.	Connecticut	Mich.	Michigan	Sgt.	Sergeant
d.	died	Minn.	Minnesota	sq mi	square miles
Dec	December	Miss.	Mississippi	SSE	south-southeast
Del.	Delaware	mm	millimeters	SSW	south-southwest
E	east, eastern	Mo.	Missouri	SW	southwest
EC	European Com-	MP	Member of	Tenn.	Tennessee
	munity		Parliament	Tex.	Texas
e.g.	for example	mp	melting point	UN	United Nations
est	estimated	mph	miles per hour	US	United States
F	Fahrenheit	N	north, northern	USSR	Union of Soviet
Feb	February	NATO	North Atlantic		Socialist
Fl. Lt.	Flight Lieutenant		Treaty		Republics
Fla.	Florida		Organization	Va.	Virginia
ft	feet	NE	northeast	Vt.	Vermont
Ga.	Georgia	Neb.	Nebraska	W	west, western
Gen.	General	N.H.	New Hampshire	wt	weight
Gov.	Governor	N.J.	New Jersey		

Torah (Hebrew: instruction) The five books of Moses (Genesis, Exodus, Leviticus, Numbers, and Deuteronomy), which constitute the first of the three divisions of the Hebrew *Bible. In Judaism, the term is also applied more widely to the whole body of religious teachings, viewed as the revealed word of God and including both the written and the oral Torah. The reading of the Torah, from a manuscript scroll (*sepher Torah*), occupies a central place in *synagogue services.

TORAH *Worshipers wearing prayer shawls and phylacteries (on their foreheads and left hands, as on left of illustration) surround the scrolls of the Torah.*

Tories Members of a British political group that became the *Conservative party in the 1830s; Tory is still used synonymously with Conservative.

tormentil A perennial herb, *Potentilla erecta*, native to Europe, W Asia, and N Africa. Its slender stems, 4–12 in (10–30 cm) long, bear yellow flowers and grow from a woody rootstock, which has astringent properties. The trailing tormentil (*P. anglica*) has creeping flower stems up to 28 in (70 cm) long and larger flowers. Family: *Rosaceae*.

tornado A violently rotating column of air, small in diameter, characterized by a funnel-shaped cloud, which may reach ground surface. Wind speeds of more than 200 mph (325 kph) have been experienced. Occurring over land, tornadoes cause large-scale destruction and are a considerable problem in the central US and Australia, where they frequently occur as groups.

Toronto 43 42N 79 25W A city and port in E Canada, the capital of Ontario on Lake Ontario. Canada's second largest city, with a metropolitan area population of more than 2,300,000, it is very prosperous, housing a stock exchange and the headquarters of banks, insurance companies, and large corporations. With Canada's busiest airport, Toronto is also a water, road, and rail hub. Its diversified industries include heavy engineering, electrical, chemical, and wood products, foods, clothing, sporting goods, publishing and films. With theaters, orchestras, museums, opera, ballet, three universities, and a cosmopolitan population, Toronto is the cultural center of English-speaking Canada. *History*: established as Upper Canada's capital and military center (1793), Toronto was burned by American troops (1813) and was the scene of the Mackenzie Rebellion (1837) against oligarchic government. It became an industrial and commercial center with the development of railroads (1850s). Population (1991): 635,395.

torpedo (armament) A self-propelled guided underwater missile carrying a high-explosive warhead. They can be launched by ships or aircraft but have been used most successfully by submarines. Designed in 1866 by British engineer Robert Whitehead, they were extremely effective against shipping in World Wars I and II. Modern torpedoes are driven by steam turbines or by battery-powered electric motors and have sophisticated active or passive acoustic homing systems. (Active devices send out sounds and are guided by the echo from the target; passive devices are guided by sounds from the target.)

torpedo (fish). *See* electric ray.

Torquemada, Tomás de (1420–98) Spanish Dominican friar and Grand Inquisitor. Confessor to Ferdinand and Isabella, he was appointed head of the Spanish *Inquisition in 1483. His sentences were extremely harsh and he was responsible for the expulsion of the Jews from Spain in 1492.

Torrance 33 50N 118 19W A city in SW California, SW of Los Angeles. Founded in 1912 by Jared L. Torrance, it was a planned industrial and residential city. Oil is drilled and refined there, and aircraft, missiles, metals, electronic parts, chemicals, and foodstuffs are produced. Population (1990): 133,107.

Torreón 25 34N 103 25W A city in NE Mexico. It is the center of La Laguna, a vast state-controlled agricultural cooperative producing cotton and wheat. Population (1980): 328,086.

Torres Strait A channel between New Guinea and Cape York Peninsula, N Australia, linking the Arafura Sea and Coral Sea. It was explored (1606) by the Spanish navigator, Luis Vaez de Torres. Width: about 90 mi (145 km).

Torricelli, Evangelista (1608–47) Italian physicist, who succeeded *Galileo as professor of mathematics at Florence University. He discovered that the atmosphere exerts a pressure and demonstrated it by showing that it could support a column of mercury in a tube, thus inventing the mercury barometer (1643). He also created the first man-made vacuum in his simple barometer, the space above the mercury still being called a Torricellean vacuum.

tort In law, a civil wrong that constitutes a breach of a duty established by law rather than by *contract. It is distinguished from a crime in that it affects the interests of the injured person rather than of the state. Thus in tort the offender may be sued for damages.

Tortelier, Paul (1914–90) French cellist. He won first prize at the Paris conservatory at the age of 16. After playing in orchestras in the US he began a career as a soloist, composer, and teacher. He made many recordings and wrote a book on cello playing.

tortoise A slow-moving herbivorous reptile belonging to the family *Testudinidae* (40 species), occurring in deserts, grassland, and forests of the Old and New Worlds, especially in Africa. Tortoises have a protective high-domed shell, tough scaly legs, and range in size from about 4–60 in (.10–1.5 m) (*see* Galápagos giant tortoise). Tortoises lay eggs and have long lifespans, reputedly up to 150 years in some cases. The common Mediterranean tortoise (*Testudo graeca*) is a popular pet; in colder climates, it must hibernate during the winter. *Compare* turtle; terrapin.

tortoise beetle A *leaf beetle with a carapace-like shield. Tortoise beetles are 0.35–0.47 in (9–12 mm) long and many tropical species are brilliantly colored (the South American species *Desmonota variolosa* is emerald green). The flat spiny larvae have a forked appendage at the rear end of the body to which they attach excrement for camouflage.

tortoiseshell butterfly A *nymphalid butterfly whose wings are mainly orange with black markings. Tortoiseshells are found in Europe, Asia, and North America. The caterpillars feed mainly on nettles and willows. The adults hibernate. Chief genera: *Aglais, Nymphalis*.

tortoiseshell cat A breed of cat whose coat consists of distinct evenly spread patches of black, red, and cream. All tortoiseshells are female (any males produced are sterile); they have compact bodies, short legs, and yellow or orange eyes. There are both long- and short-haired breeds.

Tortuga Island (French name: Île de la Tortue) 1 00S 90 55W A West Indian island, N of Haiti in the Greater Antilles. It was a haunt of buccaneers during the 17th century. Area: 70 sq mi (180 sq km).

Toruń (German name: Thorn) 53 01N 18 35E A city in N central Poland, on the Vistula River. The astronomer Copernicus was born there (1473). Its university was founded in 1945. Industries include precision engineering and chemicals. Population (1992 est): 202,000.

Toscanini, Arturo (1867–1957) Italian conductor. He began his career as a cellist. He made his debut in Rio de Janeiro in 1886 in Verdi's *Aida* and subsequently conducted at La Scala, Milan, and at the Metropolitan Opera in New York. From 1937 until his death he conducted the NBC (National Broadcasting Company) Symphony Orchestra.

Tosks One of the two divisions of the Albanian people living in the S of the country. *See also* Ghegs.

totemism In primitive societies, the common occurrence of a special relationship of ritual significance between certain animal and plant species or other natural phenomena and certain social groups or individuals. Features of this relationship are belief in descent from the totem species (which may include animal worship), a *taboo on killing or eating it except at special ritual feasts, and clan exogamy, but only among Australian aborigines do all these occur together. The Indians of the NW Pacific coast of America also practice totemism, as did the ancient Indo-European peoples.

totem pole Among the Indians of the NW Pacific coast, a carved and painted pole used to commemorate important events, as a house post, or to mark or contain funerary remains. The carvings are largely of animals associated with particular families and their histories and legends.

Totila (d. 552 AD) King of the Ostrogoths (541–52), who temporarily recovered much of central and S Italy from the Eastern Roman Empire. He took Rome in 546, lost it to *Belisarius, and then recaptured it. He was finally defeated and killed by *Narses.

toucan A noisy forest-dwelling bird belonging to a family (*Ramphastidae*; 37 species) occurring in tropical America; 10–24 in (25–60 cm) long, toucans have huge brightly colored bills and typically black plumage with a brightly colored breast. They feed on fruit. Order: *Piciformes* (woodpeckers, etc.).

touch-me-not A European annual herbaceous plant, *Impatiens noli-tangere*, 8–40 in (20–100 cm) high. It has narrow leaves and bright-yellow tubular flowers, each with a large lower lip and a long curled spur, borne on slender drooping stalks. The ripe fruits split open at the slightest touch to expel the seeds explosively. Family: *Balsaminaceae*.

touchstone A black or gray flintlike stone, formerly used for testing the purity of gold and silver. The metal to be tested and one of known purity are both rubbed with the touchstone and compared. The color of the marks left indicates the impurities present. Treatment with nitric acid highlights the marks. The method is still sometimes used to test the purity of gold.

Toulon 43 07N 5 55E A port in SE France, in the Var department on the Mediterranean Sea. In 1942 most of the French fleet was scuttled there to prevent its capture by the Germans. Toulon is one of France's principal naval bases and has marine engineering, chemical, oil, and textile industries. Population (1975): 185,050.

Toulouse 43 33N 1 24E A city in S France, the capital of the Haute-Garonne department on the Garonne River. A major commercial and industrial center, it has aircraft, armaments, chemical, and textile industries. It is also an important agricultural trading center. Notable buildings include the basilica (11th–13th centuries), the gothic cathedral, and the university (1230). *History*: capital of the Visigoths and later of the kingdom of Aquitaine, it passed to France in 1271. It suffered badly during the campaign against the Albigenses. Population (1990): 365,933.

Toulouse-Lautrec, Henri (Marie Raymond) de (1864–1901) French artist, born in Albi of aristocratic descent. Stunted in growth by a childhood accident, he settled in Paris, where he trained under two conservative artists in the early 1880s and led an unconventional life among the music halls and cafés of Montmartre. His comic but sympathetic studies of popular entertainers (for example Jane Avril and Aristide Bruant), circus life, and prostitutes in posters, lithographs, and paintings were influenced by *Degas and Japanese prints. Characteristic paintings are *At the Moulin Rouge* and *La Toilette*.

touraco. *See* turaco.

Touraine A former province of France. Once independent, later under Angevin control, and in 1641 incorporated into the French kingdom, Touraine was famous until the late 17th century for its Huguenot silk weavers. The region is noted for its royal chateaux.

Tourcoing 50 44N 3 10E A city in N France, in the Nord department. Together with its twin town, Roubaix, it forms the center of the French woolen industry. Population (1983): 102,000.

Tour de France The main European professional cycling race. Founded in 1903, the road race, of some 20 stages, lasts three weeks or more and has a maximum length of approximately 2480 mi (4000 km). The race starts in a different town each year but always ends in Paris. The teams are commercially sponsored.

Touré, (Ahmed) Sékou (1922–84) Guinean statesman; president (1961–84). Active in trade unionism in French West Africa, in 1956 Touré was elected to the French National Assembly. He opposed de Gaulle's plan of federalism in French West Africa and lost French support on independence (1958), when he became head of state and then president.

tourmaline A group of minerals composed of complex cyclosilicates containing boron. There are numerous varieties, some being used as gemstones and some for their piezoelectric and polarizing properties. Tourmalines are found in veins and pegmatites in granite rocks.

Tournai (Flemish name: Doornik) 50 36N 3 24E A city in W central Belgium, on the Scheldt River. It has a notable cathedral (11th–14th centuries). Industries include carpets, textiles, and leather. Population (1981 est): 69,718.

tournament In medieval Europe, a festival at which knights competed in various military tests of skill and courage. The best-known example was jousting, in which mounted knights charged each other with lances. Combatants were usually limited to members of noble families and weapons were usually blunt. Tournaments originated in France in the 11th century and had died out by the end of the 16th century. In modern times, the word refers to a military display and to competitions in various sports.

Tournefort, Joseph Pitton de (1656–1708) French botanist, who proposed a system of plant classification that used a single Latin name to distinguish a particular genus. This was later incorporated in the binomial system of nomenclature developed by *Linnaeus.

TOULOUSE-LAUTREC *A lithograph of the popular singer Yvette Guilbert (1867–1944), one of a series of 16 studies for a poster (1894).*

Tourneur, Cyril (c. 1575–1626) English dramatist. He published several poems, including the satire *The Transformed Metamorphosis* (1600), and is the presumed author of *The Atheist's Tragedy* (1611) and *The Revenger's Tragedy* (1607). The latter play has also been attributed to Thomas *Middleton. He died in Ireland after taking part in an expedition to Cádiz.

Tours 47 23N 0 42E A city in central France, the capital of the Indre-et-Loire department situated between the Loire and Cher rivers. Its prosperous silk industry declined following the revocation of the Edict of Nantes (1685) and the exodus of the Huguenot weavers. Notable buildings include the gothic cathedral, the archiepiscopal palace (17th–18th centuries), and the university (1970). Tours is a tourist center for the Loire Valley and has varied manufacturing industries. Population (1990): 133,403.

Toussaint-L'Ouverture, François Dominique (c. 1743–1803) Haitian slave, who led a slave rebellion in Haiti that achieved self-government under French protection. L'Ouverture became lieutenant governor of Haiti in 1794 and established a free society, expelling the Spanish and British landowners. He became governor general in 1801 but the French, afraid of his power, forcibly retired him in 1802. He was then arrested for plotting a rebellion and imprisoned.

Tower of London A royal fortress on the N bank of the River Thames, to the E of the City of London. It was begun in the 11th century, with the White Tower (1078), and added to in subsequent centuries. It was a royal palace until the 17th century and a state prison, which held such famous prisoners as Lady Jane *Grey and Anne *Boleyn. It is now a barracks, armory, and museum, containing the British crown jewels and regalia.

Townes, Charles Hard (1915–   ) US physicist, who constructed the first *maser (1953). For this work he shared the 1964 Nobel Prize with Nikolai Bosov and Aleksandr Prokhorov, two Soviet physicists, who independently worked out the theory of the maser.

town planning. *See* Urban Planning.

Townshend Acts (*or* American Import Duties Act; 1767) Four acts passed by Britain to assert its authority over the American colonies by imposing revenue duties on tea, paper, glass, and painters' colors. They were named for Charles Townshend (1725–67), chancellor of the exchequer (1766–67). The acts, the uses to which the resulting revenues were put, and their repressive enforcement provoked violent resentment that contributed to the outbreak of the *American Revolution.

Townsville 19 13S 146 48E A port in Australia, in NE Queensland on Cleveland Bay. It is the commercial center; industries include sugar processing, copper refining, and meat packing. Population (1991 est): 115,600.

toxemia The presence of bacterial toxins, such as those of diphtheria and tetanus, in the blood. However, the term is most often used to describe a condition affecting pregnant women, formerly thought to be due to toxins but is now known to be caused by *hypertension (raised blood pressure). Hypertension in pregnancy is often accompanied by protein in the urine and *edema (fluid in the tissues). In very severe cases the patient may develop fits.

toxicology. *See* poisons.

toxin A poison produced by a living organism. Many microorganisms, including bacteria and fungi, produce toxins. In diphtheria and tetanus the toxin is produced by the bacteria within the body of the infected person; in botulism the toxin is produced in contaminated food and ingested by the patient. Some toxins are useful: penicillin is a toxin, produced by fungi, that kills bacteria.

Toyama 36 42N 137 14E A city in Japan, in central Honshu on the Sea of Japan. It has been known since the 17th century for its pharmaceutical industry. Population (1991): 321,254.

Toynbee, Arnold (Joseph) (1889–1975) British historian. After holding several university posts, he was director of studies at the Royal Institute of International Affairs (1925–55). His major work, *A Study of History* (12 vols, 1934–61), structured according to the rise and fall of civilizations, embodies his theory of historical progress.

Trabzon (former name: Trebizond) 41 00N 39 43E A port in NE Turkey, on the Black Sea. It was the capital of the Comnenian empire (1204–1461) and has a university (1963). Population (1990): 143,941.

trace element A chemical element required by an organism for normal healthy growth but only in minute amounts. Higher plants, for instance, require traces of copper, zinc, etc. Many trace elements are constituents of vitamins and enzymes.

tracer bullet A bullet that when ignited by the propellant emits light or smoke. In flight, its path appears as a continuous streak enabling the gunner to correct his aim. Mixed with other types of bullets during loading, tracer bullets are used in aircraft and by ground troops both during combat and as an aid to maintaining direction during a night attack.

tracery In *gothic architecture, decorative stonework supporting the glass in windows. Molded stone bars were introduced as an ornamental element in 13th-century France and England. Designs were at first geometric but later became curvilinear (*see* Decorated; Flamboyant). In England the regular rectangular tracery of the *Perpendicular style enabled windows of enormous size to be built.

trachea 1. The windpipe: a tube that conducts air from the larynx to the left and right bronchi, which continue to the *lungs. The trachea is lined by *mucous membrane and supported by hoops of cartilage in its wall. **2.** One of the air passages in insects, which lead directly to the tissues. Each trachea has an external opening (spiracle) that can be opened and closed.

trachoma An eye disease that occurs in dry poor parts of the world and is caused by a large viruslike organism of the genus *Chlamydia*. It is a severe form of *conjunctivitis in which the membrane lining the eyelids and covering the cornea becomes scarred and shrunken and the eyelids become deformed. Trachoma is the world's most common cause of blindness; it is treated with antibiotics.

tractor A self-propelled vehicle designed to provide high power and traction at relatively low speeds for use in agriculture, construction, etc. Tractors were developed from mobile versions of the steam engines used in the 19th century. The American Burger tractor of 1889 was the first to use an internal-combustion engine. The modern tractor is usually powered by a diesel engine and equipped with a cab that insulates the driver from weather and noise. A power take-off (PTO) and hydraulically operated fittings enable powerful and versatile implements to be operated by the tractor, including shovels, loaders, mowing machines, spreaders, and cultivators.

Tracy, Spencer (1900–67) US film actor. He began his film career in the 1930s by playing gangsters, but later costarred with Katherine *Hepburn in nine films, including *Woman of the Year* (1942), *Adam's Rib* (1949), *Pat and Mike* (1952), *Desk Set* (1956), and *Guess Who's Coming to Dinner* (1967). Other notable films include *The Old Man and the Sea* (1958), *Inherit the Wind* (1960), and *Judgement at Nuremberg* (1961).

Trade and Navigation Acts. *See* Navigation Acts.

trade cycle The repeated cycle of *boom, *recession, *depression, recovery, and boom in an economy. In the 19th century, the trade cycle displayed regularity and stability; in the 20th century, it has fluctuated more. The *Depression of the 1930s was severe and a protracted world slump followed, after World War II, by a period of boom, interrupted by only minor recessions, which persisted until a serious recession began in the 1970s. The causes of the cycle are uncertain, but it may result from the persistence of erratic shocks to the economy, such as wars, political increases in the prices of essential commodities (such as oil), etc. Governments have tried to temper the effects of the trade cycle by imposing government spending policies.

trademarks Distinctive emblems owned by a manufacturer or trader and applied to his goods to identify them as produced or sold by him. The owner of a trademark has the right to its exclusive use in connection with the goods associated with it. Any trademark can be protected against infringement by legal action and registered trademarks enjoy additional statutory protection.

Tradescantia A genus of flowering plants (about 60 species), native to North and Central America and popular as ornamentals. Varieties of the wandering jew (*T. fluminensis*) are popular houseplants, having oval green leaves, tinged with pink or mauve or with silver stripes. Spiderworts, derived from *T. virginiana*, have three-petaled blue, purple, red, or white flowers and grasslike leaves; they are attractive border plants. Family: *Commelinaceae*.

trade union. *See* labor union.

trade winds (*or* tropical easterlies) The predominantly easterly winds that blow in the tropics. They blow generally from a NE direction in the N hemisphere and from a SE direction in the S hemisphere, converging toward the equator. They are noted for their constancy of direction and speed.

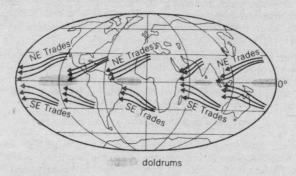

doldrums

TRADE WINDS

trading stamps Stamps given by a retailer to customers in proportion to the price of goods purchased. The customer can exchange these stamps (when he has collected enough of them) for merchandise. The retailer buys the stamps from a trading-stamp company and seeks to recover his cost from higher profits resulting from increased turnover.

Trafalgar, Battle of (Oct 21, 1805) The naval battle in the Napoleonic Wars in which the British under Nelson (in the *Victory*; □ships) defeated the French W of Cape Trafalgar, between Cádiz and Gibraltar (SW Spain). Nelson's skillful tactic of attacking enemy lines at right angles was an important element in the British success, which was tragically marred by Nelson's death. It ended the threat of a French invasion of Britain and established conclusively British naval supremacy.

tragacanth. See gums.

tragedy A form of drama recounting the fall (usually, the death) of a noble protagonist. The form evolved in ancient Greece from the *dithyramb, a choral song, and was fully developed in the plays of Aeschylus, Sophocles, and Euripides. Little tragic drama of worth was then written until the Elizabethan period of English literature, when Marlowe prepared the way for the tragedies of Shakespeare and his followers. In 17th-century France the neoclassical tragedies of

Racine and Corneille were carefully based on principles derived from Aristotle's *Poetics* (*see* unities). During the 19th century the essential elements of tragedy were more apparent in the novel than in drama. Ibsen and Strindberg in Europe and Eugene O'Neill in the US contributed to the development of tragic drama, but few 20th-century dramatists have attempted to write tragedies in the classical or Elizabethan sense.

tragicomedy A genre of drama developed by European writers in the late 16th and early 17th centuries. Its combination of tragic and romantic elements was pioneered by the Italian dramatist *Guarini in *Il pastor fido* (c. 1583) and was further developed in France and by several Jacobean and Restoration dramatists in England. The term is often applied to any play containing both tragic and comic elements, such as those of Chekhov.

tragopan A short-tailed *pheasant belonging to a genus (*Tragopan*) occurring in wet forests of the Himalayas. Male tragopans have vivid plumage, including long crown feathers, and two erectile blue fleshy "horns" on the head; a fold of skin beneath the bill forms a large bib during display.

Trail of Tears The journey of the Indian tribes, forced to migrate (1829–43) to new homes in Oklahoma Territory. The long hard trip to the West produced severe hardships for the Indians; one of every four who started out died as a result of disease, famine, or abuse.

Trajan(us), Marcus Ulpius (53–117 AD) Roman emperor (98–117). Trajan's early military successes led to his adoption by *Nerva in 97 AD. After his arrival in Rome as emperor his virtues were praised by Pliny in the *Panegyric*. His domestic policies were munificent and humane: corn was freely distributed, taxes were lessened, and much public building was carried out. He conducted two important wars: a successful Dacian campaign and a fruitless Parthian war. He died in Cilicia on his way back to Rome. □sculpture.

tranquilizers A group of drugs used to quiet aggressive, restless, or anxious patients. The major tranquilizers are powerful drugs used in the treatment of schizophrenia and other mental disorders. They include reserpine, the *phenothiazines, and the butyrophenones (e.g. haloperidol). Minor tranquilizers, which include the *benzodiazepines, are used for the treatment of neuroses and anxiety. Side effects of the major tranquilizers may be severe, and these drugs are usually prescribed only for serious psychological disorders.

Transcaucasia A region in Georgia, Azerbaijan, and Armenia. The Great *Caucasus range is in the N and the Little Caucasus, in the S. Its resources include oil and it is an important agricultural region. In 1918, Georgia, Azerbaijan, and Armenia formed the short-lived Transcaucasian Federative Republic, the basis of the Transcaucasian Soviet Federated Republic (1922–36) of the Soviet Union.

transcendentalism A philosophy that emphasizes the modes of thought and apprehension beyond the world of experience. In the philosophy of *Kant, everything beyond man's limited experience is transcendental and essentially unknowable. Human intuitions about time and space and understanding of quality and quantity are vital for experience, but are transcendent in that they do not come from that experience. *See also* transcendentalists.

transcendentalists A group of mid-19th century US writers and philosophers united by their philosophic idealism and their trust in the moral value of intuition. Their beliefs derived from the philosophy of Kant, especially as interpreted by Carlyle and Coleridge. Leading members of the group included Ralph Waldo *Emerson, Henry David *Thoreau, Margaret Fuller, Bronson Alcott, and George Ripley. They advocated social, political, and religious reforms, and many of their writings were published in the periodical *The Dial* (1840–44).

transducer Any device that changes a signal or physical quantity into another form. *Microphones, *loudspeakers, and *thermocouples are examples. It is also usually the primary sensor in a measurement or sensing system.

transformer A device for converting alternating current from one voltage to another. The input is fed to a primary winding, a coil of wire around a soft iron core, creating an oscillating magnetic field in the core. This field induces a secondary current of the same frequency in the secondary winding wound on the same core. The ratio of primary to secondary voltage is equal to the ratio of the number of turns in the secondary coil to that in the primary. The device is widely used both in electronic circuits and in the transmission and distribution of electric power (*see* electricity supply).

transhumance A form of pastoral nomadism in which livestock are moved seasonally between mountain summer pastures and lower-lying winter pastures, or between northern and southern or wet and dry season grazing areas.

transistor A *semiconductor device with three or more electrodes. Transistors form the basic elements of electronic *amplifiers and logic circuits, often combined with other components in *integrated circuits. They were first developed in 1948 by William *Shockley and his coworkers at the Bell Telephone Co. and now replace *thermionic valves in most applications. The term transistor usually refers to the **bipolar junction transistor**, which consists of two junctions between p-type and n-type semiconductors forming either a p-n-p or n-p-n structure. Current is carried across these junctions by both negative and positive charge carriers (electrons and holes). The current between the emitter and the collector electrodes varies not only with the voltage drop across them, but also with the voltage or current level at the base (the third electrode). Depending on how it is connected into a circuit, the junction transistor can act as a voltage or current amplifier in much the same way as a triode valve. Transistors, however, work at a much lower voltage than valves, are more compact and robust, emit less heat, and are cheaper to make.

Originally, junction transistors were made by alloying the impurity metal onto the semiconductor crystal or by adding impurities as the crystal was being grown. Now the doping is diffused in as a gas, introduced by ion implantation, or, more commonly, achieved by a combined process of etching and diffusion, known as the planar process.

The **field effect transistor** (FET) is a unipolar device, in which current is carried by only one type of charge. There are two types: the junction FET (JFET) has a region of semiconductor of one doping type flanked by two highly doped layers of the opposite type. Current flows parallel to the junctions, between the so-called source and drain electrodes, through a narrow channel between the highly doped regions (the gate); it is controlled by the electric field arising from the gate input voltage, which alters the width of the conducting channel. The JFET is used as a separate component in amplifiers and switches. In the insulated-gate FET (IGFET) the source and drain electrodes are highly doped regions in a substrate of the opposite type. The gate electrode is a conductor separated from the substrate by a thin insulating layer across the surface. The electric field caused by the gate voltage controls the source-drain current on the other side of the insulator. The IGFET is used mainly in metal-oxide semiconductor (MOS) integrated circuits. It is smaller than the equivalent bipolar junction transistor and uses less power.

TRANSISTOR

Germanium is a typical semiconductor. The four outer electrons in each of its atoms form covalent bonds with adjacent atoms. In the pure state it acts as an insulator as no electrons are available to carry current.

Arsenic atoms have five outer electrons. Germanium containing arsenic atoms as an impurity can carry current because the fifth electron is available as a carrier. This is an n-type semiconductor because current is carried by negative electrons.

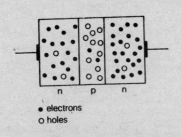

- electrons
o holes

In the bipolar junction transistor a piece of p-type material is sandwiched between two n-type pieces, making an n-p-n structure (p-n-p transistors are also used).

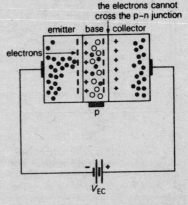

In an n-p-n transistor, a negative voltage is applied to one end (the emitter) and a positive to the other (the collector). No current flows, however, because a potential barrier forms at the junction between the emitter and the central region (the base).

TRANSISTOR

Indium atoms have three outer electrons. Germanium doped with indium, therefore, has holes in its electronic structure. These can be filled by electrons from neighboring atoms, creating new holes; this has the effect of positive charge moving through the crystal in the opposite direction to electrons. This is p-type germanium.

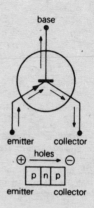

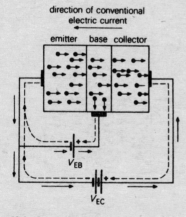

If the base region is positively biased, the free electrons in the emitter are attracted to the p-type base and current flows through the thin base to the collector. As the collector current depends on the amount of bias to the base, the device can be used as an amplifier.

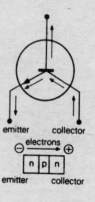

In the symbolic representation of a transistor, the direction of the arrow on the emitter indicates current direction and the type of transistor (n-p-n or p-n-p).

TRANSISTOR *The operation of the bipolar junction transistor.*

transit instrument A telescope theodolite, or similar device, that can be adjusted over a range of angular settings and is used to measure angular position. In astronomy, for instance, transit telescopes measure the vertical angles of stars or planets.

transition elements A large group of metallic elements, including most of the commonly used metals, the inner electron shells of which are incomplete. The *lanthanides and the *actinides are sometimes included in this definition. The elements show considerable similarities to their horizontal neighbors in the *periodic table. In general, they are hard, brittle, high-melting, and excellent conductors of heat and electricity. Their chemistry is complicated; they have multiple valences and tend to form colored compounds.

Transjordan. *See* Jordan, Hashemite kingdom of.

Transkei, Republic of A small country in South Africa, consisting of three separate areas. Most of the population is *Xhosa. *Economy*: chiefly subsistence agriculture, especially livestock, although such cash crops as tea, coffee, and flax are now being developed. Many adult males still work and live in South Africa. *History*: created in 1963, when South Africa granted self-government to the Xhosa nation, as the first of the Bantu Homelands, it became independent in 1976. All black Africans of Transkeian origin became its citizens, simultaneously losing their South African citizenship. Its independence is, however, recognized only by South Africa. In 1978, after constant disputes, especially over territorial rights, it broke off diplomatic relations with South Africa, in spite of continuing economic dependence on it. President: Paramount Chief Botha Jongilizwe Sigcau. Prime minister: Paramount Chief Kaiser Matanzima. Official currency: South African rand. Area: 16,675 sq mi (43,188 sq km). Population (1983 est): 2,775,000. Capital: Umtata.

translucence One of the degrees of transparency used by geologists for classifying minerals. A mineral is translucent if it transmits light but not sufficiently so to enable the outline of an object to be seen.

transmigration of souls. *See* reincarnation.

transmutation The conversion of one element into another. It was originally the (unfulfilled) aim of alchemists to bring about the transmutation of base metals into gold (*see* alchemy). Transmutations were achieved in the 20th century by bombarding elements with *alpha particles or *neutrons. An example is the production of oxygen17 when nitrogen14 is bombarded with alpha particles.

transpiration The loss of water vapor from the surface of a plant, which occurs primarily through small pores (stomata) in the leaves but also (slowly) through the cuticle of the *epidermis. The rate of water loss is controlled by the opening and closing of the stomata, greater loss occurring during the day than at night.

transplantation The surgical implantation of a tissue or organ derived either from another part of the body of the patient himself or from another individual (the donor). Skin grafting is an example of the former type of operation: it is used particularly to repair damage and disfigurement caused by burns and other injuries. Transplantation of donor organs is usually far less successful since the body's immune system reacts against and rejects the foreign tissue. These operations require careful matching of the donor's and recipient's tissues together with the use of drugs that suppress the recipient's immune responses (*see* immunosuppression). The first successful heart transplant operation was performed by Christiaan *Barnard in 1967, and since then many such operations have been performed in various countries, especially the US. Other organs that have been transplanted include the kidneys, lung, and liver, of which kidney transplants have been the most successful. Transplantation of bone marrow, heart valves, and pieces of bone have also been attempted.

transponder In telecommunications, a combined transmitter and receiver that sends out a signal automatically on receiving a predetermined trigger signal.

transportation In British law, the practice of sending a convicted criminal to some place outside Britain, usually to one of the colonies, to be kept in hard labor. Transportation was replaced by imprisonment at the end of the 18th century.

Transportation, Department of (DOT) US cabinet-level agency that establishes the country's overall transportation policy, including that of highway planning and construction, urban mass transit, railroads, aviation, and the safety of waterways, ports, highways, and oil and gas pipelines. Established in 1966, it is headed by the secretary of transportation, who oversees the US Coast Guard (*see* Coast Guard), the Maritime Administration, the St Lawrence Seaway Development Corporation, and the various transportation administrations.

transsexualism. *See* transvestism.

Trans-Siberian Railway The world's longest railroad, running 5800 mi (9335 km) from Moscow to Vladivostok, known as Siberia's lifeline. Double track, largely electrified, has replaced the original single track line built between 1891 and 1905. The complete journey with nearly a hundred stops takes nine days.

transubstantiation In Roman Catholic theology, the doctrine that the substance of the elements of bread and wine in the *Eucharist is changed at consecration into the substance of the body and blood of Christ. Only the accidents (i.e. the qualities apparent to the senses) of the bread and wine remain. *Compare* consubstantiation.

transuranic elements Elements with higher atomic number than uranium. Apart from traces of neptunium and plutonium, none of them has ever been detected in nature, since no isotopes of sufficient *half-life exist; they have been created since 1940, usually in minute amounts, in nuclear reactions. At present, over a dozen are known. *See also* actinides.

Transvaal The most northerly province in South Africa. Much of it is plateau with rolling country and high ridges, including the Witwatersrand. Heavily populated in the S, it is the most prosperous province and contains the country's main industrial area, centered on the Witwatersrand; iron, steel, and chemicals are produced. Mineral deposits include gold, diamonds, uranium, coal, chromite, and tin, and it has important deposits of platinum. It has a well-developed agriculture producing maize, wheat, peanuts, citrus fruit, cotton, and tobacco; sheep and cattle are raised. Forestry is also important. *History*: originally an Afrikaner republic, it fought in the *Boer Wars against Britain (1880–81, 1899–1902). It joined the Union of South Africa in 1910. Area: 109,621 sq mi (283,917 sq km). Population (1991): 8,630,396. Capital: Pretoria.

transvestism The practice of wearing clothes appropriate to the opposite sex, usually for sexual pleasure. Many transvestites are heterosexual males and do not wish to change their sex. Psychotherapy and aversion therapy can provide effective treatment for those requiring it. **Transsexualism** is the settled belief that one's psychological gender is opposite to one's physical sex, and this can cause considerable suffering. Psychological treatments are usually unhelpful. Some transsexuals manage to pass successfully as members of the opposite sex; hormone therapy and plastic surgery on genitals and breasts can help this adjustment by effecting an apparent sex change.

Transylvania A region of SE Europe, bounded by the Carpathian Mountains and the Transylvanian Alps, now in Romania. Transylvania retained its distinctive character under successive Roman, Magyar, and Hungarian rulers; during the 16th and 17th centuries, it was a self-governing princedom within the Ottoman Empire. Restored to Hungary, within the Holy Roman Empire, in 1687, Transylvania became part of Romania after World War I.

Transylvanian Alps (*or* Southern Carpathian Mountains; Romanian name: Carpaţii Meridionali) A mountain range extending 227 mi (360 km) E–W across S central Romania and rising to 8343 ft (2543 m) at Mount Moldoveanu.

Trapani 38 02N 12 32E A seaport in Italy, in NW Sicily. A Carthaginian naval base, it was ceded to Rome after the first Punic War. Its industries include fishing, fish processing, salt production, and marble working. Population (1981): 72,000.

trap-door spider A *spider, especially one of the family *Ctenizidae*, that constructs a silk-lined burrow in the ground covered by a tight-fitting silk-hinged door. Ctenizids are dull brown, with short stout legs. They occur in tropical and subtropical regions and only leave their burrows to hunt.

Trappists A Roman Catholic monastic order, officially known as the *Cistercians of the Strict Observance. It was founded in 1664 at the abbey of La Trappe in Normandy by D. A. J. le B. de Rancé (1626–1700). When the monks were expelled during the French Revolution, the order established houses in other countries; there are now monasteries in Britain, Ireland, North America, and elsewhere. The order is notable for its austerity, which includes the observance of strict silence, manual labor, and a simple vegetarian diet.

Trasimeno, Lake (*or* Lake Perugia) A lake in central Italy. It is drained via an artificial tunnel by the Tiber River. Area: 50 sq mi (129 sq km).

traveler's-tree A palmlike tree, *Ravenala madagascariensis*, native to Madagascar. It grows over 90 ft (27 m) tall and bears a crown of banana-like leaves, 48–72 in (120–180 cm) long, on stalks 7–13 ft (2–4 m) long. Each leaf base, shaped like a huge cup, holds about 1 qt (1 l) of water, which can provide a drink for thirsty passers-by (hence the name). Family: *Strelitziaceae*.

Traven, B(en) (Berick Traven Torsvan; 1890–1969) US novelist. Despite much speculation, his identity remains uncertain. He was probably born in Chicago of German ancestry, worked in Germany in 1918–19, and lived in Mexico from the 1920s. His allegorical novels include *The Death Ship* (1926) and *The Treasure of the Sierra Madre* (1927).

Travis, William Barret (1809–36) US lawyer and soldier, instrumental in the fight for Texas independence. A practicing lawyer in Alabama, he moved to Texas in 1831. During the war for independence in Texas he died leading the volunteer troops at the *Alamo, having replaced an ill James *Bowie.

trawler A vessel equipped for catching fish by towing nets. Such vessels are often designed with cold storage facilities for the catch for extended voyages at sea.

treadmill A penal device used in 19th-century prisons. It consisted of a hollow cylinder with a series of steps. A prisoner treading on the steps would set the cylinder in motion, which could then be used for grinding corn, etc.

treason The violation by a citizen of his allegiance to the sovereign or the state. Treason consists of two elements: adherence to the enemy, and rendering him aid and comfort.

Treasury, Department of US cabinet-level agency that formulates and rec-
ommends economic, financial, tax, and fiscal policies, serves as a financial agent
for the federal government, enforces the law, and manufactures coins and currency. Established in 1789, it is headed by the secretary of the treasury, who is a
major policy adviser to the president and who oversees such divisions of the department as the US Customs Service, the Bureau of Printing and Engraving, the
US Mint, and the Internal Revenue Service.

Treaty of Paris (1898) Treaty signed in Paris, France, that ended the *Spanish-
American War. The US acquired the Philippines, Puerto Rico, and Guam; Cuba
became independent.

treaty ports The five Chinese ports that were opened to British consuls and
merchants in 1842 at the end of the first *Opium War. They were Canton, Amoy,
Fuzhou, Ningbo, and Shanghai.

Trebizond. *See* Trabzon.

tree A tall perennial woody plant, usually with a single main stem (the trunk)
and secondary stems (the branches) arising some distance above ground level.
(Shrubs are smaller bushier woody perennials without a distinct trunk.) Most
tree species are either *dicotyledons (angiosperms)—the broad-leaved trees—or
*conifers (gymnosperms). These are the only trees that form true *wood and
they are of economic importance as producers of hardwoods and softwoods, respectively. Other groups containing trees are the cycads (gymnosperms), mono-
cotyledons (notably the *palms), and the ferns. Trees grow wherever the annual
rainfall exceeds 30 in (76 cm) but a few have adapted to desert conditions. The
conifers and tropical trees are mostly *evergreen plants, while broad-leaved
trees growing in regions with marked seasonal changes in climate are typically
deciduous.

The tallest existing tree on record is a Californian redwood, which has attained a
height of 364 ft (111 m). The study of the ecology and classification of trees is
called **dendrology**. *See also* forest.

treecreeper A small songbird belonging to a family (*Certhiidae*; 5 species)
occurring in Europe and Asia and occasionally in North America. It has a
brownish streaked plumage with pale silvery underparts, long claws, and a slender down-curved bill. The European treecreeper (*Certhia familiaris*), 5 in
(12.5 cm) long, occurs mainly in coniferous woods, where it creeps up tree
trunks to probe for small beetles, spiders, woodlice, etc.

tree fern A tropical *fern belonging to the genus *Cyathea* (600 species), found
mainly in moist mountainous regions. It has a trunklike stem, 10–80 ft (3–25 m)
high, and a crown of large tapering branched fronds. Family: *Cyatheaceae*.

tree frog A small toad belonging to a widely distributed family (*Hylidae*;
about 500 species). They have adapted to living in trees and have adhesive pads
on their toes that enable them to cling to leaves and branches, leaping acrobati-
cally to capture insects. Most species breed in water although some carry the developing eggs on their backs.

treehopper A winged insect, less than 1.5 in (13 mm) long, belonging to the
mainly tropical family *Membracidae* (2600 species). An enlargement of the thorax extends over the body to form a "hood," which varies in color and shape to
camouflage the insects against the background vegetation on which they live
and feed. Suborder: *Homoptera*; order *Hemiptera*.

tree kangaroo A *wallaby of the genus *Dendrolagus* (9 species) of Australia
and New Guinea. The black tree kangaroo (*D. ursinus*) is an agile climber that
feeds at night on the ground and sleeps during the day in trees.

TREE

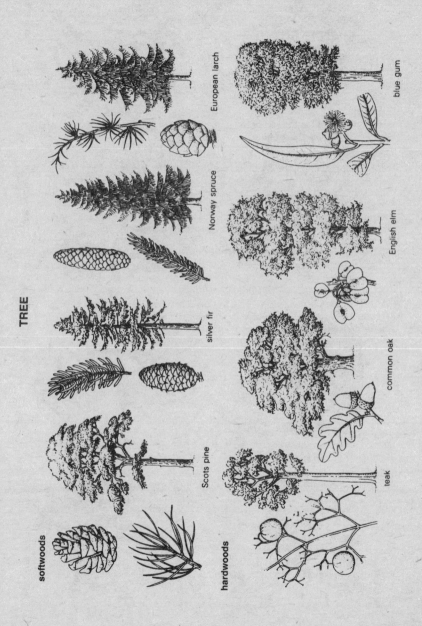

softwoods

European larch

Norway spruce

silver fir

Scots pine

hardwoods

blue gum

English elm

common oak

teak

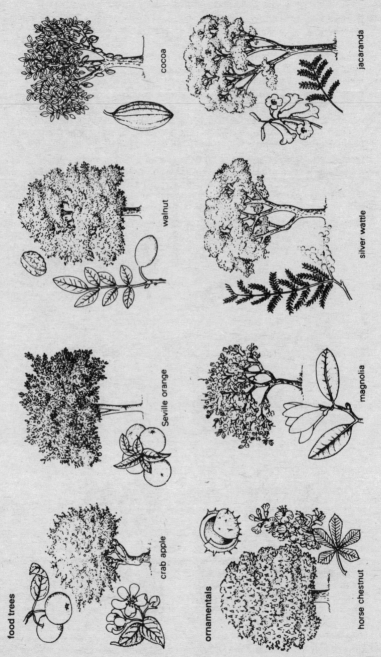

TREE

cocoa

jacaranda

walnut

silver wattle

Seville orange

magnolia

food trees

crab apple

ornamentals

horse chestnut

tree of heaven A tree, *Ailanthus altissima*, native to central Asia and planted elsewhere as an ornamental. Growing to a height of 100 ft (30 m), it has compound leaves, up to 40 in (1 m) long, composed of paired leaflets. Male and female flowers appear on separate trees, forming greenish-white clusters; the female flowers produce winged fruits. The trees are resistant to pollution and hence popular in urban areas. Family: *Simaroubaceae*.

tree shrew A primitive *prosimian primate belonging to the family *Tupaiidae* (18 species), found in Java, Borneo, Sumatra, the Philippines, and S Asia. The common tree shrew (*Tupaia glis*) is 12–18 in (30–45 cm) long including the tail (6–9 in; 15–23 cm) and has a slender pointed face. It darts among the branches, feeding chiefly on insects with some fruit and seeds.

tree snake Any of a number of slender tree-dwelling snakes that hunt birds, frogs, and lizards in tropical forests. The blunt-headed tree snake (*Imantodes cenchoa*) of Central and South America can stiffen most of its 24–36 in (60–90 cm) body length to reach another branch while supported by only a single coil of the tail. *See also* flying snake; vine snake.

trefoil One of several annual herbs of the genus *Trifolium* (which also includes the *clovers), characterized by leaves consisting of three leaflets. The hop trefoil (*T. campestre*), found on grassland and roadsides of Europe, W Asia, N Africa, and North America, grows to a height of 14 in (35 cm) and has compact globular heads of yellow flowers. The birdsfoot trefoils belong to the genus *Lotus* (about 70 species), of temperate Eurasia, Africa, and Australia. The leaves have five leaflets and the yellow or reddish flowers have a prominent keel resembling a lip. A common species is *L. corniculatus*, a perennial grassland herb growing to a height of 4–16 in (10–40 cm). Family: *Leguminosae*.

Trematoda. *See* fluke.

Trengganu A state in NE Peninsular Malaysia, on the South China Sea. Mountainous and forested inland, it is settled mainly along the coast, with fish, rice, rubber, and copra being the chief products. Area: 5002 sq mi (12,955 sq km). Population (1990): 752,000. Capital: Kuala Trengganu.

Trent, Council of (1545–63) The 19th general council of the Roman Catholic Church, an expression of the *Counter-Reformation, which was summoned by Pope Paul III to strengthen the Church in its confrontation with Protestantism. It was held in Trento (N Italy). There were three sessions (1545–47, 1551–52, 1562–63), which clarified doctrine and instituted reforms: the Council condemned Luther's doctrine of justification by faith alone and defined *transubstantiation. It also strengthened episcopal authority and issued decrees on clerical abuses and education.

Trent, River A river in central England. Flowing mainly NE from Staffordshire through Nottingham, it joins the Ouse River to form the Humber estuary. The Midlands' main river, it is linked to the Mersey by the Trent, Mersey, and Grand Union Canals. Length: 170 mi (270 km).

Trent Affair (1861) US–British incident during the Civil War that established policy regarding freedom of the seas. US naval officers aboard the *San Jacinto* seized two Confederate commissioners, traveling on the British ship *Trent* in waters off Havana, Cuba. The British government, angered at the violation of neutrality, demanded that the Confederates be released. More than a month later, the US government condemned the act and ordered the prisoners released.

Trentino-Alto Adige (Former name: Venetia Tridentina)) An autonomous region in N Italy. Formerly part of Austria, it passed to Italy after World War I and has a large German-speaking population. It is a mountainous forested region, situated entirely within the Alps. The fertile valleys of the Adige River and its tributaries produce wine, fruit, and dairy products. Timber is an important industry. Numerous hydroelectric plants have encouraged the development of manufacturing industry. Tourism is an important source of revenue. Area: 5256 sq mi (13,613 sq km). Population (1988 est): 882,000. Capital: Trento.

Trento (German name: Trent) 46 04N 11 08E A city in N Italy, the capital of Trentino-Alto Adige on the Adige River. Dating from pre-Roman times, it has a romanesque cathedral (12th-century) and the 16th-century Church of Sta Maria Maggiore, where the Council of *Trent met. Its products include chemicals, electrical goods, and silk. Population (1988 est): 101,000.

Trenton 40 15N 74 43W The capital city of New Jersey. George Washington defeated the British there in 1776. Industries include the manufacture of pottery, cable, rope, and metal. Population (1990): 88,675.

trepang (or bêche-de-mer) The boiled, dried, and smoked body wall of certain *sea cucumbers, used to make soup in the East. It is produced mainly from animals of the genera *Holothuria, Stichopus*, and *Thelonota*, found on coral reefs of the SW Pacific.

trephine A surgical saw used to remove a circular section of the skull in order to release pressure caused by bleeding within the skull or to provide access to the brain. The use of trephines dates from ancient times.

Trevelyan, Sir George Otto (1838–1928) British statesman and historian, nephew and biographer of Lord Macaulay. He was a member of Parliament from 1868 to 1897 and held various political posts.

Trèves. *See* Trier.

Trevino, Lee (1939–) US golfer, who was US Open champion (1968, 1971), British Open champion (1971, 1972), and US Professional Golfers Association champion (1974).

Treviso 45 40N 12 15E A city in Italy, in Veneto. Dating from Roman times, it has an 11th-century cathedral and other historic buildings, including several ancient palaces. Its manufactures include ceramics and agricultural machinery. Population (1981): 88,000.

Trevithick, Richard (1771–1833) British engineer, who developed high-pressure steam engines that were sufficiently light and powerful to be used in locomotives. He built the first steam-driven carriage to carry passengers (1801) and the first locomotive to run on smooth wheels on smooth rails (1804). He died penniless.

Trevor-Roper, Hugh Redwald, Baron Dacre (1914–) British historian. Trevor-Roper's many books, notable for their literary merit, include *Archbishop Laud* (1940) and *The Last Days of Hitler* (1947).

triangle A percussion instrument consisting of a steel rod bent into the shape of a triangle. The triangle was first used in late 18th-century orchestral works to provide a "Turkish" atmosphere. □musical instruments.

Triangle trade A trading system among the West Indies, American colonies, and Africa. The New England and Middle Atlantic colonies manufactured rum from West Indian molasses. The rum was brought to Africa and traded for slaves who were then taken to the West Indies and sold for molasses.

Trianon, Grand and Petit Two villas in the grounds of the Palace of Versailles, near Paris. The Grand Trianon was built in 1687 for Louis XIV by *Mansart and the Petit Trianon from 1762 to 1768 for Louis XV by Jacques Ange Gabriel (1698–1782).

Triassic period (*or* Trias) A period of geological time at the beginning of the Mesozoic era, lasting from about 240 to 200 million years ago. The rocks of the period, laid down mainly under continental conditions, so greatly resemble those of the preceding *Permian period that the two are often considered together as the Permo-Trias(sic). The dinosaurs, ichthyosaurs, and plesiosaurs appeared in the Triassic.

tribes of Israel In the Bible, the Hebrew people. The 12 tribes, descended from the sons of Jacob, were *Reuben, *Simeon, *Judah, *Issachar, *Zebulun, *Benjamin, *Dan, *Naphtali, *Gad, *Asher, Levi (*see* Levites), and *Ephraim and *Manasseh. These last two were counted as one, except in parts of the Bible where the tribal lists omit either Levi or Simeon. After the death of Solomon, 10 of the tribes broke away from Benjamin and Judah to form the northern kingdom of Israel (*see* Ten Lost Tribes of Israel).

tribology The study of *friction and such allied topics as lubrication, abrasives, surface wear, etc. The effects of friction, such as triboluminescence and frictional electricity, are also studied.

tribune In ancient Rome, a plebeian magistrate appointed to protect *plebeians' rights. Instituted during the 5th-century political struggles between *patricians and plebeians, the tribunes, first two, later 10 in number, could veto legislative proposals of the Senate or popular assemblies and could themselves propose legislation without senatorial approval. This power, to obstruct and circumvent the Senate, considerably influenced Roman politics from the Gracchi's revolutionary times (*see* Gracchus, Tiberius Sempronius) to Augustus's assumption of tribunicial power in the late 1st century BC.

Triceratops A three-horned dinosaur of the late Cretaceous period (about 100–65 million years ago) and one of the last of the dinosaurs; 26 ft (8 m) long and weighing 8.5 tons, it had an enormous head with one horn on the snout and one (up to 40 in [1 m] long) over each eye. It also had a large bony neck frill and short limbs with hoofed feet and browsed on tough plants. Order: *Ornithischia*. □fossil.

Trichinopoly. *See* Tiruchirappalli.

Trier (French name: Trèves) 49 45N 6 39E A city in SW Germany, in Rhineland-Palatinate on the Moselle River. Founded by the Emperor Augustus, it has important Roman remains including the amphitheater. The cathedral (11th–12th centuries) was built around the 4th-century basilica. It shares a university with Kaiserslautern (1970) and is the birthplace of Karl Marx. It is a wine-trading and industrial center. Population (1984): 95,000.

Trieste (Serbo-Croat name: Trst) 45 39N 13 47E A seaport in Italy, the capital of Friuli-Venezia Giulia, situated on the Gulf of Trieste at the head of the Adriatic Sea. An important transit port for central Europe, it has shipyards, oil refineries, and a steel industry. It has a 14th-century cathedral and a university (1938). *History*: an important Roman port in the 1st century AD, it passed to Austria in 1382. It expanded rapidly in the 19th century as an outlet for Austrian goods and in 1920 was ceded to Italy. Following World War II it became the capital of the Free Territory of Trieste, which was established by the UN (1947) following a dispute between Italy and Yugoslavia. In 1954 most of the N of the Territory (including Trieste) passed to Italy and the remainder to Yugoslavia, becoming part of independent Slovenia in 1991. Population (1991 est): 231,047.

triggerfish A shallow-water fish, belonging to a family (*Balistidae*) related to *puffers, that occurs in tropical seas. Its deep laterally flattened body, up to 24 in (60 cm) long, is covered with large scales. The strong spine of the first dorsal fin is erected and locked into position by the second dorsal fin, forming a "trigger" that wedges the fish into crevices. It feeds on mollusks and crustaceans.

trigonometry A branch of mathematics founded by Hipparchus in the mid-2nd century BC, concerned originally with the measurement of triangles. The ratios of the lengths of the sides of a right-angled triangle are used to define the sine, cosine, and tangent of one of the angles of the triangle. Trigonometry deals with the properties of these and related functions. Its study is essential to most branches of physics and mathematics, particularly those involving cyclic quantities.

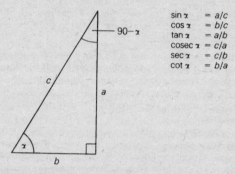

$$\sin x = a/c$$
$$\cos x = b/c$$
$$\tan x = a/b$$
$$\operatorname{cosec} x = c/a$$
$$\sec x = c/b$$
$$\cot x = b/a$$

TRIGONOMETRY *Definitions of the trigonometric functions sine, cosine, and tangent and of their reciprocals cosecant, secant, and cotangent.*

Trilling, Lionel (1905–75) US literary critic. In *The Liberal Imagination* (1950), *Sincerity and Authenticity* (1974), and other works, he expressed a moral concern with all aspects of modern culture. His novel *The Middle of the Journey* (1947) is concerned with moral and political issues of the 1930s and 1940s.

trilobite An extinct marine *arthropod belonging to a subphylum (*Trilobita*; over 4000 species) that flourished between Cambrian and Permian times, i.e. 500–200 million years ago. Trilobite □fossils are abundant in rocks of this period. Its flattened oval body, 0.40–26.5 in (10–675 mm) long, was divided by two longitudinal furrows into three lobes. The head bore a pair of antennae and usually a pair of compound eyes and each segment of the thorax and tail region carried a pair of forked appendages. Many trilobites burrowed in sand or mud, preying on other animals or scavenging.

trimaran A modern sailing vessel with three parallel hulls, a larger central one and two smaller ones used as stabilizers or outriggers. Trimarans are usually rigged as sloops. It is modeled on the outrigger canoe, or **proa**, of the SW Pacific. *See also* catamaran.

Trimurti The Hindu triad of gods, *Brahma, *Vishnu, and *Shiva, representing the creative, sustaining, and destructive aspects of reality respectively, sometimes portrayed as one body with three heads.

Trinidad and Tobago, Republic of A country off the N coast of South America, consisting of the islands of Trinidad and Tobago. Both are hilly and wooded. Most of the population is of African and East Indian descent. *Economy*: oil and asphalt have replaced cocoa and sugar as the main source of the country's wealth and reserves of offshore gas have also been discovered. Other industrial developments include aluminum smelting, plastics, electronics, iron and steel, and petrochemicals. Tourism is a growing industry. It is a member of CARICOM. *History*: Trinidad was inhabited by Arawak and Carib Indians when it was discovered by Columbus in 1498. It was a Spanish colony from the 16th century until 1802, when it was ceded to Britain; it joined with Tobago in 1809. During World War II bases were leased to the US but most have since been given up. The country was a member of the short-lived Federation of the West Indies from 1958 to 1961 and became an independent state within the British Commonwealth in 1962. In 1970 there was considerable unrest, partly because of the black power movement. In 1976 it became a republic with the former governor general, Ellis Clarke, as its first president. Eric Williams of the People's National Movement (PNM) served as prime minister from independence until his death in 1981. He was succeeded by PNM's George Chambers. In 1986, the National Alliance for Reconstruction won the majority vote and installed Arthur Robinson as prime minister. In 1990, Muslim militants attempted a coup, holding Robinson hostage for several days. Robinson was defeated in 1991 by PNM's Patrick Manning. Prime minister: Patrick Manning. Official language: English. Official currency: Trinidad and Tobago dollar of 100 cents. Area: 1980 sq mi (5128 sq km). Population (1990 est): 1,270,000. Capital and main port: Port-of-Spain.

Trinity, the A central doctrine of Christian theology, stating that God is one substance but with three distinct, coequal, and coeternal "persons," the Father, the Son, and the *Holy Spirit. The belief is based on a number of passages in the New Testament. It was given a first formal definition by the Council of *Nicaea (325), which asserted that the Son was "of the same essence (*homoousios*) as the Father." In the West, St Augustine and St Thomas Aquinas developed the doctrine. The Eastern Church rejects the so-called "double procession" of the Holy Spirit from the Father and the Son, which is accepted by the Western church (*see* Filioque).

triode. *See* thermionic valve.

Triple Alliance (1882) An alliance between Germany, Austria-Hungary, and Italy, which with the opposing *Triple Entente shaped European diplomacy in the decades before World War I. At the outbreak of war (1914) Italy declared its neutrality, thus breaking the alliance.

Triple Alliance, War of the (*or* Paraguayan War; 1865–70) The war between Paraguay and a coalition of Argentina, Brazil, and Uruguay. Conflict was precipitated by the belligerent diplomacy of Paraguay's dictator, F. S. *López, toward Argentina, which with Brazil and Uruguay invaded Paraguay. López refused to surrender and following the capture of Asunción in 1868 waged a guerrilla war in the N until taken prisoner in 1870. The war shattered the economy of Paraguay, which lost about half its population.

Triple Crown The three major races for three-year-old horses in the US: the Kentucky Derby, the Preakness Stakes, and the Belmont Stakes.

Triple Entente An informal combination of France, Russia, and Britain resulting from the Franco-Russian alliance (1893), the Franco-British *Entente Cordiale (1904), and the Anglo-Russian agreement (1907). It was formed in opposition to the *Triple Alliance.

triple jump (former name: hop, step, and jump) A field event for men in athletics, similar to the *long jump but executed as a continuous series of three jumps. The jumper lands first on the takeoff foot and then on the other, which becomes the takeoff foot for the final jump.

Tripoli (Arabic name: Tarabulus) 32 58N 13 12E The capital and main port of Libya, on the Mediterranean Sea. Originally founded as Oea by the Phoenicians, it has come under the rule of many different countries through the ages. It became the capital of Libya on independence in 1951. Its notable buildings include a Spanish fortress and it has a university (1973). Exports include fruit and olive oil and it is a transshipment center. Population (1988 est): 591,062.

Tripoli (Arabic name: Tarabulus) 34 27N 35 50E A port in NW Lebanon, on the Mediterranean Sea. It was the capital of a Phoenician federation of three other cities (hence its name, from Greek *tripolis*). Iraqi oil is brought by pipeline to the refinery here. The city was heavily damaged in 1983 as a result of fighting between Syrian forces and the Palestine Liberation Organization during Lebanon's civil war. Population (1985 est): 500,000.

Tripolitania A region of N Africa, between Tunisia and Cyrenaica. Colonized in the 7th century BC by the Phoenicians, who founded three cities, including Tripoli, the coast was controlled by a succession of foreign powers, including Romans, Arabs, Ottoman Turks, and Italians, while the nomadic Berbers of the interior were generally unaffected by political changes. Since 1951 Tripolitania has been part of Libya.

Tripura A state in NE India, in tropical jungle and plains E of Bangladesh. Rice, jute, tea, and bamboo are produced. Local cottage industries are flourishing. *History*: the Moguls ended 1000 years of Hindu monarchy (18th century) before Britain won Tripura. In 1949 it entered the Indian Union. Area: 4044 sq mi (10,477 sq km). Population (1991): 2,744,827. Capital: Agartala.

tri-ratna (Sanscrit: three jewels) In Buddhism, the *Buddha, *Dharma, and *sangha, that is, the spiritual ideal, the truth regarding the means to its attainment, and the monastic order of those who strive toward it.

trireme. *See* ships.

Tristan The tragic hero of several medieval romances. After accidentally drinking a magic love potion, he becomes the lover of Iseult (Isolde), who is betrothed to his uncle, King Mark of Cornwall. He later renounces Iseult and goes to Brittany, where he marries the duke's daughter. Dying from a wound, he sends a ship to bring back Iseult to nurse him. By his wife's treachery, she arrives too late and dies of grief at his side. Of Celtic origin, the legend appeared in a French poem, written in about 1150 (now lost). Other 12th-century versions include one by an Anglo-Norman poet, Thomas, and *Gottfried von Strassburg's *Tristan und Isolde*, the source of Wagner's opera. In a 13th-century prose romance the story was incorporated into the *Arthurian legend.

Tristan da Cunha 37 15S 12 30W A group of four small islands in the S Atlantic Ocean, a dependency of St Helena. The only settlement, Edinburgh, which is on Tristan (the largest island), grew from a British garrison (established 1816). Situated on the main sailing route, it originally flourished but became isolated when steam replaced sail. In 1961 the inhabitants were evacuated to the UK to escape a volcanic eruption but most chose to return in 1963. The economy is based on crawfish canning and postage stamps. Area: about 40 sq mi (100 sq km). Population (1980): 323.

tritium (T *or* ^{3}H) A radioactive isotope of hydrogen, the nucleus of which contains one *proton and two *neutrons. It does not occur naturally but is produced in nuclear reactors and is used as a radioactive tracer and in nuclear weapons. Tritium decays with a half-life of 12.3 years, emitting beta-rays.

Triton In Greek mythology, a sea deity, the son of Poseidon and Amphitrite. He is usually portrayed as human above the waist and as a dolphin below; he blows a shell in order to control the waves.

triton shell A *gastropod mollusk of the family *Cymatiidae* (about 100 species), occurring mainly in tropical seas. Triton trumpets (genus *Charonia*) grow to 16 in (40 cm) and have ribbed shells, often with prominent knobs. They are carnivorous, feeding on mollusks and echinoderms. Hairy tritons have a rough hairy shell.

triumvirate In Roman affairs, a board of three men officially appointed for special administrative duties. The so-called first Triumvirate (60 BC) of Caesar, Pompey, and Crassus was merely a private arrangement for mutual convenience. The triumvirate, or triple dictatorship, of Mark Antony, Lepidus, and Octavian was unique; appointed in 43 BC to maintain public order in Rome, they held office with absolute powers until Lepidus was ousted in 36 and power was divided between Mark Antony and Octavian.

Trivandrum 8 41N 76 57E A city in India, the capital of Kerala. A cultural, commercial, and communications center, it processes minerals and is the site of the University of Kerala (1937). Population (1991): 523,733.

Trnova. *See* Tŭrnovo.

Trobriand Islands A group of coral islands in the SW Pacific Ocean, in Papua New Guinea. The largest is Kiriwana (Trobriand). It produces yams, mother-of-pearl, and trepang (edible sea cucumber). The islands became famous through the studies of the anthropologist Bronisław Malinowski. Area: about 170 sq mi (440 sq km).

trogon An insectivorous bird belonging to a family (*Trogonidae*; 35 species) occurring in forested regions of Africa, Asia. and America; 9.5–18 in (24–46 cm) long, trogons have iridescent plumage, which in males is usually dark with a bright red or yellow belly. They have rounded wings, a short curved bill, and a long tail and are the sole family of the order *Trogoniformes*. *See also* quetzel.

Troilus In Greek mythology, a son of King Priam of Troy who was killed by Achilles. The story of his love for Cressida, who deserted him for the Greek Diomedes, first appeared in the *Roman de Troie* by the 12th-century French poet Benoît de Sainte-Maure.

Trois-Rivières 46 21N 72 34W A city and deepwater port in E Canada, in Quebec on the St Lawrence River. Founded in 1610, it is a transport and industrial center, producing a large proportion of the world's newsprint. Population (1986): 129,000.

Trojan Horse In Greek legend, a gigantic hollow wooden horse devised by Odysseus or by its builder, Epeius, in the *Trojan War. The Trojans hauled it inside their city, believing it to be a gift to Athena, and Greek warriors then emerged from it to open the gates to their army.

Trojan War In Greek legend, a 10 years' war waged by the Greeks against *Troy after the abduction of *Helen, wife of King Menelaus of Sparta, by Paris, a Trojan prince. Its history, probably based on an actual war fought in the 12th century BC, is related in Homer's *Iliad*. The Greeks were led by *Agamemnon and their champions included *Achilles, *Diomedes, and *Odysseus. The chief Trojan warriors were *Hector and *Paris, sons of King Priam. Most of the action in the *Iliad* is concentrated in the final year of the war and culminates in the capture of Troy by the stratagem of the *Trojan Horse.

troll In Scandinavian folklore, originally a gigantic ogre-like creature imagined as guarding treasure, inhabiting a castle, and stalking through the forest only at night since they are destroyed or turned to stone if they see the sun. In later folklore, trolls were conceived as dwarflike cave- and mountain-dwellers who were skilled craftsmen.

Trollope, Anthony (1815–82) British novelist. He worked for the post office (1834–67). He established his reputation with a series of novels set in the imaginary county of Barsetshire with a cast of predominantly clerical characters. These books include *The Warden* (1855), *Barchester Towers* (1857), and *The Last Chronicle of Barset* (1867). A second series of novels, set against a political background, includes *Phineas Finn* (1869) and *The Eustace Diamonds* (1873).

trombone A brass musical instrument, consisting of a cylindrical tube, about 10 ft (3 m) long, turned back upon itself, a cup-shaped mouthpiece, and a flaring bell. By means of a slide that is used in seven positions and by varying lip pressure, seven different harmonic series can be produced, covering a chromatic range of almost three octaves above E below the bass stave in the tenor trombone. A bass instrument also exists. The trombone has been part of the symphony orchestra since the late 18th century and is frequently used in jazz. The old English name for the trombone was the **sackbut**.

Tromp, Maarten (Harpertszoon) (1598–1653) Dutch admiral. He defeated a numerically superior Spanish fleet at the battle of the Downs (1639). His encounter with the English (1652) began the first *Dutch War, during which he defeated the English off Dungeness (1652). He died in action. His son **Cornelis (Martenszoon) Tromp** (1629–91) was an admiral in the second and third *Dutch Wars and was briefly commander in chief of the Dutch fleet (1665), being replaced by de *Ruyter.

trompe l'oeil (French: fool the eye) A method of painting figures and objects to create the illusion that they are real rather than painted. The elaborate arches, vistas, doors, etc., painted on walls in Pompeii are an example of this visual illusion. It is also associated with Italian *baroque art.

Tromsø 69 42N 19 00E A seaport in N Norway, on an island just off the mainland. The largest town N of the Arctic Circle, its industries include fishing, sealing, and fish processing. Its university was established in 1968. Population (1981 est): 46,454.

Trondheim 63 36N 10 23E A city and seaport in W Norway on Trondheim Fjord. It has a famous cathedral (12th–14th centuries) where Norwegian sovereigns have been crowned since early times. The Technical University of Norway was established there in 1900 and the University of Trondheim in 1968. Its industries include ship building and fishing; the main exports are timber, wood pulp, fish, and metal goods. Population (1992 est): 139,660.

tropic bird A white seabird belonging to a family (*Phaethontidae*; 3 species) occurring in tropical and subtropical waters. Tropic birds have black eye and wing markings and are up to 20 in (50 cm) long excluding the long streamerlike tail feathers. Tropic birds spend most of their lives at sea. Order: *Pelecaniformes* (cormorants, pelicans, etc.).

tropics The area of the earth's surface lying roughly between the Tropic of Cancer on the 23°30″ N parallel of latitude and the Tropic of Capricorn on the 23°30″S parallel.

tropism The growth of a plant or sedentary animal in response to a directional external stimulus: a growth movement toward the stimulus is a positive tropism;

the opposite response is a negative tropism. Different forms of tropism are named according to the type of stimulus. For example, positive **hydrotropism** is growth toward water, observed in plant roots; negative **geotropism** is growth away from the pull of gravity, which occurs in plant stems.

troposphere. *See* atmosphere.

Trossachs, the 56 13N 4 23W A picturesque glen in central Scotland, in the Central Region between Loch Katrine and Loch Achray. It was popularized by Sir Walter Scott in his poem *The Lady of the Lake.*

Trotsky, Leon (Lev Bronstein; 1879–1940) Russian revolutionary and Marxist theorist. Trotsky became a Marxist in the 1890s and was imprisoned and exiled for participating in revolutionary activities. He lived in W Europe from 1902 until the Revolution of 1905. Again imprisoned and exiled, he escaped abroad (1907), where he remained until 1917. On the outbreak of the Russian Revolution, he returned to Russia and abandoned his previous *Menshevik loyalties to become a *Bolshevik. He played a major role in the October Revolution, which brought the Bolsheviks to power, and as war commissar during the civil war (1918–20) directed the Red Army to victory. Under Lenin, Trotsky was Russia's second most powerful man but lost to Stalin the power struggle that followed Lenin's death and was banished from the Soviet Union. He moved eventually to Mexico, where he was murdered, probably by a Soviet agent. *See also* Trotskyism.

Trotskyism The form of Marxism developed by Leon *Trotsky, who advocated world revolution in opposition to the view that socialism could be achieved in one country in isolation. Stalin sought to secure the Soviet Union against the counterrevolutionary forces of capitalism, primarily by military and economic means. Trotskyists believed that the revolution could only be maintained and capitalism defeated by developing the strength and solidarity of the working class throughout the world, since the main struggle was against the capitalist class and not between states. To this end Trotsky and his supporters founded the Fourth International in 1937, after what they saw as the degeneration of the Third International under the influence of Stalinism. Despite Trotsky's murder in 1940 and various subsequent internal splits, in 1979 the Fourth International had functioning sections in over 60 countries. These and other revolutionary groups with Trotskyist aims were regarded as dangerous and counterrevolutionary by the leaders of communist states.

troubadours Provençal poets of the 12th to 14th centuries whose lyric poetry had a profound influence on both the subject matter and form of subsequent European verse. A number of the troubadours were of noble birth and were enthusiastically patronized by several European courts. Both poets and composers, the troubadours wrote songs introducing a new concept of love, later labeled *courtly love (although they were also noted for their satires and poems on political subjects). They developed several poetic genres and verse forms, including the *canso d'amor* (a love song in five or six stanzas), the *pastorela* (a narrative relating a meeting between a knight and a shepherdess), the *alba* (a song of lovers parting at dawn), the *tenso* or *partimen* (a debate on love), and the *sestina* (a poem of six stanzas with the same end-words repeated in each stanza according to a shifting pattern). The earliest troubadour was Guillaume, 9th duc d'Aquitaine (1071–1127). Other famous troubadours were Marcabru (mid-12th century); Bertrand de Born, vicomte de Hautefort (c. 1140–c. 1207); Arnaut Daniel (c. 1180), who was credited with inventing the *sestina* and was considered the greatest craftsman by Dante; and Bernard de Ventadour (late 12th century), in whose lyrics the conventions of courtly love were most clearly developed. *See also* trouvères.

trout One of several predatory fish belonging to the family *Salmonidae*, especially the genus *Salmo*, that are native to the N hemisphere but introduced elsewhere as food and game fish. It has a stout body with a blunt head and varies in color from blackish to light olive with characteristic black or red spots or X-shaped markings. Trout occur mainly in fresh water but in some cases the young migrate to the sea to mature and return annually to streams to spawn. The common European brown trout (*S. trutta*), up to 55 in (140 cm) long, has a migratory variety called the sea trout. The North American rainbow trout (*S. gairdneri*), up to 27.5 in (70 cm) long, is distinguished by a broad purple band along its sides. Order: *Salmoniformes*.

trouvères Medieval poets of N France, especially Picardy, who were contemporary with, and influenced in subject matter and style by, the *troubadours. Notable trouvères include Conon de Béthune (d. 1224), Thibaud (IV) de Champagne, king of Navarre (d. 1253), *Adam de la Halle, and Rutebeuf (13th century).

Troy An ancient city in Asia Minor, near the Dardanelles. According to legend, when the Trojan prince *Paris abducted *Helen, her husband's brother, *Agamemnon, led a Greek force to recover her, captured Troy by the stratagem of the wooden horse after 10 years' fighting, and destroyed it (traditional date: 1184 BC.) □Schliemann's excavations (1870) identified Troy at Hissarlik. Excavations have revealed nine superimposed cities, the seventh of which (not the second, as Schliemann thought) was contemporary with the legendary siege and had met a violent end. *See also* Homer; Trojan War.

Troy 42 43N 73 40W A city in E central New York where the Mohawk River flows into the Hudson River, NE of Albany. Rensselaer Polytechnic Institute (1824) and Russell Sage College (1916) are there. Founded in 1789, the city became the starting point of the Erie Canal in 1825 and is now the beginning of the New York State Barge Canal. Industries include textiles and clothing, especially shirts; automotive supplies, steel, machinery, paper, and food processing. Population (1990): 54,269.

Trudeau, Garry (1948–   ) US satirical cartoonist. While at Yale University, he began publishing cartoons and in 1970 began the syndicated strip "Doonesbury," which often satirized national political figures and events. Trudeau won a Pulitzer Prize for the strip in 1974, and his readership expanded dramatically to more than 400 newspapers. His subject matter often sparked controversy. Collections of "Doonesbury" often appeared in book form, such as *But This War Had Such Promise* (1975), and he also wrote plays, including *Doonesbury* (1983).

Trudeau, Pierre Elliott (1919–   ) Canadian statesman; Liberal prime minister (1968–79, 1980–84). A French Canadian, he nevertheless opposed French separatism and in 1970 briefly introduced martial law to deal with separatist agitation in Quebec. In the same year his government recognized the People's Republic of China. Trudeau's dashing image was reinforced by his young wife, Margaret Trudeau, but the couple finally separated in 1977 after a series of much publicized estrangements. Defeated in 1979 by Joseph *Clark, he was reelected in 1980. Trudeau retired from office in 1984, and his Liberal party lost the subsequent general election.

Truffaut, François (1932–84) French film director. He wrote for the magazine *Cahiers du Cinéma* during the 1950s and was an influential member of the *New Wave. His films, noted for their visual charm and elegance, include *The 400 Blows* (1959), *Shoot the Piano Player* (1960), *Jules et Jim* (1961), *L'Enfant* *sauvage* (1970), *Day for Night* (1973), *The Story of Adele H.* (1975), and *Love on the Run* (1978).

truffle A fungus belonging to the order *Tuberales*. Up to 4 in (10 cm) across, truffles are rounded, often with a rough pitted surface, and occur in chalky soils, usually in association with tree roots. Having a strong smell and taste, they are unearthed and eaten by squirrels, rabbits, etc., which disperse the spores in their feces. Several species are regarded as delicacies, including the black Périgord truffle (*Tuber melanosporum*) and the white Piedmont truffle (*T. magnatum*). They are collected in oak woods using trained pigs or dogs. The bluish-black English truffle (*T. aestivum*) is found mainly in beech woods. Class: *Ascomycetes*.

Trujillo 8 06S 79 00W A city in Peru, situated 8 mi (13 km) from its port, Salaverry, on the Pacific coast. Founded in 1535, it has many colonial buildings and a university (established in 1824 by Simón Bolívar). Trujillo is the commercial center for an area producing sugarcane and rice. Population (1990 est): 532,000.

Trujillo (Molina), Rafael (Leónidas) (1891–1961) Dominican dictator, who governed the Dominican Republic, directly or indirectly, from 1938 to 1961, aided by a powerful police force. His tyranny led to his assassination.

Truman, Harry S. (1884–1972) US statesman; 33rd president of the United States (1945–53). After service in World War I, Truman studied law and began his political career as presiding judge of Jackson County, Mo. (1926–34). Elected to the US Senate in 1934, Truman was chosen as the vice-presidential running mate of Pres. Franklin *Roosevelt in 1944. After Roosevelt's death the following year, Truman succeeded to the presidency and inherited the responsibility of bringing World War II to an end.

During his first year in office he authorized the atomic bombing of Hiroshima and Nagasaki to force Japan's surrender and played an important part in the *Potsdam Conference that determined the fate of the postwar world. Later in his administration, he introduced the **Truman Doctrine** to provide economic and military aid to countries threatened by interference from other states (1947) and the *Marshall Plan of postwar economic aid to Europe (1948). In 1948 he also ordered a massive airlift to prevent the Communist takeover of West Berlin. Winning reelection by his victory over the Republican candidate, Thomas E. *Dewey, in the 1948 elections, Truman began his second term in office by announcing his *Fair Deal program of domestic social reform. During his second term, however, Truman was increasingly preoccupied by foreign affairs. In 1949 he helped to establish the *North Atlantic Treaty Organization, and beginning in 1950, he directed the American military participation in the *Korean War, which included a dramatic confrontation with Gen. Douglas *MacArthur. Truman retired from public office at the end of his second term in 1953.

trumpet A brass □musical instrument. The modern trumpet consists of a cylindrical tube, 5 ft (1.5 m) long, turned back on itself, a cup-shaped mouthpiece, and a flaring bell. Three valves alter the effective length of the tube, allowing the notes of the harmonic series on six successive semitones to be played. With varying lip pressure the B-flat trumpet has a chromatic range of two and a half octaves below E below middle C. The early trumpet (from the Renaissance to the early 19th century) could only produce the notes of its natural harmonic series. The upper notes of the series were known as the *clarino* (Italian: clarinet) register, much used for brilliant effects by such composers as Bach.

trumpet creeper A vine of the genus *Campsis*. The American trumpet creeper (*C. radicans*) is native to the S US and the Chinese trumpet creeper

(*C. grandiflora*) is of Asian origin. Both produce trumpet-shaped orange flowers and are cultivated as ornamentals. Family: *Bignoniaceae*.

HARRY S. TRUMAN *President (1945–53) who ended World War II by ordering the atomic bomb dropped on Japanese cities.*

trumpeter A long-legged ground-dwelling bird belonging to a family (*Psophiidae*; 3 species) occurring in forests of N South America; 20 in (50 cm) long, trumpeters have a small head, soft dark plumage, and short bills, feeding on insects and berries. They travel in small flocks and have a loud trumpeting call. Order: *Gruiformes* (cranes, rails, etc.).

trunkfish A tropical fish, also called boxfish or cowfish, belonging to a family (*Ostraciidae*) related to *puffers, that occurs in the Atlantic and Pacific Oceans. Its body is often brightly colored and encased in a boxlike shell of fused bony plates with spaces for the fins, etc.

trust In law, a binding arrangement between two persons (or groups) in which one (the trustee, who may be an individual or a corporation) has control of property (the trust property), which he administers for the benefit of the other (the beneficiary). The trustee may himself be one of the beneficiaries. Trusts developed in the Middle Ages when certain parties, such as religious orders, had the use or benefit of property that they were not allowed to own.

trust territory A territory being prepared for self-government, for which the UN is responsible. There is now only one—Micronesia. The trust territories replaced the *mandates of the League of Nations.

Truth, Sojourner (Isabella Baumfree; ?1797–1883) US evangelist and reformer. A former slave (?1797–1827) in New York state, she took her symbolic name and traveled the country, preaching in favor of the emancipation of slaves and women's rights. She claimed to have had visions and heard voices instructing her in her work. She later was appointed by President Lincoln to aid freedmen.

trypanosomiasis Any infection caused by parasitic protozoa of the genus *Trypanosoma*. In Africa the parasite is transmitted by the tsetse fly and causes *sleeping sickness. In South America another species is transmitted by a bug and causes *Chagas' disease.

trypsin A digestive enzyme, secreted by the pancreas, that breaks down dietary proteins in the small intestine. It is secreted in an inactive form, which is converted to trypsin by the enzyme enterokinase in the intestine.

Ts'ao Chan. *See* Cao Chan.

tsar The title (derived from the Latin, Caesar) of the rulers of Russia from 1547 to 1721. It was first adopted by Ivan the Terrible and, though commonly used until 1917, was officially replaced with the title emperor by Peter the Great.

Tsaritsyn. *See* Volgograd.

Tselinograd (name until 1961: Akmolinsk) 51 10N 71 28E A city in W Kazakhstan. It produces agricultural machinery and is a railroad junction. Population (1991 est): 286,000.

tsetse fly A fly, 0.25–0.6 in (6–16 mm) long, belonging to a genus (*Glossina*; 22 species) restricted to tropical Africa. Both sexes bite and suck the blood of mammals, transmitting trypanosomes to man and domestic animals. Thus *G. palpalis* carries human sleeping sickness and *G. morsitans* transmits nagana in cattle. The larvae develop to maturity within the female before being deposited in the soil to pupate. Family: *Muscidae*.

Tshombe, Moise (Kapenda) (1919–69) Congolese statesman; prime minister (1964–65) of the Congo (now Zaïre). He led the secession of the copper-rich Katanga (now Shaba) province of the Congo in 1960, which for three years maintained its independence under Tshombe's presidency. On its collapse Tshombe fled to Spain but was recalled briefly to become the Congo's prime minister. Dismissed by President Kasavubu in 1965, he returned to Spain and died of a heart attack in Algeria.

Tsinan. *See* Jinan.

Tsinghai. *See* Qinghai.

Tsingtao. *See* Qingdao.

Tsiolkovski, Konstantin Eduardovich (1857–1935) Russian aeronautical engineer, who pioneered space and rocket research. Becoming deaf as a child he studied mathematics and physics. In 1892 he built the first wind tunnel in Russia, which he used for testing his designs of dirigibles. He then went on to investigate the use of rockets in space travel and anticipated many of the ideas that Robert *Goddard was later to develop, especially liquid-fueled rockets.

Tsushima A group of five Japanese islands, in the Korea Strait. During the Russo-Japanese War, Russia suffered a major naval defeat nearby (1905). Fishing is the chief industry. Area: 269 sq mi (698 sq km). Population (1991): 46,064. Capital: Izuhara.

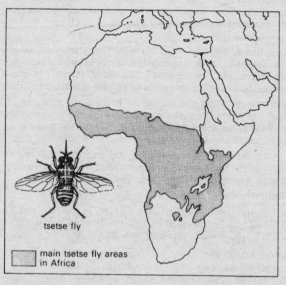

tsetse fly

main tsetse fly areas in Africa

TSETSE FLY *Several species of tsetse fly carry the parasites causing sleeping sickness in man and cattle. The tsetse areas in Africa correspond to the areas where sleeping sickness is endemic.*

Tsvetaeva, Marina (1892–1941) Russian poet. Her highly original and emotionally powerful poetry was praised by Akhmatova, Pasternak, and other contemporaries. She opposed the Revolution and left Russia in 1922 to live in Prague, Berlin, and Paris. In 1939 she followed her husband back to Russia. He was shot, and she later committed suicide.

Tuamotu Archipelago A chain of about 80 coral atolls in the S Pacific Ocean, in French Polynesia. Rangiroa is the largest island and Fakarava, the most important economically. French nuclear tests were held there during the 1960s. Mother-of-pearl, phosphate, and copra are produced. Area: 332 sq mi (860 sq km). Administrative center: Apataki atoll.

tuatara A lizardlike reptile, *Sphenodon punctatus*, that is the only living representative of the primitive order *Rhynchocephalia*, which lived 200 million years ago. It is found only on islands off the North Island of New Zealand and has a brown-black to greenish body with a crest of spines running from head to tail; up to 27.5 in (70 cm) long, it may live 100 years. Tuataras live in burrows during the day and emerge at night to feed on spiders, insects, and birds' eggs. The clutch of 8 to 14 eggs is incubated for 13 to 14 months before hatching.

Tuatha Dé Danann (Old Irish: people of the goddess *Danu) In Old Irish mythology, a divine race, one of the several mythological groups believed to have invaded and settled in Ireland. According to the *Book of Invasions*, they came from the east in the mid-15th century BC and were learned in science and the arts of the Druids. Sometimes they are portrayed as mortal men but exceptionally strong, beautiful, learned, etc.

tuba A valved brass instrument with a conical bore and low pitch, derived originally from the *saxhorn. Various types of tuba exist under a variety of names; the instrument is used in the symphony orchestra as well as in the military band. The **Wagner tuba** is not a true tuba but a bass version of the *French horn.

tuber A swollen underground plant stem in which carbohydrates (often in the form of starch) are stored. Some tubers, for example potatoes and yams, are important human foods. Tuber-bearing plants may reproduce vegetatively from buds on the tuber, and tuber crops are usually grown from tubers rather than seed.

tuberculin A protein derived from tuberculosis bacilli that have been killed. In the Mantoux test tuberculin is injected into the skin to test whether a person has been in contact with tuberculosis. The appearance of an inflamed patch (a positive reaction) indicates previous exposure to the bacilli (and therefore some immunity) but not necessarily active infection.

tuberculosis An infectious disease caused by the bacillus *Mycobacterium tuberculosis* (which was first recognized by Robert *Koch in 1882). In pulmonary tuberculosis the bacillus is inhaled into the lungs, where it forms a primary tubercle that usually heals without trouble. Alternatively the disease may smolder for months without showing any symptoms: affected people can act as carriers without being aware that they are infected. Reactivation of the primary disease, or reinfection, may lead to active tuberculosis ("consumption"), characterized by a cough (often producing some blood), fever, lassitude, weight loss, and breathlessness. The infection may also spread to other organs. The TB bacillus can also enter the body through drinking infected cows' milk, setting up a primary tubercle in the abdominal lymph nodes. Improved environmental conditions, pasteurization of milk, X-ray screening, and *BCG vaccinations have all reduced the incidence of TB in developed countries. Treatment consists of rest, isolation, and such antibiotics as streptomycin, isoniazid (INH), and para-aminosalicylic acid (PAS).

tuberose A perennial summer-flowering garden plant, *Polianthes tuberosa*, native to SW North America. It has tuberous roots, long narrow bright-green leaves clustered at the base of the stem, and smaller clasping leaves along the stem. Its fragrant waxy-white flowers are arranged in pairs on a terminal spike and are used to manufacture perfume. Family: *Amaryllidaceae*.

tubifex A freshwater *annelid worm, also called bloodworm, belonging to the widely distributed family *Tubificidae*. Found along muddy rivers and estuaries, the most common species is the bright-red extremely active *Tubifex tubifex*, up to 3.34 in (85 mm) long. Class: *Oligochaeta*.

Tübingen 48 32N 9 04E A city in SW Germany, in Baden-Württemberg on the Neckar River. The university (1477) is famed for its theological facility established in the 19th century. Industries include publishing and textile manufacture. Population (1985): 75,000.

Tubman, Harriet (Araminta T.; c. 1820–1913) US abolitionist. An escaped (1849) slave herself, she aided other slaves in escaping to the North via the *Underground Railroad. In all, she is credited with guiding more than 300 slaves to freedom along a dangerous South-to-North route. During the Civil War she worked for the Union Army.

Tubman, William V(acanarat) S(hadrach) (1895–1971) Liberian statesman; president (1943–71). A lawyer and Methodist lay preacher, he was largely responsible for welding together into a modern nation-state the peoples of diverse origins in Liberia and passed much social and political reform.

Tubuai Islands (*or* Austral Is) 23 23S 149 27W A group of seven islands in S French Polynesia, including Tubuai and Rurutu. Coffee, copra, and arrowroot are produced. Area: 67 sq mi (173 sq km).

tubular bells A tuned percussion instrument consisting of a row of metal tubes, graduated in length, hung on a frame and struck with a leather-covered hammer.

Tucson 32 15N 110 57W A city and health resort in Arizona. Its growth came with the arrival of the Southern Pacific Railroad (1880) and the discovery of silver at nearby Tombstone. Tucson is an industrial center for the surrounding agricultural and mining district and site of the University of Arizona (1885). Population (1990): 405,390.

Tucumán. *See* San Miguel de Tucumán.

Tudors The ruling dynasty of England from 1485 to 1603. Owen Tudor (c. 1400–61), a Welshman, entered the service of Henry V and married (1422) his widow Catherine of Valois (1401–37). Their eldest son Edmund, earl of Richmond (c. 1430–56), married Margaret *Beaufort, the great-great-grand-daughter of Edward III, and their son became the first Tudor monarch Henry VII. Subsequent Tudor monarchs were Henry VIII, Edward VI, Mary I, and Elizabeth I.

tufted titmouse. *See* tit.

Tu Fu. *See* Du Fu.

Tugela River A river in South Africa, flowing generally E from the Drakensberg Mountains, where it forms the **Tugela Falls**, 2810 ft (856 m) high, to the Indian Ocean. Length: about 310 mi (500 km).

tui A black *honeyeater, *Prosthemadera novaeseelandiae*, occurring in mountain forests of New Zealand. It is about 10.6 in (27 cm) long and has a white tufted throat. Once common, it has been extensively captured for its ability to mimic human speech and is now very rare.

Tula An ancient *Toltec city in central Mexico. Adopted as the Toltec capital around 980 AD, Tula was destroyed in 1168. Distinctive Toltec features there include a terraced pyramid, colonnaded buildings, and extensive use of militaristic motifs in relief sculptures.

Tula 54 11N 37 38E A city in Russia, 105 mi (169 km) S of Moscow. An important ironworks center since the 17th century, it also has food-processing industries. Tolstoy lived at nearby Yasnaya Polyana. Population (1991 est): 544,000.

tulip A perennial herbaceous plant of the genus *Tulipa* (about 100 species), native to the Old World but widely cultivated for ornament. Growing from bulbs, most tulips have a solitary bell-shaped flower, with bluish-green leaves—ranging from long and narrow to oval and pointed—clustered at the base of the plant. There are nearly 4000 varieties of garden tulips, which show enormous variation in color and type: the older varieties are descended from *T. gesneriana* and *T. suaveolens*; the newer ones often have *T. kaufmanniana, T. greigi*, or *T. fosteriana* as one of the parent species. The Netherlands, the Channel Islands, and Lincolnshire (England) are main commercial growing areas. Family: *Liliaceae*.

tulip tree A tree, *Liriodendron tulipifera*, native to E North America and widely planted for ornament. Reaching a height of 190 ft (58 m) in the wild, it has three-lobed blunt-ended leaves, which turn golden yellow in autumn. The flowers are large and tuliplike, greenish white or yellow, and produce papery cones containing winged fruits. The wood, known as white wood, is used for furniture, plywood, paper, and boxes. The Chinese tulip tree (*L. chinense*) is similar but smaller. Family: *Magnoliaceae*.

Tull, Jethro (1674–1741) English agriculturalist, best known for his invention in 1701 of the seed drill. The drill planted seeds in straight lines, thus facilitating weeding, and automatically covered them with soil to protect them from birds. He made many other innovations in agricultural methods.

Tulsa 36 07N 95 58W A city in Oklahoma, on the Arkansas River. Oil was discovered in 1901 and today over 800 oil companies have established plants there. It has also developed as a port since the opening of a waterway (1971) linking Tulsa to the Gulf of Mexico. Population (1990): 367,302.

Tulufan Depression (Turpan Depression *or* Turfan Depression) A mountain basin in NW China. Known for its fruit, it was the center of an Indian-Persian civilization (3rd–4th centuries AD). Lowest point: 505 ft (154 m) below sea level.

tumor Any swelling in the body caused by the abnormal proliferation of cells. Tumors that do not spread to other parts of the body (i.e. are noncancerous) are described as benign. They are usually harmless but may become very large, exerting pressure on neighboring tissues: in such cases they are often surgically removed. Tumors that destroy the tissue in which they arise and spread to other parts of the body are described as malignant (*see* cancer).

tuna A carnivorous food and game fish, sometimes called tunny, belonging to a family (*Scombridae*) found in warm seas. Its elongated robust body is generally dark above and silvery below, with a keeled tail base and finlets behind the anal and dorsal fins. The large bluefin tuna (*Thunnus thynnus*) reaches 14 ft (4.3 m) in length. Large quantities of canned tuna are consumed throughout the world. Order: *Perciformes*. *See also* albacore; skipjack; yellowfin tuna. □oceans.

tundra The level, virtually treeless, areas in the N hemisphere (in Eurasia and North America) lying between the most northerly region in which trees grow and the polar regions of perpetual snow and ice. Winters are long and severe with brief summers in which temperatures remain below 50°F (10°C); *permafrost is a feature. Vegetation is able to grow in summer and includes mosses, lichens, dwarf shrubs, herbaceous perennials, and a few stunted trees, such as willows and birches. Through freeze-thaw processes on the ground a variety of patterns can form, such as stone polygons and soil circles.

T'ung-chih. *See* Tong Zhi.

tung oil (*or* wood oil) A pale-yellow oil obtained from the seeds of the tung tree (*Aleurites fordii*; family *Euphorbiaceae*), found in China. It polymerizes spontaneously (and on heating) to a hard gel and is used in paints and varnishes.

tungsten (*or* wolfram; W) A gray brittle metal with the highest melting point of any element. It was discovered in 1779 and is obtained from the ores wolframite ($FeWO_4$) and scheelite ($CaWO_4$) by reduction with hydrogen or carbon. It oxidizes readily when heated, forming the oxide WO_3. The metal is used extensively as filaments in electric light bulbs, as well as in television tubes, contact breakers, and X-ray tubes. It is also used in many hard alloys for high-speed cutting tools. Tungsten carbide (WC) is very hard and is used for tipping drill bits. At no 74; at wt 183.85; mp 6176 ± 36°F (3410 ± 20°C); bp 10,230°F (5660°C).

Tung-t'ing, Lake. *See* Dongting, Lake.

Tunguska River Three rivers in Russia, in Siberia comprising tributaries of the Yenisei River. These are the **Lower** (Nizhnyaya) **Tunguska**, 1670 mi (2690 km) long, the **Stony** (Podkammenaya) **Tunguska**, 960 mi (1550 km) long, and the **Upper** (Verkhnyaya) **Tunguska**, the lower course of the Angara River.

tunicate A small marine animal belonging to the subphylum *Urochordata* (or *Tunicata*; about 2000 species). Tunicates are cylindrical, spherical, or irregular in shape, ranging from several millimeters to over 12 in (30 cm) in size. They have a saclike cellulose tunic covering the body; water is drawn in through a siphon at the top and expelled through a second siphon. Food particles are filtered out and propelled along flagellated grooves to the mouth. Individuals are hermaphrodite and produce free-swimming tadpolelike larvae that show the major characteristics of all *Chordates. They subsequently undergo metamorphosis, losing their chordate features and becoming adults. The class *Larvacea* retain their larval characteristics throughout life. Sea squirts (class *Ascidacea*) live attached to rocks, etc., singly or in colonies, while the salps (class *Thaliacea*) float in the sea, sometimes as chains of several hundred individuals.

tuning fork A two-pronged metal fork that vibrates at a fixed frequency when struck. It is used by musicians to verify *pitch. Electrically maintained tuning forks, operated by an electromagnet, are also used in scientific experiments.

Tunis (Arabic name: Tunus) 36 48N 10 13E The capital of Tunisia, on the Gulf of Tunis. It was developed by the Arabs in the 7th century AD. It came under French rule in the late 19th century, and became the capital on independence in 1956. The Islamic university was founded in 1960. Industries include chemicals, lead smelting, and textiles. Population (1989 est): 620,000.

Tunisia, Republic of (Arabic name: al-Jumhuriyah at-Tunisiyah) A small country in N Africa, bordering on the Mediterranean Sea. Its narrow coastal zone, where over half the total population live, extends into desert in the S and rises to uplands in the N. The population is largely Arabic with a Berber minority. *Economy*: predominantly agricultural, the chief products include wheat, olive oil, citrus fruits, dates, and wine; livestock, including sheep, cattle, and goats, is also important. Mining is a major source of revenue and Tunisia is one of the world's largest producers of phosphates. Oil reserves were discovered in 1964 and exploitation began in 1972; iron ore and lead are also mined. Manufacturing industry is based largely on processing the local raw materials and includes oil refining, cement, and steel processing. Fine beaches and notable architecture contribute to Tunisia's popularity with tourists. *History*: first settled by the Phoenicians, it developed into the empire of Carthage and was later absorbed into the Roman Empire, becoming "the granary of Rome." Under the dynasty of the Berber Hafsids (1207–1574) it became powerful. During the 19th century Tunisia's strategic importance aroused European interest and in 1883 it became a French protectorate. It was the scene of fierce fighting in World War II and gained independence from France (1956) following the nationalist agitation of the postwar years. Habib Bourguiba was elected president in 1957 and re-elected as life president in 1975. Bourguiba was deposed in 1987 by Zine el Abidine Ben Ali, who was reelected in 1989 in the first free, although still one-party, elections in 33 years. In 1990–91, Tunisia denounced the West's role in the Persian Gulf crisis. Civil strife continued between the government and Islamic fundamentalist groups, and many Tunisians were dissatisfied with the slow pace of democratic reform through the early 1990s. Official religion: Islam. Official language: Arabic; French is widely spoken. Official currency: Tunisian dinar of 1000 millimes. Area: 63,362 sq mi (164,150 sq km). Population (1990 est): 8,094,000. Capital: Tunis.

tunnel effect The passage of an electron or other particle through a potential barrier when, according to classical mechanics, it has insufficient energy to do so. It is explained by *wave mechanics on the basis that the electron is not completely localized in space, part of the energy of the associated wave being able to tunnel through the barrier. The effect has a negligible probability in large-scale systems, but a finite probability in microscopic systems. It is the basis of some radioactive decay processes and is made use of in the **tunnel diode**, a semiconductor device that has a negative resistance over part of its operating range.

tunnels Underground passages for roads, railroads, sewers, or aqueducts for power stations. Tunnels through rock are formed by first drilling holes for explosive, blasting out the rock, removing the debris, and then lining the inside of the tunnel. Tunneling through softer substances requires special techniques: a tunnel shield with a diameter slightly larger than that of the finished tunnel is forced into the ground by hydraulic piston jacks, the earth inside the shield is removed, and the tunnel is then lined, often with concrete sections. *See also* Channel tunnel; Simplon Pass; Mont Blanc.

Tunney, Gene (James Joseph) (1897–1978) US boxer. Although a natural light heavyweight, Tunney defeated heavyweight champion Jack Dempsey in 1926, retaining his title until his retirement from boxing in 1928. Tunney's most famous and controversial title defense came in his 1927 rematch against Dempsey. Known as the "Battle of the Long Count," this bout was highlighted by the referee's delay in beginning the count for a Tunney knockdown until Dempsey went to a neutral corner. Tunney recovered and went on to win the fight.

tunny. *See* tuna.

Tupac Amarú (José Gabriel Condorcanqui; ?1742–81) Peruvian revolutionary. A direct descendant of the last Inca emperor, he led an unsuccessful Indian revolt against Spanish rule in 1780 and was executed. The Tupamaros, the 20th-century South American urban guerrillas, derived their name from his.

Tupi A group of South American Indian peoples and languages including the *Guarani. They are mainly a tropical rain forest people who practice slash and burn agriculture. They also fish in the rivers and off the coast where their villages are located. In some areas, these were fortified against warfare. Cannibalism was common. Culture varied considerably from one region to another. Religion emphasized nature spirits and the "Grandfather Cult," associated with thunder, often led to migrations in search of a promised paradise.

Tupolev, Andrei Niklaievech (1888–1972) Soviet designer of the first supersonic passenger aircraft, the TU-144, tested in 1969. He also designed supersonic bombers, such as the TU-22, and swing-wing bombers. His TU-104, first produced in 1955, was one of the first passenger jet aircraft.

turaco (*or* touraco) A brightly colored arboreal bird belonging to a family (*Musophagidae*; 18 species) occurring in Africa; 13.7–27.5 in (35–70 cm) long, turacos have short rounded wings, a short down-curved bill, and are often crested. Most species have a greenish plumage. They feed on fruit and insects. Order: *Cuculiformes* (cuckoos and turacos).

turbine A device in which a moving fluid drives a wheel or motor, converting the kinetic energy of the fluid into mechanical energy. In its simplest form it is known as a **waterwheel**, which has been in use since ancient times to drive mills, pumps, etc. The principle of the waterwheel forms the basis of the hydraulic turbine, used in the generation of *hydroelectricity. The most widely used types are the Pelton wheel, patented in 1889 by Lester Allen Pelton (1829–1918), the radial Francis turbine, designed in 1849 by J. B. Francis

(1815–92), and the Kaplan turbine, designed by Viktor Kaplan (1876–1937). The Pelton wheel, consisting of a ring of buckets or bucket-shaped vanes arranged around the periphery of a wheel, is known as an impulse turbine as it is only the impulse of the water that makes the wheel turn. The Francis turbine, with its outer ring of stationary guide vanes and inner ring of curved vanes on the surface of one side of the wheel, is a reaction turbine; part of the energy is derived from the impulse of the water and part from the reaction between the water and the blades.

The steam-driven turbine was invented in the 1st century AD by *Hero of Alexandria. However, the first practical turbine to be driven by steam was a reaction device with several rows of turbine wheels (enabling the energy of the expanding steam to be utilized in stages) invented in 1884 by Sir Charles *Parsons. An impulse turbine using several steam nozzles was invented by Carl de Laval (1845–1913) in the 1890s. Since the beginning of the 20th century steam turbines based on these designs have replaced the *steam engine as the prime mover in *power stations. *See also* gas turbine.

TURACO *The feathers of the white-cheeked turaco (Tauraco leucotis), like those of other members of its family, contain a pure-green pigment, turacoverdin (in most birds green is a combination of two pigments—melanin and yellow carotenoid).*

turbot A *flatfish, *Scophthalmus maximus*, that occurs off European shores down to 230 ft (70 m) and sometimes in brackish water. It has a broad circular body, up to 40 in (1 m) long, which is usually light- or gray-brown on the upper (left) side and whitish underneath. It is a valuable food fish. Family: *Bothidae*.

turbulence Any random irregularity in the distribution of velocity or pressure in a fluid. Most flows of rivers and winds are turbulent and turbulence in the atmosphere affects aircraft. Turbulence also causes the laminar layers of flow around an irregular object, or a smooth object at high velocities, to be disturbed, creating a sharp increase in drag. It is to avoid turbulent flow that such objects as airfoils are streamlined (*see* streamlining; aerodynamics). In some cases turbulence is desirable; in the combustion chamber of a gasoline or diesel engine the designer seeks to create turbulence to improve mixing of the fuel and air to improve combustion.

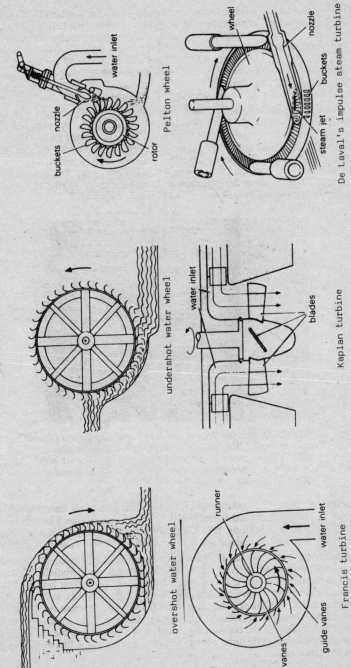

TURBINE

overshot water wheel

undershot water wheel

Pelton wheel
- water inlet
- nozzle
- buckets
- rotor

Francis turbine
- runner
- vanes
- guide vanes
- water inlet

Kaplan turbine
- water inlet
- blades

De Laval's impulse steam turbine
- wheel
- nozzle
- buckets
- steam jet

TURBINE

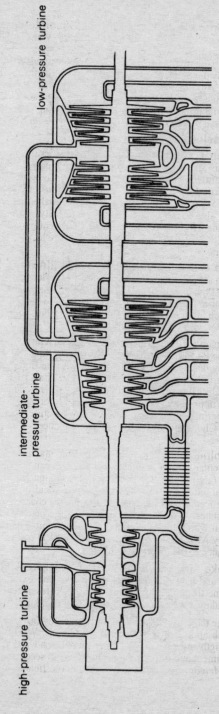

high-pressure turbine

intermediate-
pressure turbine

low-pressure turbine

multistage steam turbine

Turenne, Henri de la Tour d'Auvergne, Vicomte de (1611–75) French marshal, who made his name in the *Thirty Years' War. At the outbreak (1649) of the rebellion against Mazarin (*see* Fronde) he supported the rebels, who were led by his rival *Condé, but in 1652, after transferring his loyalties to the crown, he received a royal command and by 1653 had brilliantly suppressed the revolt. In 1658, at the battle of the Dunes, he again defeated Condé, who now held a Spanish command. He subsequently fought in the War of *Devolution (1667–68) and the third *Dutch War (1672–75), dying in action at Sasbach. He was much admired by Napoleon.

Turfan Depression. *See* Tulufan Depression.

Turgenev, Ivan (1818–83) Russian novelist. His criticism of the Russian social system in his *Sportsman's Sketches* (1852) led indirectly to his brief imprisonment and confinement to his family estate at Spasskoye. His later works, of which the best known are the novel *Fathers and Sons* (1862) and the long story *The Torrents of Spring* (1872), are noted for their analysis of intellectual and social trends. He also wrote poetry and plays, notably *A Month in the Country* (1870). A lifelong admirer of Western society, he went into self-imposed exile in Baden Baden (1862–70) and Paris (1871–83), where he was befriended by many European writers.

Turgot, Anne Robert Jacques, Baron de l'Aulne (1727–81) French economist, who served under Louis XV and XVI. Educated at the Sorbonne, he was one of the *Physiocrats and an advocate of *laissez-faire. He became comptroller general in 1774. There was great opposition to his reforms, especially the Six Edicts, which included the abolition of forced labor, and he was dismissed in 1776.

Turin (Italian name: Torino) 45 04N 7 40E A city in NW Italy, the capital of Piedmont on the Po River. Dating from Roman times, it was associated with the House of Savoy during the Middle Ages. It was the first capital (1861–65) of united Italy. Turin has an ancient university (1404), a 15th-century cathedral, a 17th-century palace, and other notable buildings. It is a center of commerce and industry and is important for the production of motor vehicles. Other industries include engineering, publishing, and the manufacture of textiles, paper, and leather goods. Chocolate and wine are also produced. Population (1991 est): 991,870.

Turing machine A hypothetical computing machine used to determine whether a particular type of mathematical problem can be solved by a computation procedure (algorithm). It is postulated that the machine has an infinite tape that stores characters in a number of discrete locations. The machine goes through a set procedure of scanning and altering the characters, regarded as a series of active states. If the problem is soluble, the machine finally settles in a passive state, in which the tape contains the solution. The concept was developed in 1936 by Alan Mathison Turing (1912–54) and others and represented an important advance in the theory of computer logic.

Turkana, Lake (name until 1979: Lake Rudolph) A lake in Kenya and Ethiopia. Fish and birds abound and, since it has no outlet, it has become increasingly saline through evaporation. Significant fossil finds were made there by Richard Leakey. Area: about 2473 sq mi (6405 sq km).

turkey A large terrestrial bird belonging to a family (*Meleagrididae*; 2 species) native to North and Central American woodlands. Wild turkeys reach 50 in (130 cm) in length and have green-bronze plumage, a warty red neck, and a long fleshy bill ornament and throat wattle. They feed on seeds and insects. The common turkey (*Meleagra gallopavo*) was first domesticated by Mexican Indians and is now raised on large farms for meat. Order: *Galliformes* (pheasants, turkeys, etc.).

Turkey, Republic of A country in the Middle East. The large Asian area, Anatolia, lies between the Mediterranean Sea and the Black Sea. The small European area, Thrace, is bordered by Greece and Bulgaria. Anatolia consists of a central plateau surrounded by mountains, the Pontic Mountains in the N and the *Taurus Mountains in the S. The plateau is semiarid and contains several shallow salt lakes. The high E range contains Mount *Ararat. The coastal areas are the most populous. Minority population groups include Kurds, Arabs, Greeks, Circassians, Georgians, Armenians, Lazes, and Jews; 98% of the population is Muslim. *Economy*: mainly agricultural. Wheat, barley, sugar beet, potatoes, and rice are grown in the interior, and cotton, tobacco, and citrus fruit are grown for export around the coast. Cattle, sheep, and goats are kept for skins, wool, and mohair, which are exported. Copper, chromium, borax, coal, bauxite, and oil are produced, although minerals are not greatly exploited. The main industries are steel, cement, textiles, and fertilizers. Machinery, chemicals, and metals are imported, chiefly from W Europe and the US. Turkey is an associate member of the EEC. Many Turks work in Europe, mainly Germany, for long periods at a time. *History*: Anatolia, formerly known as *Asia Minor, was dominated by the *Seljuqs (1055–1243) and later became the core of the *Ottoman Empire (c. 1300–1922). Under Kemal *Atatürk, who ruled as a virtual dictator, the new Republic of Turkey (declared 1923) was rapidly Westernized; religious orders were abolished and Islam was disestablished; polygamy was forbidden and women were enfranchised; the Arabic alphabet was replaced by the Roman; and relations with W Europe became closer. Economic problems were tackled by the establishment of new industries under state ownership. After the death of Kemal (1938) and World War II, in which Turkey was neutral until finally siding with the Allies in 1945, it became less stable politically, although more democratic. The Democratic party, previously in opposition, came to power in 1950 but grew increasingly reactionary; unrest increased until a military coup took place in 1960. The army again intervened in 1971, when martial law was imposed (until 1973). Violence continued with clashes between left- and right-wing students, and trouble also between Kurds and Turks and between Sunni and Shiite Muslims. Economic difficulties continued during the 1970s and early 1980s with rapid inflation, a large trade deficit, high unemployment, and a reduction in the amount of money sent home by Turks abroad. Relations with Greece have been a further problem; apart from rivalry over Cyprus, which almost resulted in war in 1974, when the island was invaded by Turkish troops, there has also been friction (1976) over Turkey's exploration for oil in the Aegean Sea. A military coup in 1980, led by Gen. Kenan Evren, overthrew the government of Suleiman Demeril. Evren assumed the powers of head of state and a new constitution was introduced in 1982. Turgut Ozal was returned as prime minister following elections held in 1983. In 1989, Ozal became Turkey's first civilian president in 29 years. Yildirim Akbulut became prime minister, but was replaced by Mesut Yilmaz in June 1991. In November 1991, Yilmaz lost the election to Demeril, who formed a coalition government. Unsuccessful Kurdish uprisings in Iraq after the Persian Gulf War caused an influx of Kurdish refugees in 1991, and by 1992 fighting between Kurdish separatist factions and Turkish government troops had increased. In 1993 elections after Ozal's death, Demeril won the presidency. Official language: Turkish; Kurdish and Arabic are also spoken. Official currency: Turkish lira of 100 kurus. Area: 330,883 sq mi (779,452 sq km). Population (1990 est): 56,549,000. Capital: Ankara.

Turkic languages A group of languages of the *Altaic language family, related to *Mongolian and *Manchu-Tungus. Spoken by more than 66 million people, the languages are spread over a geographical area extending from Turkey to Siberia. Originally written in the Arabic script in the 9th century, the languages are now written in the *Cyrillic alphabet in Russia and other countries of the former Soviet Union and in Latin script in Turkey. Phonological processes are characterized by vowel harmony and morphological processes by agglutination.

Turkish A *Turkic language, spoken mainly in Turkey. Since 1929 it has been written in a modified Latin alphabet, replacing Arabic script. Its grammatical system is based on the use of suffixes.

Turkish cat A breed of long-haired cat originating from Turkey. They have long sturdy bodies, chalk-white coats with auburn markings on the face and an auburn tail, and amber-colored eyes. Unusually for cats, they are fond of swimming.

Turkistan (or Turkestan) A region of central Asia, now comprising the Xinjiang Uygur AR of the People's Republic of China, Kazakhstan, Kyrgyzstan, Tajikistan, Turkmenistan, and Uzbekistan. A historic route of travel, migration, and invasion between Asia and Europe, Turkistan has come under many different rulers. The W has been ruled by the Persians from the 6th century BC, Islam from the 7th century AD, and the Russians from the 18th century; the E was long disputed between Chinese dynasties and nomadic tribes.

Turkmen (or Turkoman) A people of SW Asia speaking a language that is part of the *Turkic language group. The majority live as settled farmers in Turkmenistan, but groups in Iran, Afghanistan, E Turkey, N Syria, and N Iraq retain their traditional nomadic existence. Rug making is still an important craft. Their main social division is between those engaged in agriculture and the more prestigious livestock farming. They are Sunni Muslims.

Turkmenistan, Republic of (or Turkmenistan) A republic in central Asia, a constituent republic known as the Turkmen SSR in the Soviet Union until 1991. Some 90% of Turkmenistan comprises desert, including the *Kara Kum, and most of the population (66% of which comprises *Turkmen) are concentrated in oases. The principal occupation is agriculture, mainly cotton, wool, and Karakul pelts. Turkmenistan (founded in 1925) is rich in minerals, including oil and natural gas, and industry is being developed, especially chemicals, textiles, and food. It became independent in 1991 with the collapse of the Soviet Union. Turkmenistan became a member of the Commonwealth of Independent States (CIS) in 1991 and the UN in 1992. Area: 186,400 sq mi (488,100 sq km). Population (1992 est): 3,859,000. Capital: Ashkhabad.

Turks and Caicos Islands A British crown colony consisting of a series of over 30 islands in the Atlantic Ocean, to the SE of the Bahamas. The most important are Grand Turk, Grand Caicos, and Salt Cay. Most of the inhabitants are of African descent. *Economy*: mainly based on fishing, with exports of conchs, conch shells, crawfish, salt, and fishmeal. Tourism is being developed. *History*: the islands were discovered by the Spanish in 1512, but remained uninhabited until 1678, when a Bermudan salt-panning industry was set up. A dependency of Jamaica (1874–1959), they became a crown colony after the dissolution of the Federation of the West Indies in 1962, and gained internal self-government in 1976. Official language: English. Official currency: US dollar of 100 cents. Area: 192 sq mi (430 sq km). Population (1980): 7436. Capital: Grand Turk.

Turku (Swedish name: Åbo) 60 27N 22 15E A seaport and third largest city in Finland, on the Gulf of Bothnia. Capital of Finland until 1812, it has Finnish (1920) and Swedish (1917) universities. Its industries include ship building, saw milling, and engineering. Population (1992 est): 159,541.

turmeric A perennial herbaceous plant, *Curcuma longa*, native to S India and Indonesia and cultivated for its underground rhizomes. It has narrow leaves, 12–18 in (30–45 cm) long, and bears yellow flowers in dense heads, 4–7 in (10–18 cm) long. The rhizomes are boiled and dried in the sun for 5–7 days, then polished and usually sold in ground form. Turmeric is used as a spice in curries, etc., and as a yellow dye. Family: *Zingiberaceae*.

Turner, Frederick Jackson (1861–1932) US historian. A history professor at the University of Wisconsin (1891–1910) and Harvard University (1910–24), he developed the "frontier thesis" as a way of interpreting history. He maintained that Americans were the way they were because of their pioneering way of life for the previous 300 years. His theories, which greatly influenced the teaching of history through the 1930s, were outlined in many books, including *The Significance of History* (1891), *The Significance of the Frontier in American History* (1920), and *The Significance of Sections in American History* (1932; Pulitzer Prize, 1933).

TURNER Peace: Burial at Sea *(1842), oil painting showing the artist's fascination with light.*

Turner, Joseph Mallord William (1775–1851) British landscape and marine painter, born in London, the son of a barber. After studying at the Royal Academy schools and painting many topographical watercolors, he achieved success in the late 1790s with his first landscapes in oil. In 1809 he made the first of several continental tours, which were to provide him with such scenic subjects as the Alps, Venice, and Rome. While supervising the publication of his *Liber Studiorum* (1807–19), a series of engravings based on his works, his style evolved from the Dutch landscape tradition and the classicism of the landscapists *Poussin and *Claude Lorraine into a romantic vision of color, light, and weather anticipating French *impressionism. This vision becomes the real subject of such late paintings as *Rain, Steam, and Speed* (National Gallery, London) and *Interior at Petworth* (Tate Gallery). He bequeathed most of his works to the nation.

Turner, Nat (1800–31) US slave, who led the only substantial US slave revolt. Believing himself to be a divine instrument, he instigated the so-called **Southampton Insurrection**, an attempt by 75 slaves to capture a Virginia armory. More than 50 whites were killed before Turner and many of the rebels were captured and executed. Resulting uneasiness in the South led to repressive antislave legislation.

turnip A biennial plant, **Brassica rapa*, probably native to Asia and widely cultivated for its thick fleshy root, which is used as a vegetable. An erect branching stem, up to 40 in (1 m) high, grows out of the basal leaf rosette in the plant's second season and produces clusters of bright-yellow flowers. However, turnips are usually harvested in the first season. Family: **Cruciferae.*

turnstone A small **plover, Arenaria interpres*, that breeds around Arctic coasts and migrates to the S hemisphere to winter; 8 in (20 cm) long, it has a black-and-brown upper plumage, becoming tortoiseshell in summer, and white underparts. Turnstones have short black bills used to turn over pebbles and shells in search of mollusks, small fish, and sandhoppers.

turpentine An oily liquid extracted from pine resin. Its main constituent is pinene ($C_{10}H_{16}$); it is used as a solvent for paints.

turpentine tree One of several trees yielding a viscous resin. The Australian turpentine tree (*Syncarpia glomuliferae*) grows to a height of about 150 ft (45 m) and has deeply furrowed bark. The timber, which is durable and resistant to fire and wood-boring **shipworms, is used to construct piers, ships, etc. The brush turpentine tree (*S. leptopetala*) is smaller. Family: *Myrtaceae.*

The tropical African tree *Copaifera mopane* (family *Leguminosae*) is also called turpentine tree.

Turpin, Dick (1706–39) British highwayman. He was hanged at York for murder and horse stealing. The story of his ride from London to York on his horse Black Bess, popularized in Harrison Ainsworth's novel *Rookwood* (1834), is probably based on a much older legend.

turquoise An opaque greenish-blue mineral used as a gem. It consists of a basic aluminum phosphate, traces of copper providing the color. Fine specimens have been found in Iran. Birthstone for December.

turtle An aquatic reptile belonging to the order **Chelonia*, which also includes **tortoises and **terrapins; 4–80 in (10–200 cm) long, turtles have broad paddle-like flippers and a streamlined shell and occur in most seas, often migrating long distances to lay eggs on traditional nesting beaches. They are graceful and swift swimmers but clumsy on land. Their diet consists of worms, snails, crustaceans, and fish. Some turtles live in fresh water. *See also* green turtle; leatherback turtle; snake-necked turtle; soft-shelled turtle.

turtle dove A small slender dove, *Streptopelia turtur*, occurring in S Europe and N Africa, visiting N Europe in the summer; 10 in (26 cm) long, it has a checkered red-brown back, gray wings, a pink breast, a black-and-white striped neck patch, and a long white-tipped tail. It feeds on seeds. Family: *Columbidae* (pigeons).

Tuscaloosa 33 13N 87 33W A city in W central Alabama, on the Black Warrior River, SW of Birmingham. The University of Alabama (1831) is there. Settled in 1809 as Tuscaloosa, an Indian word for "black warrior," it served as the state capital (1826–46). Industries include chemical, rubber, lumber, and cottonseed products, paper, and metal pipes. Population (1990): 77,759.

Tuscan order. *See* orders of architecture.

Tuscany (Italian name: Toscana) A region in N central Italy, consisting mainly of hills and mountains with coastal lowlands in the W. It is a predominantly agricultural region producing cereals, wines (Chianti), olives, and fruit. The major manufacturing industries are iron, steel, and ship building. The most important mining region in Italy, it produces lignite, iron, mercury, salt, borax, and marble. Florence is an important tourist and cultural center. Area: 8876 sq mi (22,989 sq km). Population (1991): 3,599,085. Capital: Florence.

Tuscarora War (1711–13) Series of battles between US colonists and the Tuscarora Indians over continuing encroachment by the settlers upon Indian lands and the capturing and selling of young Indians as slaves. Militias from North Carolina, South Carolina, and Virginia finally defeated the Tuscarora, who had attacked the settlers; the Indians relocated to W Pennsylvania and joined the Iroquois League (*see* Iroquois).

Tusculum An ancient city of central Italy, near modern Frascati. A rival of *Rome before about 480 BC but later a staunch ally, Tusculum was granted Roman citizenship in 381 BC. In the 1st century BC Tusculum became a fashionable resort: *Lucullus, *Maecenas, and *Cicero owned villas nearby.

Tuskegee Institute A private coeducational nonsectarian university in Tuskegee, Ala. It was founded (1881) as the Tuskegee Normal and Industrial Institute for training African-American teachers by Booker T. *Washington, who was its president until 1915. It became Tuskegee Institute in 1937 and by 1943 offered graduate studies. It contains an extensive library, with special concentration on information pertaining to African Americans, and houses the George Washington *Carver Museum.

tusk shell A marine *mollusk of the class *Scaphopoda* (about 200 species), also called tooth shell. The common tusk shell (*Dentalium entale*) grows to 2 in (5 cm); its shell is tusk-shaped and open at both ends and it lives partly buried in sand. The mollusk has a digging foot and tentacles around the mouth for collecting microscopic plants and animals. It has no head or gills.

Tussaud, Marie (Marie Grosholtz; 1761–1850) French wax modeler, who went to London in 1802 and founded the famous waxworks museum there. She had previously worked as tutor to Louis XVI's sister and had been imprisoned during the French Revolution.

tussock moth A moth belonging to the family *Lymantriidae*, occurring in both the Old and New Worlds and including the vaporers, tussocks, and *gypsy moths. The caterpillars, cocoons, and adults are typically hairy, frequently causing skin irritation and swelling if handled. Some can be economic pests. Hairs of the caterpillar are arranged in tufts or tussocks.

Tutankhamen King of Egypt (c. 1361–1352 BC) of the 18th dynasty. Tutankhamen, perhaps Akhenaton's son, became king at the age of 11 after the brief reign of *Akhenaton's immediate successor. He abandoned Akhenaton's worship of the sun-god Aton, reinstating that of *Amon and transferring the capital once more to Thebes. His splendid and elaborate tomb, discovered by Howard *Carter in 1922, is the only Egyptian royal tomb to remain substantially intact to modern times. The beauty and craftsmanship of its contents have continued to fascinate the world. □Osiris.

Tutu, Desmond (Bishop) (1931–) South African clergyman; Nobel Peace Prize (1984). A member of the Anglican Church, he attended a teachers' college where he was strongly influenced by Bishop Trevor Huddleston, an outspoken opponent of apartheid. Tutu left teaching and was ordained a minister in 1960.

By 1975 he became Anglican dean of Johannesburg and, in 1978, general secretary of the South African Council of Churches, which has a membership of 12 million. He was the first black to achieve either position. He continued to express his opposition to apartheid and worked to eliminate segregation.

Tutuola, Amos (1920–   ) Nigerian writer. Drawing on Yoruba tribal myths and legends, he created vivid fantasies in which the real and the supernatural co-exist. His works include *The Palm-Wine Drunkard* (1952) and the short-story collection *Feather Woman of the Jungle* (1962).

Tuva Autonomous Republic An administrative division in S Russia. The region is mostly mountainous. Some 50% of the population comprise Tuvinians, a Turkic-speaking people, who are mainly herdsmen and cattle farmers. Industry is rapidly developing. Area: 65,800 sq mi (170,500 sq km). Population (1991 est): 306,600. Capital: Kizyl.

Tuvalu, State of (name until 1976: Ellice Islands) A small country in the SW Pacific Ocean. It consists of a group of nine islands, the main one being Funafuti. Most of the population is Polynesian. *Economy*: subsistence agriculture and fishing are the chief occupations. The main export is copra. *History*: formerly part of the Gilbert and Ellice Islands colony, it became a separate colony after a referendum in 1974 and gained independence in 1978. Tuvalu is a member of the Commonwealth of Nations. Prime minister: Bikenibeu Paeniu. Official language: Tuvalu. Official currency: Australian dollar of 100 cents. Area: 9.5 sq mi (24 sq km). Population (1990 est): 9000. Capital: Funafuti.

Tver. *See* Kalinin.

Twain, Mark (pen name of Samuel Langhorne Clemens; 1835–1910) US journalist and novelist. Early in his career, Mark Twain worked as a steamboat pilot on the Mississippi River and later settled in California, where he became a newspaper reporter. A skillful short-story writer, he first gained a national reputation with "The Celebrated Jumping Frog of Calaveras County" (1865), a humorous tale of life in the Far West. Twain later served as a foreign correspondent, collecting his colorful travel experiences in *The Innocents Abroad* (1869). Returning to the US, he began to lecture widely. His most famous novels, written after his retirement from journalism in 1871, portray characters drawn from his childhood in Missouri. They include *The Adventures of Tom Sawyer* (1872), *Life on the Mississippi* (1883), *The Adventures of Huckleberry Finn* (1884), and *The Tragedy of Pudd'nhead Wilson* (1894). In a completely different vein are his historical novels, *The Prince and the Pauper* (1882) and *A Connecticut Yankee in King Arthur's Court* (1889). Mark Twain's dry idiomatic wit had a lasting effect on the American literary scene. Late in life, however, suffering from the tragedies of the sudden deaths of his wife and daughter, Twain became embittered and his last works, *What is Man?* (1906) and *The Mysterious Stranger* (1916) reflected his deep pessimism. His personal memoir, *Mark Twain's Autobiography*, was published in 1924.

twayblade The most common European orchid, *Listera ovata*, which grows in damp woods, meadows, etc. Up to 24 in (60 cm) high, it has a pair of rounded leaves situated about halfway down the stem. The flowering stalk, which is sticky with glands, carries a long narrow head of small greenish flowers.

tweed A woolen fabric, more closely woven than *cheviot. Hardwearing, often with a roughened surface texture, tweed is manufactured in various weave patterns, such as checks, stripes, flecks, and herringbones. Coats, skirts, and suits are made from famous traditional tweeds, such as Harris and Donegal cloth. It derives its name from "tweel," a Scottish word for *twill.

MARK TWAIN *Author whose best-known works,* Tom Sawyer *and* Huckleberry Finn, *tell of boyhood on the Mississippi river.*

Tweed, William Marcy (1823–78) US politician. He entered politics as a Democrat in the 1850s and by 1861 he was considered head of *Tammany Hall, the Democratic organization that, at the time, controlled New York City's government. "Boss" Tweed's "ring" members made inroads into all phases of city and state government. Corruption and plunder of taxpayers' money was rampant, and in 1873 Tweed, then a multimillionaire, was convicted of fraud. He jumped bail and fled to Spain (1875), but was arrested and returned to New York (1876), where he spent the rest of his life in jail.

Tweed River A river in SE Scotland and NE England. Flowing E from the Tweedsmuir Hills to the North Sea at Berwick, it forms part of the border between England and Scotland. Length: 97 mi (156 km).

Twelfth Day. *See* Epiphany.

Twelve Tables (450 BC) The earliest codification of *Roman law, in full known as the Law of the Twelve Tables (*Lex duodecim tabularum*). The laws were engraved on bronze tablets, which were permanently displayed in public. None of the original text survives, although fragments have been preserved in quotations. The tables dealt with (1) proceedings preliminary to trial; (2) trial; (3) enforcing judgments; (4) rights of fathers; (5) inheritance; (6) ownership of property; (7) land law; (8) *trusts; (9) public law; (10) sacred law (burials, etc.); (11 and 12) supplementary matters.

twelve-tone music. *See* serialism.

twill Any woven fabric with a diagonal rib, produced by varying the regular weave of plain cloth (*see* weaving); herringbone is a common variation. Twilled fabrics are much used for making suits and pants. *See also* tweed.

twins Two individuals born from the same pregnancy: 1 out of every 83 human pregnancies results in twins. Identical twins are produced when a fertilized egg splits in two and develops as two fetuses of the same sex; identical twins are very difficult to tell apart and they usually have a great emotional affinity for each other. More commonly, nonidentical (or fraternal) twins are produced when two eggs are fertilized at the same time; they may be of different sexes and are no more alike than other siblings. *See also* Siamese twins.

Tyche A Greek goddess personifying fortune, daughter of Oceanus or Zeus and Tethys. She is identical with the Roman *Fortuna.

Tyler, John (1790–1862) US statesman; 10th president of the United States (1841–45). A planter from Virginia, Tyler began his political career as a state legislator (1811–16), US congressman (1817–21), governor of Virginia (1825–27), and as US senator (1827–36). Initially a strong supporter of Pres. Andrew *Jackson, Tyler split with him over the *Bank of the United States controversy and joined the Whig party. In 1840 he received the Whig vice-presidential nomination, joining William Henry *Harrison in the successful campaign that became famous for its slogan, "Tippecanoe and Tyler Too." Harrison's sudden death only a month after taking office brought Tyler to the presidency. The most significant achievement of his single term in office was the annexation of Texas to the US in 1844. Tyler was not renominated by the Whig party and retired to private life. At the outbreak of the *Civil War, he supported the cause of the Confederacy and was elected to the Confederate Congress, but died before it convened.

Tyler, Wat (d. 1381) English rebel, who led the Kentish peasants during the *Peasants' Revolt (1381). He was the peasants' most influential spokesman until his murder during negotiations with Richard II.

Tylor, Sir Edward Burnett (1832–1917) British anthropologist. The first professor of anthropology at Oxford (1896) and the foremost 19th-century British anthropologist, Tylor developed his interest in the subject when he visited Mexico with the US ethnologist Henry Chrysty. His *Primitive Culture: Researches into the Development of Mythology, Philosophy, Religion, Language, Art, and Custom* (1871) became the standard English-language work on anthropology.

Tyndale, William (c. 1494–1536) English biblical translator. His influential translation of the New Testament, begun at Cologne in 1525 and completed at Worms, was a major source of the later Authorized or King James Version. In 1520 he published a translation of the Pentateuch. Accused of heresy, he was taken by imperial officers at Antwerp in 1535 and strangled and burned at Vilvorde, Belgium.

Tyndall, John (1820–93) Irish physicist, who in 1869 discovered the scattering of light by microscopic particles, such as those in dust and colloids (**Tyndall effect**). He used this effect to explain the blue of the sky and was also the first to demonstrate that the air contains microorganisms, which helped to refute the theory of spontaneous generation of fungi, etc.

Tyne River A river in N England. Flowing E from the SW Cheviot Hills to the North Sea at Tynemouth, it passes through Newcastle, Gateshead, and Jarrow. Length: 30 mi (48 km).

Tyne and Wear A metropolitan county of NE England, created in 1974 from SE Northumberland and NE Durham. It comprises the districts of Newcastle-upon-Tyne, North Tyneside, Gateshead, South Tyneside, and Sunderland. It was the first major industrial region in Great Britain, developing long before the industrial revolution. Industries grew up along the Tyne River allied to the large coal fields. In the 19th century most of the region became industrialized; the development of the shipyards was especially important. During the Depression of the 1930s it suffered severely due to its dependence on heavy industry. The whole county is now designated a special development area. Area: 208 sq mi (540 sq km). Population (1981): 1,143,245. Administrative center: Newcastle-upon-Tyne.

Tynemouth 55 01N 1 24W A city in NE England, in Tyne and Wear at the mouth of the Tyne River. It includes the port of North Shields and is itself a resort. Population (1981): 60,022.

typesetting The process by which type is assembled for *printing. Until the 15th century, type was cut or engraved, a page at a time, in blocks of wood or metal; with **movable type**, invented by *Gutenberg, each character is cast on a separate piece of metal for assembling by hand and is reusable. This was the only method available until 1884 when the American Ottmar Mergenthaler (1854–99) invented the **Linotype** machine, on which the compositor operates a keyboard to assemble character matrices from a magazine; when a line is complete, molten *type metal is pumped into the matrices to form a solid line of type. The **Monotype** system, invented in 1885 by the American Tolbert Lanson (1844–1913), comprises separate keyboard and casting machines: as the compositor operates the keyboard, a punched paper tape is produced; when this is fed through the caster, the punched codes select characters in a matrix into which type metal is pumped to form individual pieces of type, which are accumulated, in the correct sequence, in a tray. Since the 1950s **phototypesetting** (photosetting *or* filmsetting) machines have revolutionized printing. Instead of casting type from hot metal, they create images of characters on photographic paper or film, which is then used for *platemaking. The compositor operates a keyboard to produce a punched paper tape or magnetic tape, which then drives the phototypesetter. Some machines flash light through an actual negative image of each character onto the paper or film; others build up its shape with tiny dots of light from a *cathode-ray tube controlled by a computer memory. The latter kind can set 20,000 or more characters per second.

typewriter A hand-operated machine for producing printed symbols. The first machine was invented in the US in 1867 but the commercial success of the typewriter began in 1874 with the machines produced by the arms manufacturers Remington and Sons. With minor modifications this design, with the paper held in a moving platen, remained the basis of the typewriter until the advent of electric golf-ball machines, with a stationary platen, in the early 1960s. These golf balls consist of spheres carrying the type in circles around their surface—they are easily replaced to provide additional typefaces (e.g. italic) or symbols (e.g. mathematical). More sophisticated machines are now available providing, in conjunction with a microcomputer, proportional spacing, justification, and word processing.

typhoid fever An infectious disease of the digestive tract caused by the bacterium *Salmonella typhi*. This disease (and paratyphoid fever) are usually contracted by drinking infected water and occur predominantly in places without a clean water supply. The symptoms, which begin 10–14 days after ingesting the bacterium, include fever, headache, cough, loss of appetite, and constipation; a characteristic red rash may appear. If untreated, the patient may develop bowel hemorrhage or perforations. Treatment is by administration of fluids and the antibiotic chloramphenicol. A vaccine provides temporary immunity.

Typhon In Greek mythology, a monster with a hundred heads, the son of Tartarus and Gaea. He was conquered by Zeus and buried under a volcano, usually identified as Mount Etna. His monstrous children included the *Chimera, the *Hydra, and *Cerberus.

typhoon A tropical cyclone or *hurricane with winds above force 12 on the *Beaufort scale, occurring in the China Sea and the W Pacific Ocean. The name is derived from a Chinese word meaning great wind.

typhus An infection caused by certain bacteria-like microorganisms (*see* rickettsia), which are transmitted to man by lice, fleas, mites, or ticks. There are many different forms of typhus, caused by different species of rickettsiae, but they share the symptoms of fever, headache, pains in muscles and joints, delirium, and a rash. These symptoms may be very mild throughout the disease. Treatment is with tetracycline antibiotics or chloramphenicol. Epidemic (or classical) typhus is carried by lice and was formerly very prevalent in overcrowded unhygienic conditions, with a high mortality rate. A vaccine against it is now available.

typography **1.** The art of *printing from movable type. **2.** The aspect of printing concerned with the design and composition of printing type. Early typefaces, which imitated handwriting, belonged to three main groups: gothic (or black-letter), used by N European printers such as *Gutenberg and *Caxton; roman, introduced at Venice about 1470; and *italic, also Venetian, first used in 1501 (*see* incunabula). Holland dominated typefounding for most of the 16th and 17th centuries but England produced two outstanding typographers in the 18th century: William Caslon (1692–1766) and John Baskerville (1706–75). Between 1800 and 1850 the so-called modern-face type designs predominated; they differed from the preceding old-face designs by their pronouncedly upright appearance and horizontal serifs (short finishing strokes on the ends of the main lines of letters). Sanserif (i.e. without serifs) typefaces originated in early 19th-century designs but only came into their own in the 1920s and 1930s through the work of the German *Bauhaus typographers. In England, William *Morris revitalized book design at the end of the 19th century, producing several handsome typefaces for his Kelmscott Press. Influential 20th-century typographers include the Dutchman Jay van Krimpen, the Englishmen Eric Gill and Stanley Morison, and the American F. W. Goudy.

Tyr (*or*, in Old English, Tiw) In Teutonic mythology, the god of war; with *Odin and *Thor, he is one of the three main Germanic gods. His name is linguistically related to *Zeus* (although Latin writers, beginning with Tacitus, identified him with Mars) and survives in *Tuesday.*

Tyrannosaurus A huge bipedal dinosaur that lived in North America during the late Cretaceous period (about 100–65 million years ago). This animal was 50 ft (15 m) long, stood 20 ft (6.5 m) tall, and weighed up to 10 tons. It had a massive body with a short thick neck supporting a large head, large muscular hind limbs with clawed feet, and tiny fore legs. It was a carnivore with long daggerlike teeth but was probably quite rare and fed infrequently. Order: *Saurischia.*

tyrant In antiquity, a ruler who obtained absolute power without election or right of succession. In the Greek city-states tyrants were often leading members of oligarchies who obtained popular support. Generally they ruled benevolently, conforming to established institutions, and were often significant patrons of the arts. Famous tyrants include *Aristagoras of Miletus, *Agathocles and *Dionysius I of Syracuse, *Phalaris of Agrigento, *Pisistratus of Athens, and *Polycrates of Samos.

tyrant flycatcher A passerine bird belonging to the New World family *Tyrannidae* (365 species), ranging from 3.5–10.6 in (9–27 cm) in length, often with a long tail, and generally gray, brown, or olive-colored with paler underparts. They are typically arboreal and dart out from a perch to seize flying insects. Tyrant flycatchers are very aggressive and will attack large birds that enter their breeding territories. *Compare* flycatcher.

Tyre (modern name: Sur) 33 12N 35 11E A port in SW Lebanon, on the Mediterranean Sea. It was important to the Phoenicians for several centuries and was taken by Alexander the Great after a seven-month siege in 322 BC and by the Romans in 68 BC. The city was long held by the Crusaders but fell to Muslim forces in 1291.

Tyrol. *See* Tirol.

Tyrone A county of W Northern Ireland, bordering on the Republic of Ireland. It is predominantly hilly, descending in the E to Lough Neagh. Agriculture is important with cattle and sheep farming and the production of barley, potatoes, flax, and turnips. Small-scale manufacturing is carried out in the larger towns. Area: 1260 sq mi (3263 sq km).

Tyumen 57 11N 65 29E A port in central Russia, on the Tura River. It serves as a transport center for the oil and natural gas that are mined nearby. Population (1991 est): 494,200.

Tzu-ch'eng. *See* Zibo.

Tz'u-hsi. *See* Zi Xi.

Tzu-po. *See* Zibo.

U

Ubangi-Shari. *See* Central African Republic.

Uccello, Paolo (P. di Dono; 1397–1475) Florentine painter and craftsman. He trained in the *Ghiberti workshop. From 1425 to 1431 he worked in St Mark's, Venice, as master mosaicist. His frescoes for Sta Maria Novella, Florence, include the famous *Flood*, which shows his preoccupation with perspective and foreshortening. In the three paintings of the battle of San Romano, commissioned by the Medici, he combines a geometric structure with the rich decoration of the *international gothic style.

Udaipur 24 36N 73 47E A city in India, in Rajasthan. Formerly the capital of Udaipur (*or* Mewar) princely state, its lake contains an island with a marble palace. Udaipur has chemical, asbestos, and zinc-smelting industries and a university (1962). Population (1991): 307,682.

Udall, Nicholas (1505–56) English dramatist. He was headmaster of Eton College and later of Westminster School. *Ralph Roister Doister* (c. 1553), influenced by classical Roman drama and probably written for his pupils, was the first full-length English comedy.

Udine 46 04N 13 14E A city in NE Italy, in Friuli-Venezia Giulia. It was partially damaged in an earthquake in 1976. There are textile and leather industries. Population (1987 est): 100,200.

Udmurt Autonomous Republic (*or* Udmurtia) An administrative division in central Russia. The Udmurts, comprising about 50% of the population, speak a Finno-Ugric language. The region has rich oil, shale, timber, and peat resources and manufactures locomotives, machine tools, and other engineering products. Cereals, flax, and some vegetables are grown. Area: 16,250 sq mi (42,100 sq km). Population (1985): 1,559,000. Capital: Izhevsk.

Ufa 54 45N 55 58E A city in central Russia, the capital of the Bashkir autonomous republic. Situated in the Ural Mountains, it has oil refineries and a large chemical industry; its university was founded in 1957. Population (1991 est): 1,097,000.

Uffizi An art gallery in Florence, containing the art treasures of the Medici. Built by *Vasari in the 16th century to house government offices, the Uffizi was opened as a museum in 1765. The major part of its collection comprises Italian Renaissance paintings, although it also includes sculpture and Flemish, Dutch, German, and French paintings.

UFOs. *See* unidentified flying objects.

Uganda, Republic of A landlocked country in East Africa. It consists chiefly of a high plateau rising to mountains, including the Ruwenzori Mountains in the W and Mount Elgon in the E, and a considerable proportion of the total area is occupied by lakes, notably Lake Victoria. The majority of the population is African, especially *Ganda, with dwindling minorities of Europeans and Asians. *Economy*: chiefly agricultural, the main food crops being maize, millet, yams, and other tropical plants. Cash crops include coffee (the main export), tea, tobacco, and cotton; livestock is also important. There has been an increase in forestry production, almost all hardwood. Uganda's freshwater fishing industry is one of the largest in the world, and fish farming is being developed. The chief mineral resource is copper, much of which is exported to Japan. Hydroelectric-

PAOLO UCCELLO

PAOLO UCCELLO *Detail from* A Hunt in a Forest *(c. 1460).*

ity is a valuable source of power and there is some industry, including food processing, textiles, and cement. *History*: the area was dominated by the kingdom of *Buganda from the 18th to the late 19th centuries, becoming a British protectorate in 1894. It became an independent state within the British Commonwealth in 1962 and the following year a republic was established with *Obote as prime minister. In 1971 the government was overthrown in a military coup that brought Gen. Idi *Amin to power. His repressive regime was overthrown in April 1979, by Ugandan exiles aided by Tanzanian troops. The subsequent provisional government was headed by Yusuf Lule (1912–85) until June 1979. A military coup in 1980 overthrew his successor, Godfrey Binaisa, and Obote was reelected president. Battling for control of the government by opposition groups, which included several of the former political heads (who denied contact with Amin), followed Obote's assumption of the presidency. Obote was unable to restore stability and to repair the devastations inflicted by the Amin regime, and he was overthrown in a military coup in 1985. Obote fled the country, and army leader Yoweri Museveni came to power at the beginning of 1986. Under Museveni and with general international monetary support, Uganda's economy grew, but, by the early 1990s, domestic economic crises forced the government to cut spending and resort in some cases to a barter system. Many Ugandans fled to Kenya in 1992 to escape regional guerrilla fighting and ensuing political turmoil. Official language: English; Swahili is widely spoken and the most important local language is Luganda. Official currency, since 1967: Ugandan shilling of 100 cents. Area: 91,343 sq mi (236,860 sq km). Population (1990 est): 17,593,000. Capital: Kampala.

Ugarit An ancient town on the Syrian coast (now Ras Shamra). Repeatedly destroyed and rebuilt from Neolithic times, Ugarit became a great international port between 1500 BC and its ultimate destruction about 1200. Pottery, carvings, and diplomatic correspondence recovered there bear witness to strong Mycenaean, Hittite, and Egyptian links. There were temples to *Baal and his father Dagon, and a set of religious texts, written in a type of alphabetic *cuneiform unique to Ugarit, throw light on religious cults in ancient *Canaan.

ugli A hybrid cross between a *grapefruit and a *tangerine. The fruit resembles a small grapefruit with brownish-yellow warty skin and orange-colored flesh. It is grown in the West Indies.

Ujjain 23 11N 75 50E A city in India, in Madhya Pradesh. An ancient city, it lay on the first meridian of Hindu geographers and was the capital of the Avanti kingdom (6th–4th centuries BC). One of the seven sacred Hindu cities, it is the scene of a bathing festival (Kumbh Mela) held every 12 years. It is an agricultural trading center with textile industries and has a university, founded in 1957. Population (1991): 366,787.

Ujung Padang (Makassar *or* Macassar) 5 09S 119 08E A port in central Indonesia, in SW Sulawesi. Already a flourishing port when the Portuguese arrived in the 16th century, its exports now include coffee, copra, resins, and vegetable oils. There is some manufacturing industry. Its university was established in 1956. Population (1980): 709,038.

ukiyo-e (Japanese pictures of the floating world) A Japanese art style concerned with the depiction of everyday life. It was popular among the middle classes in the 17th and 18th centuries. Favorite subjects included prostitutes, women engaged in domestic tasks, actors, etc. Ukiyo-e began as a style of painting but it is most closely associated with Japanese color woodblock prints. The first ukiyo-e printmaker was probably Hishikawa Moronobu (c. 1618–94). The art culminated in the landscapes of *Hokusai and *Hiroshige, which were highly influential on *impressionism, *Postimpressionism, and the *Nabis in 19th-century France.

Ukraine, Republic of (*or* Ukraine) An independent country in E central Europe, a constituent republic of the Soviet Union until 1991. It is a very fertile wooded region. Some 96% of the population comprises Slavs, mostly Ukrainians. There are major coal fields and iron-ore mines (including the *Donets Basin), resulting in the development of a large ferrous metallurgical industry. The machine-building, chemical, consumer-goods, and food industries are also important. Crops grown include wheat, sugar beet, cotton, and tobacco. *History*: it was dominated by the Khazars from the 7th to the 9th centuries and then by the Rurik princes of Kiev. In the 13th century the Golden Horde overran the region, which subsequently came under the rule of Lithuania and, in the 16th century, Poland. In the 17th century many Ukrainians fled the harsh Polish government, becoming *Cossacks. Polish domination was followed by Russian rule. After a national and cultural revival in the late 19th century the Ukraine declared independence in 1918 but subsequently submitted to Soviet armies, becoming (1922) one of the original constituent republics of the Soviet Union. It became independent in 1991 with the collapse of the Soviet Union. Ukraine was one of the first members of the Commonwealth of Independent States (CIS) in 1991. It has been a member of the UN since 1945. Economic reform and defense agreements with Russia were the greatest concerns during the early years of independence. Area: 231,990 sq mi (603,700 sq km). Population (1991 est): 51,945,000. Capital: Kiev.

ukulele A small guitar, patented in Hawaii in 1917. The fingerboard of a ukulele is fretted; the four gut or nylon strings are strummed with fingers or a small plectrum. Originally used to play chordal accompaniments to folk songs, the ukulele became popular in US jazz.

Ulan Bator (*or* Ulaanbaatar; former name: Urga) 47 54N 106 52E The capital of the Mongolian People's Republic, situated on a plateau in the N of the country. Built around a monastery, in the 17th century it developed as a center of trade between China and Japan. It became the capital when Outer Mongolia declared its independence in 1911. It is Mongolia's main center of industry. The Mongolian State University was founded in 1942. Population (1990 est): 550,000.

Ulanova, Galina (1910–   ) Russian ballet dancer. From 1928 she danced with the Leningrad Kirov Ballet, where she excelled in classical ballets, such as *Swan Lake* and *Giselle*, and from 1944 with the Moscow Bolshoi Ballet, for which she made several films. She retired from the stage in 1962.

Ulan Ude 51 55N 107 40E A city in SE Russia, in the Buryat autonomous republic on the Selenga River. It is a transport center and has boat building, ship-repairing, and machinery-manufacturing industries. Population (1991 est): 362,000.

Ulbricht, Walter (1893–1973) East German political figure. A fervent Stalinist, Ulbricht rose rapidly in the Communist party ranks. He lived in the Soviet Union during the Nazi period and after World War II was the leading architect of the German Democratic Republic. He was general secretary of the Socialist Unity party from 1950 and in 1960 became chairman of the newly established council of state. In 1961 he ordered the construction of the Berlin Wall.

ulcer An inflamed eroded area of skin or mucous membrane. There are many forms of ulcer, one of the most prevalent being *peptic ulcers, which affect the stomach and duodenum. Ulcers may also occur in the mouth—small irritating aphthous ulcers affect many people—and in the intestine in inflammatory bowel disease (*see* colitis). Varicose ulcers may develop in the skin, particularly around the ankles, of patients with chronic *varicose veins.

Ulm 48 24N 10 00E An industrial city and port in SW Germany, in Baden-Württemberg on the Danube River. Its gothic cathedral (1377) escaped damage during World War II. Napoleon defeated the Austrian army there in 1805 and it is the birthplace of Einstein. Population (1991 est): 109,000.

Ulm, Battle of (Sept 25–Oct 20, 1805) A battle in which Napoleon with 210,000 men defeated 72,000 Austrians in Bavaria. The Austrians were taken by surprise in the rear and capitulated. Napoleon thus prevented a union between Austrian and Russian forces.

Ulster An historic province in the Republic of Ireland and former kingdom of N Ireland. The land passed to the English crown in 1461 and during the 17th century most was confiscated and given to English and Scottish settlers (*see* Plantation of Ireland). It was partitioned in 1921 to form the six counties of Northern Ireland and the Ulster province of the Republic of Ireland, consisting of the counties of Cavan, Donegal, and Monaghan. Area: 3094 sq mi (8013 sq km).

ultramicroscope A type of microscope, invented by *Zsigmondy in 1902, used to study colloidal particles in a liquid medium. A beam of light illuminates the particles from the side, the scattered light enabling the movements of the particles to be observed as flashes against a dark background (dark-field illumination).

Ultramontanism (Latin: beyond the mountains, i.e. within Italy) A tendency within the Roman Catholic Church that supports the centralized power of the pope and the *Roman Curia as against nationalist movements, such as *Gallicanism, or greater independence at the diocesan level. The high point of Ultramontanism was the promulgation of papal *infallibility (1870). The Second *Vatican Council encouraged a devolution of authority.

ultrasonics The study of *sound waves the frequencies of which are too high to be audible to the normal human ear, i.e. above about 20,000 hertz. Such waves are known as ultrasound and may be produced by *magnetostriction or by applying a rapidly alternating voltage across a *piezoelectric crystal. Ultrasound now has a number of applications, for example utilizing its rapid vibrations to destroy bacteria in milk, break up large molecules, and clean surfaces.

ultraviolet radiation *Electromagnetic radiation the frequency of which lies between that of the violet end of the visible spectrum and *X-rays, i.e. between about 380 and 5 nanometers. Ultraviolet radiation is produced during arc discharges and by gas-discharge tubes (e.g. the mercury-vapor lamp). It is also produced in large quantities by the sun, although the radiation below 200 nm is absorbed by the *ozone layer of the atmosphere.

Ulyanovsk (name until 1924: Simbirsk) 54 19N 48 22E A port in W Russia on the Volga River. Industries include food processing, vodka distilling, and motor-vehicle manufacture. It was renamed in honor of Lenin (originally V. I. Ulyanov), who was born there. Population (1991 est): 668,000.

Ulysses. *See* Odysseus.

Umayyads (*or* Omayyads) The first dynasty of *caliphs, which ruled Islam from 661 to 750 AD. Their capital was Damascus. After reluctantly accepting Islam, the family obtained some of the leading positions in the state and one of them, *Mu'awiyah, became caliph (661) on the death of his rival *Ali. The dynasty reached its peak with *'Abd al-Malik (reigned 685–705). The Umayyads were overthrown by a rebellion of discontented Arabs and pious Muslims and were replaced by the *Abbasids, a rival family. In Muslim Spain, an Umayyad,

*'Abd ar-Rahman, seized power in 756 and established a dynasty that ruled until 1030.

Umbelliferae A widely distributed family of plants (2850 species), most abundant in N temperate regions. Most species are herbaceous, with much-divided leaves and umbrella-shaped heads (umbels) of tiny flowers, each usually with five petals and five sepals. A few species have dome-shaped flower heads. The fruits are ridged, splitting into two parts when ripe. The family includes vegetables, such as the carrot, celery, and parsnip, and many culinary herbs and spices, such as angelica, caraway, chervil, coriander, dill, fennel, and parsley.

Umberto I (1844–1900) King of Italy (1878–1900). He commanded with distinction in the war against the Austrians (1866). As king he led Italy into the *Triple Alliance with Germany and Austria (1882) and encouraged Italian colonialism in Africa. Defeat by the Ethiopians at Adowa (1896) and economic difficulties led to unrest at home and the imposition of martial law in 1898. Two unsuccessful attempts on Umberto's life were followed by his assassination at Monza.

Umberto II (1904–83) The last king of Italy (1946), following the abdication of his father Victor Emmanuel III. He himself was forced to abdicate after a referendum approved the establishment of republican government and he retired to Portugal as the count of Sarre.

umbilical cord The structure, about 50 cm long, that connects a fetus to the *placenta in the uterus. It contains three blood vessels (two arteries and one vein) that convey blood to and from the placenta. At birth the umbilical cord is tied off and cut; the part connected to the baby subsequently degenerates, leaving a scar on the abdomen (*see* navel).

umbrella bird A fruit-eating songbird of the genus *Cephalopterus* of tropical American forests. Male birds have a large umbrella-shaped crest that is raised over the head during display. They also have fleshy wattles hanging from the chest—ranging from the short naked red wattle of the bare-necked umbrella bird (*C. glabriollis*) to the feather-covered pendulous wattle of the ornate umbrella bird (*C. ornatus*). Family: *Cotingidae* (90 species).

umbrella tree A small North American tree, *Magnolia tripetala*, up to 40 ft (12 m) high, that has umbrella-like clusters of large leaves (16 in; 40 cm long) at the ends of the branches. The large flowers are creamy white with a strong scent and the fruits are scarlet; the tree is grown as an ornamental in temperate regions. Family: *Magnoliaceae*.

Umbria A landlocked mountainous region in central Italy. Its agriculture produces cereals, vines, and olives. Hydroelectricity powers modern industries producing iron, steel, chemicals, engineering, and food products. The Umbrian school of painting, which included Perugino and Raphael, was established there during the Renaissance. Area: 3265 sq mi (8456 sq km). Population (1991): 822,972. Capital: Perugia.

Umtali. *See* Mutare.

Umtata 31 35S 28 47E The capital of the Transkei, in S Africa. It has an Anglican cathedral. Population (1985): 80,000.

Un-American Activities Committee, House (HUAC) US House of Representatives committee established in 1935 to investigate subversive organizations in the US. Headed by Representative Martin Dies, the committee investigated nazism, fascism, and communism in the US, as well as those liberals, many of them involved in *New Deal programs, thought to have Communist connections. It was responsible for the blacklisting of Hollywood writers and directors alleged to be Communists and for the investigations in 1948 of government officials, especially Alger Hiss. The *Internal Security Act of 1950 originated from these committee hearings. Before being abolished (1975) its name had been changed to the Internal Security Committee (1969).

Unamuno y Jugo, Miguel de (1864–1936) Spanish writer and philosopher, of Basque parentage. Unamuno's chief philosophical work, *The Tragic Sense of Life* (1913), reflects the influence of *Kant, *Hegel, and *Kierkegaard. This work and his novels are concerned with the themes of faith, free will, the immortality of the soul, and the struggle for moral integrity.

uncertainty principle. *See* Heisenberg uncertainty principle.

Uncle Sam A personification of the people or government of the US, usually portrayed as a lean figure with white hair and whiskers, wearing a tall hat, swallow-tail coat, and striped trousers. The name is associated with a certain meat inspector, Samuel Wilson (1766–1854), who confused the initials of the United States with those of his own nickname.

unconscious In *psychoanalysis, the part of the mind that includes ideas and impulses of which the individual is unaware and which cannot readily be brought back into awareness. (It is distinguished from the **subconscious**, which comprises ideas and impulses that can readily be recalled to consciousness.) The unconscious mental processes are unacceptable to the conscious mind and are kept unconscious by the process of *repression. Psychoanalytic *psychotherapy attempts to bring these processes back into consciousness by overcoming the resistances to them.

Underground Railroad A pre–Civil War secret organized system that helped escaped slaves in the South reach freedom in the North. Because the Fugitive Slave laws of 1793 and 1850 made it legal for owners to recapture slaves, sympathetic Northerners set up a loose network of safe hiding places called stations, usually in the homes of supporters, for slaves making their way north as far as Canada. The slaves were led by conductors, the most famous of whom was Harriet *Tubman.

underground railroads Apart from short sections of tunnel on main-line railroads, the world's first urban underground railroad (1863) was built in London using the cut and cover method (cutting a trench from above and filling in over the railroad). The first "tube" railroad (1890), cut by boring through the earth, was also in England and used electric trains. Other major cities to have an underground railroad include New York (subway), Paris (*métro*), Moscow, Tokyo, Buenos Aires, Madrid, and Hong Kong.

underwing moth A moth whose brightly colored hindwings are hidden by the camouflaged forewings when at rest. When disturbed the moth flies off flashing its bright colors, which startles and confuses predators. Underwings belong to several families and are found in Europe, Asia, and North America.

underwriting. *See* insurance; Lloyd's.

Undset, Sigrid (1882–1949) Norwegian novelist, best known for *Kristin Lavransdatter* (1920–22), a trilogy of historical novels set in 14th-century Norway. She wrote a number of other novels, most of them dealing with themes that reflect her conversion to Roman Catholicism in 1924. She also wrote essays and lives of the Norwegian saints.

undulant fever. *See* brucellosis.

unemployment The total number of people unable to find work at a given time. A certain amount of **frictional unemployment**, i.e. unemployment due to people changing jobs, etc., is inevitable. **Structural unemployment** is due to people having the wrong skills, living in different areas from vacancies, etc. The proportion of the workforce unemployed also increases with a downturn in the *trade cycle (this is **demand-deficient unemployment**); it hit an all-time high in the *Depression of the 1930s reaching over eight million in the US. While it is accepted that even with "full" employment up to about 3% of the workforce may be out of work (as a result of frictional and structural unemployment) considerable controversy remains as to the extent of structural unemployment as compared to demand-deficient unemployment. Monetarists (*see* monetarism) believe that, provided the *money supply is adequate, unemployment is largely due to structural problems and they advocate such measures as mobility allowances and retraining schemes. They claim that attempts to boost the economy by *deficit financing, as advocated by *Keynesianism, will not help the problem and will merely fuel *inflation.

UNESCO. *See* United Nations Educational, Scientific and Cultural Organzation.

Ungaretti, Giuseppe (1888–1970) Italian poet. He was born in Egypt and studied in Paris, where he met *Apollinaire, *Valéry, and other avant-garde writers and artists. His poetry, beginning with the war poems of *Il porto sepolto* (1916) and *L'allegria* (1919), was highly experimental, dispensing with rhyme and other conventions. The difficult language and symbolism of a later volume, *Sentimento del tempo* (1933), led a critic to describe Ungaretti's verse as *ermetico* (obscure), a term that was soon applied to the style of *Montale and *Quasimodo as well, the three being the leading practitioners of *La poesia ermetica*. Ungaretti's later volumes include *La terra promessa* (1950) and *Morte delle stagioni* (1967).

Ungava A region in E Canada, in N Quebec E of Hudson Bay. A rocky plateau with many lakes, it is rich in minerals (especially iron ore) but sparsely populated. Area: 351,780 sq mi (911,110 sq km).

ungulate A hoofed mammal. The term is not used in modern scientific classifications, the hoofed mammals being grouped into the orders *Perissodactyla* (horses, tapirs, and rhinoceroses) and *Artiodactyla*, which includes pigs, camels, deer, cattle, etc.

uniat churches Various churches of Eastern Orthodox Christianity that are in full communion with the Roman Catholic Church. Although completely Catholic in faith and doctrine, they retain their own traditional liturgies and canon law. Generally they differ from Rome in giving communion under both kinds, practicing baptism by immersion, and allowing marriage of the clergy.

UNICEF. *See* United Nations International Children's Emergency Fund.

unicorn A mythical animal described by classical writers as living in India and resembling a white horse, but with one long straight horn on its forehead. In the Middle Ages it was symbolically associated with chastity or virginity (and thus could be captured only by a virgin) and also with Christ's love of mankind. Its horn was supposed to reveal the presence of poison in food or drink. In heraldry it figured in the arms of Scotland and was combined with the lion in the arms of the British crown after the accession of James I.

unidentified flying objects (UFOs) Objects reported to have been seen in the sky (usually at night) that have not been identified as aircraft, satellites, balloons, or known astronomical bodies. Often described as saucer shaped (and known as "flying saucers"), they have been taken by some observers to be spacecraft from extraterrestrial sources—a view for which there is little credible evidence. They have, however, provided a source of considerable speculation and excitement among those who believe that they have witnessed an event that has passed unnoticed by the rest of mankind.

UNICORN *A representation of a unicorn from a 15th-century tapestry in the Musée Cluny, Paris.*

Unification Church A religious sect founded in South Korea in 1954 by a millionaire Korean businessman, Sun Myung Moon (1920–   ). In the early 1960s it was introduced into the US as a right-wing Christian Youth Crusade and is now also active in other countries. The ideology of the cult is summarized in Moon's book, *Divine Principle*, which he claims was revealed to him by Christ in 1936. Moon is presented as the Second Messiah, the head of a family of perfect children (i.e. his followers, the Moonies), who will succeed in redeeming mankind from Satan. Absolute obedience is demanded of members, who spend most of their waking hours earning money for the organization by selling such items as artificial flowers in the streets. The large tax-exempt sums realized in this way have enabled Moon to build an extensive property and business empire in the US, where he has lived since 1972, but he was sentenced to prison for tax evasion in 1984.

unified field theory A theory that encompasses the four fundamental interactions—*strong, *weak, *electromagnetic, and *gravitational—in terms of a single field, analogous to the electromagnetic or gravitational fields. Einstein failed after many attempts to unify gravitation and electromagnetism and it may be that no simple unification is possible.

uniformitarianism The generally accepted theory that all geological changes have occurred through gradual processes operating over a long period and continuing today, although not necessarily at the same rate or intensity. *Compare* catastrophism.

Union, Acts of 1. The acts (1536–43) uniting England and Wales. They imposed English law and administration on Wales and made English the language of officialdom. **2.** The act (1707) uniting England and Scotland to form Great Britain. **3.** The act (1800) that united Great Britain and Ireland to form (1801) the United Kingdom. After the establishment of the Irish Free State (1921; *see* Home Rule), the act united Britain with Northern Ireland.

Union, Act of (1841) Act that began self-government in Canada by uniting Upper and Lower Canada. Proposed by Britain's governor-general, Lord *Durham, and fashioned by Lord Russell, the act provided equal representation for British and French Canadians.

Union of Soviet Socialist Republics. *See* Soviet Union.

Unitarians A group of Christians who reject the doctrine of the Trinity and the divinity of Christ, believing instead in the single personality of God and regarding Christ as a religious teacher. They have no formal creeds but stress reason and conscience as the bases of religion and view human nature as essentially good; they therefore also reject orthodox Christian teaching on original sin and atonement. Modern Unitarian thought dates from the Reformation, but congregations were first formed in Britain and the US in the 18th century. These are now associated in the General Assembly of Unitarian and Free Christian Churches.

unitary symmetry A method of classifying *hadrons. It is found that by plotting *isotopic spin against hypercharge (the sum of *strangeness and *baryon number) on a graph for particular values of *spin and *parity, a symmetric pattern of hadrons is obtained. In this way families of hadrons can be constructed. The theory was used to predict the existence and properties of the omega-minus particle, which were later confirmed.

United Arab Emirates (UAE; former name: Trucial States) A federation of seven sheikdoms in the Middle East, in *Arabia on the S coast of the Persian Gulf and the Gulf of Oman, comprising Abu Dhabi, Ajman, Dubai, Fujairah, Ras al-Khaimah, Sharjah, and Umm al-Qaiwain. Abu Dhabi occupies 87% of the total area and Abu Dhabi and Dubai each have about one-third of the population, which is mainly Arab and Sunnite Muslim. The terrain is flat sandy desert, below 656 ft (200 m) except for a slight rise to the NE. *Economy*: fishing and pearls are still important, but the oil of Abu Dhabi and Dubai, both underground and offshore, is the chief product and export: it has made Abu Dhabi one of the richest per capita political units in the world. *History*: the sheikdoms signed several common treaties with Britain from 1820; that of 1892 made them protectorates—the Trucial States—and British troops were stationed there until independence. The federation was formed in 1971 (Ras al-Khaimah not joining until 1972) and is a member of OPEC. The UAE contributed heavily to the UN-coalition forces during the Persian Gulf War in 1991, and, for the first time, allowed women to join its army later that year. President: Sheik Zayed bin Sultan al-Nahayan of Abu Dhabi. Prime minister: Sheik Rashid bin Said al-Maktum. Official language: Arabic. Official currency: UAE dirham of 10 dinars and 1000 fils. Area: 32,290 sq mi (83,650 sq km). Population (1992 est): 1,989,000. Provisional capital: Abu Dhabi. Chief port: Dubai.

United Arab Republic (UAR) The state created by the union of Egypt and Syria in 1958. Joined by North Yemen in the same year, it collapsed in 1961, when Syria withdrew, but Egypt retained the name until 1971.

United Australia party (UAP) A political party, comprising the Nationalist party and ex-members of the *Labor party, that governed Australia (sometimes in coalition with the Country party) from 1931 to 1941. It was dissolved in 1944 to be succeeded by the *Liberal party.

United Empire Loyalists Those Americans who remained loyal to England in the American Revolution and were forced after the colonists' victory in 1783 to migrate to Canada.

United Fronts In China, two periods of cooperation between the Chinese Communist party and its opponent, the *Guomindang. The first United Front (1924–27) was brought about, under Soviet influence, to defeat the *warlords and dissolved as relations between the two parties declined into civil war. The second United Front (1937–45) was formed following the *Xi An incident, which forced *Chiang Kai-shek to abandon civil war with the communists for an alliance against the Japanese invasion (*see* Sino-Japanese Wars).

United Irishmen, Society of An Irish secret society established in Belfast in 1791 by Wolfe *Tone to press for an independent Irish republic. Hopes of French aid in the 1790s were frustrated but in 1798 the United Irishmen rose in Ulster and Wexford, being suppressed with some difficulty.

United Kingdom (UK) A country in N Europe, consisting of *England, *Scotland, *Wales, and the province of Northern Ireland (*see* Ireland). The United Kingdom of Great Britain and Ireland, formed in 1801, became the United Kingdom of Great Britain and Northern Ireland in 1922, following the creation of the Irish Free State. Head of state: Queen Elizabeth II. Prime minister: John Major. Languages: English, with Gaelic and Welsh minority languages. Area: 94,214 sq mi (244,014 sq km). Population (1991): 55,486,800. Capital: London.

United Nations (UN) An organization established to maintain international peace and to foster international cooperation in the resolution of economic, social, cultural, and humanitarian problems. The UN was founded on Oct 24, 1945 (United Nations Day), when the major powers ratified a charter that had been drawn up earlier in the year in San Francisco. There were 51 founder members, including the US, which thus abandoned the isolationist stance it had taken to the UN's predecessor, the *League of Nations. Most of the countries of the world are now members of the UN, the chief exceptions being Switzerland and *Taiwan, which lost its seat to the People's Republic of *China in 1971.

The headquarters of the UN are in New York City. The organization's main deliberative organ is the **General Assembly**, which meets for three months every year. Each member state has one equal vote in the Assembly, which can only adopt recommendations: as a body of independent sovereign states, it cannot impose its will upon members. The **Security Council** bears the chief responsibility for maintaining international peace. Its permanent members are China, France, Russia, the UK, and the US; a further 10 members are elected by the General Assembly for two-year terms. Decisions, except on procedure, must be agreed by 9 members, including all the permanent members (the so-called veto privilege). In the event of a breach of international peace the Council may commit military forces to an attempt to reestablish peace, as for example during the *Korean War. The **Economic and Social Council** (ECOSOC) coordinates the economic and social work of the UN and has regional commissions in Europe, Asia and the Pacific, Latin America, Africa, and Western Asia. The **Trusteeship Council** is responsible for the one remaining *trust territory (Micronesia). The principal judicial organ of the UN is the *International Court of Justice. The **Secretariat**, headed by the secretary general (currently Javier Pérez de Cuellar), is responsible for administration.

The UN maintains other bodies around the world. The **United Nations Development Program** (UNDP) fosters the economic growth of the *developing countries; its headquarters are in New York. The **United Nations Conference on Trade and Development** (UNCTAD) encourages international trade, especially for the purpose of accelerating the economic development of developing countries; its headquarters are in Geneva. The **United Nations Industrial Development Organization** (UNIDO) promotes industrial development in the developing countries; its headquarters are in Vienna. The **United Nations Environment Program** (UNEP) is concerned with international cooperation in the protection of the environment; its headquarters are in Nairobi. Others include the Office of the *United Nations High Commissioner for Refugees; the *United Nations International Children's Emergency Fund; and the *United Nations Relief and Works Agency for Palestine Refugees in the Near East. There are in addition a number of specialized agencies, each charged with a specific function. These include the *Food and Agriculture Organization, *International Civil Aviation Organization, *International Labor Organization, *International Monetary Fund, *International Telecommunication Union, *United Nations Educational, Scientific and Cultural Organization, *International Bank for Reconstruction and Development, *World Health Organization, and the *World Meteorological Organization.

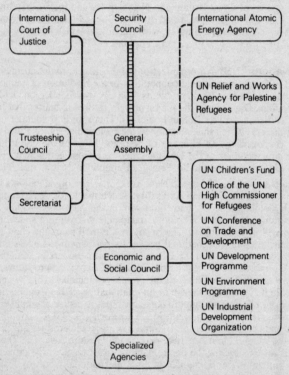

UNITED NATIONS *The structure of the organization.*

United Nations Educational, Scientific and Cultural Organization
(UNESCO) A specialized agency of the *United Nations established in 1945 to promote international cooperation in education, science, and culture. It collects and distributes information, provides operational assistance (e.g. funds for teacher training) to *developing countries, and sponsors research. Its headquarters are in Paris.

United Nations High Commissioner for Refugees, Office of the (UNHCR) A *United Nations body established in 1950 to provide international protection for refugees. It seeks permanent solutions to their problems through voluntary repatriation, resettlement in other countries, or integration into the country of present residence. The UNHCR has recently been concerned with refugees from Chile, Cyprus, Angola, and Vietnam. Its headquarters are in Geneva. It won the Nobel Peace Prize in 1981.

United Nations International Children's Emergency Fund (UNICEF) A *United Nations body established in 1946 to carry out postwar relief work in Europe. It is now chiefly concerned with providing health care, education, and improved nutrition to *developing countries. Most of UNICEF's funds come from voluntary government contributions. Its headquarters are in Geneva. It won the Nobel Peace Prize in 1965.

United Nations Relief and Works Agency for Palestine Refugees in the Near East (UNRWA) A *United Nations body founded in 1950 to provide relief, health, education, and welfare services for Palestinian refugees in the Middle East (*see* Palestine). Its permanent headquarters are in Beirut (Lebanon).

United Provinces of the Netherlands The northern provinces of the Netherlands, which united (1579) during the *Revolt of the Netherlands against Spain and formed (1581) a self-governing independent federation. The so-called Dutch Republic survived until conquered by the French (1795) during the Revolutionary Wars.

United States of America (USA) A country in North America, the fourth largest country in the world. The USA is a federal republic comprising 50 states, including two separated from the others: Alaska, in the extreme NW of the continent, and Hawaii, in the central Pacific Ocean. The US borders on Canada in the N and Mexico in the S. The Pacific mountain system and the Rocky Mountains, the watershed of the country, extend N–S in the W with an arid area between, while the Appalachian Mountains extend N–S in the E. In the center lie vast plains. The population is of mixed ethnic stock, the majority being of European descent; other groups include African Americans, Latin Americans, Chinese, Japanese, and American Indians (many of whom live on reservations). *Economy*: the US is the world's greatest industrial producer, with a highly diversified economy. Its large resources of minerals and fuels make it the leading producer of natural gas, lead, copper, aluminum, and sulfur and of electrical and nuclear energy. It is almost self-sufficient in raw materials, although as its mineral resources are depleted it is having to increase its imports, notably of petroleum. The chief manufactures are steel, motor vehicles, chemicals, electronic equipment, and consumer goods. Although only 4% of the workforce are employed in agriculture, 15% of all exports are agricultural products. Farming is highly mechanized, with efficient control of disease and pests. Cereals, cotton, and tobacco are the main crops. Main exports include motor vehicles, aircraft, machinery, grain, and chemicals, while main imports include petroleum and petroleum products, chemicals, metals, machinery, cars, and newsprint. *History*: extensively explored following its discovery by Columbus in 1492, America was settled from 1565, chiefly by the Spanish, French, and British. The British colonies, in the E, had the greatest religious and economic freedom and were therefore the most attractive and successful. However, during the 18th century conflict developed between local colonial assemblies and their British governors, particularly over taxation. The colonists' confidence in themselves was strengthened by their success against the French in the *French and Indian Wars (1754–1763) and the 13 colonies finally won independence in the *American Revolution (1775–83). The US rapidly expanded W from this time, acquiring vast territories with the Louisiana Purchase (1803). Through the *Mexican War (1846–48) California and other western lands were added. The discovery of gold in California (1848) further encouraged settlement in the W. By 1820 conflict was developing between the cotton-growing states of the South (where African slaves had worked since the late 17th century) and the commercial North (where the industrial revolution was under way and slavery was opposed). As the new states of the West aligned themselves with the North, the South felt increasingly threatened. This led to the *Civil War (1861–65), which ended in victory for the North and the abolition of slavery. It was followed by a period of rapid industrial and economic expansion, while territorial expansion continued with the purchase of Alaska (1867), the annexation of Hawaii (1898), and the *Spanish-American War (1898), in which the US acquired the Philippines, Puerto Rico, Guam, and a measure of control over Cuba.

Intervention in Colombia led to the construction of the Panama Canal (opened 1914). Economic and territorial expansion made the US a world power, a status confirmed by its role in World War I, which it entered reluctantly (1917) because of its policy of isolationism. The 1920s saw another industrial and commercial boom, which ended in the *Depression that followed the Crash of 1929. The US was also reluctant to enter World War II but was forced to do so by the Japanese bombing of Pearl Harbor in Hawaii (Dec 7, 1941). US troops and weapons played a major part in defeating the Axis powers in Europe and its development and use of the atom bomb ended the war against Japan. The key US role in the establishment of the United Nations (1945) involved it inextricably in international affairs, in which it has since played a leading role. Postwar fear of Soviet expansion resulted in the Marshall Plan (1947), designed to render Europe less susceptible to communism by bolstering it economically, in involvement in the *Cold War, and in the harassment of supposed communists at home (*see also* McCarthy, Joseph R.). Fear of the spread of communism led also to military involvement in Korea (1950–53), Cuba (1961–62), and Vietnam (1961–75) and in the use of foreign aid to maintain the status quo in developing countries. After 1963 relations with the Soviet Union improved, with strategic arms limitation discussed (*see* disarmament), and diplomatic relations were established with China in 1979. Interventionist policy continued, however, with the role of the CIA in foreign affairs criticized and investigated (1975–76) following the government's loss of credibility resulting from the *Watergate affair (1972–74). US support of Israel, the linchpin of its Middle East policy, embroiled the US further in the war in Lebanon. In Central America the US supported an unpopular conservative government in El Salvador and aided enemies of the leftist Sandinista regime in Nicaragua in the early 1980s. In the Caribbean US troops invaded (1983) the tiny island of Grenada to help overthrow the governing Marxist regime. Nuclear arms control talks with the Soviet Union broke down as the US deployed missiles in Western Europe in response to the threat of increasing Soviet missile development. Domestic problems since World War II have included the difficulties of effecting racial integration, with race riots in the mid- and late 1960s followed by extensive opposition to the *Vietnam War. The postwar economic boom was followed by decline in the early 1970s, with continuing inflation. Depletion and pollution of natural resources is making such measures as energy saving a necessary part of the economy. With its increasing dependence on petroleum imports the country suffered through the drying up of supplies from Iran (1978–79) and rises in world petroleum prices. Relationships with Iran were further strained when Iranian students took 52 US diplomats hostage in the American Embassy, Tehran, in 1979, only releasing them in January 1981, soon after Reagan's inauguration. In the early 1980s the country experienced the worst recession since the Great Depression. By the end of Reagan's first term reduced spending on social programs and tax cuts resulted in economic revival, but the country's huge deficit evoked increasing concern. Reelected in 1984, President Reagan faced both domestic and foreign problems. Vice Pres. George Bush, who succeeded Reagan in 1989, soon faced another severe recession, and trade deficits increased tension with Japan. In 1990–91, Iraq's invasion of Kuwait provoked a Middle East crisis that involved US military forces in *Operation Desert Storm, which expelled Iraq from Kuwait. In fall 1991, Bush's appointment of Clarence *Thomas to the Supreme Court triggered major controversy. Democrat Bill *Clinton won the 1992 elections and faced major issues in health reform, deficit reduction, and trade after taking office. Civil wars in Somalia and Bosnia became foreign affairs issues in 1993–94. President: William Clinton. Official language: English. Official currency: US dollar of 100 cents. Area: 3,614,343 sq mi (9,363,123 sq km). Population (1990): 248,709,873. Capital: Washington, D.C.

United States Air Force Academy A four-year higher-education institution that trains men and women to be officers in the *Air Force. Located in Colorado Springs, Colo., it was established in 1958. Graduates receive a bachelor of science degree and a commission as a second lieutenant in the air force.

United States Military Academy A four-year higher-education institution that trains men and women to be officers in the US *Army. Located at West Point, N.Y., it was established in 1802 for men only; women have been admitted since 1976. Graduates receive a bachelor of science degree and a commission as a second lieutenant in the army.

United States Naval Academy A four-year higher-education institution that trains men and women to be officers in the US *Navy or *Marine Corps. Located in Annapolis, Md., it was established in 1845 for men only; women have been admitted since 1976. Graduates receive a bachelor of science degree and a commission as a navy ensign or Marine Corps second lieutenant.

United States v. E. C. Knight Company (1895) US Supreme Court decision that defined the *Sherman Anti-Trust Act and confirmed the law's intent of applying only to interstate trade.

unities Three principles concerning the representation in drama of action, time, and space. According to the interpretation of Aristotle's *Poetics* by 16th and 17th-century neoclassical critics, a play must represent a single action occurring in a single setting during the course of a single day. The unities were strictly observed in much 17th-century French drama, notably in the tragedies of *Racine and *Corneille, but were largely ignored in England.

universe The sum of all potentially knowable objects—the earth, sun, and other solar-system bodies, the stars and other members of our *Galaxy, countless millions of other *galaxies, and the matter between these objects. The universe is thought to be 10–20 thousand million years old and is at present expanding (*see* big-bang theory; cosmology). Its unimaginable vastness in both space (about 10^{10} light years across) and time (about 10^{10} years old) has only been accepted in this century. The possibility of life elsewhere in the universe is fairly high (i.e. there is a high probability that there are millions of stars with similar planetary systems and conditions to those of the solar system), but because distances are so enormous there is very little chance of ascertaining the existence of life elsewhere.

universities Independent degree-awarding institutions of higher education. They evolved in Europe in the Middle Ages from the *studia generalia*, schools open to scholars from all parts of Europe, and by the end of the 14th century consisted of lawful communities of teachers and scholars, recognized by civil or ecclesiastical authorities. Among the earliest were those founded at Bologna (1088), Paris (c. 1150), Prague (1348), Vienna (1365), and Heidelberg (1386). The first universities in England were established at Oxford and Cambridge in the 12th century. In the US the first universities evolved from institutions established prior to the American Revolution, such as *Harvard (1636), *Yale (1701) and *Princeton (1746). Following industrialization during the 19th century, many new universities were established, a process that continued into the 20th century, especially after World War II. Increasing emphasis was placed upon the development of technical studies. Two-year community (junior) colleges developed, offering liberal arts and vocational training.

Upanishads About 200 prose and verse treatises on metaphysical philosophy, produced as commentaries on the *Vedas* and dating from around 400 BC. They deal with the nature of *Brahman and the soul and are reputedly divinely inspired. Many different, sometimes contradictory, views are represented.

upas An evergreen tropical tree, *Antiaris toxicana*, native to SE Asia. Up to 100 ft (30 m) high, it has a crown of short spreading branches and long simple leaves; the flowers give rise to fleshy red pear-shaped fruits. The milky latex is a source of arrow poison. Family: *Moraceae*.

Updike, John (Hoyer) (1932–) US novelist and short-story writer. Until 1959 he worked for the *New Yorker* magazine. In novels such as *Rabbit, Run* (1960), *Couples* (1968), *Rabbit Redux* (1970), *Bech: A Book* (1971), *Marry Me* (1976), *Bech Is Back* (1982), *The Witches of Eastwick* (1984), *Roger's Version* (1986), and *S.* (1988), he has explored the moral confusions of contemporary US society. He has moved beyond the suburban setting of much of his writing in *The Coup* (1979), a novel set in an emergent African country. His novel *Rabbit is Rich* (1981) won a Pulitzer Prize. *Self Consciousness* (1989) is a memoir and *Odd Jobs* (1991) is a collection of his criticism and essays.

Upolu The most populous island in Western Samoa. It is fertile and copra, cacao, bananas, and rubber are produced. Area: 430 sq mi (1114 sq km). Chief town: Apia.

Upper Canada A former province (1791–1841) in SE Canada, corresponding to the S half of modern Ontario province. Including the area west of the Ottawa River and north of the Great Lakes, it became Canada West in 1841 and part of Ontario in 1867.

Upper Volta, Republic of. *See* Burkina Faso.

Uppsala 59 55N 17 38E A city in E central Sweden. It is a historic and cultural center, with a famous library, a gothic cathedral, and Sweden's oldest university (1477), where *Linnaeus taught. Population (1992 est): 170,750.

Ur An ancient city of *Sumer (S Iraq). Mentioned in Genesis as *Abraham's homeland, its site remained unidentified until 1854. Sir Leonard *Woolley's excavations (1922–34) made famous the spectacularly rich royal burials of about 2500 BC and seemed to provide historical evidence for *Noah's flood. The leading city in Sumer when it was sacked by barbarians about 2000 BC, Ur was superseded by *Babylon. Ur remained a center for the worship of the moon god Nanna until changes in the course of the Euphrates forced its remaining inhabitants away (5th century BC).

Ural River A river in Russia and Kazakhstan, rising in the S Ural Mountains, and flowing mainly S to the Caspian Sea near Guryev. Length: 1575 mi (2534 km).

Uralic languages A major language family comprising two related groups of languages, the *Finno-Ugric and the Samoyedic (*see* Samoyed). Originating from a common source over 10,000 years ago in an area N of the Ural Moun-

UR The "Standard" of Ur (c. 2500 BC; British Museum, London). It consists of a hollow box, the sides of which depict a king's campaign, decorated with lapis lazuli, shell, and red limestone. The side shown depicts animals being taken to be killed for the victory banquet.

tains, the two branches of the Uralic language family have developed into multiple forms covering an extensive geographical area in Europe, Scandinavia, and Asia.

Ural Mountains A mountain range extending 1243 mi (2000 km) N–S from the Kara Sea in Russia to the steppes of Kazakhstan NE of the Caspian Sea and traditionally dividing Europe from Asia. The highest point is Mount Narodnaya, in the N, at 6214 ft (1894 m). Most industrial metals are obtained there, as well as some precious stones, such as emerald and amethyst, and the S part is an important industrial area, including the towns of Sverdlovsk and Magnitogorsk.

Urania In Greek mythology, one of the nine *Muses, the patron of astronomy. She was often portrayed with a globe and compass.

uranium (U) The radioactive metallic element used as a fuel for nuclear reactors (*see* nuclear energy). Uranium is a silvery-white metal, almost as hard as steel and very dense (relative density 18.95). Before the development of nuclear power, one of its major uses was in making yellow glass. Uranium has the highest atomic number of the naturally occurring elements. It was first isolated in 1841 by E. Péligot (1811–90), although it had been identified before this in pitch-blende. It is also found in the ores uranite, carnotite, and monazite; it is mined primarily in Canada, Australia, and South Africa. Natural uranium contains three isotopes: ^{238}U (99.283%), ^{235}U (0.711%), and ^{234}U (0.006%). ^{238}U has a half-life of 4.51×10^9 years and is useful in dating rocks, as well as in fuel for fast reactors. The most important isotope in the nuclear industry is ^{235}U, which is used in *thermal reactors. Some reactors use metallic fuel, others uranium dioxide (UO_2). Other oxides include U_3O_8 and UO_3. The volatile gas uranium hexafluoride (UF_6) is used to separate uranium isotopes by gaseous diffusion. At no 94; at wt 238.029; mp 2072°F (1132°C); bp 6911°F (3818°C).

uranium series One of three naturally occurring series of radioactive decays. The uranium series is headed by uranium 238, which undergoes a series of alpha and beta decays ending with the stable isotope lead 206. *See also* actinium series; thorium series.

Uranus (astronomy) A giant planet, orbiting the sun every 84 years (between Saturn and Neptune) at a mean distance of about 1.8 billion mi (2.9 billion km). Its axis of rotation is close to its orbital plane. It is somewhat larger (32,540 mi [52,400 km] in diameter) than Neptune and exhibits a similar greenish featureless disk in a telescope. In its equatorial plane lie 15 *satellites and a system of 10 narrow rings (similar to, but less visible than, Saturn's rings), discovered in 1977 and examined in detail in a 1986 flyby. Composed predominantly of hydrogen and helium, with cloud layers of methane and possibly ammonia, its atmospheric and interior structure are similar to Neptune's. Uranus was discovered telescopically in 1781 by Sir William Herschel.

Uranus (Greek mythology) The personification of Heaven. He was the son of Gaea (Earth), and his children by her included the *Titans and the *Cyclops. He was castrated by his son Cronus and his genitals were thrown into the sea, which gave birth to *Aphrodite.

Urartu (biblical name: Ararat) A kingdom flourishing between about 850 and 650 BC in E Turkey. The inhabitants, of *Hurrian stock, made their capital at Van (ancient Tushpa). Their metalwork was famous, examples even reaching Etruscan Italy. Urartu was frequently at war with neighboring Assyria.

Urban II (Odo of Lagery; c. 1042–99) Pope (1088–99). Until 1094 his rule was challenged by Guibert of Ravenna (d. 1100), the antipope set up by Emperor Henry IV. A Cluniac monk, he was made a cardinal by *Gregory VII, whose reform policies he continued. Councils at Melfi (1089) and at Piacenza and Clermont (1095) condemned simony, lay investiture, and clerical marriage. At Clermont he also proclaimed the First *Crusade. He was beatified in 1881. Feast day: July 29 or 30.

Urban VI (Bartolommeo Prignano; c. 1318–89) Pope (1378–89). His anti-French policies and dictatorial behavior inspired the French cardinals to declare his election void and to elect an antipope, thereby beginning the *Great Schism.

Urban VIII (Maffeo Barberini; 1568–1644) Pope (1623–44) during the *Thirty Years' War, in which he supported Richelieu against the Hapsburgs. A great scholar, Urban supported new religious orders and reforms, including the revision of the Missal and new canonization procedures. He promulgated several measures against heresy and condemned the writings of Galileo and Jansen.

urban planning The designing of town and city areas with a view to providing adequate public facilities, healthy and pleasant surroundings, and good communications. Among the first urban planners were the Romans, who evolved a characteristic grid plan for many of their towns. Interest in the subject revived during the *Renaissance but it only became of major importance during the 19th-century urban expansion, when the need for an assured supply of housing and services became urgent. As a branch of the social sciences urban planning has become highly sophisticated in the 20th century, now having to deal not only with unprecedented concentrations of people but also with large quantities of traffic.

Urbino 43 43N 12 38E A city in Italy, in Marche. The birthplace of Raphael, Urbino possesses a 15th-century ducal palace and a university (1506). Its manufactures include textiles and majolica. Population: 16,296.

Urdu An *Indo-Aryan language of N India and Pakistan, where it is an official language. Like *Hindi it arose from *Hindustani, but since it was used largely by Muslims in this region, while Hindi has been progressively influenced by *Sanskrit, the two now differ considerably. It is written in a modified Arabic script.

urea (*or* carbamide) A white crystalline compound $(CO(NH_2)_2)$ derived from ammonia and carbon dioxide. It is widely used as a nitrogen fertilizer, a feed supplement for ruminant animals, and in the plastics and pharmaceutical industries. Urea is the excretory product of nitrogen metabolism in mammals and is present in *urine.

urea-formaldehyde resins Synthetic thermosetting resins that are made by the condensation in aqueous solution of urea and formaldehyde with an ammonia catalyst. Cellulose filler is added to the colorless syrupy solution produced and a molding powder forms when it dries. This powder can be colored with pigment and used to make cups, bathroom fittings, electrical fittings, etc.

uremia The accumulation of *urea in the blood due to kidney failure. Kidney failure can occur suddenly due to shock, obstruction of both ureters, injury, or acute kidney disease or it may arise slowly due to *nephritis or other diseases. In acute kidney failure the kidneys will often recover after *dialysis with a kidney machine. In chronic conditions, requiring long-term dialysis, a kidney transplant (if available) is preferred.

urethane A white crystalline solid, $(CO(NH_2)(OC_2H_5))$, made by heating ethanol with urea nitrate. It is soluble in water and alcohol and is used to manufacture *polyurethane foam.

Urey, Harold Clayton (1893–1981) US physicist, who received the Nobel Prize in 1934 for his discovery of deuterium. He also did valuable work on the separation of isotopes, which was useful in the manufacture of the hydrogen bomb. In postwar years, as professor at the University of Chicago (1945–52) and then at the University of California, he turned to geophysics.

Urfa (ancient name: Edessa) 37 08N 38 45E A city in S Turkey, near the Syrian border. It was the birthplace of Abraham. It has changed hands frequently, being occupied by Crusaders from 1098 to 1637. Population (1990): 276,528.

Urfé, Honoré d' (1568–1625) French novelist. His major work was the prose romance, *L'Astrée* (1607–27), which is set in his native Lyonnais in the 5th century and combines elements of pastoral and adventure; it is considered to be the first French novel. He also wrote the pastoral dramas *Sireine* and *Sylvanire* (1627).

Urga. *See* Ulan Bator.

uric acid A compound ($C_5H_4N_4O_3$) formed during the nitrogen metabolism of animals and the chief nitrogenous excretory product of reptiles and birds. In man, raised levels of uric acid in the blood are associated with gout.

urine The fluid that is formed by the kidneys and contains the waste products of metabolism and surplus water and salts. In man the kidneys normally produce 1–1.6 qt (0.9–1.5 l) of urine per day, containing some 1.75–2.5 oz (50–70 g) of solids—mostly urea, creatine, uric acid, and inorganic salts. The composition of urine depends on the type of animal and the need to conserve body water.

Uris, Leon Marcus (1924–   ) US writer. His best-known work is *Exodus* (1958), about the founding of present-day Israel; it was made into a successful movie in 1961. His works, usually incorporating history with fiction, include *Battle Cry* (1953), *Armageddon* (1964), *Topaz* (1967), *QB VII* (1970) and *Trinity* (1976). He wrote the scripts for those of his works that were made into films.

Urmia, Lake A shallow lake in NW Iran, the largest in the country, lying 4265 ft (1300 m) above sea level. It has no outlet and consequently is salty and varies in size. Average area: 1930 sq mi (5000 sq km).

Urnfield A group of Bronze Age cultures originating in central Europe. Urnfield peoples characteristically cremated their dead and buried the ashes in cemeteries of pottery urns. Their culture spread to most of Europe before being displaced by Iron Age *Hallstatt or Roman influence. Urnfields are commonly associated with groups who later became identifiable as the *Celts.

Ursa Major (Latin: great bear) A large conspicuous constellation in the N sky. The brightest stars, all of 2nd magnitude, are Alioth, Alcaid, and Dubhe. The seven brightest stars form the Big Dipper.

Ursa Minor (Latin: little bear) A constellation in the N sky that contains the N celestial pole. The brightest star is *Polaris, the present pole star.

Ursula, St A legendary British martyr. According to tradition, she and 11,000 virgins were murdered by the Huns at Cologne while returning from a pilgrimage to Rome in the 3rd or 5th century. She is first mentioned in the 10th century. She has given her name to numerous religious establishments, including the *Ursulines. Feast day: Oct 21.

Ursulines A Roman Catholic religious order for women, named for its patron St *Ursula, founded in Brescia in 1535 by St Angela Merici (1474–1540). It is devoted to educational work and is the oldest teaching order of women.

urticaria (*or* hives) An acute or chronic allergic disorder in which itching white raised patches surrounded by red areas appear on the skin: they resemble nettle stings (hence the alternative name—nettle rash). Acute urticaria usually arises from allergy to food or drugs and usually disappears quickly if the cause is removed. Chronic urticaria occurs in young people and its cause is not certain. Urticaria is treated with *antihistamines.

Uruguay, Oriental Republic of A country in the SE of South America, on the Atlantic Ocean and the Río de la Plata, bounded by Argentina and Brazil. Coastal plains rise to higher ground, especially in the N. The Uruguay River forms its W boundary and the other main river is the Negro. Most of the population is of Spanish and Italian descent. *Economy*: the traditional livestock industry was badly affected by the 1974 EEC ban on meat imports, although new markets have subsequently been found. The cultivation of the principal crops (wheat, corn, sorghum) has been intensified and the fishing industry has been expanded with government assistance. The principal industries include food processing, hides and leather, textiles, construction, metallurgy, and rubber. Hydroelectricity is a valuable source of power. *History*: explored by the Spanish in the 16th century, its early history was one of rivalry between Spanish and Portuguese settlements. In the 18th century Spain established its control of Uruguay, which in 1776 became part of the viceroyalty of the Río de la Plata. Under the leadership of Artigas, Uruguay joined Argentina in the movement for independence against Spain but was subsequently fought over by Argentina and Brazil. In 1828, with British help, Uruguay achieved independence; politics have since been dominated by two parties, the Colorados (liberals) and the Blancos (conservatives). The late 19th century saw the beginning of considerable immigration from Europe, which was encouraged by the establishment in the first decades of the 20th century of what is regarded as Latin America's first welfare state. Uruguay is renowned for its literature and art. In the late 1960s there was considerable unrest caused partly by the Tupamaro urban guerrillas (*see* Tupac Amarú). In 1972 they were crushed by the army, which subsequently imposed repressive measures that led to international protests against violations of human rights. In 1982 a limited form of democracy was introduced with the approval of the organization of three political parties. An election was held in 1984. However, dissent was still repressed, and the economy continued to be unstable. The military president Gen. Gregorio Alvarez Armelino resigned in 1985 in favor of a democratically elected president, Sr Julio Sanguinetti, who signed an amnesty decree for all the military accused of human rights violations. In 1989, Luis Alberto Lacalle was elected president and inaugurated in March 1990. When the opposition voted against many of his economic reform programs, Lacalle in 1992–93 instituted changes by decree, ignoring opposition. Uruguay is a member of the OAS and LAFTA. Official language: Spanish. Official currency: new Uruguayan peso of 100 centésimos. Area: 72,172 sq mi (186,926 sq km). Population (1990 est): 3,002,000. Capital and main port: Montevideo.

Uruguay River (Portuguese name: Rio Uruguai; Spanish name: Río Uruguay) A river in South America. Rising in S Brazil, it flows generally SW forming the Argentina-Brazil and Argentina-Uruguay borders before joining the Rio Paraná to form the Río de la Plata. Length: about 1000 mi (1600 km).

Uruk (biblical name: Erech; modern name: Warka) An ancient city in S Mesopotamia. The site testifies to the beginnings of Sumerian civilization in the 4th millennium BC; significant finds include pictographic writing and pottery made on a wheel. In the 3rd millennium, Uruk was a center for the worship of the god *Anu. *Gilgamesh was one of its rulers. Supplanted by *Ur (c. 2100), Uruk nevertheless remained inhabited until the early Christian era.

Ürümqi (*or* Urumchi; former name: Tihwa) 43 43N 87 38E A city in NW China, the capital of Xinjiang Uygur AR, and the site of its university. Industries include iron and steel and machine building. Population (1987 est): 1,040,000.

ushabti A figurine of faience, wood, or stone placed in an ancient Egyptian tomb to serve the deceased in the afterlife. Called "answerers," they carried inscriptions asserting their readiness to answer the gods' summons to work.

Ushant (French name: Ouessant) 48 28N 5 05W A French island off the W coast of Brittany. Two naval battles (1778 and 1794) between the British and the French were fought off its coast. Area: about 6 sq mi (16 sq km).

Üsküdar (former name: Scutari) 41 02N 29 02E A town in NW Turkey, a suburb of Istanbul on the opposite side of the Bosporus. The British military base there during the Crimean War included the hospital in which Florence Nightingale worked.

Uspallata 32 43S 69 24W A pass through the Andes, in S South America at the foot of Mount Aconcagua, linking Santiago (Chile) with Mendoza (Argentina). The statue *Christ of the Andes* was erected there in 1904. Height: 12,600 ft (3840 m).

USSR. *See* Soviet Union.

Ussuri River A river in E Asia, rising in extreme E Russia and forming part of the border with China as it flows N to the Amur River at Khabarovsk. Border fighting between Soviet and Chinese forces occurred there (1964, 1972). Length: about 500 mi (800 km).

PETER USTINOV *As an unsavory legionnaire in the comedy film* The Last Remake of Beau Geste *(1977).*

Ustinov, Peter (Alexander) (1921–) British actor, director, and dramatist of Russian descent. In the theater he acted mostly in his own plays, which include *The Love of Four Colonels* (1951) and *Romanoff and Juliet* (1956); his many films include *Spartacus* (1960, for which he won an Academy Award), *Death on the Nile* (1978), and *Evil Under the Sun* (1981). He has written novels and an autobiography; he is also well known as an impersonator and television personality.

Ust-Kamenogorsk 49 58N 82 36E A port in E Kazakhstan, on the Irtysh River. It is the center of a zinc-, copper-, and lead-mining region. Population (1991 est): 333,000.

Ustyurt Plateau (*or* Ust Urt Plateau) A desert upland lying between the Caspian and Aral Seas, in Kazakhstan and Uzbekistan at an average height of about 656 ft (200 m). Area: about 77,000 sq mi (200,000 sq km).

Usumbura. *See* Bujumbura.

usury In medieval canon law, the charging of interest for the loan of money. Although Christians were precluded from being moneylenders, the profession was permitted to Jews by the fourth Lateran Council (1215). Since Jews were allowed by the Pentateuch to lend money at interest to strangers, and were excluded from many alternative occupations, they comprised the majority of moneylenders. By the late Middle Ages, however, with growing demand for credit to meet the needs of trade, many Christians, notably at Cahors and in Lombardy, ignored canonical prohibition and became moneylenders and usury came to mean the charging of extortionate interest.

Utagawa Kuniyoshi (Igusa Magosaburo; 1797–1861) Japanese painter and printmaker of the *ukiyo-e movement. He is known for his warrior and landscape prints.

Utah US mountain state, bordered by Nevada (W), Idaho and Wyoming (N,NE), Colorado (E), and Arizona (S). The Wasatch Range of the Rocky Mountains divides the state into two arid regions: the Great Basin, which includes the Great Salt Lake, and the Great Salt Lake Desert in the W and the Colorado Plateau in the E. The raising of livestock is the principal agricultural activity but further growth in this sector is limited by the lack of irrigation and by soil erosion. Manufacturing is increasing in importance, especially food products, fabricated steel, spacecraft and, more recently, electronics equipment. There are significant deposits of copper, oil, natural gas, and uranium. Scenic attractions, such as Bryce Canyon and Zion National Park, make it a popular tourist area. *History*: the area was inhabited from c. 9000 BC. Europeans (Spanish missionaries) first entered the area in 1776 and the region was held by the Spanish until ceded to the US by Mexico in 1848. The persecuted Mormons, who had emigrated from New York, began major settlements in 1847, thereby dispossessing the Ute Indians, and their religion continues to exert a dominating influence over the life of the state. After conflict between the Mormons and the federal government over the issue of polygamy was resolved, Utah was finally admitted to the Union in 1896. Area: 84,916 sq mi (219,931 sq km). Population (1990): 1,722,850. Capital: Salt Lake City.

Utamaro. *See* Kitagawa Utamaro.

uterus The part of a woman's reproductive tract in which the fetus develops. The uterus is a hollow muscular organ, about 3 in (7.5 cm) long in the absence of pregnancy. It is connected by the vagina to the outside and to the ovaries by the Fallopian tubes. In a nonpregnant woman the lining of the uterus is shed at monthly intervals (*see* menstruation). During *childbirth the uterus, which is greatly enlarged (about 12 in [30 cm] long), undergoes strong contractions to expel the baby. *See* also cervix.

Utica 43 06N 75 15W A city in New York, on the Mohawk River. F. W. Wool-worth opened his first store there in 1879. There is an annual eisteddfod (festival of the arts), sponsored by its many Welsh inhabitants. Industries include dairy farming and textiles. Population (1990): 68,637.

utilitarianism An ethical doctrine holding that the best action is the one that will result in the greatest happiness and least pain for the greatest number of people. Utilitarianism flourished in Britain from the mid-18th century to the mid-19th century. *Hume, *Bentham, and James *Mill propounded it and John Stuart Mill defended it. It influenced all thought in politics and morals and was the most widespread British contribution to such thought. Both *intuitionism and *idealism have developed critiques of the doctrine, based on its inherent un-fairness, the difficulty of assessing consequences, and the belief that some acts are intrinsically good or intrinsically bad, regardless of outcome.

utopianism A program of total social and political reform with the object of establishing a perfect society. The term derives from the imaginary state de-picted in Thomas *More's *Utopia* (1516). Utopian schemes have sometimes found practical expression in social experiment, such as Robert *Owen's com-munities. Others, such as *Utopia* itself, are literary satires attacking existing in-stitutions by comparing them unfavorably with imaginary ideals. Utopianism advocates a communistic organization of society, but the concomitant authori-tarianism reveals that no way has been found of reconciling individual freedom and happiness with social justice.

Utrecht 52 06N 5 07E A city in the central Netherlands, the capital of Utrecht province. The Union of Utrecht (1579) united the northern provinces of the Netherlands against Spain. The Treaties of *Utrecht were concluded there. Its notable buildings include the gothic cathedral (14th century) and its famous university (founded 1636). An important railroad center, its industries include textiles, chemicals, and metallurgy. An annual trade fair is held. Population (1991 est): 231,200.

Utrecht, Treaties of (1713–14) A series of treaties between France and, re-spectively, Britain, the Netherlands, Prussia, Portugal, and Savoy that concluded the War of the *Spanish Succession. Further treaties arranged settlements with Spain and the Holy Roman Empire. The effect of the treaties was to end Louis XIV's attempts at European expansion.

Utrillo, Maurice (1883–1955) French painter, the illegitimate son of Suzanne Valadon (1867–1938), an artist's model who later became an artist. For almost his entire life, he suffered from alcoholism and drug addiction. He specialized in painting often deserted street scenes, notably of Montmartre, which are distin-guished by their near-monochrome colors and precise drawing. These were often based on picture postcards and after 1916 became somewhat repetitive.

Uttar Pradesh A state in N India, stretching from highlands N across the Ganges plain into the Himalayas. The most populous state, it produces grains, pulses, and sugarcane. Forestry is important but there is little industry. *History*: the center of N Indian culture, Uttar Pradesh was also the core of the Mogul Em-pire. It was the center of the Indian Mutiny (1857–59) against British rule and of Indian nationalism. Area: 113,643 sq mi (294,413 sq km). Population (1991): 139,031,130. Capital: Lucknow.

Uzbekistan, Republic of (*or* Uzbekistan) A republic in E central Asia, a constituent republic of the Soviet Union until 1991. The NW comprises desert but fertile land is found in the SE. The Uzbeks, who are Turkic-speaking Sun-nite Muslims, make up two-thirds of the population. Uzbekistan is rich in min-eral deposits, including oil, coal, and copper, and has more than 20 hydroelectric plants and three natural gas pipelines in operation. Industries include mining, chemicals, textiles, and paper. The region is a chief cotton-growing area, the third most important in the world. Rice is also produced. *History*; the region was invaded by the Persians under Darius I, by the Macedonians under Alexander the Great, and then by the Arabs (8th century AD) and the Mongols (13th century). In the 16th century the Uzbeks became the dominant people in the region, which was annexed by Russia in the 19th century. The Uzbek SSR was formed in 1924. It became independent in 1991 with the collapse of the Soviet Union. Uzbekistan became a member of the Commonwealth of Independent States (CIS) in 1991 and the UN in 1992. Area: 173,546 sq mi (449,600 sq km). Population (1987): 19,026,000. Capital: Tashkent.

V

V-1 A German World War II unguided missile, also called a flying bomb. It carried about 2000 pounds (900 kg) of high explosive. Some 8000 missiles were launched against London between June 1944 and March 1945, killing over 5500 civilians. The "V" stands for the German *Vergeltungswaffe*, retaliation weapon.

V-2 A German World War II *ballistic missile powered by a rocket engine using alcohol and liquid oxygen as fuel. It carried about 2000 pounds (900 kg) of high explosive. Some 4000 were used against Britain and the Low Countries in 1944 and 1945. It became the basis for both US and Soviet postwar rocket design.

Vaal River A river in South Africa, rising in the SE Transvaal. It flows generally W and SW, to join the Orange River and forms part of the Orange Free State–Transvaal border. The **Vaal Dam**, near Vereeniging, supplies water to the mines of the Witwatersrand. Length: 750 mi (1210 km).

Vaasa (Swedish name: Vasa) 63 06N 21 36E A seaport in W Finland, on the Gulf of Bothnia. Founded in 1606, it was rebuilt nearer the sea following a fire in 1852. Its industries include ship repairing, textiles, and food processing. Population (1980): 53,758.

vaccination (or inoculation) The introduction of inactivated or dead disease-causing microorganisms (vaccine) into the body to stimulate the formation of *antibodies to these agents without producing the disease (*see also* immunity). The first vaccination (against smallpox) was performed by Edward *Jenner in 1798. Vaccination is now routinely used to prevent such life-threatening infections as poliomyelitis, diphtheria, tetanus, and tuberculosis. It is also used to protect visitors to areas where such infections as yellow fever, cholera, and typhoid fever are endemic. Vaccines are usually given by injection but some can be administered through skin scratches and some are taken by mouth. Vaccination against German measles (rubella) may be given to nonpregnant women of childbearing age to prevent the malformations in the fetus that this disease can cause. The use of the whooping cough vaccine is controversial as in very rare cases it has caused brain damage.

vacuum A region of space that contains no matter. In practice, a perfect vacuum is impossible to obtain and any region in which the pressure of the gas is less than about one millimeter of mercury may be considered a vacuum. In technical work a soft (*or* low) vacuum goes down to a pressure of 10^{-4} mmHg, a hard (*or* high) vacuum is between 10^{-4} and 10^{-9} mmHg, and an ultrahigh vacuum is below 10^{-9} mmHg. Vacuum technology is used in making cathode-ray tubes, lightbulbs, etc., and is used in certain forms of food preservation. **Vacuum gauges** include the *McLeod gauge and *Pirani gauge.

vacuum flask. *See* Dewar flask.

Vadodara. *See* Baroda.

Vaduz 47 08N 9 32E The capital of the principality of Liechtenstein. It is a tourist center and its castle (restored 1905–16) is the residence of the ruling prince. Population (1991 est): 4870.

vagina The part of the reproductive tract of women and other female mammals into which the *penis is inserted during sexual intercourse. It connects the uterus to the exterior and is readily distensible to allow for childbirth.

vagus nerve An important nerve that connects the brain with the throat, larynx, heart, lungs, stomach, and gut. Surgical cutting of a branch of the vagus nerve (**vagotomy**) is sometimes carried out to reduce the secretion of acid by the stomach in the treatment of a peptic ulcer.

Valdemar I (*or* Waldemar; 1131–82) King of Denmark (1157–82). His defeat of rival claimants to the throne ended a prolonged civil war in Denmark. His campaigns against the Wends (1159–69), assisted by his minister *Absalon, ended in victory with the seizure of Rügen. He subsequently repressed internal unrest.

Valdemar II (*or* Waldemar; 1170–1241) King of Denmark (1202–41); the son of Valdemar I. Before becoming king he conquered Holstein and Hamburg (1200–01) and later conducted successful campaigns in the E Baltic region. In 1219 he conquered Estonia but from 1223 to 1225 was imprisoned by a German vassal. At home he introduced military and legal reforms, issuing a revised legal code, the Law of Jutland (1241).

Valdemar IV Atterdag (*or* Waldemar; c. 1320–75) King of Denmark (1340–75). He was brought up at the court of Emperor Louis IV, Denmark being in the hands of foreign princes. Recognized as king in 1340, his reunification of Danish territories was completed by the recovery of Skåne from Sweden in 1360. His conquest of Gotland in the Baltic (1361) brought opposition from the Hanseatic League, which defeated Valdemar (1368) and forced him to accept the unfavorable Treaty of Stralsund (1370). His daughter *Margaret became queen of Denmark, Norway, and Sweden.

Valdivia 39 46S 73 15W A port in S Chile, on the Río Valdivia near the Pacific coast. It was badly damaged by earthquake (1960). Industries include tanning, ship building, and sugar refining. It contains the Southern University of Chile (1954). Population (1991 est): 123,580.

valence (*or* valency) The combining power of an atom, ion, or radical. It is equal to the number of hydrogen atoms that the atom, ion, or radical can combine with or replace in forming compounds, i.e. it is the number of single covalent or electrovalent bonds (*see* chemical bonds) that an atom, etc., can make. Many elements have more than one valence, for example phosphorus has valences of three and five. A **valence electron** is an electron in the outer shell of an atom that participates in forming chemical (valence) bonds. *See also* energy band.

Valence 44 56N 4 54E A city in SE France, the capital of the Drôme department on the Rhône River. It has a cathedral (11th–12th centuries) and is a commercial center for agricultural produce. Population (1982): 68,100.

Valencia 39 29N 0 24W The third largest city in Spain, on the Guadalaviar estuary. In 1021 it became the capital of the Moorish kingdom of Valencia. El Cid, the legendary Spanish hero, took the city from the Moors and held it from 1094 until his death in 1099. Its many notable buildings include the cathedral (1262–1482); the university was founded in 1500. The center of a productive agricultural area, Valencia has an important trade in oranges, rice, and silk. Population (1991): 752,909.

Valencia 10 14N 67 59W The third largest city in Venezuela. It is the focus of the country's most productive agricultural area and is a major industrial center. The University of Carabobo was founded there in 1852. Population (1990 est): 903,076.

Valencia A former kingdom in E Spain, corresponding approximately to the present-day province of Valencia. It was taken from the Moors by El Cid during the 11th century and came under the rule of Aragon in 1238.

Valenciennes 50 22N 3 32E A city in N France, in the Nord department. It has metallurgical and textile industries and an oil refinery. Its once famous lace industry is being revived. Population (1982): 35,000.

Valens (d. 378 AD) Eastern Roman emperor (364–78). Valens owed his accession to his brother *Valentinian, emperor in the West. During Valens's reign the Visigoths crossed the Danube and killed Valens at the battle of *Adrianople.

valentine A greeting card sent anonymously on Feb 14 as a declaration of affection. In ancient Rome boys drew girls' names from a love urn on Feb 15 and the early Christian Church transferred this popular pagan custom to St Valentine's feast day rather than abolish it. Paper valentines date from the 16th century.

Valentine, St (died c. 269) Roman priest and martyr, known as the patron of lovers. The customs practiced on his feast day (Feb 14) have no connection with his life (*see* valentine).

Valentinian I (d. 375 AD) Western Roman emperor (364–75). Valentinian became emperor by the acclamation of the army at Nicaea and shortly afterward made his brother *Valens emperor in the East. Reputedly of cruel disposition, he fought campaigns in the north of the Empire, restoring the Rhine frontier and Hadrian's Wall.

Valentino, Rudolph (Rodolpho Gugliemi di Valentina d'Antonguolla; 1895–1926) US film actor, born in Italy. He held various laboring jobs between arriving in the US in 1913 and going to Hollywood in 1918. His performances in *Four Horsemen of the Apocalypse* (1921), *The Shiek* (1921), *Blood and Sand* (1922), *Son of the Sheik* (1926), and other romantic dramas of the early silent cinema established him as the leading cinema idol of the 1920s.

RUDOLPH VALENTINO *In one of his most popular films,* Blood and Sand *(1922).*

Valera, Eamon De. *See* De Valera, Eamon.

valerian A perennial or (rarely) annual herb of either of the genera *Valeriana* (200 species) or *Centranthus* (12 species), native to the N hemisphere. Up to about 40 in (1 m) high, the plants usually have lobed leaves and small fragrant pink, red, or white five-lobed funnel-shaped flowers clustered into terminal heads. The root of the common valerian (*V. officinalis*), of Eurasia, has sedative properties. Family: *Valerianaceae*.

Valéry, Paul (1871–1945) French poet, essayist, and critic. After publishing some early symbolist verse he devoted himself for many years to abstract metaphysical study. *Cahiers* (29 vols, 1957–60) is a record of his daily speculations from 1894 until his death. His later poetry in *La Jeune Parque* (1917) and *Charmes* (1922) combines sensuous lyricism with intellectual force. He published many collections of essays on literary, scientific, and political topics.

Valhalla In Teutonic mythology, one of the three homes of *Odin, imagined as an enormous hall, the rafters of which are spears and the walls shields. Half of the warriors who die in battle are brought by the *Valkyries to Valhalla, where they spend their days in battle and their nights in feasting and listening to songs of their heroic exploits.

Valium. *See* benzodiazepines.

Valkyries In Teutonic mythology, beautiful maidens, between 3 and 27 in number, who are the personal attendants of *Odin. They wear helmets and armor, carry spears and, led by *Freyja, ride on horseback over battlefields in order to find and carry away the slain warriors whom Odin has chosen to live with him in *Valhalla.

Valla, Lorenzo (1405–57) Italian Renaissance humanist. He was a violent opponent of *scholasticism and an able scholar. In his *De voluptate* (*On Pleasure*; 1431), he argued that the pleasures of the senses were the greatest good. Valla's iconoclastic views had a considerable influence upon later Renaissance thought.

Valladolid 41 39N 4 45W A city in central Spain, in Old Castile. It was formerly the capital of Castile and León (14th–15th centuries). It has a 16th-century cathedral and contains Cervantes' house; its university was founded in 1346. Christopher Columbus died there (1506). An industrial center, its industries include brewing and textiles. Population (1991): 328,365.

Valle d'Aosta An autonomous region in NW Italy, consisting of the upper basin of the Dora Baltea River. Created in 1945, it has a large French-speaking population. Industry is replacing agriculture as the main activity and there are valuable hydroelectric resources. Tourism is important. Area: 1260 sq mi (3262 sq km). Population (1980 est): 114,469. Capital: Aosta.

Valletta 35 54N 14 32E The capital of Malta, a port on the N coast with one of the finest harbors in the world. Founded in 1566 by the Knights of St John, its main buildings include the 16th-century St John's Co-Cathedral and the University of Malta (1769). Formerly an important British naval base, its dockyards have been converted to commercial use and it is now an important transit center for Mediterranean shipping. Population (1991 est): 9,199.

valley An elongated depression in the earth's surface. It is usually occupied by a river or stream at its base and terminates on joining another river, lake, or the ocean. Valleys have various origins but the common **V-shaped valley** is formed as the result of erosion by a river. Those that originated through glacial erosion are **U-shaped valleys**, with steep sides and broad floors, often occupied by deep lakes (*see* fjord). *See also* rift valley.

Valley Forge The site, 22 mi (35 km) NW of Philadelphia, of the headquarters of Gen. *George Washington's forces in the winter of 1777–78 during the *American Revolution. Despite a severe lack of food and warm clothing, Washington's men remained loyal to the cause of American independence and emerged ready for an offensive against the British forces in the spring of 1778. Their fighting capacity was greatly improved by the training they received from Baron Friedrich Wilhelm Von *Steuben, a former Prussian officer, who became inspector general of the Continental army.

Valley of Ten Thousand Smokes A volcanic area in S Alaska. Its name derives from the many fissures spouting smoke, gas, and steam.

Valley of the Kings The cemetery of the Egyptian pharaohs from about 1580 to about 1085 BC, W of the Nile, near *Thebes. Tombs were tunneled in the limestone cliffs while mortuary temples were built in the valley below. All the tombs were robbed, except that of *Tutankhamen.

Valois The royal dynasty of France from 1328 to 1589, succeeding the *Capetians. The *Hundred Years' War (1337–1453) nearly destroyed Valois power, which was saved by *Charles VII (reigned 1422–61). He and his son *Louis XI vigorously extended royal authority. Their successors, *Charles VIII and *Louis XII, waged disastrous wars in Italy, where they opposed the *Hapsburgs. The last Valois were the victims of rival religious factions at court (*see* Wars of Religion) and were succeeded by the *Bourbons.

Valois, Dame Ninette de. *See* de Valois, Dame Ninette.

Valona. *See* Vlora.

Valparaíso 33 05S 71 40W The second largest city in Chile, on the Pacific Ocean. Founded by the Spanish (1536), it has suffered several earthquakes. Notable surviving buildings include the cathedral. It is the site of two universities (1926 and 1928). Valparaíso is a major port, handling most Chilean imports, and is an important industrial and commercial center. Manufactures include chemicals, textiles, and vegetable oils. Population (1991 est): 295,954.

value-added tax (VAT) An indirect tax on goods calculated by adding a percentage to the value of a product as it increases at each stage of production; the whole cost of the tax is eventually passed on to the consumer.

vampire In folklore, a soulless or "undead" corpse that rises from its coffin at night, sometimes taking the form of a vampire bat, and sucks the blood of living victims (who are thus also transformed into vampires). The vampire cannot lie at rest but must continually find new victims. It attacks only at night and is repelled by crucifixes, garlic, and the light of day. The body of a vampire can be destroyed by being beheaded, burned, having a stake driven through its heart, or by exposure to sunlight. Although appearing in many cultures, the vampire legend is particularly associated with E European folklore and was popularized by Bram Stoker's *Dracula* (1897), the source of many modern vampire films.

vampire bat A bat of the family *Desmodontidae* (3 species), of Central and South America. The most common species is *Desmodus rotundus*, 3–3.5 in (7.5–9 cm) long. Vampire bats feed on the blood of mammals or birds. They make a small incision in the skin with their sharp incisor teeth and lap up the blood of their sleeping victim with a grooved tongue. Vampire bats are too small to cause serious blood loss to their host; they do, however, transmit dangerous diseases, including rabies.

Van, Lake A lake in SW Turkey. It has no outlet and is therefore salty; sodium carbonate is extracted by evaporation, and the lake is fished for darekh. Area: 1443 sq mi (3738 sq km).

VAMPIRE BAT *Its chisel-like incisor teeth are used to cut the flesh of the victims to cause a flow of blood.*

vanadium (V) A transition metal, named for the Norse goddess Vanadis. The metal is isolated by reduction of the trichloride (VCl_3) with magnesium or of the pentoxide (V_2O_5) with calcium. It is an important additive to rust-resistant *steels and high-speed tool steels. The pentoxide is a useful catalyst in the oil industry. Complex vanadate ions (for example $VO_4^{3/}-$) exist in solution. At no 23; at wt 50.942; mp 3288°F (1890°C); bp 6116°F (3380°C).

Van Allen, James Alfred (1914–) US physicist, who during World War II developed a proximity fuse for antiaircraft shells. After the war he used rockets for research into the upper atmosphere, being especially interested in cosmic rays. In 1958, while professor of physics at Iowa University, he used the results of the Explorer satellites to deduce the existence of belts of charged particles (*see* Van Allen radiation belts) above the earth.

Van Allen radiation belts Two regions of charged particles in the earth's *magnetosphere. The toroidal inner belt lies 620–3,105 mi (1000–5000 km) above the equator and contains protons and electrons captured from the *solar wind or derived from cosmic-ray interactions. The outer belt lies 9,315–15,525 mi (15,000–25,000 km) above the equator, curving down toward the earth's magnetic poles, and contains mainly electrons from the solar wind. The belts were discovered in 1958 by James *Van Allen on his analysis of observations by early Explorer satellites.

Vanbrugh, Sir John (1664–1726) English architect and dramatist. England's most successful *baroque architect, his most impressive buildings were Castle Howard (1699–1726), Blenheim Palace (begun 1705), and Seton Delaval (begun 1720). Highly imaginative and extravagant in his designs and costs, Vanbrugh rarely finished buildings. His plays include *The Provoked Wife* (1690–92) and *The Relapse* (1697).

Van Buren, Martin (1782–1862) US statesman; 8th president of the US (1837–41). After serving as a New York state senator (1812–20) and US senator (1821–28) Van Buren was elected governor of New York in 1828. Since he had helped to establish the *Democratic party and was a strong supporter of Pres. Andrew *Jackson, Van Buren resigned the governorship after only three months in office to accept appointment as secretary of state. During Jackson's second term, Van Buren served as vice president and was Jackson's personal choice to succeed him as the Democratic presidential nominee in 1836. Victorious in the general election, Van Buren began his administration during the Panic of 1837, the country's first great economic depression, which was caused largely by a wave of land speculation in the West. His conservative fiscal policies and his refusal to provide government aid to prop up the economy led to his defeat in the 1840 election.

Vance, Cyrus (1917–) US statesman; secretary of state (1977–80). He represented President Johnson in Cyprus (1967) and Korea (1968) and was US negotiator at the Paris peace talks on Vietnam (1968–69). He resigned as secretary of state in opposition to President Carter's attempt to rescue the US hostages held in Tehran (Iran).

Vancouver 49 13N 123 06W A city and port in W Canada, in British Columbia on Burrard Inlet and the Fraser River delta. Established in 1862 on a beautiful site at the S end of the Coast Mountains, it has developed a rich tourist industry. Vancouver is Canada's largest Pacific port and railhead. With a large airport, it is a center for international trade and warehousing. It is the commercial and industrial center of British Columbia, important especially for its timber, paper, and associated industries. Other industries include food processing, ship repairing, and fishing. Vancouver has two universities and a thriving cultural life. Population (1991): 471,844.

Vancouver, George (c. 1758–98) British navigator. He served his apprenticeship under Captain *Cook and in 1791 set out on a long voyage in the Pacific. He visited Australia and then proceeded NW, charting the W coast of America and circumnavigating the island named for him.

Vancouver Island A Canadian island off the Pacific coast of British Columbia. Its E coastal plain rises to glaciers and forested mountains. The economy depends on timber, mining, fishing, and tourism; it is also a popular retirement area. Area: 12,408 sq mi (32,137 sq km). Chief town: Victoria.

Vandals A Germanic tribe that during the first four centuries AD migrated southward from Scandinavia and the S Baltic coast through Europe to Spain and Africa. There, in 429, they established a kingdom under Genseric and in 455 sacked Rome. The devastation they caused gave rise to the term vandalism. In 534, however, their kingdom was destroyed by the Byzantine general *Belisarius.

Van de Graaff generator A type of *electrostatic generator, invented by the US physicist Robert Jemison Van de Graaff (1901–67), that produces static potentials of millions of volts. Charge from an external source is fed onto a continuously moving belt, which transfers it to the inside of a large hollow conducting sphere. The charge moves to the outer surface of the sphere, leaving the inside neutral and able to collect more charge. This type of generator can be used to provide a high-voltage source for the Van de Graaff *accelerator.

Vanderbilt, Cornelius (1794–1877) US financier. Establishing a small ferry service in New York harbor at the age of 16, Vanderbilt gradually expanded his maritime interests to include regular schooner service in Long Island Sound and steamboat service on the Hudson River. At the time of the California *Gold Rush (1848–49), Vanderbilt eagerly sought to transport would-be miners to the gold fields, and he negotiated with the Nicaraguan government to obtain transit rights that made his New York-to-San Francisco sea and land route shorter than the routes of any of his competitors. In 1855 he also established transatlantic service. By the time of the Civil War, Vanderbilt had become increasingly interested in railroad investments, and after selling off his various shipping lines, he purchased several railroads that he combined into the New York Central R. R. Late in life, he endowed Vanderbilt University in Nashville, Tenn. (1873).

Van der Post, Laurens (1906–) South African novelist. His travel books include *Venture to the Interior* (1952) and *The Lost World of the Kalahari* (1958). His novels, often imbued with deep feeling for the African landscape, include *The Hunter and the Whale* (1967) and *A Story Like the Wind* (1972).

Van der Waals, Johannes Diderik (1837–1923) Dutch physicist, who was professor at Amsterdam University (1877–1907). He was awarded the 1910 Nobel Prize for his work on the intermolecular forces (Van der Waals' forces) and his equation of state (*see* Van der Waals' equation), which takes these forces into account.

Van der Waals' equation A modification of the ideal gas equation, $pV = RT$, where p is the pressure exerted by a gas with volume V and absolute temperature T. R is the *gas constant. Van der Waals adjusted V to $(V - b)$ to take account of the volume occupied by the gas molecules. He also assumed that forces of attraction exist between the gas molecules and therefore adjusted the pressure term to $(p - a/V^2)$. Both a and b are constant for a particular gas. The intermolecular forces are known as **Van der Waals' forces** and are caused by molecules inducing electric *dipole moments in neighboring molecules.

van de Velde A family of 17th-century Dutch painters. **Willem van de Velde the Elder** (1611–93) and his eldest son **Willem van de Velde the Younger** (1633–1707) were both marine artists, who lived in England after 1672 in the service of Charles II. His younger son **Adriaen van de Velde** (1636–72) was a landscape painter, who was often employed by such artists as *Ruisdael and *Hobbema to paint the figures in their landscapes. **Esaias van de Velde** (c. 1591–1630), the landscape painter, was probably the brother of Willem van de Velde the Elder. He is best known as the teacher of the landscape painter Jan van *Goyen and for such works as *Winter Scene*, which herald the realistic landscapes of the later 17th-century Dutch school.

van de Velde, Henry (1863–1957) Belgian *Art Nouveau architect and interior designer. A painter until about 1890, he took up design under the influence of William *Morris and the *Arts and Crafts movement. In 1901, after working in Paris and Berlin, he settled in Weimar, where he directed (1901–14) its School of Arts and Crafts, later part of the *Bauhaus.

Van Dieman's Land. *See* Tasmania.

van Dieman, Anthony. *See* Dieman, Anthony van.

Van Dyck, Sir Anthony (*or* Vandyke; 1599–1641) Flemish *baroque painter, born in Antwerp. Early in his career, he was assistant to *Rubens, who greatly influenced his work. After working in England for James I, he visited Italy (1621–27). In 1632 he returned to England as painter to □Charles I. Although he painted many religious and mythological subjects, such as *Cupid and Psyche*, his reputation rests largely on his portraits of the English court. Many of these are in Britain's Royal Art Collection. *Charles I on Horseback*, and *Thomas Killigrew and Lord Croft* demonstrate the elegance and grandeur of his style. He had a profound influence on the development of British portraiture.

Vänern, Lake The largest lake in Sweden. It drains into the Kattegat via the Göta River, a major source of hydroelectric power. Area: 2141 sq mi (5546 sq km).

Vane the Elder, Sir Henry (1589–1655) English politician. He represented Charles I in negotiations with Parliament (1640) but fought against the king in the English Civil War. His son **Sir Henry Vane the Younger** (1613–62), a staunch Puritan, emigrated to New England in 1635 but returned to England in 1637 and was prominent in the opposition to the king. A member of the state council during the Commonwealth (1649–53) he then retired (1653), participated in the overthrow of Richard Cromwell (1659), and was executed after the Restoration.

van Eyck, Jan (c. 1390–1441) Flemish painter, who also served as diplomatic envoy of Philip the Good, duke of Burgundy. The controversial *Adoration of the Lamb* altarpiece (Cathedral of S Bavon, Ghent) was probably begun by his elder brother **Hubert van Eyck** (d. 1426) and completed by Jan after Hubert's death. Jan is noted for his realistic portraits, particularly *The Arnolfini Marriage* and *Man in a Red Turban.* He certainly perfected and possibly invented the Flemish technique of oil painting, in which the pigment is mixed with oil and turpentine and applied in thin glazes.

Van Gogh, Vincent (1853–90) Dutch postimpressionist painter, born at Zundert, the son of a pastor. He worked as an art dealer, a teacher in England, and a missionary among coal miners before taking up painting in about 1880. His early works were chiefly drawings of peasants. After a limited training in The Hague and in Antwerp, where he studied the works of *Rubens and Japanese prints, he moved to Paris (1886). Here he briefly adopted the style of *impressionism and later of *pointillism. In Arles in 1888 he painted his best-known works—orchards, sunflowers, and the local postman and his family—but only one painting was sold during his lifetime. The visit of his friend *Gauguin ended in a quarrel during which Van Gogh cut off part of his own left ear. In 1889 he entered a mental asylum at Saint-Rémy. The ominous *Wheatfield with Crows* was painted shortly before his suicide, in Auvers. His letters to his brother (Theo) contain the best account of his life and work. *See* expressionism.

Vanilla A genus of climbing *orchids (about 90 species), native to tropical Asia and America. They have long fleshy stems attached to trees by aerial roots and produce large white and yellow flowers. Several species are cultivated commercially for the flavoring agent vanilla, the most important being *V. planifolia.* The fruit—a pod—contains an oily pulp and minute seeds and reaches a length of 8 in (20 cm). The aroma of vanilla is due to vanillin, a volatile oil resulting from curing and fermentation of the pods.

Van't Hoff, Jacobus Henricus (1852–1911) Dutch chemist, who pioneered the field of stereoisomerism, showing that the bonds of a carbon atom are arranged in a tetrahedron. This enabled him to explain *optical activity in terms of molecular structure. He also contributed to chemical thermodynamics and to the theory of solutions, for which he won the 1901 Nobel Prize. He was professor at Amsterdam University from 1878 to 1896, when he moved to the Academy of Sciences in Berlin.

Vanua Levu A volcanic island in the S Pacific Ocean, the second largest in Fiji. Sugar, copra, and gold are exported. Area: 2137 sq mi (5535 sq km). Chief town: Lambasa.

Vanuatu (formerly New Hebrides; French: Nouvelles-Hebrides) Republic in the SW Pacific Ocean, consisting of 12 main islands and 60 smaller islets comprising a chain about 500 mi (800 km) long. The largest of the islands, most of which are heavily forested and volcanic, are Espiritu Santo and Malikula. Discovered by the Portuguese (1606), they were jointly administered as a condominium by France and the UK (1906–80). In 1978 they became partially self-governing as a preliminary to their independence as the Republic of Vanuatu in 1980. Copra, cocoa, coffee, and beef are exported. Industries include tourism, fishing, and mining of manganese. The population is primarily Melanesian. Area: about 5700 sq mi (14,760 sq km). Population (1992 est): 154,000. Capital: Vila, on Efate.

vapor pressure The pressure of the vapor given off by a liquid or solid. The vapor pressure increases with temperature; when it equals the external pressure, the liquid boils. If the liquid or solid is in an enclosed space the number of molecules leaving it eventually reaches an equilibrium with the number of molecules returning to it. At this point the vapor is saturated and the pressure is the **saturated vapor pressure**.

Varanasi (*or* Benares) 25 20N 82 00E A city in India, in Uttar Pradesh on the Ganges River. A major place of pilgrimage for Hindus, Jains, Sikhs, and Buddhists, it has 3 mi (5 km) of ghats (steps), from which thousands of Hindus bathe in the sacred river. There are also burning ghats, from which the ashes of the cremated are scattered over the water. The city contains 1500 temples and two universities. Industries include engineering and brassware. Population (1971): 583,856.

Varèse, Edgard (1883–1965) French composer. He settled in the US in 1915. Pursuing his concept of music as "organized sound," he composed music characterized by dissonance, the use of unpitched sounds, and complex rhythms. His works include *Ionisation* (for 41 percussion instruments and two sirens; 1931), *Density 21.5* (for solo flute; 1935), and *Déserts* (for wind instruments and tape; 1949–54).

Vargas, Getúlio (1883–1954) Brazilian statesman; president (1934–45, 1951–54). He came to power in the revolution of 1930, which he led after losing the presidential election. In 1937 he announced the fascist New State, modeled on that of Portugal. He was overthrown in 1945 and reelected in 1950 but, threatened with a military coup, he committed suicide.

variable A mathematical symbol for a quantity that can take any value from a set of values called the range. A variable that can take any value between two given values is called continuous; otherwise it is discrete. A quantity that can only take one value is called a constant.

variable stars Stars the brightness of which varies with time, the variations being regular, irregular, or a mixture of the two. In regular variables the brightness completes a cycle of changes in a period ranging from hours to years. The brightness variation can be up to several *magnitudes. The three major groups are: eclipsing *binary stars, which include *Algol variables; cataclysmic variables, such as *novae; and pulsating stars, which periodically brighten and fade as their surface layers expand and contract and which include *Cepheid variables, *RR Lyrae stars, and Mira stars (*see* Mira Ceti).

variance In a set of numbers, usually measurements, the quantity obtained by summing the squares of the differences between each number and the average value of the set and then dividing by the number of members of the set. Variance and, more often, its square root, called the **standard deviation**, are used to estimate scatter or random error in experimental results.

varicose veins Swollen tortuous veins in the legs caused by malfunctioning of the valves in the veins, which obstructs blood flow. Varicose veins tend to run in families and are commoner in older and overweight people, women, and those who are constantly standing. They may produce a dull ache and later may be the cause of thrombosis or infection. To avoid these complications and for cosmetic reasons the veins are often injected with a substance that makes them shrivel up or they may be surgically removed.

Varna 43 12N 27 57E A city and port in E Bulgaria, on the Black Sea. Founded in the 6th century BC, it finally passed to Bulgaria in 1878. Processed foods and livestock are exported and it has engineering and boat building industries. Population (1991 est): 314,913.

Varna, Battle of (Nov 10, 1444) The battle in which the Hungarians were decisively defeated by the Turks. It enabled the Turks to expand further into the Balkans and ultimately to capture Constantinople (1453).

varnish A resinous solution in oil or alcohol that dries to form a hard transparent coating on wood, metal, etc. The *resins may be natural, synthetic, or mixed. The natural resins used include *shellac, copal, dammar, and congo. *Polyurethane is a particularly durable and chemical-resistant synthetic resin used for protecting wood and metal in harsh environments. Polyesters and alkyds are also used, for example for coating paper containers or as a protective finish for ink.

varnish tree. *See* lacquer tree.

Varro, Marcus Terentius (116–27 BC) Roman scholar and poet. After a varied public career he was appointed public librarian by Julius Caesar in 47 BC. He wrote scholarly works on many subjects as well as satires and other poems. Only a 3-volume work, *On Agriculture*, and parts of a 25-volume work, *On the Latin Language*, survive.

varve dating A technique used in geology and archeology to give the age of a sediment and to provide information about the climate during which it was formed. Varves are layers of claylike sediment deposited from a melting glacier into a lake. Each varve represents a single year's deposition; a thick varve indicates that the sediment was deposited during a hot summer (since the glacier would melt more quickly and therefore deposit more material). Varves are particularly well developed in Scandinavia and in some regions their formation has continued from the Pleistocene Ice Age to the present: by counting the varves the absolute age of a particular sediment can be calculated.

Vasa The ruling dynasty of Sweden (1523–1818) and of Poland (1587–1668) founded by *Gustavus I Vasa. John III (1537–92; reigned 1568–92) married into the Polish royal house and his son Sigismund III (1566–1632) became king of both Poland (1587) and Sweden (1592). Sigismund was deposed (1599) in Sweden, where he was succeeded by his uncle *Charles IX, and the Vasa split into two competing lines. The best-known Vasa monarchs in Sweden were *Gustavus II Adolphus and *Christina.

Vasarely, Victor (1908–   ) Hungarian-born painter. After training in Budapest, he moved to Paris (1930), where his abstract paintings of geometric forms were initially influenced by *constructivism. By the 1950s and 1960s he was painting dazzling patterns that appear to move; these works are regarded as leading examples of *Op art.

Vasari, Giorgio (1511–74) Italian painter, architect, and writer. In Florence, under Medici patronage, he painted fresco cycles in the Palazzo Vecchio and built the *Uffizi, both works showing his respect for *mannerism. He is, however, best known for his *Lives of the Most Eminent Italian Architects, Painters, and Sculptors*, tracing the history of Renaissance art from Giotto to Michelangelo. First published in 1550, it is still popular and useful today, despite some inaccuracies.

vasectomy. *See* sterilization.

Västerås 59 36N 16 32E A city in central Sweden, on Lake Mälar. An important city in medieval times, it has a 12th-century castle and a gothic cathedral. It is a major center of the electrical industry. Population (1992 est): 120,354.

VAT. *See* value-added tax.

Vatican City, State of the A small independent state within the city of Rome, the seat of government of the Roman Catholic Church. St Peter's Square, St Peter's Basilica, the Vatican Palace, and Papal Gardens are within its area, and it includes 12 buildings outside its boundary, notably several churches and the pope's summer palace at Castel Gandolfo. It has its own army, police, diplomatic service, coinage, postal facilities, and radio station (Radio Vaticano, which provides an all-day service in 31 languages giving information on the Church). *History*: it came into being in 1929, when Pius XI signed the *Lateran Treaty with Mussolini, thereby ending a dispute between church and state dating from the incorporation of the *papal states into newly unified Italy in 1870. The state is governed by a commission appointed by the pope. Supreme pontiff: John Paul II. Official language: Italian. Area: 109 acres (44 hectares). Population (1992 est): 750.

Vatican Councils The 20th and 21st ecumenical councils of the Roman Catholic Church, held at Rome. **1.** (1869–70) The council that was convoked by *Pius IX to deal with a variety of topics but was overshadowed by the question of papal authority and resulted in the promulgation of the doctrine of papal *infallibility. The council was suspended because of the Franco-Prussian War. **2.** (1962–65) The council that was convoked by *John XXIII and continued by *Paul VI. Its main purpose, in Pope John's words, was *aggiornamento*, a bringing-up-to-date of the Church. It promulgated no dogmas but instead initiated fundamental changes, including reform of the liturgy and commitment to the *ecumenical movement and to greater collegiality in Church government. It established an atmosphere in which progressive critics could freely express their views.

Vatnajökull An icefield in SE Iceland. Several peaks protrude above the ice level rising to 6952 ft (2119 m) at Öræfajökull, the highest point on the island. Area: 3139 sq mi (8133 sq km).

Vauban, Sébastian Le Prestre de (1633–1707) French military engineer, who revolutionized siege warfare. Appointed engineer to Louis XIV of France in 1655, he directed sieges at Gravelines (1658), Maastricht (1673), and Luxembourg (1684).

vaudeville A type of popular entertainment featuring a variety of performers including singers, dancers, comedians, magicians, jugglers, and acrobats. It developed from entertainments given in taverns and from the music halls of 19th-century England. Vaudeville declined in the 1920s and 1930s with the rise of the rival attractions of motion pictures and radio. Celebrated vaudeville performers, many of whom later became film and television performers, include W. C. *Fields, Will *Rogers, Bob *Hope, George Burns (1896–   ), Gracie Allen (1906–64), Jack *Benny, Jimmy *Durante, and Fanny Brice (1891–1951).

Vaughan, Henry (c. 1622–95) English poet. After producing two volumes of secular verse, he turned to metaphysical poetry, expressing a mystical religious awareness in vivid colloquial language. His best-known volumes are *Silex Scintillans* (1650; enlarged 1655) and *The Mount of Olives* (1652), a book of prose meditations.

Vaughan Williams, Ralph (1872–1958) British composer. He had lessons from Ravel. Influenced by English folk songs and Tudor music, he developed a modal style that found its first full expression in *Fantasia on a Theme by Tallis* (for string orchestra; 1910). His works include nine symphonies of which the first, *A Sea Symphony* (1903–09), is choral. He also wrote the ballet *Job* (1931) and the opera *The Pilgrim's Progress* (1951).

vault An arched roof usually in brick or stone and first developed in ancient Egypt. The simplest and oldest type is the barrel or tunnel vault, a single continuous arch, which originally had to be supported by very thick walls. A more complicated type is the groin vault of the Roman and medieval periods, using a series of mutually supporting interlocking arches, which could span greater distances. The rib vault, consisting of a skeleton of diagonal ribs to support the interlocking arches, was developed by gothic builders. Its decorative counterpart is the fan vault with its multiplication of radiating ribs, a principal feature of the *Perpendicular style. With the invention of reinforced concrete, vaulting has advanced enormously, allowing huge distances to be covered without much support.

Vavilov, Nikolai Ivanovich (1887–1943) Soviet plant geneticist. He traveled widely, amassing a vast collection of plant varieties, particularly varieties of wheat. His researches into the origins of cultivated plants led him to propose 12 world centers of plant origin. Although a leading administrator of Soviet science, Vavilov's views brought him into conflict with *Lysenko and Stalinist ideology. He was arrested and imprisoned in 1940.

Veblen, Thorstein Bunde (1857–1929) US economist. He coined the term "conspicuous consumption" to define his theory that people make purchases for status, not for practical application of the product or service. The higher the cost of an article, the more exclusive it becomes. As the exclusive filters down to the lower classes, the upper class adopts new exclusive articles that filter down, continuing the cycle. He described this concept in *The Theory of The Leisure Class* (1899) and *Theory of Business Enterprise* (1904).

vector (mathematics) A quantity that has both magnitude and direction. Examples of vectors include velocity, force, magnetic flux density, etc. A vector needs three numbers (called components) to be defined, each number representing its magnitude in one of three mutually perpendicular directions. Two vectors are added by adding the corresponding components and may be multiplied to give either a *scalar quantity or another vector.

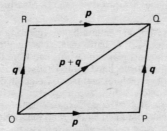

VECTORS *The two vectors OP (**p**) and PQ (**q**) add to give the resultant vector OQ (**p** + **q**). OR = PQ = **q**; OP = RQ = **p**. OQP is a vector triangle and ORQP is a parallelogram of vectors.*

vector (medicine) An organism capable of transmitting a disease-causing organism (pathogen) from one organism to another. Transmission may be accidental, for example the housefly carries bacteria picked up from its food, or the vector may play a significant role in the life cycle of the pathogen, for example the malarial parasite spends part of its life cycle in the mosquito, which transmits it to man.

Vedanta The various philosophical schools of Hinduism, which derive from the commentaries on the *Vedas*, especially the *Upanishads*, the *Brahmasutras*, and the *Bhagavadgita*. The schools differ in their views on the nature of *Brahman and the individual soul, but have in common the belief in reincarnation, the truth of the *Vedas*, the law of *karma, and the need for spiritual release. Believing Brahman to be the cause of the world, they condemn Buddhism and Jainism.

Vedas (Sanskrit: divine knowledge) The basic Hindu scriptures, written in archaic Sanskrit (Vedic) around 1500 BC. It comprises hymns, invocations, mantras, spells, and rituals, mostly concerning the sacrificial worship of gods representing various natural forces. The canon comprises four main collections: the *Rigveda*, the *Samaveda*, the *Yajurveda*, and the *Atharvaveda*. The *Brahmanas*, the *Aranyakas*, and the *Upanishads*, which are later commentaries, may also be considered canonical. These scriptures are widely revered among Hindus.

veduta (Italian: view) A painting, drawing, or print of a view of a town or city. Examples of vedute are *Piranesi's engravings of Rome and *Canaletto's paintings of Venice. The **capriccio** is a specialized form of veduta consisting of various architectural elements combined to produce an imaginary setting. A famous capriccio is the etching of *St Paul's Cathedral in London with the Grand Canal of Venice* by William Marlow (1740–1813).

Vega A conspicuous white star, apparent magnitude 0.03 and 26.5 light years distant, that is the brightest star in the constellation Lyra.

Vega (Carpio), Lope Félix de (1562–1635) Spanish poet and dramatist. After serving with the Spanish Armada (1588) he became secretary to the duke of Alba in Toledo, and settled in Madrid in 1610. His numerous love affairs continued after his ordination as priest in 1614, but his later years were saddened by the deaths of his wife, children, and mistresses. Most of his numerous plays, such as *Fuenteovejuna* (1612–14) and *El caballero de Olmeda* (1615–26), were based on Spanish history.

vegetarianism The practice of abstaining from eating animal flesh for ethical, religious, or nutritional reasons. Some vegetarians will not eat any animal products, including milk, cheese, eggs, etc., and are called **vegans**. Vegetarianism occurs in many religious traditions, including Buddhism, Jainism, and Hinduism, and it was advocated by *Pythagoras, *Plato, and many other thinkers.

vein (physiology) A thin-walled blood vessel that carries oxygen-depleted blood from the tissues to the *heart. Most of the smaller veins have valves to prevent backflow of blood. Damage to these valves leads to dilation of the veins (*see* varicose veins). The veins opening directly into the heart are the superior and inferior vena cavae and the pulmonary veins from the lungs, which are unique in carrying oxygenated blood.

Velázquez, Diego Rodriguez de Silva (1599–1660) Spanish painter, born in Seville. He trained under Francisco de *Herrera the Elder and Francisco Pacheco (1564–1654), his father-in-law, although he was most strongly influenced by *Titian. Initially he specialized in painting religious subjects and scenes from everyday life with still lifes, before becoming (1623) court painter to Philip IV (1605–65; reigned 1621–65) and thereafter painting chiefly portraits of the royal family and the chief minister Olivares. Other works include his famous *Pope Innocent X* and the *Rokeby Venus*, painted during his second visit to Italy (1649–51). *Las Meninas* (c. 1656) is typical of the informality of his later court portraits.

veld (*or* veldt) A tract of open grassland on the plateau of S Africa. It includes the Highveld (over 4900 ft; 1500 m), Middleveld (4900–2950 ft; 1500–900 m), and Lowveld (below 2950 ft; 900 m).

velocity The rate of change of a body's position in a given direction. The speed of a body is not in a specified direction. Velocity is thus a *vector quantity and speed is a scalar quantity. **Angular velocity** is the rate of change of a body's motion about an axis. It is measured in radians per second.

velocity of light (*c*) The speed with which all *electromagnetic radiation travels through a vacuum, equal to $2.997,925 \times 10^8$ meters per second. It is one of the *fundamental constants and, according to the special theory of *relativity, is independent of the speed of the observer and cannot be exceeded by any material body.

velocity ratio. *See* mechanical advantage.

Venda, Republic of Nominally independent country in mainland Africa, within South African territory. Most of the population is Venda. *Economy*: chiefly agricultural, the main crop being maize; the timber industry is also developed. *History*: it was the third *Bantu Homeland to be granted full independence from South Africa (1979), but this is not recognized elsewhere in the world. Official currency: South African rand. Area: 2861 sq mi (7410 sq km). Population (1992 est): 567,000. Capital: Thokoyandou.

Vendée A department in W France, in Pays de la Loire region. A series of peasant-royalist insurrections, the **Wars of the Vendée**, took place here (1793–1832). The first rebellion, catalyzed by the Republican government's introduction of conscription, was also fueled by loyalty to the Roman Catholic Church. After initial success the rebels were decisively defeated at Savenay (December 1793). Subsequent abortive uprisings (1796, 1815, and 1832) failed to attract popular support. Area: 2709 sq mi (7016 sq km). Population (1991 est): 512,000. Capital: La Roche-sur-Yon.

Vendôme, Louis Joseph, duc de (1654–1712) French marshal under Louis XIV. He fought in the Wars of the *Grand Alliance (1689–97) and of the Spanish Succession (1701–14). He was victorious at Luzzara (1702) and Cassano (1705) but was defeated by Marlborough at Oudenaarde (1708) and was then recalled. From 1710 until his death he campaigned successfully in Spain.

Venera probes A series of Soviet *planetary probes to Venus, first launched in 1961. Veneras 4 to 8 sent capsules into the hostile atmosphere, those of 7 and 8 surviving to reach the surface (1970, 1972). The lander sections of Veneras 9 and 10 (1975), 11 and 12 (1978), and 13 and 14 (1982) all successfully reached the surface, relaying photographs back to earth via the orbiter sections. Veneras 15 and 16 were launched in 1983.

venereal disease A disease spread predominantly by sexual intercourse, the most important of which are *syphilis and *gonorrhea.

Venetia A region of NE Italy between the Po River, the Alps, and the Adriatic Sea. The mainland territory of the Republic of Venice until 1797, Venetia then came under Austrian control and in 1815 formed part of the new kingdom of Lombardy-Venetia. Venetia was incorporated into the kingdom of Italy in 1866 and after World War I formed the "Three Venices"—Venezia Tridentina, Venezia Euganea, and Venezia Giulia. Most of the latter was lost to Yugoslavia after World War II and Italian Venetia was divided into the regions of Friuli-Venezia Giulia, Veneto, and Trentino-Alto-Adige.

Venezuela, Republic of A country on the N coast of South America bounded by the Caribbean Sea (N), Guyana (E), Brazil (S), and Colombia (SW and W). The plains of the Orinoco basin in the N rise to the Guiana Highlands in the SE, and in the NW the N end of the Andean chain reaches heights of over 16,000 ft (5000 m). Also in the NW is Lake Maracaibo. Most of the population is of mixed European and Indian descent. *Economy*: based chiefly on oil, first discovered in 1917 and of which Venezuela is now one of the world's largest producers and exporters. The industry was nationalized in 1976. Efforts are being made to diversify the economy, including plans to use the country's vast iron-ore deposits to increase steel production. Another major project is the construction of the world's largest aluminum smelter, which will be able to utilize the recent discovery of bauxite. Venezuela is also rich in diamonds, gold, zinc, copper, lead, silver, phosphates, manganese, and titanium. The agricultural sector remains relatively underdeveloped, although a large share of the oil revenues has been spent in attempts to develop this area. Crop growing in the N includes coffee, cocoa, sugar, corn, and rice, while further S stock raising is the principal agricultural activity. The vast forests remain largely unexploited. *History*: sighted by Columbus in 1498, it was visited in 1499 by Vespucci, who named it Venezuela ("Little Venice") on seeing Indian villages built on stilts over Lake Maracaibo. Spanish settlement began in 1520 and Venezuela remained under Spanish rule until liberated by Bolívar in 1821. It then formed part of Colombia until 1830. Independent Venezuela was ruled by a succession of dictators, notably *Guzmán Blanco and *Gómez, until the post-World War II period, which witnessed the development of more democratic and stable governments, made possible in part by oil revenues. In the early 1980s oil revenues declined sharply, foreign debt increased, and an economic crisis ensued. Violent demonstrations in Caracas accompanied the enactment of an austerity program in 1989. Emergency foreign aid and a rise in oil prices boosted the economy in 1990 and 1991. Protesting government austerity programs, rebel army troops attempted two coups in 1992. Martial law was declared, and Pérez was forced to institute political and economic reforms. Continued unrest in 1993 led to Pérez's suspension and new elections, with former president Rafael Caldera taking the presidency with a campaign to roll back economic reform. Venezuela is a member of the OAS, LAFTA, and OPEC. President: Carlos Andrés Pérez. Official language: Spanish. Official currency: bolívar of 100 céntimos. Area: 352,143 sq mi (912,050 sq km). Population (1990 est): 19,753,000. Capital: Caracas. Main port: Maracaibo.

VENICE *St. Mark's Square, flooded with rainwater. Venice in Peril, an international organization, raises money to help save the threatened city.*

Venice (Italian name: Venezia) 45 26N 12 20E A city in NE Italy, the capital of Veneto. It is a seaport built on over 100 islands in the Lagoon of Venice (an inlet of the Gulf of Venice at the head of the Adriatic Sea). Venice is a center of commerce and tourism and its manufactures include glassware, textiles, and lace. The rise of the industrial suburbs of Mestre and Marghera on the mainland, however, has led to the economic decline of the old city. The Grand Canal and about 170 smaller canals provide waterways for the city transport, which includes water buses (*vaporetti*) and gondolas. Famous bridges include the Rialto Bridge and the *Bridge of Sighs. Situated at the center of Venice is the famous St Mark's Square (Piazza San Marco) overlooked by *St Mark's Cathedral, the 15th-century Clock Tower, the Campanile, and the Doge's Palace. An outstanding collection of Venetian paintings, including works by Bellini, Mantegna, Canaletto, and Titian, is housed in the Accademia. The fashionable seaside resort, the Lido, is situated 2 mi (3 km) to the SE, on the outer edge of the lagoon. *History*: originally settled by refugees fleeing the barbarian invasions on the mainland (5th century AD onward), Venice was united under the first *doge in 697. Strategically positioned between Europe and the East, it became an independent republic and a great commercial and maritime power, defeating its greatest rival Genoa in 1380. Its decline began in the 16th century following the discovery of the Cape route to India. Venice is currently endangered by floods, pollution, and subsidence. Population (1991 est): 317,837.

Venizélos, Eleuthérios (1864–1936) Greek statesman; prime minister (1910–15, 1917–20, 1924, 1928–32, 1933). During the *Balkan Wars (1912–13), Venizélos expanded Greek territory by acquiring the Aegean islands and Crete. In 1917 he succeeded in drawing Greece into World War I on the side of the Allies. His unsuccessful attempt to instigate a revolt in Crete led to his exile in 1935.

Venn diagram. *See* set theory.

ventricle. *See* brain; heart.

Ventris, Michael (1922–56) British architect and scholar, famous for his decipherment of *Linear B. First inspired by hearing Sir Arthur *Evans lecture in 1936, Ventris studied tablets from *Knossos and *Pylos. In 1952 he realized that their language was a form of Greek. After his death in an automobile accident, his results were consolidated by his collaborator, John Chadwick.

Venturi tube A device consisting of an open-ended tube with a central constriction, used to measure the rate of flow of a fluid, which can be calculated from the pressure difference between the center and the ends. It is extensively used to measure the airspeed of aircraft. Invented by G. B. Venturi (1746–1822).

Venus (goddess) A Roman goddess originally of gardens and fertility who became identified with the Greek *Aphrodite as goddess of love. This identification followed the introduction into Rome of the cult of Aphrodite of Eryx in Sicily and was further established by the Julian family, whose members included the emperors from Augustus to Nero and who claimed descent from *Aeneas, son of Aphrodite. Having no myths of her own, she assumed those of Aphrodite.

Venus (planet) The second planet in order from the sun, orbiting the sun every 225 days at an average distance of 67 million mi (108 million km). It is 7,515 mi (12,102 km) in diameter and has an extremely long period of axial rotation (243 days). It can be one of the most brilliant objects in the sky, reaching a *magnitude of −4.4, and like the moon exhibits *phases. Its surface is totally obscured by dense swirling yellowish clouds of sulfuric acid droplets and sulfur particles. The atmosphere is primarily (98%) carbon dioxide. *Planetary probes have shown that the surface temperature is a hostile 879°F (470°C) and the surface atmospheric pressure is about 90 times that of earth. The surface has now been carefully mapped and photographed by the Pioneer Venus orbiter and the *Venera probes.

Venus flytrap A *carnivorous plant, *Dionaea muscipula*, native to the eastern US. The upper part of each leaf is hinged at the midrib and an alighting insect triggers the leaf to snap shut, with its spined margins interlocking, thus trapping the prey. A cluster of five-petaled white flowers is borne on a long stalk. Family: *Droseraceae*.

Venus's flower basket A *sponge of the genus *Euplectella*, found in parts of the Pacific and Indian Oceans. They form enclosed cylindrical colonies, up to 12 in (30 cm) long, with a delicate skeletal lattice of silica.

Venus's girdle A marine invertebrate animal, *Cestum veneris*, belonging to an order (*Cestida*) of *ctenophores. Its transparent ribbonlike body is about 2 in (5 cm) wide and 40 in (1 m) or more long. It occurs in the Mediterranean Sea and Atlantic Ocean and swims with an undulating motion.

Veracruz (*or* Veracruz Llave) 19 11N 96 10W A major port in E Mexico, on the Gulf of Mexico. Industries include iron and steel processing, ship building, and sugar refining; the chief exports are coffee, chicle, and tobacco. It contains the Regional Technical Institute of Veracruz (1957). Population (1980): 284,822.

Verbena A genus of herbaceous plants or dwarf shrubs (about 250 species), chiefly native to North and South America. The leaves are simple, often with narrow lobes, and the funnel-shaped flowers have five spreading often two-lipped lobes and form dense elongated or flat-topped clusters. Several species are grown as ornamentals, especially *V. × hybrida* from South America. Lemon verbena (*Lippia citriodora*) is a related shrub from tropical America, the lemon-scented leaves of which yield an oil used in perfumery. Family: *Verbenaceae*. *See also* vervain.

Vercelli 45 19N 8 26E A city in NW Italy, in Piedmont. An ancient Ligurian and later a Roman city, it has an outstanding library of manuscripts (notably the *Codex Vercellensis*, an early English manuscript dating from the late 10th century, which contains the texts of several poems and other literature). Vercelli lies at the center of Europe's main rice-producing area. Population: 56,494.

Vercingetorix (d. 46 BC) Gallic chieftain, who led the revolt of the tribes of Gaul against Julius Caesar in 52. After early successes Vercingetorix was besieged at Alesia and his capture ended Gallic resistance to Rome. He was subsequently executed.

Verde, Cape (French name: Cap Vert) 14 43N 17 33W The westernmost point of Africa, in Senegal, consisting of a promontory extending into the Atlantic Ocean.

Verdi, Giuseppe (1813–1901) Italian composer of operas. He studied privately in Milan before beginning a career as a composer. He had an early success with *Nabucco* (1842) but his first mature work was *Rigoletto* (1851); this was quickly followed in 1853 with *La Traviata* and *Il Trovatore*. In 1869 he was commissioned to write an opera for the opening of the Suez Canal; the result was *Aida* (1871). His last works were the *Requiem* (in memory of Alessandro Manzoni; 1874) and the operas *Otello* (1887) and *Falstaff* (1893), with librettos, based on Shakespeare's plays, by Arrigo *Boito.

verdigris A green copper acetate used as a paint pigment. The term is also applied to the green coating, consisting of copper sulfate or carbonate, that forms on copper roofs, etc.

Verdun 49 10N 5 24E A city in NE France, in the Meuse department on the Meuse River. Strategically positioned on the E approach to the Paris Basin, Verdun has long been an important fortress. It was the scene of a major battle in 1916 (*see* World War I). It has brewing, textile, and metallurgical industries. Population: 26,927.

Vereeniging 26 41S 27 56E A city in South Africa, in the S Transvaal, on the Vaal River. Founded in 1892, it was the site for negotiations to end the second Boer War (1902). It is an important coal-mining center with iron and steel industries. Population (1980 est): 149,410.

Verhaeren, Émile (1844–96) The chief Belgian poet associated with symbolism (*see* symbolists). Beginning with the realistic verse of *Les Flamandes* (1883), he published many volumes of poetry the themes of which included his patriotism, his socialism, and his love for his wife. He was also a distinguished art critic.

Verlaine, Paul (1844–96) French poet. His early poetry, notably *Fêtes galantes* (1869), reflects his association with the *Parnassians. His tempestuous relationship with *Rimbaud, who influenced his more experimental *Romances sans paroles* (1874), resulted in the break-up of his marriage, and in 1873 he was imprisoned for shooting and wounding Rimbaud. His later poetry concerned the conflicts inherent in his attempts to lead a reformed life. After the publication of *Les Poètes maudits* (1884), which included studies of Corbière, Mallarmé, Rimbaud, and "Pauvre Lelian" (Verlaine's anagram for himself) among others, Verlaine was the acknowledged leader of the symbolist poets.

JAN VERMEER The Music Lesson (*c. 1660*). *The woman, whose face can be seen in the mirror, stands to play the virginals. The instrument on the floor is a bass viol.*

Vermeer, Jan (1632–75) Dutch painter, who spent his entire life in Delft and whose importance was only established in the 19th century after centuries of obscurity. Despite his everyday subject matter, favorite themes being women reading or writing letters and playing musical instruments, his works are remarkable for their motionless figures, technical finish, and skillful use of light. His best-known paintings include *The Milkmaid*, *The Lacemaker*, and *Allegory of Painting*, showing himself at work.

vermiculite A *clay mineral with the property of expanding up to 22 times its original thickness on heating, when the water molecules between the silicate layers are driven off. In this form it is light and water-absorbent, and is used as a heat- or sound-insulating material, packaging material, fire extinguisher, and a growing medium for plants. Vermiculite results from the hydrothermal alteration of biotite and the intrusion of acid magma into basic rock.

vermilion Red mercuric sulfide (HgS). It sublimes readily on heating and occurs naturally as the mineral cinnabar. It is used as a pigment, often mixed with red lead and ferric oxide.

Vermont A state in the NE US, in New England bordered by New York (W), Quebec, Canada (N), New Hampshire (E), and Massachusetts (S). The extensively forested Green Mountains run N–S through the center of the state, with the lowlands of the Champlain Valley in the NW and the Connecticut Valley in the E. Small manufacturing industries and tourism are the main sectors of the economy and a variety of goods are produced, particularly wood and paper products. Mining is important, especially the extraction of stone, asbestos, sand, and gravel. The state's farmers produce dairy products, hay, potatoes, and corn. Vermont is famous for its maple syrup. *History*: settled by the British in 1724, it declared its independence in 1777 and joined the Union in 1791, the first state admitted after the signing of the Constitution. It has maintained a staunch independence from federal intervention in state affairs. Area: 9609 sq mi (24,887 sq km). Population (1990): 562,758. Capital: Montpelier.

vermouth An alcoholic drink made from white wine distilled with herbs. The best-known vermouths are French and Italian and are drunk as aperitifs either neat, with soda or tonic water, or with *gin.

Verne, Jules (1828–1905) French writer. He studied law in Paris but chose to follow a literary career. Verne's *Voyages extraordinaires*, beginning with *Five Weeks in a Balloon* (1863), introduced such scientific and technological marvels as the submarine, space travel, and television. They included *Journey to the Center of the Earth* (1864), *From the Earth to the Moon* (1865), and *Twenty Thousand Leagues Under the Sea* (1873). One of the precursors of *science fiction, Verne wrote over 100 adventure stories, including *Around the World in Eighty Days* (1873).

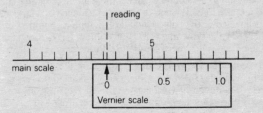

VERNIER SCALE *An auxiliary scale used to measure accurately to two places of decimals.*

Vernier scale A device for measuring subdivisions of a scale, such as those on a pair of calipers. The auxiliary Vernier scale is divided so that 10 of its subdivisions correspond to nine of those on the main scale. If the reading falls between two main-scale divisions, say between 4.6 and 4.7, the zero mark on the Vernier scale is slid along so that its zero is lined up with the reading. By noting the division on the Vernier scale that is exactly in line with a main-scale division, the second decimal place of the measurement is obtained. If the fourth Vernier division is in line with a main-scale division, the reading would be 4.64. Named for Pierre Vernier (1580–1637).

Verona 45 26N 11 00E A city in N Italy, in Veneto on the Adige River. Strategically situated at the junction of major routes between Italy and N Europe, its history dates from Roman times. It possesses a Roman amphitheater, a 12th-century cathedral, and the medieval Castelvecchio. A popular tourist center, its manufactures include textiles, paper, furniture, and leather goods. Population (1991 est): 258,946.

Veronese, Paolo (P. Caliari; 1528–88) Italian painter of the Venetian school, born in Verona. After training for his father's trade of stonecutter, he studied under minor artists but was chiefly influenced by *Titian. In 1553 he settled in Venice, where he worked on decorations in the Ducal Palace and S Sebastiano. In the Villa Barbaro at Maser, designed by *Palladio, he painted illusionistic landscapes, mythological scenes, and portraits. His religious works, for example *Marriage at Cana*, were often pretexts for depicting contemporary banquets in impressive architectural settings and were sometimes the cause of controversy. Thus the *Last Supper* was condemned by the Inquisition for its irreverence; Veronese thereupon retitled the painting *Feast in the House of Levi*.

Veronica. *See* speedwell.

Verrocchio, Andrea del (Andrea del Cione; c. 1435–88) Florentine Renaissance sculptor, painter, and goldsmith, who ran a large and influential workshop. His only known painting is the *Baptism of Christ*, in which his famous pupil *Leonardo da Vinci reputedly assisted. As a sculptor Verrocchio enjoyed great success, his major works being *Doubting Thomas* (c. 1481), *David*, and the equestrian monument of Bartolommeo Colleoni in the Campo SS Giovanni e Paolo, Venice.

verruca. *See* wart.

Versailles 48 48N 2 08E A city in N Central France, in the Yvelines department. Versailles is chiefly famed for its baroque palace, the residence of the French kings from 1678 to 1769. It was built for Louis XIV between 1676 and 1708 on the site of a hunting lodge; the design includes architecture by J. H. Mansart (1646–1708), interior decoration by *Le Brun, and formal gardens by *Le Nôtre. In addition to the Grand Château, there are two smaller chateaux: the Grand Trianon and the Petit Trianon (a favorite residence of Marie Antoinette). Historic events enacted at the palace include Britain's recognition of American independence (1783), the crowning (1871) of William I as German emperor, and the signing of the Treaty of *Versailles (1919). Population (1982): 95,240.

Versailles, Treaty of (1919) The treaty, signed at the *Paris Peace Conference after World War I, between the Allied and Associated powers and defeated Germany. Versailles declared Germany guilty of causing the war, imposed heavy reparations payments, and limited the German army and navy to nominal strength. Territorial provisions included the return of Alsace and Lorraine to France, the cession of parts of Germany to Poland, and the Allied occupation of the Rhineland. Further, most of Germany's colonies were to become *mandates of the *League of Nations, which was established by the treaty. The US refused to ratify the treaty and did not make peace with Germany until 1921.

vertebra. *See* spine.

Vertebrata (*or* Craniata) A subphylum of animals that includes the fish, amphibians, reptiles, birds, and mammals. They are characterized by a backbone consisting of interlocking vertebrae, which forms the main support for the body and protects the nerve cord (spinal cord). The skeleton may be of cartilage or bone and includes two pairs of fin or limb elements that articulate with girdles attached to the backbone. The brain is large and housed in a protective skull. Their highly versatile skeleton has enabled vertebrates to develop many specializations and adaptations for a wide variety of lifestyles in water, on land, and in the air. Phylum: *Chordata*.

vervain A slender erect branching perennial herb, *Verbena officinalis*, found on waste ground throughout Eurasia and N Africa; 12–30 in (30–75 cm) high, it has deeply lobed leaves and narrow spikes of tiny pinkish flowers. The fruit splits into four nutlets. Cultivated forms of *Verbena* may also be called vervain.

vervet. *See* grass monkey.

Verwoerd, Hendrik Frensch (1901–66) South African statesman; prime minister (1958–66). Verwoerd's commitment to *apartheid sparked demonstrations among blacks, including one at *Sharpeville during which the police fired on the crowd. He took South Africa out of the Commonwealth in 1960. He was assassinated in parliament in Cape Town.

Vesalius, Andreas (1514–64) Flemish anatomist, whose major work, *The Seven Books on the Structure of the Human Body* (1543), contained some of the first accurate descriptions of human anatomy together with illustrations of his dissections. Vesalius's observations challenged the prevailing theories of the Greek physician *Galen, opening up a new era of scientific investigation.

Vespasian (9–79 AD) Roman emperor (69–79). He was acclaimed emperor by the army in Egypt (July 69) but he was not recognized at Rome until the death in December of his rival Vitellius (15–69). Vespasian's decisive policies brought an end to civil war and he increased taxes and reformed the army. He was deified after his death.

Vespucci, Amerigo (1454–1512) Italian navigator, after whom America is named. In 1499 he explored the NE coast of South America, discovering the mouths of the Amazon, and in 1501, under Portuguese auspices, he explored the E coast as far as Rió de La Plata, which he discovered.

Vesta (goddess) The Roman goddess of the hearth, identified with the Greek *Hestia. She was worshiped in private households, and her annual festival, the Vestalia, was held in June. The **Vestal Virgins**, her priestesses, tended the eternal fire at her shrine in Rome. They served for periods of 30 years under strict vows of chastity.

Vesta (astronomy) The third largest *asteroid, 334 mi (538 km) in diameter, and the only one occasionally visible with the naked eye. Its orbit lies between those of Mars and Jupiter.

Vestmannaeyjar (*or* Westman Islands) A group of rocky islands off the S coast of Iceland. In 1963 the volcanic island of Surtsey emerged from the ocean and the volcano, Helgafell, erupted in 1974 destroying part of the chief settlement of Vestmannaeyjar on the island of Heimaey.

Vesuvius 40 49N 14 26E A volcano in S central Italy, in Campania region near Naples. It was presumed to be extinct until it erupted in 79 AD engulfing the towns of *Herculaneum and *Pompeii; the last eruption was in 1944. Wine is made from the grapes grown on its exceptionally fertile slopes. Average height: 4003 ft (1220 m).

vetch A climbing or trailing annual or perennial herb of the genus *Vicia* (about 150 species), native to N temperate regions and South America. The leaves comprise several pairs of leaflets, often modified into tendrils, and the blue, purple, yellow, or white flowers are borne either in long spikes or singly in the leaf axils. Some species are grown as fodder crops or for green manure. Family: *Leguminosae*.

Veterans' Administration (VA) US federal agency that administers a system of benefits for veterans and their dependents, including military service-related death or disability compensation, pensions for non-service-related disabilities or deaths, medical programs, home loans, and education, rehabilitation, and burial benefits. Established in 1930, it consolidated existing separate veterans' benefits organizations; it is headed by the administrator of veterans' affairs who is appointed by the president.

veterinary science The scientific discipline concerned with animal health and welfare. Some of the earliest descriptions of animal diseases were made by *Aristotle and, by the Middle Ages, veterinary practice was an established trade. Control and eradication of livestock diseases have enabled improved productivity and the introduction of modern intensive farming methods. The care of domestic pets utilizes many of the diagnostic and surgical techniques of human medicine.

vetiver A perennial *grass, *Vetiveria zizanioides*, also known as khus-khus, native to tropical Asia and introduced to South Africa. Its thick fragrant roots contain an oil used in perfumes.

Viareggio 43 52N 10 15E A city and resort in Italy, in Tuscany on the Ligurian Sea. Shelley was cremated in Viareggio and Puccini is buried there. Population: 55,737.

Viborg 56 28N 9 25E A city in N central Denmark, in Jutland. It has a 12th-century cathedral and its industries include iron founding, distilling, and the manufacture of textiles and machinery. Population (1981): 28,700.

vibraphone A type of *xylophone in which a characteristic vibrato effect is produced by electrically operated fans installed at the upper ends of the resonator tubes. □musical instruments.

Vibrio A genus of freshwater and marine bacteria. They are rod-shaped, either straight or curved, and swim by means of whiplike flagella at one end of the cell. *V. cholerae* causes *cholera in man and other types may cause gastroenteritis.

Viburnum A genus of shrubs and small trees (about 200 species), mostly native to N temperate regions. They have rounded heads of small funnel-shaped white or pink flowers, each with five spreading white lobes. Many species and varieties are grown as garden shrubs and pot plants, including the snowball tree (*see* guelder rose) and *laurustinus. Family: *Caprifoliaceae. See also* wayfaring tree.

Vicente, Gil (c. 1465–1536) Portuguese dramatist. He wrote court entertainments, plays based on religious and chivalric stories, and comedies satirizing the clergy and nobility, including *Comedia de Rubena* (1521) and *Auto da Mofina Mendes* (1534). He wrote in both Portuguese and Spanish, and has been identified with a goldsmith of the same name. His plays were published by his son and daughter in 1562.

Vicenza 45 33N 11 33E A city in NE Italy, in Veneto. It was the home of the 16th-century architect Andrea Palladio and many of his finest works are sited there. Vicenza has iron, steel, and textile industries. Population (1988): 110,000.

Vice President of the United States Second-ranking executive branch officer. Elected by the voters on the same ticket as the president, the vice president holds office for four years and succeeds to the presidency in case of death, disability, resignation, or impeachment of the president. He presides over the Senate, but only votes (not being a member of the Senate) in cases of a tie vote. He attends cabinet meetings and is, by law, a member of the National Security Council and the Board of Regents of the Smithsonian Institution.

Vichy 46 07N 3 25E A spa in central France, in the Allier department on the Allier River. From 1940 until 1944, during World War II, it was the seat of the French government of Marshal Pétain. Its waters, which were known to the Romans, are bottled and exported worldwide. Population (1982): 30,500.

Vicksburg 32 21N 90 51W A city in Mississippi, on the Mississippi River. During the Civil War it was the site of the Vicksburg campaign, a 47-day siege in 1863 in which General Grant successfully gained control of the Mississippi River after the city fell and thereby split the Confederacy. Vicksburg is an important distribution center for cotton, timber, and livestock. Population (1990): 20,908.

Vico, Giambattista (*or* Giovanni Battista Vico; 1668–1744) Italian historical philosopher. Vico was one of the first philosophers to attempt a critical philosophy of history. He rejected Descartes's negative attitude to the study of history and argued that philosophers had underrated "the study of the world of nations, which since men made it, men should come to know." Language, ritual, and myth were, he maintained, essential clues to an understanding to the past. His ideas were particularly influential in the later 18th century.

Victor Emmanuel II (1820–78) King of Italy (1861–78). He succeeded to the throne of Sardinia-Piedmont in 1849, following the abdication of his father Charles Albert. His appointment (1852) of *Cavour as prime minister was crucial to the achievement of Italian unification (*see* Risorgimento). Victor Emmanuel fought at Magenta and Solferino against the Austrians, freeing Lombardy, and coordinated with *Garibaldi in the campaign that freed S Italy. After becoming king of Italy he completed its unification by the acquisition of Venetia (1866) and of Rome (1870), which he made the Italian capital.

Victor Emmanuel III (1869–1947) King of Italy (1900–46) following the assassination of his father Umberto I. He acquiesced in Mussolini's seizure of power (1922) and after Mussolini's fall (1943) relinquished his powers to his son Umberto II. He formally abdicated in 1946, shortly before Italy became a republic.

Victoria A state of SE Australia, bordering on the Tasman Sea, Bass Strait, and the Indian Ocean. It consists of central uplands, an extension of the *Great Dividing Range, descending to plains in the N and S. Agriculture is diverse with fruit and vineyards in the Murray Basin and wheat and sheep farming to the SW. Gippsland is a noted dairying area; 50% of the country's cattle are now concentrated in S Victoria. Brown coal is mined in Central Gippsland and gas and oil are piped from fields in the Bass Strait. Industry, concentrated on Melbourne, includes engineering, oil refining, and the manufacture of cars and textiles. Area: 87,884 sq mi (227,600 sq km). Population (1992 est): 4,456,000. Capital: Melbourne.

Victoria 22 16N 114 13E Also called Hong Kong City, the capital of Hong Kong colony, situated on the N of the island. The University of Hong Kong was established there in 1911. Population: 1,100,000.

Victoria 48 26N 123 20W A city and port in W Canada, the capital of British Columbia on S Vancouver Island. Founded in 1843, it is a commercial and distribution center. Victoria's mild climate attracts tourists and retired people. It has some industry, but the provincial government and federal dockyards are the main employers. Victoria University (1963) is situated there. Population (1991): 71,228.

Victoria (1819–1901) Queen of the United Kingdom (1837–1901), whose sense of duty and strict moral code came to symbolize the ethos of the mid- and late 19th century, a period that came to be known as the Victorian Age. The granddaughter of George III, Victoria succeeded her uncle William IV. In 1840 she married her cousin Prince *Albert of Saxe-Coburg-Gotha, who exerted considerable, and generally beneficial, influence over her. They had nine children, including Victoria, who became empress of Germany as the wife of Frederick III, and Edward, later Edward VII. Prince Albert's death in 1861 was a severe blow to Victoria, and she resolved thereafter to act exactly as he would have wished.

She had an exalted view of the monarch's role in government, failing to appreciate the limitations of constitutional monarchy. Her close friendship with *Disraeli, who made her empress of India (1876), contrasted with her strained relations with his rival *Gladstone. In the last years of her reign, especially after her Golden Jubilee (1887), she enjoyed enormous popularity and greatly enhanced the prestige of the crown.

VICTORIA *The queen is photographed at a country estate in 1891, reviewing state papers and attended by her Indian servant.*

Victoria, Lake (*or* Victoria Nyanza) The largest lake in Africa, in Uganda, Tanzania, and Kenya. The second largest freshwater lake in the world (after Lake Superior), it was discovered for Europeans in 1858 by Speke in his search for the source of the River Nile, of which Lake Victoria is the chief reservoir. The level was raised by the construction of the *Owen Falls Dam. There is fishing there and the main ports are Jinja, Kisumu, Mwanza, and Bukoba. Area: 26,826 sq mi (69,485 sq km).

Victoria, Tomás Luis de (c. 1548–1611) Spanish composer. He studied in Rome and in 1571 succeeded Palestrina as maestro di cappella at the Roman Seminary. In about 1582 he returned to Spain as chaplain to the dowager Empress Maria, the sister of *Philip II. He composed many motets and more than 20 masses in the polyphonic style.

Victoria and Albert Museum A London museum founded in 1853 to house and collect examples of applied arts of all periods and cultures. It was given its present name in 1899.

Victoria Falls 17 55S 25 52E A waterfall in the Zambezi River on the border of Zimbabwe and Zambia. The river flows over an abrupt rock edge 1 mi (1.6 km) wide, dropping as much as 420 ft (128 m), and then through a narrow gorge known as the **Boiling Pot**. A major tourist attraction, the falls also provide hydroelectric power.

Victoria Island A Canadian island in the Arctic Ocean, in Franklin district. The third largest island in Canada, its lowlands rise to high cliffs in the NW. The scanty population is clustered in a few settlements. Area: 212,199 sq mi (81,930 sq km).

vicuna A hoofed mammal, *Vicugna vicugna*, of high Andean plateaus. Resembling a small camel, the vicuna is 30 in (75 cm) at the shoulder and has a tawny-brown coat with a white bib and underparts. Hardy and aggressively territorial, they have never been domesticated but their wool is highly valued and wild herds are rounded up for shearing. Family: *Camelidae* (camels, etc.).

Vidal, Gore (1925–   ) US novelist and essayist. His moral concern with contemporary society is expressed with wit and elegance in both his essays and his novels, which range from historical studies, such as *Burr* (1974), *1876* (1976), *Lincoln* (1984), *Empire* (1987), and *Hollywood* (1990), to satires, such as *Myra Breckinridge* (1968) and essays, in *The Second American Revolution* (1982).

Vidal de la Blache, Paul (1845–1918) French geographer. A professor at the Sorbonne, Paris (1898–1918), Vidal was the most eminent French human geographer of his day. His work includes *États et nations de l'Europe* (1889) and *Principes de géographie humaine* (1922). He was the founding editor of *Annales de géographie* in 1891.

video games Electronic games played by one or more people, in which the players manipulate figures or objects over a screen, typically a television or computer screen in home use. Originated as relatively simple games similar to table tennis, video games soon became more complicated, with intriguing plots, numerous characters, multiple layers of difficulty, and dramatic color graphics.

video recording The storage of a *television program on magnetic tape. Because the demodulated video (vision) signal can have frequencies in the megahertz range, a videotape cannot be used like a sound tape in which the highest frequencies will be less than 20 kilohertz. It would not be practical to run the tape one thousand times faster than a sound tape; instead the signal is recorded diagonally on the tape (each diagonal line representing one line of the picture) and the tape is run slowly over a drum on which the recording and reading heads rotate at high speeds. Such devices are available for use with domestic television sets. Videodiscs are discs for the storage of television pictures from which the optically stored signal can be retrieved by a laser system.

Vienna (German name: Wien) 48 12N 16 20E The capital of Austria, in the NE at the foot of the Vienna Woods (Wienerwald) on the Danube River. With its musical and theatrical life, its museums, and parks, it is a popular tourist attraction. Trade and industry, however, form the basis of the economy, the major industrial products being machinery, textiles, chemicals, and furniture. Most of the chief buildings lie on or within the Ringstrasse, the boulevard built in 1857 to replace the old city ramparts. These include the Cathedral of St Stephen (begun about 1135); the Hofburg (the former imperial palace); the Rathaus (1873–83); the Parliament buildings (1883); the Opera House and Burgtheater; and the university (1365). *History*: seat of the Hapsburgs (1278–1918) and residence of the Holy Roman Emperor (1558–1806), Vienna became an important political and cultural center in the 18th and 19th centuries, having associations with many composers, including Haydn, Mozart, Beethoven, Schubert, and the Strauss family. At the end of World War I it became the capital of the small republic of Austria. It suffered considerable damage during World War II and was jointly occupied by the Allied powers (1945–55). Population (1991): 1,533,175.

Vienna, Congress of (1814–15) A conference of European powers that met following the fall of Napoleon. The chief countries represented were Austria (by *Metternich), Britain (by *Castlereagh and Wellington), Russia, Prussia, France (by *Talleyrand), and the papacy. Its Final Act created a kingdom of the Netherlands, a German confederation of 39 states, Lombardy-Venetia subject to Austria, and the *Congress Kingdom of Poland. Legitimate monarchs were restored in Spain, Naples, Piedmont, Tuscany, and Modena, and Louis XVIII was confirmed as king of France.

Vienna Circle The group of scientific philosophers who developed the doctrine of *logical positivism (*or* logical empiricism). Founded by *Schlick in 1924, the Vienna Circle flourished until 1939. Philosophers and scientists cooperated to analyze and clarify both philosophical and scientific concepts and to set up criteria of meaningfulness for propositions other than the truths of logic. Members included *Carnap, *Gödel, and Otto Neurath (1882–1945). They did not consciously set out radically to revise traditional views about philosophy, but they had this effect, notably in America and Britain. *See also* Ayer, Sir Alfred (Jules).

Vienne River A river in W central France, flowing mainly NNW from the Correze department to the Loire River. Length: 220 mi (354 km).

Vientiane 18 06N 102 30E The capital of Laos, a port on the Mekong River on the border with Thailand (formerly Siam). Founded in the 13th century, it came under Siamese control in the 18th century and was destroyed (1828) following a revolt against Siamese rule. It became capital of the French protectorate of Laos in the late 19th century. The Université Sisavangvong was founded there in 1958. Population (1985 est): 178,200.

Vierwaldstättersee. *See* Lucerne, Lake.

Viet Cong Communist guerrillas who fought the government of South Vietnam during the *Vietnam War (1954–75). Dedicated to the union of North and South, in 1960 they established a political organization, the National Liberation Front, which amalgamated the various groups committed to the overthrow of the South Vietnamese Government.

Viet Minh The Vietnam League for Independence, formed in 1941 by *Ho Chi Minh to overthrow French rule and to create an independent Vietnamese republic. Officially a multiparty movement, the Viet Minh was dominated by the communists and opposed by many nationalist leaders. Following the refusal of the French to recognize Vietnamese independence after World War II, the Viet Minh played a prominent role in the *Indochina war against France (1946–54).

Vietnam, Socialist Republic of A country in SE Asia, occupying the E part of the Indochina peninsula on the South China Sea. It is bordered by China (N), the South China Sea (E and S), and by Cambodia and Laos (W). Fertile coastal lowlands rise to forested plateaus and mountains, the most populated areas being around the Mekong delta in the S and the Red River delta in the N. The inhabitants are mainly Vietnamese, with minorities of Chinese and others. *Econ-*

omy: seriously affected by the wars of recent decades, some progress has been made since 1975. Agriculture remains the most important sector and there have been further moves toward greater collectivization of the land. Irrigation schemes have helped to increase production although self-sufficiency in the staple food, rice, has not yet been achieved. Other important crops include sugarcane, tea, maize, coffee, and rubber. Teak and bamboo are the chief forest products and fishing is also important. Industrial developments, including steel, have been concentrated mainly in the N, based on the coal, tin, zinc, and other metals to be found there, but recent discoveries of offshore oil SE of Ho Chi Minh City open up the possibility of industrial expansion in the S. The principal exports are coal, rubber, wood, tea, spices, and coffee. *History*: the northern kingdom of Nam Viet was conquered in 111 BC by the Chinese. In 939 AD it broke free and re-sisted further Chinese invasions until the 15th century, when it was again briefly occupied. Its southward expansion culminated in the establishment (1802) of a united Vietnamese empire, which incorporated the three historic regions of Annam, Cochinchina, and Tonkin. The subsequent French conquest resulted in the institution of protectorates over Cochinchina, Tonkin, and Annam, which were joined with Cambodia (and later Laos) to form (1887) the Union of *In-dochina. Vietnam was occupied by the Japanese in World War II, during which Ho Chi Minh formed the Viet Minh league to fight for independence. France's refusal in 1945 to recognize his government led to war (1946–54) after which, following defeat at Dien Bien Phu, the French withdrew. The Geneva Confer-ence (1954) divided Vietnam along the seventeenth parallel into communist North Vietnam and noncommunist South Vietnam, between which civil war en-sued. In 1961 the US extended assistance to the South and remained involved in the conflict until 1973 (*see* Vietnam War). The civil war continued until 1975, when the North emerged victorious, proclaiming (1976) the reunited Socialist Republic of Vietnam. Since then attempts at reconstruction have been hindered by further political developments. A deterioration of Sino-Vietnamese relations led to the withdrawal of all Chinese aid in 1978, and following Vietnam's inva-sion of Kampuchea (December 1978–January 1979) many other nations sus-pended aid leading to an increased reliance on the Soviet Union. The Chinese invasion of Vietnam (February–March 1979) led to a massive increase in the number of Chinese refugees attempting to leave Vietnam by small craft across the South China Sea. Many of these refugees, known as the Boat People, died by drowning or from disease, and the reluctance of some countries to provide new homes for the survivors led to an international conference in Geneva to deal with the Boat People's dilemma (1979). The fifth congress of the Vietnamese Com-munist party (1982) attempted to rejuvenate Vietnam's aged leadership by dis-missals and promotions. Economic dependence on the Soviet Union and eco-nomic crises continued in the early 1980s with severe shortages of goods and services, a huge trade deficit, and an unstable market. Malnutrition was wide-spread. Hanoi announced a withdrawal of occupation troops from Cambodia, but reportedly sent in replacement troops. By the end of the 1980s, however, most of the troops had been withdrawn from both countries. By 1983 the limited private enterprise that had been permitted in Vietnam for two years was again severely restricted. Internally, Vietnam had a hard time recovering in the post-war economy; the transition to a market economy remained stalled, and inflation skyrocketed. In 1990, Vietnam expressed a desire to improve relations with China and the US. The US held back until 1991 when Vietnam, having lost an ally when the Soviet Union was dissolved, agreed to support UN peace efforts in Cambodia. Relations with the US gradually improved, to the point where eco-nomic sanctions were lifted in early 1994. Official language: Vietnamese. Offi-cial currency: dong of 100 hao. Area: 329,466 sq mi (127,180 sq km). Popula-tion (1990 est): 68,488,000. Capital: Hanoi. Main port: Haiphong.

Vietnam War (1954–75) The war between South Vietnamese communist insurgents, supported by North Vietnam, and the government forces of South Vietnam, aided from 1961 by the US. It resulted in communist victory and the union (1976) of North and South Vietnam. From 1954 guerrilla warfare was waged against South Vietnam by the communist *Viet Cong, who were reinforced by North Vietnamese troops in 1959. In 1961 the US, seeking to halt the spread of communism in SE Asia, dispatched troops (numbering 550,000 by 1969) in support of the beleaguered South; in 1965 US air raids on the North had begun. US participation was lessened after peace negotiations were initiated in 1969, but the war again escalated following the US–South Vietnamese invasion of Cambodia in 1970. A massive communist offensive in 1972, together with the strength of domestic opposition to US involvement in the war, prompted the US to reopen negotiations for peace. These led to the Paris Agreement (January 1973) and the withdrawal of US troops. By 1975 the North had emerged victorious. About 900,000 Viet Cong and North Vietnamese, 50,000 Americans, and some 400,000 South Vietnamese died in the war. *See also* Indochina.

viewdata An information storage and retrieval system in which pages of text are transmitted as coded signals along telephone wires and displayed on a domestic television receiver. The user has direct access to a central computer store via a keyboard, and there is therefore no delay in response, unlike the alternative *teletext system.

Vignola, Giacomo da (1507–73) Roman mannerist architect (*see* mannerism). Vignola was the leading architect of his day in Rome, carrying on the building of *St Peter's Basilica after the death of *Michelangelo. Among his other works were the Palazzo Farnese (1564) in Piacenza and the influential church of Il Gesù, Rome (begun 1568). He was also the author of a popular architectural treatise.

Vigny, Alfred de (1797–1863) French poet, novelist, and dramatist. He associated with many romantic writers while serving as an army officer from 1814 to 1827. His fiction includes the historical novel *Cinq-Mars* (1826) and his plays include *Chatterton* (1835), his masterpiece, and several adaptions from Shakespeare. His poetry, especially in *Les Destinées* (1867), expresses through impersonal symbolic techniques his philosophy of stoical pessimism.

Vigo 42 15N 8 44W A port and naval base in NW Spain, in Galicia on the Atlantic coast. In 1702 an English-Dutch fleet sank a Spanish treasure fleet there. Population (1991): 274,629.

Viipuri. *See* Vyborg.

Vijayanagar A Hindu empire established from the town of that name in S India during the first half of the 14th century. It enjoyed a reputation for trade, opulence, and cultural and artistic distinction. Its Muslim neighbors, with whom it had always had uneasy relations, defeated Vijayanagar at the battle of Talikota in 1565 and totally destroyed the city.

Vijayawada (former name: Bezwada) 16 34N 80 40E A city in India, in Andhra Pradesh on the Krishna River. Industries include engineering and rice milling. Population (1991): 701,351.

Viking probes Two identical US spacecraft that went into orbit around Mars in 1976. The lander sections landed on the surface in July and September and performed various experiments, including tests for possible microorganisms; none were found. The orbiter sections took extensive measurements and photographs of Mars's surface and two satellites.

Vikings Scandinavian sea warriors active from the late 8th to the mid-11th centuries. They established important settlements in the British Isles (especially at York and Dublin), where an Anglo-Danish dynasty was founded (1016) by *Canute, and in Normandy. Swedish Vikings raided, and then settled, in the E Baltic, established the Russian Kievan state, and traded with Constantinople, where they provided the imperial guard. They also established settlements in *Vinland and Greenland. Viking literature (the sagas) and art are noted for their dynamic vitality.

villa A country house in Italy or the south of France. Villas date back to Roman times, when they were used as vacation retreats or as farmhouses. The Emperor Hadrian's Villa at Tivoli (123 AD) was built on a palatial scale with extensive parks. During the Renaissance the villa with its substantial estate was revived, particularly in Venetia in N Italy, where *Palladio designed them to combine farming and pleasure purposes. Gardens with grottoes, fountains, and sculptures became an integral part of such Renaissance villas as the Villa d'Este (1550) at Tivoli, built by Pirro Ligorio (c. 1500–83).

Villa, Pancho (Francesco V.; 1878–1923) Mexican revolutionary. An outlaw, Villa supported successive revolts against Mexican governments and came to dominate the north with an irregular army. In 1916 he raided Texas and New Mexico and a US force was sent into Mexico to capture him. It failed to do so but, after an agreement with the Mexican Government in 1920, he disbanded his army. He was later assassinated.

Villa-Lobos, Heitor (1887–1959) Brazilian composer. He toured Brazil collecting folk songs and in 1945 founded the Brazilian Academy of Music. His music is characterized by native rhythms and exotic tone colors. His vast output includes 12 symphonies, *Bachianas Brasilieras* (1930–45), a series of pieces inspired by Bach, concertos for cello, guitar, and harp, 15 string quartets, guitar music, *Rudepoema* (1921–26) for piano, and the ballet *Uirapurú* (1917).

Villanovan The earliest Iron Age culture of N Italy, named for the site of Villanova near Bologna. Emerging in the 9th century BC Villanovan culture is characterized by sophisticated metalworking, using local mineral resources. The dead were cremated and their bronze or pottery urns were often shaped like wattle and daub huts. Villanovan settlements preceded most of the important towns of the *Etruscans.

Villars, Claude Louis Hector, Duc de (1653–1734) French marshal under Louis XIV. He fought in the third *Dutch War (1672–78) but his greatest achievements came in the War of *Spanish Succession (1701–14). He rallied France's flagging fortunes after Marlborough's victory at *Blenheim (1704) and imposed devastating losses on the allies at *Malplaquet (1709). He last saw active service when well into his 80s in the War of the *Polish Succession (1733–38).

Villehardouin, Geoffroi de (c. 1150–c. 1213) French medieval chronicler. A participant in the Fourth Crusade and witness of the fall of Constantinople (1204), Villehardouin wrote the best source description of these events in his *Conquête de Constantinople*. However, his bias toward the Latins possibly distorts the account.

villein The unfree peasant of medieval Europe, holding land from the lord of the *manor in return for labor. Villeins were the most numerous class in England from the 11th to late 14th centuries, when many villeins acquired written titles to their holdings following the *Peasants' Revolt.

Villiers de l'Isle-Adam, Philippe Auguste, Comte de (1838–89) French poet, novelist, and dramatist. He was the impoverished descendant of an ancient aristocratic family. His best-known works are *Contes cruels* (1883) and the symbolist drama *Axël* (1886).

Villon, François (1431–63?) French poet. He studied at the University of Paris but thereafter led a life of vagrancy and crime. He was condemned to be hanged in 1463 but was banished from Paris instead, and nothing is known of him after that date. Only about 3000 lines of his work survive. The ballades and other poems in his *Lais* and *Grand Testament* are characterized by compassion, irony, and a fascination with death and decay. Among the best known of his poems are the *Ballade des dames du temps jadis* and his epitaph, the *Ballade des pendus*.

Vilnius (Polish name: Wilno) 54 40N 25 19E The capital city of Lithuania, on the Neris River. A commercial industrial, and educational center, it is a railroad junction and has a wide range of manufacturing industries and a university founded (1579) by Stephen Báthory. *History*: it dates back to the 14th century, when it became Gediminas's capital but declined following Lithuania's union with Poland. It was ceded to Russia in 1795. After World War I it was given to newly independent Lithuania but was seized by Poland in 1922. Restored to Lithuania in 1940, it then became part of the Soviet Union. The Germans occupied Vilnius in World War II, when its large Jewish population was virtually exterminated. Population (1991 est): 598,000.

Vimy. *See* World War I.

Viña del Mar 33 02S 71 35W A seaside resort in W central Chile, a suburb of Valparaíso on the Pacific Ocean. Its attractions include a casino, beaches, hotels, and a racecourse. Population (1991 est): 312,000.

Vincent de Paul, St (c. 1580–1660) French priest, known for his work among the poor and sick. Captured by Barbary pirates on his way to Marseilles (1605), he escaped and in 1625 founded the Congregation of the Mission Priests (*see* Lazarists). In 1633 he founded the Daughters of Charity. Feast day: July 19.

Vincent of Beauvais (c. 1190–1264) French Dominican friar, scholar, and encyclopedist. His greatest achievement was a Latin encyclopedia, the *Speculum maius*, which he compiled from the whole range of knowledge available to him. In three parts, it dealt with natural history, theological doctrine, and history.

vine Any climbing or trailing plant that requires a support for upward growth. The term is often restricted to the *grape vine (Vitis vinifera) and other plants of the genus *Vitis*, which climb by means of tendrils.

vinegar A dilute solution of *acetic acid, produced from soured wine, beer (malt vinegar), or other dilute alcoholic liquids. It is used in salad dressings, preserving, and other foods.

vinegar eel A *nematode worm, *Anguillula* (or *Turbatrix*) *aceti*, that lives in fermenting vinegar. It feeds on the microorganisms that convert alcohol to acetic acid in the formation of vinegar.

vine snake One of several species of slender venomous tree-dwelling snakes belonging to the family *Colubridae*. The South American green vine snake (*Oxybelis fulgidus*), up to 48 in (120 cm) long, moves swiftly through trees, where it is well camouflaged, preying on small lizards, which it paralyzes before eating.

Vinland The Viking name for the area of NE America, probably Newfoundland, explored and briefly settled by *Leif Ericsson (c. 1000). It is possible that the area was visited a decade earlier by Bjarni Herjolfsson. Ericsson's achievement is celebrated in an important saga.

Vinnitsa 49 11N 28 30E A city in central Ukraine. Originally Polish, it was ceded to Russia in 1793. It is the center of a sugar-beet region and food processing is the principal industrial activity. Population (1991 est): 380,000.

Vinson, Frederick Moore (1890–1953) US political leader and jurist; Supreme Court chief justice (1946–53). A Democrat from Kentucky, he served in the US House of Representatives (1924–29; 1931–38). He sat on the US Court of Appeals (1938–42), directed the war mobilization office (1943–45), and was secretary of the treasury (1945–46), before being appointed chief justice by Pres. Harry S Truman. He supported civil rights and believed in broad powers for the federal government.

Vinson Massif 78 02S 22 00W The highest peak in Antarctica, in the Ellsworth Mountains in Ellsworth Land. It was discovered in 1935. Height: 16,864 ft (5140 m).

vinyl resins. *See* polyvinyl chloride; polyvinyl acetate.

viol A bowed stringed instrument, common from the 15th until the early 18th centuries, when it was eclipsed by the *violin. Viols differ from violins in that they have six strings, tuned mainly in fourths, a shallower bridge, gut frets on the fingerboard, sloping shoulders, and flatter backs. They are held between the knees when played and the bow is held in an underhand grip. A consort of viols comprises treble, alto, tenor, and bass instruments; there is also a **violine** pitched an octave lower than the bass. The bass viol acquired the name **viola da gamba** from the Italian *gamba*, leg.

viola A ☐musical instrument of the *violin family. It is similar to the violin, although larger in size, having thicker strings and a heavier bow. It has a range of over four octaves from the C below middle C; its strings are tuned C, G, D, A. It is a member of the orchestra and the string quartet.

violet A perennial herb of the genus *Viola*, up to 16 in (40 cm) tall, whose solitary flowers, usually blue, purple, or white, have two upright petals, two horizontally spreading ones, and a lower central one with guidelines for pollinating insects seeking nectar. The toothed leaves are oval or heart-shaped, often in a basal rosette, and the seeds are released explosively from a three-valved capsule. The sweet-scented garden violets are derived from the Eurasian sweet violet (*V. odorata*). The dog violet (*V. canina*) is another common species, and the genus also includes the *pansies. Family: *Violaceae*.

violin A bowed string instrument, the soprano member of the family that includes the viola, cello, and double bass. It has four strings tuned in fifths (G, D, A, E), an arched bridge, and a smooth fingerboard. It has a range of over four octaves from the G below middle C. Early violins used gut strings; modern strings are steel or gut-covered steel. The violin is played with a bow strung with horsehair; the strings can also be plucked. The design of the violin was perfected by the Amati, Guarneri, and Stradivari families in Italy between the mid-16th and early 18th centuries. It is widely used as a solo concerto instrument, in the orchestra, in the string quartet, and in folk music. ☐musical instruments.

Viollet-le-Duc, Eugène Emmanuel (1814–79) French architect and author. He began his career as a restorer of medieval buildings, working on the Ste Chapelle and *Notre-Dame in Paris. Viollet was the champion of both the revived gothic style and contemporary developments in architecture, his *Dictionaire raisonée de l'architecture française* (1854–68) and later books indicating the similarities he saw between gothic and contemporary industrial methods of construction.

violoncello. *See* cello.

viper A venomous snake, belonging to the family *Viperidae* (150 species), that has long erectile fangs, which are folded back when not in use; 10–120 in (0.3–3 m) long, vipers feed on small animals, which are injected with venom and then trailed until they die. Most give birth to live young. Old World vipers (subfamily *Viperinae*) are stout-bodied and broad-headed and mostly ground dwelling, although some are burrowers and some arboreal. New World vipers (subfamily *Crotalinae*) are known as *pit vipers.

Virchow, Rudolf (1821–1902) German pathologist and statesman. He originated the concept that disease arises in the individual cells of a tissue and—with publication of his *Cellular Pathology* (1858)—founded the science of cellular pathology. Virchow held public office, supervising improvements in standards of public health, and he also helped develop the science of anthropology in Germany.

Virgil (Publius Vergilius Maro; 70–19 BC) Roman poet. He was born into a farming family near Mantua in N Italy. He completed his education in Rome, where he became a friend of Horace and *Maecenas. Reacting against the troubled political background of civil war, he described in his *Eclogues* (42–37 BC) an idealized pastoral landscape. His more practical vision of Italy in the *Georgics* (36–29 BC) is informed by his passionate interest in agriculture. During his final years he worked on the *Aeneid*, a national epic in 12 books describing the wanderings of Aeneas, the founding of Rome, and extolling the Julian dynasty and Augustus, who claimed descent from Aeneas. He died of fever after returning from a voyage to Greece. The supreme poet of imperial Rome, Virgil became the object of superstitious reverence to later generations. The *Aeneid* was used for divination and its author was imagined to be a magician with supernatural power. In the Middle Ages, Virgil was treated almost as a Christian prophet because of a passage in the fourth *Eclogue* that seems to predict the birth of Christ.

virginals A keyboard instrument of the 16th and 17th centuries, the earliest and simplest form of the harpsichord. Often made in the form of a box, which could be set on the table, the strings (one to each note) run parallel to the keyboard.

Virginia A state on the mid-Atlantic coast bordered by Kentucky and West Virginia (W and NW), Maryland (N), the Atlantic Ocean (E), and North Carolina and Tennessee (S and SW). The low-lying coastal plain is separated from the forested Appalachian Mountains in the W by a region of rolling upland. Manufacturing is very important and the principal industries are chemicals and tobacco processing. Fishing and mining (especially of coal) are also significant sectors of the economy. Numerous historic sites and monuments, beaches, mountains, springs, and national parks are the basis for a thriving tourist industry. The state's farmers produce tobacco, hay, corn, apples, and peaches. Timber, especially for ship building, has long been important. *History*: one of the 13 original colonies, it was named for Elizabeth I of England, the Virgin Queen. A period of expansion followed the establishment of the first permanent English settlement in the New World by the Virginia Company (1607) and demands for self-government grew. It provided many of the leaders for the American Revolution, becoming a state in 1788. Four of the first five US presidents came from Virginia and during the Civil War, Richmond was the capital of the Confederacy. Area: 105,716 sq mi (40,817 sq km). Population (1990): 6,187,358. Capital: Richmond.

Virginia Beach 36 51N 75 58W A resort city in SE Virginia, on the Atlantic Ocean, E of Portsmouth and Norfolk. The first English colonists, later settlers of Jamestown, landed there in 1607. It is an independent city that was merged with

Princess Anne County in 1963. Its 38 miles (61 kilometers) of coastline attract tourists to the many resorts, the basis of the economy. There are several military bases nearby. Population (1990): 393,069.

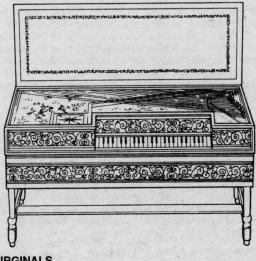

VIRGINALS

Virginia creeper A climbing shrub, also called woodbine, of the genus *Parthenocissus*, especially *P. tricuspidata* of SE Asia and *P. quinquefolia* of North America. It clings by means of branched tendrils with suckers and is often grown as an ornamental for its attractive red autumn foliage. The compound leaves have five pointed oval toothed leaflets and the tiny clustered flowers have five petals. Family: *Vitaceae*.

Virginia Plan (1787) A plan of central government presented by the Virginia delegation at the *Constitutional Convention. It called for a bicameral legislature; the upper-house members were to be elected by lower-house members, who had been elected by popular vote. The number of each state's representatives in both houses was to be based on the state's population and wealth. The president and Supreme Court members were to be chosen by the legislature. Although it was felt that this plan was advantageous to the larger states, it was adopted in part, after modification by the *Connecticut Compromise.

Virgin Islands A West Indian group of approximately 100 small islands and cays in the Lesser Antilles, administratively divided between the US and the UK. **The Virgin Islands of the United States** consist of three main islands, the largest being *St Croix, and about 50 smaller ones. They were purchased from Denmark in 1917 for their strategic importance. Tourism is the principal industry; other industries include rum distilling and textiles. Area: 133 sq mi (344 sq km). Population (1990): 101,809. Capital: Charlotte Amalie. **The British Virgin Islands** consist of about 40 islands, the largest being Tortola. They became a British crown colony following the defederation of the Leeward Islands colony in 1956. Tourism is replacing agriculture as the colony's chief source of wealth. Area: 59 sq mi (153 sq km). Population (1987 est): 13,300. Capital: Road Town.

Virgo (Latin: virgin) A large equatorial constellation that lies on the *zodiac between Libra and Leo. The brightest star is *Spica. The constellation contains the **Virgo cluster** of galaxies, which contains over 2500 members, the majority of which are spiral galaxies.

virtual particle A short-lived particle that is used in quantum mechanics to represent the interaction between stable particles. For example, in classical physics two electrically charged particles are represented as interacting by the overlapping of the two fields that surround them; in quantum mechanics this interaction would be represented by the exchange of virtual photons between them. The *strong interaction is represented by the exchange of virtual pions, the *weak interaction by the exchange of intermediate vector bosons, and the *gravitational interaction by the exchange of virtual gravitons.

virus A minute noncellular particle that can reproduce only in living cells. Viruses consist of a core of nucleic acid (either *DNA or *RNA), surrounded by a protein coat (capsule) and, in some types, a lipid-containing envelope. Some bacterial viruses have tails (*see* bacteriophage). They may be spherical, ellipsoid, rod-shaped, or polyhedral, with sizes in the range 20–450 nanometers (nm; *see* SI units), although some tailed forms may reach 800 nm. Viruses alternate between an inert virion stage and an infective stage, in which the capsule binds to the host cell and the viral nucleic acid (containing its genes) enters the cell and directs the components of the host cell to assemble replica viruses. These are finally liberated, often with damage to or death of the host cell.

Viruses are responsible for a wide range of diseases in plants and animals, including influenza, measles, rabies, and smallpox. They can also cause the formation of tumors.

Visby 57 37N 18 20E A port and resort in SE Sweden, on the W coast of Gotland Island. It was an early member of the Hanseatic League and a major commercial center in the Middle Ages. Its industries include sugar refining and metalworking.

viscacha A gregarious South American *rodent, *Lagostomus maximus*, related to *chinchillas. Over 20 in (50 cm) in length, viscachas live in warrens of 12 to 15 burrows often with piles of earth outside. They are nocturnal and feed on grasses, roots, and seeds. Family: *Chinchillidae*.

Visconti An Italian family that established (1310) lordship over Milan under **Matteo I Visconti** (1250–1322) and then, in spite of papal opposition, gained control over many Lombard cities. Skillful marriage alliances both within Italy and outside expanded their influence. By 1400, under **Gian Galeazzo Visconti** (1351–1402), the family's most brilliant representative, they controlled most of N Italy, centered on Milan and Pavia. Temporary reverses under his son **Giovanni Maria Visconti** (1388–1412) were arrested but the death of his brother **Filippo Maria Visconti** (1392–1447) without heirs led to the establishment of *Sforza control over the duchy.

Visconti, Luchino (1906–76) Italian film director. Born into a noble family, he became a committed Marxist. His late films especially are characterized by elaborate and formal visual composition. They include *The Leopard* (1963), *The Damned* (1970), and *Death in Venice* (1971). He also directed many opera and drama productions.

viscosity A measure of the degree to which a fluid resists a deforming force. Viscosity is defined by Newton's law of viscosity: if two layers of a fluid, area A and distance x apart, flow with a relative velocity v, there is a force between them equal to $\eta A v / x$. η is called the coefficient of viscosity. Viscosity is measured in newton seconds per square meter. The **kinematic viscosity** is the coefficient of viscosity divided by the density of the fluid.

Vishakhapatnam 17 42N 83 24E A city in India, in Andhra Pradesh on the Bay of Bengal. An important port, India's first steamer was launched there in 1948. Industries include ship building and oil refining. Population (1991): 750,024.

Vishnu The second member of the Hindu trinity, the *Trimurti. He is known as the Preserver, complementing *Brahma the Creator and *Shiva the Destroyer, and is married to *Lakshmi. He has 10 avatars or manifestations, the most famous of which are *Rama and *Krishna. He is often portrayed as lying asleep on a seven-headed snake in the intervals between his appearances in successive universes. His devotees are the Vaishnavas, a sect founded by the scholar and philosopher Chaitanya (1486–c. 1534 AD), who stressed devotion to the god regardless of *caste.

VISHNU *The god is portrayed reclining on Sesha, the king of the nagas. From the south face of the 6th-century temple of Vishnu at Deogarh (India).*

Visigoths A branch of the *Goths. Forced by the *Huns across the Danube (376 AD), they destroyed a Roman army at *Adrianople (378) and established themselves in the Balkans, expanding southward and, under *Alaric I, sacking Rome in 410. Moving into France and Spain, they ruled first as Roman subjects and then independently. Their rule in France was destroyed by the *Franks (507) and in Spain by the Muslims (711).

Vislinsky Zaliv. *See* Vistula Lagoon.

Vistula Lagoon (German name: Frisches Haff; Polish name: Wiślany Zalew; Russian name: Vislinsky Zaliv) An inlet of the Baltic Sea on the coast of Poland and Russia, almost totally enclosed by a narrow spit of land. Area: 330 sq mi (855 sq km).

Vistula River (Polish name: Wisła) The longest river of Poland, rising in the S of the country, in the Carpathian Mountains, and flowing generally N and NW through Warsaw and Toruń, then NE to enter the Baltic Sea via an extensive delta region near Gdańsk. It provides an important economic link in the transportation system of eastern Europe. Length: 1090 km (677 mi).

vitalism The theory that living organisms contain a vital force that distinguishes them from nonliving things. It was proposed by the French philosopher Henri *Bergson, who believed that a vital force (*élan vital*)—a form of energy—controlled the form, development, and activities of organisms.

vitamin An organic compound, other than a protein, fat or carbohydrate, that is required in small amounts by living organisms for normal growth and maintenance of life. For animals vitamins must be supplied in the diet, although some group B vitamins may be produced by microorganisms present in the digestive tract. Vitamins function as *coenzymes in many metabolic reactions; they are involved in the formation and maintenance of membranes, in the absorption and metabolism of calcium and phosphorus, and in many other essential processes. Many can now be synthesized commercially but some are easily destroyed by light or heat, e.g. in storage or cooking. Vitamins A, D, E, and K are classified as fat-soluble; group B vitamins and vitamin C are water soluble.

vitamin A (*or* retinol) A fat-soluble vitamin and an essential constituent of the visual pigments of the eyes. It also functions in the maintenance of healthy mucous membranes. Vitamin A deficiency leads to dryness of membranes lining the mouth and respiratory tract, blindness, and defective growth. Sources include liver, fish-liver oils, and egg yolk, while precursors of vitamin A, such as beta-carotene, occur in green plants and vegetables (e.g. carrots).

vitamin B complex A group of water-soluble vitamins that are all constituents of *coenzymes involved in metabolic reactions. Thiamine (B_1) is important in carbohydrate metabolism; it occurs in cereal grains, beans, peas, and pork. Deficiency leads to *beriberi. Riboflavin (B_2) is involved in carbohydrate and amino acid metabolism and sources include yeast, liver, milk, and green leafy plants. Nicotinamide (nicotinic acid *or* niacin) can be synthesized from the amino acid tryptophan; liver is a rich source of the vitamin and milk and eggs of tryptophan. Vitamin B_6 (pyridoxine) is essential for amino acid metabolism and is widely distributed in yeast, liver, milk, beans, and cereal grains. Also common in many foods are pantothenic acid, a constituent of coenzyme A; biotin, which is synthesized by intestinal bacteria; and choline, a precursor of *acetylcholine (which transmits nervous impulses). Folic acid and vitamin B_{12} (cyanocobalamin) can be synthesized by intestinal bacteria; deficiency of either causes megaloblastic or pernicious *anemia. Liver is a good source of vitamin B_{12}.

vitamin C (*or* ascorbic acid) A water-soluble compound that is required for several metabolic processes, especially for the maintenance of healthy connective tissue. It cannot be synthesized by man and certain animals, in whom it must form part of the diet. Fruit and vegetables, especially citrus fruits, are good sources. Deficiency of vitamin C leads to *scurvy. Claims that large doses of the vitamin prevent colds have not been scientifically accepted.

vitamin D A fat-soluble vitamin consisting of several related compounds (sterols), principally cholecalciferol (D_3) and ergocalciferol (D_2). Vitamin D is important in calcium and phosphorus metabolism, especially in the absorption of calcium from the gut and the deposition and resorption of bone minerals. Vitamin D_3 is produced by the action of sunlight on skin, which normally meets all the body's requirements. Fish and fish-liver oils are the main natural sources, while vitamin D_2 is added to margarine. Deficiency in infants causes *rickets.

vitamin E A vitamin consisting of a group of related compounds that function as biological antioxidants, inhibiting the oxidation of unsaturated fatty acids.

The most potent form of vitamin E is alpha-tocopherol, found in green leafy plants, cereal grains, and eggs. Deficiency (which is rare) may lead to anemia.

vitamin K A vitamin consisting of a group of quinone-based compounds that are necessary for the formation of prothrombin, important in blood clotting. Vitamin K occurs in vegetables, cereals, and egg yolk and can be synthesized by intestinal bacteria. Deficiency is rare.

Vitebsk 55 10N 30 14E A port in Belarus, on the Western Dvina River. It serves as the transport center of an agricultural region; industries include food processing. Population (1991 est): 362,000.

Viti Levu The largest Fijian island, in the S Pacific Ocean. Mount Victoria, the highest mountain in Fiji, rises to 4341 ft (1302 m). Sugar, pineapples, cotton, and rice are produced and gold is mined. Area: 4010 sq mi (10,386 sq km). Chief settlement: Suva.

Vitória 20 19S 40 21W A port in E Brazil, the capital of Espírito Santo state. It serves the coffee-growing and mining areas of the state of Minas Gerais. Its university was founded in 1961. Population (1980): 144,143.

Vitoria 42 51N 2 40W A city in N Spain, in the Basque Provinces. During the Peninsular War Wellington defeated the French under Joseph Bonaparte there (1813). A manufacturing and commercial center, it has a trade in cereals and wine. Population (1991): 204,961.

Vitruvius (Marcus Vitruvius Pollio; 1st century BC) Roman architect and military engineer, famous as the author of the only complete architectural treatise to survive from antiquity. In the 10 books of *De architectura* he describes all the main aspects of Roman architecture—public and domestic buildings, temples, the *orders of architecture, interior decoration, town planning, engineering, etc. Rediscovered in Renaissance Italy, it strongly influenced such architects as *Alberti and *Palladio.

Vittorini, Elio (1908–66) Italian novelist. He was an outspoken critic of fascism and was imprisoned in 1943 following the publication of his novel *Conversation in Sicily* (1941). Released after the German occupation of Italy, he joined the resistance. He translated the works of many US writers and in postwar Italy had great influence as a literary critic.

Vittorino da Feltre (V. Ramboldini; 1378–1446) Italian Renaissance humanist and educationalist. At his school in Mantua, Vittorino educated the children of both the aristocracy and the poor. He developed a broad curriculum, including classics, gymnastics, drawing, and science.

Vivaldi, Antonio (1678–1741) Italian composer and violinist. He was ordained priest in 1703 and taught music at the Ospedale della Pietà in Venice, for whose orchestra many of his works were written. Toward the end of his life he toured Europe; he died in poverty in Vienna. Besides operas and sacred music, Vivaldi wrote over 450 concertos for a wide range of solo instruments, including a set of four violin concertos entitled *The Four Seasons*, which are musical illustrations of four sonnets by the composer.

Vivekananda, Swami (1862–1902) Hindu philosopher. Born in Bengal, he studied Western thought and science, which he realized was required to improve conditions in India. He dedicated himself to social reforms and to amalgamating Western scientific materialism with Eastern spirituality. He founded the Vedanta movement in the West, where, as the best-known disciple of *Ramakrishna, he was well received and where his teaching has had a continuing influence.

Viverridae A family of mammals of the order *Carnivora*. The 82 species include the genets, civets, linsangs, and mongooses. Viverrids typically have a long body and tail and short legs.

Vivés, Juan Luis (1492–1540) Spanish humanist and writer. He visited England (1523, 1527–28) but lived mainly at Bruges. His *De anima et vita* (1538) is a psychological work of some depth. He also wrote a treatise on educational theory, *De disciplinis* (1531).

viviparity A reproductive process in animals in which the embryo develops within the maternal body, from which it obtains continuous nourishment. Viviparity occurs in most mammals—the embryos being nourished through the placenta—and in some snakes, lizards, and sharks. In **ovoviviparity** the embryo develops within the mother but is surrounded by egg membranes and derives its food from the yolk. It occurs in certain snakes and fish. It should be distinguished from **oviparity**, occurring in birds and many other animals, in which fertilized eggs are laid or spawned by the mother.

vivisection The use of live animals for experiments. Many animals, especially rats, mice, rabbits, guinea pigs, and monkeys, are used worldwide to determine the effects of drugs, cosmetics, food additives, and other chemicals on living organisms, often as an indication of their likely effects on man. They are also used in medical and biological research and for many standard biological tests and assays. In many countries vivisection is controlled by legislation. Alternatives to live animals include the use of test-tube (*in vitro*) techniques, tissue cultures, and computer-based mathematical models.

Vlaardingen 51 55N 4 20E A major port in the SW Netherlands, in South Holland province on the Nieuwe Waterweg (New Waterway). It has the largest shipyard in Holland; other industries include herring fishing. Population (1988 est): 75,000.

Vladimir 56 08N 40 25E A city in Russia, 115 mi (185 km) NE of Moscow. It is a rail junction and a manufacturing and tourist center. Its fine medieval buildings include the Cathedral of St Dimitrii (1197). *History*: founded in the early 12th century, it was the capital (c. 1157–1238) of the grand duchy of Vladimir. It was then virtually destroyed by the Tatars and in 1364 passed under the rule of Moscow. Population (1991 est): 356,000.

Vladimir I, St (c. 965–1015) Prince of Novgorod (970–80) and grand prince of Kiev (980–1015). In about 987 Vladimir became a Christian and introduced the Byzantine rite to Kiev and Novgorod.

Vladivostok 43 09N 131 53E A port in E Russia, on the Sea of Japan. It is the terminus of the Trans-Siberian Railway and a major naval base, also supporting fishing and whaling fleets. Ice breakers are employed to keep its harbor open in winter. Industries include ship building and food processing. Population (1991 est): 648,000.

Vlaminck, Maurice de (1876–1958) French painter. A self-taught artist, he worked with *Derain from 1899 and from 1901 was strongly influenced by *Van Gogh. He became a leading exponent of *fauvism, painted under the influence of *Cézanne from 1908, but returned after 1915 to a style expressing his aggressive temperament in numerous stormy landscapes, which hold a minor place in 20th-century *expressionism.

Vlissingen. *See* Flushing.

Vlora (*or* Vlorë; Italian name: Valona) 40 29N 19 29E An important seaport in SW Albania, on the Adriatic Sea. After centuries of foreign domination, the independence of Albania was proclaimed there on Nov 28, 1912. Industries include fishing and an olive-oil refinery. Population (1987 est): 67,500.

Vltava River A river in the Czech Republic, rising in the Forest of Bohemia and flowing mainly SE then N to join the Elbe River near Melnik. It is an important source of hydroelectric power. Length: 270 mi (434 km).

vocal cords. *See* larynx.

vodka A *liquor distilled from potatoes, rye, barley, or malt, usually in E Europe. Being colorless and without a distinctive flavor, vodka is used in many mixed drinks, such as Screwdriver (vodka and orange juice) and Bloody Mary (vodka and tomato juice).

voiceprint A graphic record of the sounds produced during speech. The record shows the range of frequencies and harmonics produced and can be used to identify any individual voice. Although there are certain standards in articulation, which are recorded on the voiceprint, individual timbre and harmonics are produced by the shape and flexibility of the larynx and the oral cavity, which are as distinctive as faces or fingerprints. Voiceprints are used in phonetics and in forensic science.

Vojvodina An autonomous province of NE Yugoslavia, in the republic of Serbia. Predominantly low lying and fertile, it is one of the chief agricultural areas of Yugoslavia, producing cereals, fruit, and vegetables. Area: 8683 sq mi (22,489 sq km). Population (1991): 2,012,605. Capital: Novi Sad.

volcanoes Vents or fissures in the earth's surface, either on land or under the sea, through which magma rises from the earth's interior and erupts as lava, gases, and pyroclastic material. Many volcanoes have cones consisting of ash, pyroclastic deposits, and lava. Basaltic lava tends to produce gently sloping cones, the lava flowing over a wide area, whereas the more viscous acid lava produces a steeper-sided cone. Volcanic cones are often topped by craters, created by volcanic explosions, and craters of over 0.6 mi (1 km) in diameter (calderas) sometimes occur through the collapse or explosive removal of the top of a volcano. Volcanoes may be active, quiescent (dormant), or extinct. The world's highest volcano (extinct) is Aconcagua (22,831 ft; 6959 m) in the Andes. Volcanoes frequently occur along plate boundaries (*see* plate tectonics).

Volcano Islands A group of three small volcanic Japanese islands in the W Pacific Ocean. Claimed in 1891, they were under US administration (1951–68). Sulfur and sugar are produced. Area: about 11 sq mi (28 sq km).

vole A small short-tailed *rodent belonging to the subfamily *Microtinae* (which also includes lemmings). Voles are found in Europe, Asia, and North America and range in size from 14–28 in (7–35 cm). They have blunt noses and their cheek teeth grow continuously. The common field voles (genus *Microtus*; 42 species) live under surface vegetation of meadowland, eating nearly their own weight in seeds, roots, and leaves every 24 hours. Family: *Cricetidae*.

Volga River A river in Russia, the longest river in Europe. Rising in the Valdai Range, it flows mainly E and S through Volgograd to the Caspian Sea. It drains much of Russia, and its many large reservoirs provide important irrigation and hydroelectric power. The Moscow–Volga Canal, the Volga–Don Canal, and the Mariinsk Canal system form navigable waterways from the capital to the White Sea, the Baltic Sea, the Caspian Sea, the Black Sea, and the Sea of Azov. Length: 2293 mi (3690 km).

Volgograd (name until 1925: Tsaritsyn; name from 1925 until 1961: Stalingrad) 48 45N 44 30E A city in Russia, on the Volga River. It has been rapidly redeveloped since its virtual destruction in World War II (*see* Stalingrad, Battle of) and it is now a major industrial city, having steel plants and factories manufacturing especially machinery, footwear, and food. Population (1991 est): 1,007,000.

volleyball A six-a-side court game invented in the US in 1895, in which an inflated ball is hit with the hands or arms. After the service each team is allowed to hit the ball three times before it crosses the net. A rally ends when the ball touches the ground or is not returned correctly. Only the serving side can score; if the receiving side wins a rally, it serves next. Players rotate on the court so that each has an opportunity of serving. A game goes to 15 points and a 2-point lead is required to win. It is an Olympic Games sport for both men and women.

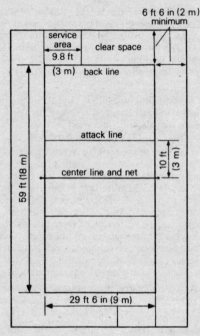

VOLLEYBALL *The dimensions of the court. The height of the ceiling is a minimum of 23 ft (7 m). The top of the center of the net is 8 ft (2.43 m) above the floor for men or 7 ft 4 in (2.24 m) for women.*

Volstead Act (1919) A US law that prohibited the production, sale, and transportation of alcoholic beverages. Written by US Representative Andrew J. Volstead (1860–1947), it gave power to the government to enforce the provisions of the 18th Amendment. *See also* Prohibition.

volt (V) The *SI unit of potential, potential difference, or electromotive force equal to the potential difference between two points on a conductor carrying a steady current of one ampere when the power dissipated is one watt. Named for Alessandro *Volta.

Volta, Alessandro Giuseppe Antonio Anastasio, Count (1745–1827) Italian physicist, who invented the electrophorus (1775), a device used to accumulate electric charge and the forerunner of the modern capacitor. His greatest invention, the Voltaic pile or cell, was the first practical battery and led to a number of important discoveries in electricity. He was professor of physics at Pavia University (1779–1815) and was made a count by Napoleon in 1801. The unit of potential difference is named for him.

Volta River A river in West Africa. Its headstreams, the Black Volta and White Volta rivers, join in N central Ghana to form the Volta River, which then flows S to enter the Bight of Benin. The Akosombo Dam, completed in 1965 as part of the Volta River scheme, provides Ghana's hydroelectric-power requirements and powers its important aluminum smelter. Length: 300 mi (480 km).

Voltaire (François-Marie Arouet; 1694–1778) French man of letters, philosopher, scientist, and moralist, whose versatile work epitomizes the age of Enlightenment. He conducted a lifelong campaign against injustice and intolerance. For offending the duc de Rohan, he was briefly imprisoned in the Bastille (1717) and then went into exile in England (1726–29). After the publication of his *Lettres philosophiques* (1734), which advocated political and religious toleration, he fled to Cirey in Champagne, where he lived with his mistress, Madame de Châtelet. He subsequently lived in Germany (1750–53) having earlier been on friendly terms with Frederick the Great through their correspondence, and in Switzerland (from 1754), chiefly at Ferney near Geneva. His voluminous writings cover history, science, philosophy, and verse drama (for which he was most popular among his contemporaries), and include the satirical and philosophical fable *Candide* (1759), *Traité de la tolérance* (1763), the *Dictionnaire philosophique* (1764), and histories of Peter the Great and Louis XV.

Volta Redonda 22 31S 44 05W A city in S Brazil, in Rio de Janeiro state on the Rio Paraíba. It has the largest steelworks in South America. Population (1980): 177,772.

voltmeter A device for measuring voltage. A voltmeter should draw as little current as possible from the circuit and therefore requires a high input impedance. In the direct-current moving-coil voltmeter the magnetic force on a coil in a magnetic field is used to deflect a needle, the high impedance being provided by a high resistance in series with the coil. *Cathode-ray oscilloscopes and digital voltmeters, used for both direct and alternating current, have high internal impedances.

Volturno River A river in S central Italy, flowing SE and SW to the Tyrrhenian Sea. In 1860 it was the scene of a battle in which Garibaldi defeated the Neapolitans during the wars for Italian unity (*see* Risorgimento). It was the German line of defense during World War II. Length: 109 mi (175 km).

Volunteers in Service to America (VISTA) US federal agency, part of the independent agency ACTION, that provides Americans with opportunities to work, on a full-time volunteer basis, to improve the lives of the economically disadvantaged in the US. Volunteers serve for one year and live and work among the poor in urban or rural areas, or on Indian reservations, sharing skills and experiences. In order to qualify for service, a volunteer must be a resident of the US or one of its territories. The VISTA program was founded in 1964.

Volvox A genus of freshwater single-celled organisms that live in hollow spherical colonies of 500–50,000 individuals, which are linked together by fine strands of cytoplasm; the center of the sphere contains a gelatinous mass. New colonies are formed asexually by division of certain cells or by sexual reproduction, in which the fertilized eggs become dormant cysts that subsequently form new colonies. *Volvox* is regarded by some authorities as an alga (it contains the green pigment chlorophyll) and by others as a protozoan of the class *Flagellata*. □Protozoa.

Von Braun, Wernher (1912–77) US rocket engineer, born in Germany. Beginning his research into the design of rocket engines in 1932, he was director of the German Rocket Test Center at Peenemünde during World War II. It was there that the *V-2 rocket was finally perfected, being launched on London in 1944. After the war Von Braun was taken to the US where he worked on space rockets, including the Saturn launch vehicles (*see* rockets).

Vondel, Joost van den (1587–1679) Dutch dramatist and poet. His works, which adhere to classical models, reflect his deep involvement in contemporary political and religious disputes and his gradual change from Calvinist to Catholic views. His masterpieces, *Lucifer* (1654), *Adam in Ballingschap* (1664), and *Jephtha* (1659), treat biblical themes.

Vonnegut, Kurt (1922–   ) US novelist. His novels and stories are noted for their satirical use of science-fiction techniques. *Slaughterhouse Five* (1969) is based on his experience as a prisoner of war during the fire-bombing of Dresden in 1945. His other works include *Cat's Cradle* (1963), *Breakfast of Champions* (1973), *Slapstick* (1976), *Jailbird* (1979), *Palm Sunday* (1981), *Deadeye Dick* (1982), *Bluebeard* (1987), and *Hocus Pocus* (1990).

voodoo Magical and animistic cults of West African origin, practiced by blacks in Haiti and elsewhere in the Caribbean and in parts of South America. Trances induced by spirit possession are central to voodoo ritual. Other elements in the nocturnal rites are animal sacrifice, drum beating, dancing, and debased elements of Roman Catholic liturgy.

Voronezh 51 40N 39 13E A city in W Russia. It is at the center of an agricultural region and food processing is an important economic activity. Its educational institutions include a university that was transferred from Tartu in 1918. Population (1991 est): 900,000.

Voroshilov, Kliment Yefremovich (1881–1969) Soviet marshal and statesman. Voroshilov was a Red Army commander in the civil war (1918–20) and then commissar for defense (1925–40). He lost his command of the NW armies in 1941 for failing to break the German siege of Leningrad. He was president of the Soviet Union from 1953 to 1960.

Voroshilovgrad (name until 1935, after 1991; Lugansk) 48 35N 39 20E A city in E Ukraine. In the coal-producing Donets Basin, it manufactures mining machinery and has iron and steel and chemical industries. Population (1991 est): 504,000.

Vorster, Balthazar Johannes (1915–83) South African statesman; prime minister (1966–78) and briefly president (1978). A lawyer, Vorster became minister of justice and police in 1960 and was known for his extreme right-wing views and strict enforcement of racial policies. Becoming prime minister after Verwoerd's assassination, he attempted to improve South Africa's relations with black Africa. He retired during investigations of financial irregularities in his term as prime minister.

vortex The circular motion of a fluid about a vertical axis. Examples include whirlpools, hurricanes, and cyclones. A vortex may be formed in a fluid at a point just behind a blunt obstacle past which it is flowing. The direction of rotation of a naturally occurring vortex is often determined by the direction in which the *Coriolis force is acting.

Vorticella A genus of microscopic aquatic single-celled animals found in dense clusters or singly; 0.002–0.6 in (0.05–0.15 mm) long, they are bell-shaped and attached to the substrate by a long coiled contractile stalk. Cilia around the mouth of the "bell" create currents that carry food particles into the mouth. □Protozoa.

vorticism A British art movement inaugurated in 1913 by the writer and painter Wyndham *Lewis. Influenced by *cubism and *futurism, it called for an art expressing the advanced technology and pace of modern life. Its journal, *Blast*, included contributions from Ezra *Pound and T. S. *Eliot. The sculptors *Gaudier-Brzeska and *Epstein were also associated with the movement.

Vosges A range of mountains in NE France. It extends roughly N–S to the W of the Rhine River between Basle and Karlsruhe, rising to 4672 ft (1423 m) at Ballon de Guebwiller, close to the source of the Moselle River.

vote The expression of a choice or opinion, by ballot or by voice, especially for the purpose of electing members to representative assemblies. In the US all persons over the age of 18 may vote in local, state, and national elections.

Voyager probes Two US *planetary probes launched in 1977 toward the outer planets. Voyager 1 approached Jupiter in 1979 before being accelerated toward Saturn, which it reached in 1980. Voyager 2 flew past Jupiter en route to Uranus (1986) and Neptune (1990).

Voznesenskii, Andrei (1933–) Soviet poet. He has traveled in the US and Europe and is, with *Yevtushenko, the best-known contemporary Soviet poet. His poems are noted for their lively originality and inventiveness. His translated poetry includes *Selected Poems* (1964) and *Antiworlds* (1967).

VTOL aircraft. *See* aircraft.

Vuillard, (Jean) Édouard (1868–1940) French artist. He was a member of the *Nabis in Paris and his work was influenced chiefly by Japanese prints. His intimate domestic scenes in paintings and lithographs featured large expanses of patterned wallpapers and textiles and became labeled intimist (*see* intimism). After 1900 he concentrated on society portraiture but also produced murals for public buildings.

Vulcan The Roman god of fire. Originally associated with purely destructive manifestations, such as volcanoes, he became patron of smiths and metal-workers after his identification with the Greek *Hephaestus, whose myths he assumed.

Vulcanite (*or* Ebonite) A hard black insulating material made by heating rubber with sulfur (which makes up about 30% of the product).

vulcanization A process in which sticky natural rubber is made into a harder useful material by heating it with sulfur. Rubber consists of polymer chains with frequent double bonds; the vulcanization process involves the formation of sulfur bridges (–S–S–) between the chains. An inert filler, such as carbon black, is incorporated at the same time.

Vulgate The Latin translation of the Bible made by St Jerome in the 4th century AD. It is the oldest surviving translation of the whole Bible and differs from earlier Latin versions in translating the *Old Testament direct from Hebrew rather than from Greek. It was adopted by the Council of Trent (1546) as the official version of the Roman Catholic Church and is the basis of later English versions, such as the *Douai Bible.

vulture A large carrion-eating bird belonging to the order *Falconiformes*; 24–40 in (60–100 cm) long with a wingspan of up to 105 in (270 cm), vultures have a fleshy naked head, a large crop, and a graceful soaring flight. New World vultures (family *Cathartidae*; 6 species) have a slender hooked bill, large feet, and are voiceless. *See also* condor. Old World vultures (subfamily *Aegypiinae*; 20 species) are widely distributed in open temperate and tropical regions except Australia. They have heavy chopping bills, strong grasping feet, and a feathered ruff at the base of the neck. Family: *Accipitridae* (hawks and eagles). *See also* griffon vulture; lammergeier.

Vyshinskii, Andrei Yanuareevich (1883–1954) Soviet diplomat and lawyer. Vyshinskii was a professor of law and chief prosecutor in Stalin's purge trials (1934–38). He became foreign minister in 1949 and remained in office until Stalin's death when he was demoted to deputy foreign minister and permanent delegate to the UN.

W

Wabash River A river of the E central US, flowing from W Ohio through Indiana to join the Ohio River. Length: 764 km (475 mi).

Wace (c. 1180–c. 1175) Anglo-Norman poet. His major works are the *Roman de Rou* (1160–74), concerning the history of Normandy, and the *Roman de Brut* (1155), which was dedicated to Eleanor of Aquitaine and contained much new material relating to the *Arthurian legend.

Waco 31 55N 97 08W A city in E central Texas, on the Brazos River, SE of Fort Worth. Baylor University (1845) is there. Settled in 1849 and named after the Waco Indians, it is a distribution center for the area's agricultural products. Cotton is important, and textiles, clothing, furniture, glass, tires, and aircraft components are manufactured. Population (1990): 103,590.

Wade-Davis Bill (1864) US law, vetoed by Pres. Abraham Lincoln, that established procedures for *Reconstruction. Drafted by senators Benjamin F. Wade and Henry W. Davis, it stated that the government of a seceded state could not be reorganized until a majority of white males pledged allegiance to the US.

Wade-Giles system. *See* Chinese.

wadi A normally dry valley in a desert or semidesert area. It will occasionally contain water following the infrequent violent downpours of rain that occur in these areas.

Wad Medani 14 24N 33 30E A city in the E central Sudan, on the Blue Nile River. Its recent growth has been due to its central position in the *Gezira irrigation scheme. Population (1983): 141,050.

Wagner, (Wilhelm) Richard (1813–83) German composer. He studied at the Thomasschule in Leipzig. His early attempts at composition were unsuccessful but productions of his operas *Rienzi* (1842) and *The Flying Dutchman* (1843) led to his appointment as conductor at the Dresden opera house. In 1845 his opera *Tannhäuser* was successfully performed there but in 1848, after the failure of the May uprising, Wagner fled to Zürich, where he began the composition of the operatic cycle *Der Ring des Nibelungen*, an epic treatment of German mythology. Wagner developed the use of composition with *leitmotifs in order to achieve an integration of music and drama in opera, having as an ideal that of the *Gesamtkunstwerk* (German: complete work of art). During the composition of the *Ring*, he fell in love with Mathilde Wesendonck (1828–1902), who inspired the opera *Tristan und Isolde*. Wagner continued to face financial difficulties until, in 1864, King Ludwig II of Bavaria befriended him, financing the first performance of *Tristan* in 1865. Shortly afterward Wagner eloped with Cosima von Bülow (1837–1930), Liszt's daughter, whom he married in 1870. In 1868 he produced his comic opera *Die Meistersinger von Nürnberg* and continued work on the *Ring*, raising money to build a theater in Bayreuth for the first performance of the cycle (1876). His last opera, *Parsifal*, was produced in Bayreuth in 1882. Wagner was also a prolific writer on music, the theory of music drama (*see* opera), art, and other subjects. His son **Siegfried Wagner** (1869–1930) and grandson **Wieland Wagner** (1917–66) directed annual productions of Wagner's music dramas at Bayreuth after his death.

Wagner von Jauregg, Julius (1857–1940) Austrian psychiatrist who, as professor of psychiatry and neurology at Vienna University, successfully treated patients suffering from progressive syphilitic brain disease by means of a controlled malarial infection. His work led to the introduction of fever therapy for various mental disorders and he was awarded the 1927 Nobel Prize.

RICHARD WAGNER *A contemporary caricature, emphasizing the composer's shortness.*

Wagram, Battle of (July 5–6, 1809) The battle in which Napoleon won a major victory over the Austrians. Fought NE of Vienna, it forced Austria to concede general defeat to the French. Wagram witnessed the largest concentration of field artillery in recorded history.

wagtail A slender fine-billed songbird noted for its constantly bobbing tail. The pied wagtail (*Motacilla alba*) is black, gray, and white, about 7 in (18 cm) long, and commonly occurs near houses. The larger gray wagtail (*M. cinerea*) lives near streams, catching flying insects. In summer the male has a bright-yellow breast, black throat, and bluish upper parts. The yellow wagtail (*M. flava*) visits Britain in the summer. Family: *Motacillidae* (wagtails and pipits).

Wahhabiyah A Muslim sect founded by Muhammad ibn Abd al-Wahhab (1691–1787). It stresses the need for a Muslim state based on strict adherence to the literal authority of the *Koran and *Hadith. It is responsible for the creation of the kingdom of Saudi Arabia.

Waikato River The longest river in New Zealand, in North Island. Rising in Mount Ruapehu, it flows generally NW through Lake Taupo to enter the Tasman Sea near Auckland. It is an important source of hydroelectric power. Length: 220 mi (350 km).

Wailing Wall Part of the western wall of the *Temple of Jerusalem; it is the only part of the wall still standing that formerly surrounded the Temple. Since late Roman times Jews have gathered there to pray and to mourn over the Temple's destruction.

Wairarapa Plain A low-lying sedimentary area in New Zealand, on SE North Island. Sheep and dairy farming are important. Area: about 320 sq mi (830 sq km).

Waitangi, Treaty of (1840) A treaty between the British government and 46 Maori chiefs in New Zealand, which gave the Maori full rights and confirmed their possession of their lands. Its infringement by settlers led to the *Maori Wars.

Waite, Morrison Remick (1816–88) US lawyer and jurist; chief justice of the Supreme Court (1874–88). A successful lawyer, he worked behind the scenes in Ohio politics and represented the US in the *Alabama* claims case (1871) in Geneva, Switzerland. He was appointed chief justice by Pres. Ulysses S. *Grant and worked to define and clarify post–Civil War legislation. He held that the due process clause of the 14th Amendment was instrumental in defining states' rights in the Granger cases (1876) and further defined the states' role in segregation in the *Civil Rights cases.

Wajda, Andrzej (1926–   ) Polish film director. He established his international reputation with *A Generation* (1954), *Kanal* (1957), and *Ashes and Diamonds* (1958), a trilogy of films concerning Poland during and after World War II. In later films, such as *Landscape after Battle* (1970), *The Wedding* (1972), *Man of Iron* (1981), *Danton* (1982), and *Korczak* (1990), he continued to explore social and political themes.

Wakamatsu. *See* Kitakyushu.

Wakashan languages A group of *North American Indian languages of the NW Pacific coast, including *Nootka and *Kwakiutl.

Wake Island 19 18N 166 36E A coral atoll in the central Pacific Ocean, a US air base. It was taken by the Japanese following the Pearl Harbor attack (Dec 7, 1941). Area: 3 sq mi (8 sq km).

Waksman, Selman Abraham (1888–1973) US microbiologist, born in Russia. Waksman coined the term antibiotic for naturally occurring antibacterial substances. His search for these among soil microorganisms led to the discovery of actinomycin (1940) and *streptomycin (1943), the first effective agent for the treatment of tuberculosis. Waksman was awarded a Nobel Prize (1952).

Walachia (*or* Wallachia) A principality in SE Europe between the lower Danube River in the E and the Transylvanian Alps in the N and NE. Founded in 1290, it was a Hungarian fief until 1330. In the late 14th century it came under Turkish domination, which lasted until the 19th century. In 1859 Walachia united with *Moldavia to form Romania, the independence of which was recognized in 1878.

Waɫbrzych (German name: Waldenburg) 50 48N 16 19E An industrial city in SW Poland, in the Sudeten Mountains. It is a coal-mining center and has engineering and chemical industries. Population (1992 est): 141,000.

Walburga, St (*or* St Walpurgis; c. 710–79 AD) English nun and missionary to Germany; the sister of the English missionary St Willibald (700–86), bishop of Eichstätt. She worked with St *Boniface in Germany, where she became abbess of Heidenheim, an important cultural center. It is not certain why *Walpurgisnacht* (May 1), the traditional German witches' sabbath, is associated with her name. Feast day: Feb 25.

Walcott, Derek (1930–   ) West Indian poet and playwright, winner of the Nobel Prize in literature in 1993. A native of the island of Saint Lucia, he reflected his Caribbean heritage in his work, which included the play *Dream on Monkey Mountain* (1970) and the poetry collections *Sea Grapes* (1976), *Collected Poems* (1986), *The Arkansas Testament* (1987), and *Omeros* (1990). He also taught extensively at US and Caribbean colleges.

Waldemar. *See* Valdemar.

Waldenses (*or* Vaudois) A Christian group founded in the 12th century by Peter Waldes (d. 1217), a wealthy merchant of Lyons, who apparently gave his wealth to the poor and formed a community known as "the poor men of Lyons." The first settlements were in the French Alps, but religious persecution, which continued sporadically to the 18th century, scattered the Waldenses to Italy, Bohemia, Germany, Spain, and eventually North America. They were supported at the Reformation by other Protestant groups. They reject many Roman doctrines (e.g. transubstantiation, purgatory, celibacy of the clergy); at present they number about 20,000.

Waldheim, Kurt (1918–   ) Austrian diplomat; secretary general of the UN (1972–81); president (1986–92) of Austria. He served in Paris and Canada before becoming Austria's permanent representative to the UN (1964–68, 1970–71). He was elected Austria's president in 1986 after a campaign that revealed his service with Nazi units in Yugoslavia during World War II. He did not run for re-election in 1992.

KURT WALDHEIM *The former UN secretary general (center) with the Greek-Cypriot president of Cyprus, Kyprianou (right), and Denktash, president of the Turkish Federated State of Cyprus.*

Wales (Welsh name: Cymru) A principality in the W of Great Britain, a political division of the *United Kingdom. It is bordered by England to the E, the Irish Sea to the N, St George's Channel to the W, and the Bristol Channel to the S. Much of the country is covered by hills and mountains, including the Brecon Beacons to the S, the Cambrian Mountains in central Wales, and the mountains of Snowdonia in the NW. The Isle of Anglesey lies off the NW coast. The principal rivers are the Usk, Rhymney, Taff, Neath, Towry, and Dovey. Central Wales is sparsely populated, most of the population living in the valleys and coastal plains of the S and along the coastal strip in the N. *Economy*: the valleys and coastal plain in the S are highly industrialized, based on the extensive coal fields. Steelmaking has long been associated with these coalfields, and Wales accounts for about half the UK's production of steel sheet and almost all its production of tinplate. Light industry has also been encouraged by the government. Milford Haven, in the far SW, is famous for its deepwater port, used for importing oil, which has given rise to oil refining and associated petrochemical industries. Towns on the coast of North Wales derive an important revenue from tourism. *History*: the Celtic inhabitants of Wales were little affected by the Roman occupation and were Christianized in the 3rd century AD. King *Offa of Mercia built a great dike (8th century) stretching from sea to sea, providing a frontier behind which the Welsh kingdoms were contained. Edward I of England defeated *Llywelyn ap Gruffud (d. 1282) and established English supremacy in Wales. Owen *Glendower's revolt in the early 14th century was also crushed and English rule was formalized with the Acts of *Union (1536–43). In common with England, Wales adopted Protestantism in the 16th century. The early 19th century was characterized by rural overpopulation and near famine, which was alleviated by industrialization in the S and NE, and Wales also suffered during the Depression of the 1930s. Politically, Welsh nationalism has been a powerful force. Area: 8016 sq mi (20,767 sq km). Population (1981): 2,790,000. Capital: Cardiff.

Walesa, Lech (1943–   ) Polish labor leader, who was awarded the Nobel Peace Prize (1983); president (1990–   ). An electrician, fired (1976) for protesting against working conditions at the Lenin Shipyard in Gdansk, he worked underground in the labor movement and eventually founded Solidarity (1980), a national federation uniting individual unions. A general strike that same year forced the Polish Communist government to grant workers the right to organize. Solidarity was outlawed in 1981, and Walesa was imprisoned until 1982. Solidarity was legalized in 1989, and, amid the reforms sweeping Eastern Europe, Walesa was elected president on the Solidarity platform in 1990.

Waley, Arthur (1889–1966) British translator and poet. His translations of Chinese and Japanese poetry influenced many Western poets, notably Ezra Pound. He also translated novels and plays and wrote several studies of Oriental literature and art.

walking (*or* race walking) In athletics, a form of racing in which a particular gait is used; the advancing foot must touch the ground before the other leaves it. Races are held on a track or on roads.

wallaby A herbivorous marsupial belonging to the *kangaroo family (*Macropodidae*). Wallabies are smaller than kangaroos. Hare wallabies (genus *Lagorchestes*; 3 species) are the smallest, measuring up to 35 in (90 cm) in length. Rock wallabies (genus *Petrogale*; 6 species) have a squarish tail and rough-soled feet for negotiating rocky ground. Scrub wallabies (genus *Protemnodon*; about 11 species) inhabit brush or open forest, browsing on leaves and grass.

Wallace, Alfred Russel (1823–1913) British naturalist, who formulated a theory of evolution by natural selection independently of Charles *Darwin. Wallace spent eight years (1854–62) assembling evidence in the Malay Archipelago, sending his conclusions to Darwin in England. Their findings were presented to the Linnaean Society in 1858. Wallace found that Australian species were more primitive, in evolutionary terms, than those of Asia, and that this reflected the stage at which the two continents had become separated. He proposed an imaginary line (Wallace's line) dividing the fauna of the two regions.

Wallace, Edgar (1875–1932) British novelist. The illegitimate son of an actress, he was the prolific and enormously successful author of over 170 popular novels and detective stories. He died in Hollywood, where he was a scriptwriter.

Wallace, George Corley (1919–) US politician; governor of Alabama (1963–67; 1971–79; 1983–87). He served in various state positions until 1962 when he was elected governor for the first time. In 1963 he became prominent nationally when he defied a court order to integrate the University of Alabama; he eventually complied when the National Guard was called out. Not eligible to run for a second consecutive term as governor, he campaigned for his wife **Lurleen Burns Wallace** (1926–68) who became governor in 1967. He campaigned for the Democratic presidential nomination three times (1964, 1972, 1976) and once ran for president on the American Independent party ticket (1968). In an assassination attempt in the 1972 campaign he was shot and left partially paralyzed. A defiant segregationist during the 1960s into the 1970s, he accepted integration and received considerable support from African Americans in his successful 1982 gubernatorial campaign.

Wallace, Henry Agard (1888–1965) US statesman and agriculturalist; vice president (1941–45). He edited *Wallace's Farmer* (1924–29) and *Iowa Homestead* (1929–33) and experimented with hybrid corn. He served as secretary of agriculture (1933–40) during which time he was responsible for implementing the *Agricultural Adjustment Act. As vice president during Pres. Franklin D. *Roosevelt's third term, he worked to better Latin American and Asian relations with the US. He was secretary of commerce (1945–46) and ran for president in 1948 on the Progressive party ticket.

Wallace, Lew(is) (1827–1905) US soldier, diplomat, and author. He served in the *Mexican War (1846–47), as a Union general in the *Civil War, as governor of New Mexico (1878–81), and minister to Turkey (1881–85). He wrote the best-seller *Ben Hur* (1880).

Wallachia. *See* Walachia.

wallaroo An Australian *kangaroo, *Macropus robustus*. Smaller than red or gray kangaroos, wallaroos are heavy-set and have long thick dark-gray fur. They are found mainly in Queensland and New South Wales.

wallcreeper A Eurasian songbird, *Tichodroma muraria*, about 7 in (17 cm) long with a gray plumage and broad black wings patched with red. It climbs rock faces, clinging with its sharp claws and square tail and probing crevices for insects with its long curved bill. Family: *Sittidae* (nuthatches).

Wallenstein, Albrecht Wenzel von (1583–1634) Bohemian-born general, who commanded the imperial forces (1625–30, 1632–34) in the *Thirty Years' War. He raised an army of 24,000 men for the emperor Ferdinand I, with which he won a series of victories, acquiring considerable territories for himself. His growing independence led Ferdinand to dismiss him in 1630 but he was recalled to deal with the Swedish threat in 1632. He subsequently betrayed Ferdinand and was murdered by a group of British officers.

Waller, (Thomas) Fats (1904–1943) US jazz musician and songwriter. Waller played the piano in cabarets and accompanied such singers as Bessie Smith. In the 1930s he organized small bands and recorded many of his own compositions, including "Honeysuckle Rose" and "Ain't Misbehavin'."

wallflower An annual or perennial herb of either of the genera *Cheiranthus* (about 10 species), native to Eurasia and North America, or *Erysimum* (about 80 species), native to Eurasia. Wallflowers have narrow leaves and four-petaled flowers, usually orange, yellow, red, or brown. Many varieties of *C. cheiri* are cultivated as garden ornamentals. The Siberian wallflower (*E.* × *marshallii*) has brilliant orange or yellow flowers. Family: **Cruciferae.*

Wallis and Futuna A French overseas territory in the SW Pacific Ocean comprising two small groups of islands. Formerly a French protectorate, its status was changed following a referendum (1959). The chief of the **Wallis Islands** is Uvéa, while the **Futuna Islands** (*or* Îles de Horne) consist of Futuna and Alofi. Copra and timber are produced. Area: 106 sq mi (275 sq km). Population (1983): 12,400. Capital: Matautu, on Uvéa.

Walloons The French-speaking inhabitants of Belgium, who live mainly in the S and E of the country. They are descended from the northernmost group of *Franks who adopted the Romance speech. *Compare* Flemings.

Wall Street The center of the financial district in New York City, in which the New York Stock Exchange is situated. Wall Street, often known as the Street, is synonymous with the stock exchange.

WALL STREET *The Depression of the early 1930s was triggered by the collapse of the New York Stock Exchange in 1929. During the severe winter of 1931, free coal was distributed to the poor in New York.*

walnut A □tree of the genus *Juglans* (about 17 species), especially the Eurasian species *J. regia*, which produces the best quality nuts. Up to 100 ft (30 m) tall, it has gray deeply furrowed bark and its leaves comprise seven oblong leaflets grouped in opposite pairs. Separate male and female catkins occur on the same tree, and the plum-sized green fruits each contain a kernel enclosed in a wrinkled pale-brown shell. The kernels are eaten as dessert nuts or used in baking and confectionery, and the whole fruits may be eaten pickled. The timber of this species and of the American black walnut (*J. nigra*) is valued for furniture. Family: *Juglandaceae*.

Walpole, Sir Hugh (Seymour) (1884–1941) British novelist. Born in New Zealand, he worked as a teacher before becoming a full-time writer. His many novels include *The Dark Forest* (1916), set in Russia, *The Cathedral* (1922), and a four-volume family saga, *The Herries Chronicle* (1930–33).

Walpole, Sir Robert, 1st Earl of Orford (1676–1745) British statesman, regarded as the first prime minister (1721–42). He became a Whig member of Parliament in 1700. After his effective handling of the *South Sea Bubble he became (1721) first lord of the treasury and chancellor of the exchequer. He maintained his position by adroit patronage and skillful management of the House of Commons but his government was weakened by legislative failures and by his unpopular foreign policy. Conflict with Spain led to the War of *Jenkins' Ear and Walpole was forced to resign.

His fourth son **Horace Walpole, 4th Earl of Orford** (1717–97) was a writer. He published memoirs, antiquarian works, and one of the most popular of gothic novels, *The Castle of Otranto* (1765).

walrus A large *seal, *Odobenus rosmarus*, of coastal Arctic waters. Males are up to 12 ft (3.7 m) long and weigh about 3100 lb (1400 kg). Walruses have tusks—elongated upper canine teeth up to 40 in (1 m) long—used in digging for mollusks on the sea bed and for fighting and display. They have an inflatable bag of skin on each side of the neck, used for buoyancy when sleeping in the sea. Family: *Odobenidae*. □mammal.

Walsall 52 35N 1 58W An industrial city in central England, in West Midlands near Birmingham. Industries include coal mining, engineering, machine tools, aircraft components, electronics, leather goods, hardware, and chemicals. Population (1981): 178,900.

Walter, Bruno (B. W. Schlesinger; 1876–1962) German conductor. He became director of the Vienna Court Opera (1901–12) and went to the US after the outbreak of World War II. There he was associated with the Metropolitan Opera and the New York Philharmonic Orchestra. He was famous as an interpreter of Mahler and conducted the first performance of *Das Lied von der Erde* in 1911.

Waltham 42 23N 71 14W A city in E Massachusetts, on the N bank of the Charles River, W of Boston. Brandeis University (1947) is there. The first US paper mill was started in Waltham in 1788, and the first power loom for the manufacture of cotton textiles was introduced by Francis Cabot Lowell in 1813. Long known as a watchmaking center, Waltham now houses many electronics and precision-instrument industries. Population (1990): 57,878.

Walther von der Vogelweide (c. 1170–c. 1230) German poet. After studying under the court poet of Vienna, he earned a precarious living as a Minnesinger at various courts until he was granted a fief by the emperor Frederick II. His finest works are love poems and poems inspired by his loyalty to the Holy Roman Empire.

Walton, Ernest Thomas Sinton (1903–) Irish physicist, who shared the 1951 Nobel Prize with Sir John *Cockcroft for their invention in 1929 of the first particle accelerator.

Walton, Izaak (1593–1683) English writer. His best-known work is *The Compleat Angler* (1653), a relaxed and entertaining treatise on fishing. He also wrote short biographies of John Donne (1640), George Herbert (1670), and other churchmen.

Walton, Sir William (Turner) (1902–83) British composer. He first became well known through *Façade* (1922), a setting of poems by Edith Sitwell for reciter and instrumental group. Later works include two symphonies (1932–35, 1960), the opera *Troilus and Cressida* (1954), concertos for viola (1929), violin (1939), and cello (1957), the oratorio *Belshazzar's Feast* (1931), and music for Laurence Olivier's films of Shakespeare's *Hamlet*, *Henry V*, and *Richard III*.

waltz A ballroom dance in $\frac{3}{4}$ time in which couples revolve round the room with gliding steps. It originated in Austria and Germany in the late 18th century from a popular folk dance, the *Ländler*. Although many considered it indecorous, it quickly spread to France and reached England in about 1812. Its variations include the skipping French waltz in $\frac{6}{8}$ time, the slow Boston waltz, and the galloping Viennese waltz, for which the Strauss family composed their most famous music.

Walvis Bay A port on the Atlantic coast of Namibia, comprising an exclave of Cape Province, South Africa. Annexed to the Cape Colony in 1884, it has been administered as part of South West Africa (now Namibia) since 1922. It is a major port, handling most Namibian imports, and has important fishing industries. Area: 434 sq mi (1124 sq km). Population (1980): 26,000.

wampum Strings, belts, or ornaments of shell-beads, made by Indians of the NE regions of the US and used by them originally as a record of a treaty or agreement and later, after contact with Europeans, as a form of money.

wandering Jew. *See* Tradescantia.

Wandering Jew In legend, a Jew who rebuked Christ as he was carrying the cross to Calvary and told him to go faster; he was condemned to wander the earth until Christ's second coming. The story is of an early date, a version being given by the English chronicler Matthew Paris (d. 1259); however, its popularity dates from 1602, when a pamphlet was published containing the story of a bishop of Schleswig who had met a certain Ahasuerus, who claimed to be the Wandering Jew.

Wang. *See* Koryŏ.

Wang An Shi (*or* Wang An-shih; 1021–86) Chinese statesman and writer. As a leading minister (1069–76) during the Song dynasty, he introduced wide-ranging economic reforms (including a fund to make loans to farmers), known as the New Policies. Conservative opposition led to his retirement from office, after which he devoted his energies to scholarship and poetry.

Wang Jing Wei (*or* Wang Ching-wei; 1883–1944) Chinese revolutionary, who attempted unsuccessfully to assassinate the Qing prime minister (1910). Wang later became a rival of *Chiang Kai-shek for the leadership of the *Guomindang (Nationalist People's party) and in 1927, in opposition to Chiang, he established a short-lived government at Wuhan. Reconciled with Chiang in 1932, Wang subsequently became prime minister of a Japanese puppet government in Nanjing and died in disgrace.

Wankel engine A four-stroke rotary *internal-combustion engine. It consists of a triangular-shaped rotating piston, with outward curved sides and rounded corners. This rotates in an oval-shaped chamber, slightly narrowed in the middle, which has inlet and exhaust ports and a spark plug. The piston has an inner toothed annulus, which rotates about a central stationary gear, the whole piston being connected via gears to an output shaft. The fuel is drawn in, compressed, and ignited in the chamber spaces provided by the pistons as it rotates. The small number of moving parts and the lack of vibration are the chief advantages of this type of engine, but gas leakage around the seals between the piston ends and the cylinder has been the principal problem. It is, however, used in some cars. It was invented by the German engineer Felix Wankel.

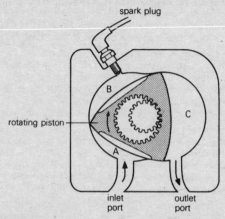

spark plug

rotating piston

B

C

A

inlet port

outlet port

WANKEL ENGINE *The rotary piston draws the fuel mixture through the inlet port into chamber A. At the same time the gas drawn into chamber B in the previous third of a cycle is compressed and ignited to drive the piston around. Meanwhile, the gas in chamber C is discharged through the outlet port.*

wapentake Any of the medieval administrative subdivisions into which the parts of England settled by the Danes (*see* Danelaw) were divided. They corresponded to the *hundreds found in the rest of England. Derived from the Old Norse words for *weapon* and *take*, the term probably refers to the Scandinavian custom of brandishing weapons in an assembly as a gesture of assent.

wapiti A large *red deer of North America, sometimes regarded as a separate species (*Cervus canadensis*). Males may exceed 5 ft (1.5 m) at the shoulder and have antlers up to 4 ft (1.2 m) high.

waratah A many-branched Australian shrub, *Telopea speciosissima*: the floral emblem of New South Wales. Up to 7 ft (2 m) tall, it has leathery sometimes toothed leaves and crimson or scarlet flowers borne in large round terminal heads surrounded by ribbonlike red bracts. The fruit is a leathery capsule containing winged seeds. Family: *Proteaceae*.

Warbeck, Perkin (c. 1474–99) Flemish-born impostor, the focus of a Yorkist plot against Henry VII of England. Pretending to be the duke of York (presumed murdered with his brother Edward V in 1483) he landed in Cornwall in 1497 but he and his 6000 followers fled in the face of Henry's troops. He was later hanged.

warble fly A parasitic fly belonging to the family *Oestridae*, widespread in Europe and North America. *Hypoderma boris* and *H. lineatum* attack cattle; eggs are laid on the legs and the larvae burrow into the tissue, coming to lie beneath the hide of the back. There they produce swellings (warbles), each pierced with a hole for breathing. When mature the larvae leave the warble and pupate in the ground. *See also* gadfly.

warbler A small active songbird belonging to a family (*Sylviidae*; 400 species) widely distributed in Old World regions and belonging to a subfamily (*Parulidae*; 109 species) widely distributed in the New World regions. The Old World warblers, ranging from 3.5–10 in (9–25 cm) in length, have slender bills, soft thick plumage, and feed on insects and berries. They are usually drab brown or olive in color and many have beautiful songs. Among the New World warblers sizes vary, with many about 5.5 in (14 cm) in length, with plumage similar to Old World varieties. *See* blackcap; chiffchaff; reed warbler; whitethroat.

war crimes Acts contrary to rules of *international law governing the conduct of war, mainly contained in the Hague Convention (1907) and the Geneva Convention (1949). Persons suspected of war crimes may be tried and punished by the state that obtains custody of them. The *Nuremberg Trials established the most important principle regarding war crimes, that "the fact that the defendant acted pursuant to the order of his government or of a superior shall not free him from responsibility. . . ."

Ward, Artemus (Charles Farrar Browne; 1834–67) US humorous writer. While working as a journalist for the Cleveland *Plain Dealer*, he wrote comic letters, the supposed author of which was an itinerant showman, Artemus Ward. He gained national fame as a lecturer using this pseudonym. His writings include *Artemus Ward: His Book* (1862), *Artemus Ward: His Travels* (1865), and *Artemus Ward in London* (1867).

Ward, Barbara, Baroness Jackson (1914–81) British economist and conservationist. She has written several books on ecology and political economy, including *Spaceship Earth* (1966) and, with US bacteriologist René Dubos, *Only One Earth* (1972).

Ward, Sir Joseph George (1856–1930) New Zealand statesman; Liberal (1906–12) and United party (1928–30) prime minister. He entered Parliament in 1887, advocated greater unity within the British Empire in foreign affairs, and led the Liberals in the coalition government (1915–19) before becoming leader of the Liberal party's successor, the United party.

war games Simulations in miniature of military maneuvers and combat, using models and rules that enable authentic situations to be reproduced on the playing table. They originated in German states in the late 18th century and were developed by the Prussian army for training purposes during the 19th century. By World War I the military staffs of many countries were using them to assist in the preparation of plans and the training of commanders. War gaming is now a popular pastime.

War Hawks Members of the *Democratic-Republicans in favor of nationalism and western expansion of the US. Led by Henry *Clay and John C. *Calhoun, they advocated and helped to precipitate the *War of 1812.

Warhol, Andy (Andrew Warhola; 1926–87) US *pop artist and film producer. Originally a commercial artist, he achieved notoriety in the early 1960s with paintings of soup cans and portraits of film stars, notably Marilyn Monroe, made with the *silk-screen printing technique. His erotic, lengthy, and controversial films include *Sleep* (1963) and *The Chelsea Girls* (1966).

warlords Local despots who seized control of China following the death of the first president of Republican China, *Yuan Shi Kai, in 1916. These local tyrants, with their own private armies, attempted to increase their personal power by engaging in civil war, which was only ended by Chiang Kai-shek's Northern Expedition against them in 1926. They continued to exert power in China until Liberation (1949).

Warm Springs 32 53N 84 42W A village in Georgia. Its water, popular as a health cure since the 19th century, was used by Franklin D. Roosevelt after his attack of poliomyelitis and he subsequently established a foundation (1927) to help other victims of the disease. He died there in 1945.

War of 1812 (1812–14) The war declared on Great Britain by the US in response to Britain's impressment of sailors from American ships, its blockade on US shipping during the Napoleonic Wars, and its assistance to Indians harassing the NW settlements (*see* Tecumseh). Despite the opposition of New England merchants who feared the severe economic consequences of the war, the *War Hawks in Congress and Pres. James *Madison authorized the beginning of hostilities against the British in Canada and on the high seas. The US forces proved to be weaker than expected, although impressive victories were won in 1813 by Comdr. Oliver *Perry on Lake Erie and by Gen. William H. *Harrison at the Battle of the Thames in Canada. In 1814 the British invaded Maryland and briefly occupied Washington, setting fire to the White House and the Capitol. In the meantime, Gen. Andrew *Jackson soundly defeated the British at the Battle of Horseshoe Bend in Alabama. Negotiations to end the war began in Ghent, Belgium, and successfully concluded with a truce in December 1814. Before the news of the truce reached the US, however, Gen. Andrew *Jackson defeated the British once more at the Battle of *New Orleans.

Warren 42 28N 83 01W A city in SE Michigan, N of Detroit. Originally called Hickory Township and then Aba, it became Warren shortly after 1838. It is the home of General Motors Technical Center, and automobile manufacturing and automobile technology are the major economic activities. Electrical components, tools and dies, and steel are also produced. Population (1990): 144,864.

Warren, Earl (1891–1974) US politician and jurist. After a long and distinguished legal career as district attorney of Alameda County, Calif. (1925–39) and state attorney general (1939–43), Warren entered politics, serving almost three terms as governor of California (1943–53). As the unsuccessful Republican vice presidential nominee in 1948, Warren became one of the national leaders of the party and in 1953 he was nominated by Pres. Dwight *Eisenhower to become chief justice of the US *Supreme Court.

Warren's tenure on the court was marked by a series of landmark decisions that dramatically affected government enforcement of *civil rights. Among the Warren Court's most important decisions were those in the cases of *Brown v. Board of Education (1954), in which it ruled that racial segregation in the public schools was unconstitutional; Engel v. Vitale (1962), in which it ruled that compulsory prayer in the public schools was a violation of the separation between church and state; Reynolds v. Sims, in which it ruled that legislative districts must be drawn to ensure proportional representation; and *Miranda v. Arizona (1966), in which it ruled that suspects in criminal investigations must be advised of their constitutional rights at the time of their arrest. Following the assassination of Pres. John F. *Kennedy, Warren was appointed to head a presidential commission (*see* Warren Commission) to investigate the crime. Warren retired from the Supreme Court in 1969.

Warren, Robert Penn (1905–89). US poet and writer. Part of the Fugitive group of poets at Vanderbilt University under John Crowe *Ransome, he wrote primarily about the South. He taught at the University of Minnesota (1942–50) and at Yale University (1950–56; 1961–73). His best-known epic poem is *Brother to Dragons* (1953) and his poetry is collected in *Promises* (1957; Pulitzer Prize, 1958), *Selected Poems: 1923–1975* (1977), *Now and Then: Poems 1976–1978* (1978; Pulitzer Prize, 1979), and *Being Here* (1980). His novel *All the King's Men* (1946) paralleled the life of Huey *Long, and won a

Pulitzer Prize in literature in 1947; the film version earned him an Academy Award in 1949. Other novels included *At Heaven's Gate* (1943), *World Enough and Time* (1950), and *A Place to Come to* (1977).

Warren Commission (1963–64) US committee, under the chairmanship of Supreme Court Chief Justice Earl *Warren, designated to investigate all aspects of Pres. John F. *Kennedy's assassination. Although the conclusions of the commission found that a conspiracy or group was not involved in the assassination, controversy still surrounds the incident and different groups continue investigations.

Warrington 53 24N 2 37W A city in NW England, on the River Mersey and the Manchester Ship Canal. There are engineering, iron-founding, brewing, tanning, chemical, and detergent-manufacturing industries. Population (1981): 135,568.

Warrumbungle Range A mountain range of Australia. It lies in N New South Wales, reaching 4028 ft (1228 m) at Mount Exmouth, and contains the Breadknife, a rock 300 ft (90 m) high but only 5 ft (1.5 m) wide.

Warsaw (Polish name: Warszawa) 52 15N 21 00W The capital of Poland, in the E on the Vistula River. Settlements in the early Middle Ages had developed into a city by the end of the 15th century and it became the capital in 1611. Thereafter it suffered a decline but it rose to power again in the 18th century. It was occupied by Russia in 1794 and later by France and Prussia. It played an important role in the Polish struggles for independence in the 19th century and, after German occupation in World War I, became the capital again when independence was achieved (1918). During the German occupation of the city in World War II, a ghetto was established (1940) for 400,000 Jews and in February 1943, the survivors (about 100,000) staged an uprising, after which they were put to death. By the end of the occupation Warsaw was almost completely in ruins. After the war much of the old town was faithfully reconstructed. It has expanded in recent years and is now an important industrial and communications center. The University of Warsaw was founded in 1818 and the Technical University in 1826. Population (1992 est): 1,654,500.

Warsaw Pact (*or* Warsaw Treaty Organization) A military treaty signed in 1955 by the Soviet Union, Albania (until 1968), Bulgaria, Czechoslovakia, East Germany, Hungary, Poland, and Romania. It was formed as a communist counterpart to NATO. The Soviet army marshal was the head of the Pact's forces and its headquarters were in Moscow. Political changes in Europe and the Soviet Union and progress on disarmament made the Pact unnecessary, and it was dissolved in 1991.

warships. *See* ships; aircraft carrier; battleship; corvette; cruiser; destroyer; destroyer escort; frigate; submarine.

Wars of Religion (1562–98) French civil wars arising out of the struggle of the Huguenots (French Protestants) for religious liberty and the rivalry between Protestants and Roman Catholic nobles for control of the crown. The main parties were the Catholic *Guise family and successive Huguenot leaders, the Dukes of *Condé, Gaspard de *Coligny, and Henry of Navarre. The wars, comprising eight distinct conflicts, were exacerbated by the weakness of the monarchy under Charles IX and Henry III, who were dominated by their mother *Catherine de' Medici. The wars ended in the victory of Henry of Navarre, who after becoming a Catholic ascended the throne as *Henry IV. In 1598 he issued the Edict of *Nantes, which gave the Huguenots religious freedom.

wart (*or* verruca) A small leathery growth on the skin, caused by viruses. Warts are commonest in children and usually appear on the hands and on the soles of the feet. The appear suddenly and may disappear without treatment. Persistent warts can be treated by cauterization, freezing, or with drugs (such as podophylline), but no treatment is entirely satisfactory.

warthog A wild pig, *Phocochoerus aethiopicus*, of tropical African woodland. Short-legged, with a large head, bulging eyes, and long curved tusks, warthogs grow to about 30 in (75 cm) high at the shoulder. They are gray-brown with sparse body hair except on the shoulders and along the spine and they feed during the day on roots, grass, etc., often sheltering in disused aardvark burrows.

wart snake A thick-bodied fish-eating aquatic snake belonging to the family *Acrochordidae* (2 species), having valves that close the mouth and nostrils when underwater. The brown Javan wart snake (*Acrochordus javanicus*), also known as the elephant's-trunk snake, is 4 ft (1.2 m) long and occurs in rivers and coastal waters of Australia and SE Asia; it is killed for its skin.

Warwick 41 43N 71 28W A resort city in E central Rhode Island on Narragansett Bay, S of Providence. Founded in 1642 it became a cotton milling center. Now chiefly a residential community, its beaches and boating facilities attract many visitors. Population (1990): 85,427.

Warwick, Richard Neville, earl of (1428–71) English statesman, known as the Kingmaker. He was the most prominent English magnate during the Wars of the *Roses. A supporter of the Yorkist cause from 1453, he was responsible for the seizure of the crown in 1461 by Edward, duke of York (Edward IV). In 1470, losing influence at court, he changed sides and briefly restored Henry VI to the throne. In 1471 the Lancastrians were routed, and Warwick was killed.

Warwickshire A county in the Midlands of England. It consists mainly of undulating countryside, drained to the SW by the River Avon. It is predominantly agricultural, dairy farming being especially important. Area: 765 sq mi (1981 sq km). Population (1987): 484,000. Administrative center: Warwick.

Wash, the A shallow inlet of the North Sea, in E England between Lincolnshire and Norfolk, into which the Rivers Witham, Welland, Nene, and Great Ouse flow. Length: about 30 km (19 mi). Width: 15 mi (24 km).

Washington One of the NW Pacific states, bordered by the Pacific Ocean (W), British Columbia (N), Idaho (E), and Oregon (S). Mountains ring the state, including the Mount St Helens volcano that erupted violently in 1980, and the Columbia Basin covers much of the central area, cut by the Columbia and Snake Rivers. The lowland around the Puget Sound in the W is highly populated, urbanized, and industrialized, while the E is predominantly rural and sparsely populated. The state's major manufacturing industry is the construction of aircraft. Washington is also a leader in nuclear research and timber production, although in 1983 construction of two of five projected nuclear power plants was halted, terminating the most costly public works project ever undertaken. Attempts to diversify the economy have led to a concentration on the growing tourist industry attracted by numerous spectacular national parks, and there is significant mineral extraction, especially of gold, silver, and uranium. Fishing is important as is foreign trade. Seattle is a major shipping center for trade with the Orient and gateway to Alaska and center of the spacecraft industry. In agriculture, wheat, potatoes, and fruit (especially apples) are grown and dairy farming is important. *History*: the British Hudson Bay Company dominated the area until the 1840s. In 1846 the boundary between Washington and Canada was agreed upon and the state (1889) was named for George Washington. Washington was the site of numerous labor disputes during the early 20th century; during and after World War II it enjoyed great prosperity as a center of the defense industry.

Area: 68,192 sq mi (176,616 sq km). Population (1990): 4,866,692. Capital: Olympia.

Washington, D.C. 38 55N 77 00W The capital of the US, in the E of the country on the Potomac River. Coextensive with the District of Columbia, it is the legislative, judicial, and administrative center of the federal government. It is nonindustrial and most of its inhabitants are government employees. Its many notable landmarks include the Washington Monument, the Lincoln Memorial, the Capitol, the □White House, the *Pentagon, the National Gallery of Art, the Hirshhorn Museum, the Phillips Gallery of Art, the Freer Gallery of Art, the Corcoran Gallery of Art, the Library of Congress, the Folger Shakespeare Library, the John F. Kennedy Center for the Performing Arts, the Washington Convention Center, the Smithsonian Institution, the Arlington National Cemetery, the Vietnam Veterans Memorial, Washington National Cathedral, and the National Shrine of the Immaculate Conception. There are five universities and most of the nation's cultural organizations have their headquarters there. *History*: its location as the nation's capital was chosen by George Washington and approved by Congress in 1790. Planned by the French engineer Pierre L'Enfant (1754–1825), its first constructions date from 1793. Almost all of the early government buildings were destroyed during the War of 1812 when British troops occupied the city in the summer of 1814 and burned all public buildings except the post office. New construction began as soon as the war ended (1815). During the Civil War Confederate forces often threatened the capital but never reached it. In the 20th century the city grew substantially as the federal government expanded. Population (1990): 606,900.

BOOKER T. WASHINGTON *Educator who founded Tuskegee Institute and who advocated education for African Americans as the doorway to equality.*

Washington, Booker T(aliaferro) (1856–1915) US educator. Son of a slave, Washington worked as a laborer at various jobs before beginning studies at the Hampton Institute in Virginia, a segregated vocational school where he later taught. In 1881, Washington was hired by the Alabama legislature to establish a technical school for African-American students at Tuskegee and in later years, this school, the *Tuskegee Institute, became one of the foremost institutions of its kind in the country. Washington served as director of the school until his death. He also became one of the most influential US African-American leaders. Traveling throughout the country on the lecture circuit, Washington supported the cause of *civil rights through education rather than political agitation. Among his most widely read published works are *The Future of the American Negro* (1899), *Sowing and Reaping* (1900), *Frederick Douglass* (1907), and his autobiography, *Up From Slavery* (1901).

GEORGE WASHINGTON

Washington, George (1732–99) US general and statesman; 1st president of the United States (1789–97). Born to a wealthy Virginia family and trained as a surveyor, Washington began his career by establishing territorial boundaries in western Virginia. During the *French and Indian Wars he served as a lieutenant colonel in the British army, playing an important role in the capture of Fort Duquesne (1758). In 1759, Washington married Martha Custis and was elected to the Virginia House of Burgesses. He later became a strong supporter of the cause of American independence and was chosen to be a member of the 1st and 2nd *Continental Congresses (1774–76).

At the outbreak of the *American Revolution, he was named commander in chief of the Continental Army. His early victories at the Battles of Trenton and Princeton (1776) were followed by defeat at the Battle of *Brandywine (1777) and the cold and hunger of the winter at *Valley Forge (1777–78), but he was able to maintain the morale of the American forces, eventually accepting the surrender of British general Charles *Cornwallis at Yorktown (1781). After briefly retiring to private life, Washington served as a delegate to the *Annapolis

Convention (1786) and presided over the *Constitutional Convention in Philadelphia (1787).

With the ratification of the US Constitution and the first national elections, Washington took office as the first president of the United States in New York City in 1789. During his two terms in office, he was able to place the federal government on a sound footing, adopting the fiscal policies of Alexander *Hamilton, suppressing the *Whiskey Rebellion (1794), and supporting the ratification of *Jay's Treaty (1795). He left office in 1797, urging future US leaders to avoid foreign entanglements. Washington's important contributions to the early history of the US earned him the familiar title "Father of His Country."

Washington Armament Conference (1921–22) A meeting of Britain, France, Japan, Italy, and the US in Washington, D.C., to discuss arms limitations. The treaties that resulted from the conference set naval limitations for the countries involved.

Washington's Farewell Address (1796) The retirement from public office speech, published in the press, of Pres. George *Washington. Because he was not seeking a third term as president, Washington advised the Federalists on the upcoming election and warned in the address against the nation dividing or becoming entangled in international politics, for there were too many important domestic issues that needed attention.

wasp A stinging insect, 0.25–1.5 in (6–40 mm) long, belonging to the order *Hymenoptera*. The social wasps (family *Vespidae*) form colonies that consist of a queen, males, and workers. The nests are built underground, in bushes, or in hollow trees. The adults feed on nectar, ripe fruit, insects, etc.; the larvae are usually fed on insects and insect larvae. Fertilized eggs produce queens or workers and unfertilized eggs produce the males. New colonies are established by young fertilized queens—the only individuals to survive the winter. Certain parasitic wasps lay their eggs in the nests of other wasps. Solitary wasps (family *Sphecidae*) lay their eggs in individual nests that are stocked with food and sealed by the parent. *See also* digger wasp; gall wasp; hornet; potter wasp; spider wasp.

Wasserman, August von (1866–1925) German bacteriologist, who invented the Wasserman test for detecting *syphilis, based on the complement-fixation studies of *Bordet. Wasserman made many other contributions to immunology, including a test for tuberculosis and an antitoxin against diphtheria.

watch A timepiece small enough to be worn by a person. Watches, as small clocks, first came into use at the beginning of the 16th century with the invention by Peter Henlein (1480–1542) of the mainspring as the energy store in place of the earlier falling weight. Based on a verge escapement, watches were then bulky devices, often cylindrical, worn on the girdle. The invention of the balance spring in 1675 converted the watch from a highly decorated ornament into a more functional article that could be concealed in the pocket. By the 18th century pocket watches had attained a high degree of accuracy. At the beginning of the 20th century wristwatches were introduced and with World War I their advantages to men in uniform made them overwhelmingly popular. Between the wars wristwatches became smaller and cheaper or boasted such features as rust and shock resistance, luminous dials, or self-winding mechanisms. In the early 1950s the first electromagnetic watches were developed (powered by tiny batteries), but it was not until the late 1960s that the first electronic watch appeared. This used the piezoelectric oscillations of a quartz crystal as the time source and an electronic circuit to reduce the frequency to that required to drive the hands. In the 1970s quartz watches were developed without moving parts: this is the solid-state digital watch in which the dial and hands are replaced by a digital dis-

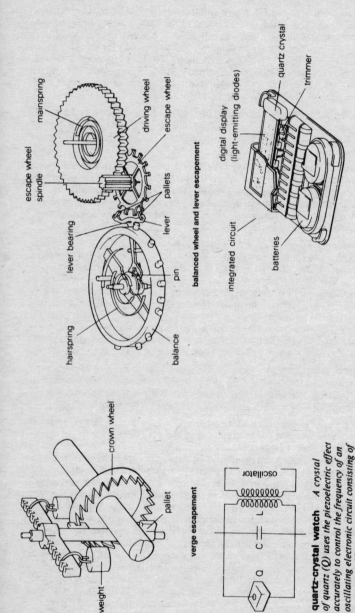

mainspring

escape wheel
spindle

driving wheel

escape wheel

hairspring

lever bearing

lever

pallets

pin

balance

balanced wheel and lever escapement

crown wheel

pallet

weight

verge escapement

digital display
(light-emitting diodes)

quartz crystal

trimmer

integrated circuit

batteries

dogital watch

quartz-crystal watch *A crystal
of quartz (Q) uses the piezoelectric effect
accurately to control the frequency of an
oscillating electronic circuit consisting of
a capacitor (C) and inductance (L).*

oscillator

L

C

Q

WATCH *Early watches used the verge escapement of clocks. The balance wheel and lever escapement dominated watch design
until the quartz-crystal and digital watch emerged in the 20th century.*

play. This can be made so small that some digital wristwatches incorporate several additional functions (e.g. date, stopwatch, alarm, reminder) as well as a tiny calculator.

water (H_2O) A colorless odorless tasteless liquid consisting of eight parts of oxygen to two parts of hydrogen by weight. Water covers 72% of the earth's surface and is found in all living matter, in minerals, and as a small but important constituent of the atmosphere. The solid form of water (ice) is less dense (916.8 kg/m^3) than the liquid at 0°C (999.84 kg/m^3), which is why ice floats and frozen water pipes burst. The maximum density (999.97 kg/m^3) occurs at 3.98°C, unlike most liquids in which the maximum density occurs at the melting point. The molecules of water are polar, i.e. they have a positive electric charge at one end and a negative at the other. This makes it an excellent solvent.

Water supplies: an adequate supply of clean water is a prerequisite of all communities. Rain is the prime source, although in arid areas *desalination of *sea water may be necessary. Rainwater for distribution is collected in reservoirs, which may also be fed by rivers, streams, etc. The stored water is purified by filtration, usually through a deep bed of sand. Most of the impurities are trapped in the top 2–2.4 in (5–6 cm), which are periodically replaced. In fast filtration processes the addition of a coagulant (e.g. aluminum sulfate) is used to cause most particle impurities to fall to the bottom. The water then passes through several tanks of coarse sand. Disinfectants, usually chlorine, are added to kill microorganisms. Sufficient chlorine is added to leave about 0.2 mg/liter of uncombined chlorine after 30 minutes. In superchlorination larger quantities are added, followed by subsequent dechlorination with sulfur dioxide. *See also* fluoridation.

water beetle A beetle of the family *Dytiscidae* (*see* diving beetle)—the so-called true water beetles. The name is also used loosely for any aquatic beetle, including the *whirligig beetles (family *Cyrinidae*); the water scavenging beetles (family *Hydrophilidae*), which resemble diving beetles but feed on algae or decaying organic matter; and the crawling water beetles (family *Haliplidae*), which crawl and feed on algae.

water boatman A *water bug belonging to the cosmopolitan family *Corixidae* (over 300 species). It has a flattened boat-shaped body with fringed oarlike hind legs and feeds on plant debris and algae, scooped up by the spoon-shaped front legs. It is normally attached to bottom vegetation of fresh and brackish waters, rising only to replenish its air store.

waterbuck A large African antelope, *Kobus ellipsiprymnus*. About 50 in (130 cm) high at the shoulder, waterbucks have a long wiry brown coat with a white rump patch and long spreading horns. Small groups spend the night in riverside cover and graze on the plains during the day.

water buffalo A large buffalo, *Bubalus bubalis*, also called Asiatic buffalo or carabao, found wild in swampy land of SE Asia and widely domesticated throughout Asia. Up to 6 ft (180 cm) at the shoulder and heavily built, water buffaloes are gray-black with long backward-curving horns and can be dangerous. Domestic breeds are more docile and have shorter horns: they are used for milk and as draft animals.

water bug An insect of the suborder *Heteroptera* (*see* Hemiptera) that lives in or on fresh or brackish water. True water bugs include the *backswimmer, *giant water bug, *water boatman, and *water scorpion. The surface water bugs include the *pond skater, water cricket (*Vellidae*), and water measurer (*Hydrometridae*).

Waterbury 41 33N 73 03W A city in Connecticut. It was the nation's largest producer of brass products in the 19th century. Other manufactures include watches, clocks, and electronic parts. Population (1990): 108,691.

water chestnut An annual aquatic plant of the genus *Trapa*, especially the Eurasian species *T. natans*, which has a rosette of diamond-shaped toothed floating leaves, feathery submerged leaves, and small white flowers. The hard spiny dark-gray fruit, up to 2 in (5 cm) across, contains edible seeds that are eaten raw, roasted, boiled, or in porridge. Family: *Trapaceae*.

The Chinese water chestnut is the tuber of an E Asian sedge, *Eleocharis tuberosa*: it is cooked and eaten in various Chinese dishes. Family: *Cyperaceae*.

watercolor A painting medium consisting of pigments bound with gum, which are diluted with water before being applied to a surface of white or tinted paper. Its special characteristics are its transparency and its white accents, which are created by leaving parts of the paper unpainted. Watercolor made opaque by the addition of white pigment and more glue is known as gouache or poster paint. Practiced since ancient times, watercolor painting in postmedieval Europe was chiefly of a monochrome variety until the late 18th century, when it was developed to perfection by a series of British landscape artists, notably *Turner and *Blake. The 19th century's outstanding watercolorists include *Horner, *Sargent, *Delacroix, and *Daumier.

watercress Either of two perennial herbs, *Nasturtium officinale* or *N. microphyllum* × *officinale*, native to Eurasia and widely cultivated for the peppery young shoots, which are used in salads. Watercress grows submerged or floating in streams or on mud; it has compound leaves, with roundish or oval leaflets, and bears clusters of four-petaled white flowers. Family: *Cruciferae*.

waterfall A steep fall of water along the course of a river or stream. It may be produced by the river crossing a band of hard rock; where the rock strata are horizontal the fall is likely to be steep. Falls also occur at the edges of plateaus or where faulting has taken place. The waterfall will continually retreat upstream through erosion. Large waterfalls and series of falls are also known as **cataracts**. The energy of a waterfall can be harnessed to provide hydroelectric power.

water flea A small freshwater *crustacean of the suborder *Cladocera* (about 430 species). Its compact body, usually 0.04–0.12 in (1–3 mm) long, is covered, behind the head, by a laterally flattened transparent carapace, which encloses 4–6 pairs of appendages. It swims by means of two large forked antennae. Common genera: *Daphnia, Leptodora*; subclass: *Branchiopoda*.

Waterford (Irish name: Port Lairge) 52 15N 7 06W A city and port in the SE Republic of Ireland, the county town of Co Waterford. It has Protestant and Roman Catholic cathedrals. It is an important trading and distribution center; industries include light engineering, papermaking, and glassmaking, for which it is famous. Population (1986): 41,054.

Waterford (Irish name: Contae Port Lairge) A county in the S Republic of Ireland, in Munster bordering on the Atlantic Ocean. Chiefly hilly, it is drained by the Rivers Blackwater and Suir. Agriculture is the main occupation with dairy farming and cattle rearing. The traditional glassmaking industry is of note. Area: 710 sq mi (1838 sq km). Population (1991): 91,608. County town: Waterford.

water gas A mixture of equal amounts of hydrogen and carbon monoxide made by passing steam over red hot coke: $H_2O + C \geq H_2 + CO$. The mixture is a useful fuel gas but the reaction producing it is endothermic and heat must be supplied to the coke. One way of doing this is to make water gas in conjunction with an exothermic reaction—that between air and carbon: $O_2 + 4N_2 + 2C \geq 2CO + 4N_2$. The mixture of carbon monoxide and nitrogen is called **producer gas**. Although it has a lower calorific value than water gas the products are hot as a result of the high temperature of the reaction. The heating value of water gas can be improved by passing it through petroleum while hot, thus cracking liquid hydrocarbons to gaseous ones, which escape with the water gas. The process, known as carbureting, can almost double the calorific value. Water gas, however, is not as effective a fuel gas as *natural gas and its use is mainly as a raw material for chemical-manufacturing processes, such as the *Haber process.

Watergate A building complex in Washington, D.C., that gave its name to a political scandal leading to the resignation of the Republican president Richard M. Nixon. Amid growing suspicion of corruption among presidential officials, the *Washington Post* exposed their involvement during the 1972 presidential election in a burglary of the headquarters of the Democratic party at the Watergate, and in subsequent arrangements (the "coverup") to buy off the convicted burglars. Amid the resignation and prosecution of top White House staff, who alleged that Nixon had connived in Watergate, he resigned under the threat of impeachment (1974). He was pardoned by Pres. Gerald Ford.

water glass (*or* sodium silicate) A mixture of silicates with the general chemical formula $xNa_2O.ySiO_2$, forming a clear viscous solution in water. It is made by fusing *sodium carbonate and sand (*silica) in an electric furnace and is used in making silica gel, detergents, and textiles.

Waterhouse, Alfred (1830–1905) British architect of the *gothic revival. His early work was done in Manchester and included the Assize Court (1859) and the Town Hall (1868). Thereafter he came to London, where he built the romanesque Natural History Museum (1881), and the gothic redbrick St Paul's School (1885) and the City and Guilds College (1879).

water hyacinth An aquatic plant of the genus *Eichhornia* (about 5 species), native to tropical America. They have slender creeping rhizomes, rosettes of stalked leaves, and clusters of flowers in the leaf axils. Some species float in shallow water; others are rooted in muddy stream banks and lake edges. *E. crassipes* is the most widely distributed species; it is used as an ornamental plant in pools and aquariums and has become a troublesome weed in the S US, Australia, and Africa. Family: *Pontederiaceae*.

water lily An annual or perennial freshwater plant of the family *Nymphaeaceae* (75 species), native to temperate and tropical regions. Water lilies have round wax-coated leaves floating on the water surface and borne on long central stalks arising from creeping stems buried in the mud below. The large showy flowers, whose stalks may rise above the water surface, are cup-shaped, with several whorls of oval pointed petals, usually white, yellow, pink, red, blue, or purple in color. Most cultivated water lilies are hybrids and varieties derived from species of *Nymphaea*. *See also* lotus.

Waterloo 43 27N 80 30W A city in E Canada, in SW Ontario on the N side of *Kitchener. Founded by Mennonites (1806), it houses several insurance companies and two universities and is a musical center. Its varied industries include distilling, brewing, furniture, and farm machinery. Population (1991): 71,181.

Waterloo, Battle of (June 18, 1815) The battle in which *Napoleon Bonaparte was finally defeated by British, Dutch, Belgian, and German forces commanded by Wellington and the Prussians under von Blücher. Napoleon caught Wellington 3 mi (5 km) S of Waterloo (Belgium) in isolation from the Prussians and attempted to smash his army by a direct offensive. The British lines held the French columns until the Prussians arrived. A concerted charge brought victory and four days later Napoleon's second, and final, abdication.

water louse A freshwater crustacean of the genus *Asellus*, related to the *woodlouse. It is found on submerged plants or the bottom of weedy streams and ponds. Order: *Isopoda*.

watermark A distinctive mark produced in *paper during manufacture by making it slightly thinner in some places than in others. In handmade paper, the watermark is formed by the wires in the bottom of the mold. In machine-made paper the mark is put in by a roller that has the mark in a raised form on its surface.

watermelon The fruit of an annual climbing plant, *Citrullus vulgaris*, native to Africa but widely cultivated. The plant has hairy deeply lobed leaves and the yellow flowers produce large oval fruits, up to 10 in (25 cm) across, with a shiny dark-green rind and red, yellow, or white flesh, which is juicy and sweet-flavored. The seeds are also edible. Family: *Cucurbitaceae*. *See also* melon.

water milfoil A submerged or floating perennial freshwater aquatic plant of the worldwide genus *Myriophyllum* (about 45 species). It has whorls of finely divided feathery leaves and the green, white, or red flowers are borne in aerial spikes. A few species are grown in aquaria. Family: *Haloragaceae*.

water moccasin A heavy-bodied venomous *pit viper *Agkistrodon piscivorus*, occurring in marshes of the S US and also called cottonmouth because it shows the white inside of its mouth when threatened. Up to 5 ft (1.5 m) long, it is brown with dark bands and hunts fish, turtles, and waterbirds.

water polo A ball game played seven-a-side (with four substitutes), usually in a swimming pool. It originated in England in the 1870s, with players riding floating barrels to resemble horses and hitting the ball with paddles; in the modern game players swim. The object is to score goals with an inflated ball that is passed between players by throwing. Except for the goalkeepers, players may not walk, jump, punch the ball, or touch it with both hands together. It is a men's sport in the Olympic Games.

water rat A large aquatic *rodent belonging to the subfamily *Hydromyinae* (13 species) found in Australia, New Guinea, and the Philippines. The Australian water rat (*Hydromys chrysogaster*) is about 14 in (35 cm) long and has otterlike fur and a white-tipped tail. Family: *Muridae*.

*Water voles and *muskrats are also known as water rats.

water scorpion A *water bug of the worldwide family *Nepidae* (about 200 species). Its scorpionlike "tail" is actually a breathing tube (siphon), which protrudes from the water while the insect hangs upside down from aquatic vegetation or the surface film of water. Water scorpions prey on small arthropods, tadpoles, and small fish.

watershed (*or* divide) The dividing line, usually a ridge, between the *catchment areas of two separate river systems. The term is also used for the entire catchment area of the drainage basin. *See also* continental divide.

water shrew A long-snouted Eurasian aquatic *shrew, *Neomys fodiens*. About 4 in (10 cm) from nose to tail, water shrews feed chiefly on aquatic invertebrates but also take small fish and frogs, aided by their venomous saliva. Their hair-fringed toes assist in swimming.

water skiing Planing on water on wooden skis (or a single ski for slalom competitions), often with fins attached for stability. It originated in the 1920s. The skier is towed by a rope usually 75 ft (23 m) long attached to a powerboat traveling at a minimum of about 15 mph (25 kph). Competitions are held for jumping, slalom (through a course of buoys), and trick riding. Barefoot water skiing is also practiced, requiring speeds of 35–40 mph (55–65 kph).

water snake. *See* grass snake.

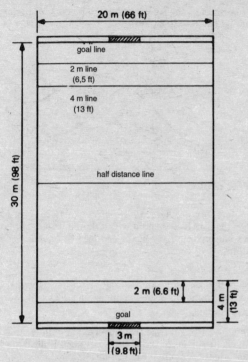

WATER POLO *The dimensions of the pool for international play. The water must be 6 ft 6 in (2 m) deep in international competition.*

water spider A European freshwater *spider, *Argyronecta aquatica*, that lives underwater in a bell-shaped structure constructed from silk and plant material and filled with bubbles of air brought down in its body hairs. It feeds inside on small animals taken from the water surface. The male (0.6 in [15 mm] long) is usually larger than the female (0.4 in [10 mm] long).

waterspout A funnel-shaped cloud extending from the base of a cumulonimbus cloud to the surface of the sea. It is a small-scale intense low-pressure system, the equivalent of a *tornado on land, characterized by intense rotating winds, which create violent agitation of the water surface and lift drops up into the cloud.

water strider. *See* pond skater.

water table The upper level of the water that has percolated into the ground and become trapped within pores, cracks, and fissures in permeable rocks. The level of the water table varies with the topography and local rainfall. *See also* artesian well.

Waterton Lakes National Park A national park (1895) in SW Alberta, Canada, in the eastern Rocky Mountains, adjoining Glacier National Park in N Montana. With Glacier National Park it forms Waterton-Glacier International Peace Park (1932) and is connected to it by highway and the Continental

Divide, which runs through the park. The highest point is Mt Blakiston (9600 ft; 2926 m). Area: 203 sq mi (526 sq km).

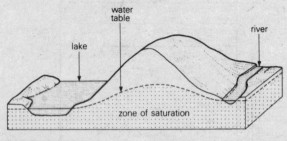

WATER TABLE

water vole A large *vole, *Arvicola terristris*, of Europe and Asia; 6–8 in (15–20 cm) long, they are heavily built with a short tail and light-brown to black fur. Water voles burrow into river banks and feed on aquatic vegetation, often during the daytime.

water wheel. *See* turbine.

Watford 51 40N 0 25W A city in SE England. It has papermaking, printing, engineering, and electronics industries. Population (1981): 74,356.

Watling Island. *See* San Salvador Island.

Watling Street The Roman road that traversed Britain from its commercial center, London, via St Albans to the strategically sited Roman town near Wroxeter, with a branch to the legionary fortress at Chester.

Watson, James Dewey (1928–   ) US geneticist, who (with Francis *Crick) proposed a model for the molecular structure of *DNA (1953). Following this fundamental breakthrough, Watson investigated the *genetic code and the way in which it is "read" by the cell. His *Molecular Biology of the Gene* (1965) has become an influential text, and *The Double Helix* (1968) gave a popular account of his work on DNA. He received a Nobel Prize (1962) with Crick and Maurice *Wilkins.

Watson, John Broadus (1878–1958) US psychologist and founder of the US school of psychology known as *behaviorism. Watson declared that speculations about animal behavior should be based entirely on observations made under laboratory conditions. In *Psychology from the Standpoint of the Behaviorist* (1919), Watson applied his principles to human behavior, which he regarded in terms of conditioned responses, excluding the possible contributions of reasoning and original thought. One of his most notable followers was B. F. *Skinner.

Watson-Watt, Sir Robert Alexander (1892–1973) Scottish physicist, who during the 1920s and 1930s pioneered the development of *radar. In 1935 the British Government, realizing the strategic importance of the invention, set up a research team working under Watson-Watt, who had put it into operation by World War II.

watt (W) The *SI unit of power equal to one joule per second. In electrical terms it is the energy per second expended by a current of one ampere flowing between points on a conductor between which there is a potential difference of one volt. Named for James *Watt.

Watt, James (1736–1819) British engineer, whose contributions to the development of the □steam engine made him one of the most important figures of the *industrial revolution. In 1764 while repairing a model of a *Newcomen engine he realized that the machine could be made more efficient if the steam was condensed in a separate chamber. Watt's steam engine, completed in 1769, soon replaced the Newcomen engine, especially after Watt had introduced a double-acting model. In 1774 he began to manufacture steam engines and by 1800 some 500 stationary Watt engines were in use for a variety of purposes. He later invented the centrifugal governor. Watt devised the unit "horsepower" and the metric unit of power is named for him.

Watteau, (Jean) Antoine (1684–1721) French rococo painter. Settling in Paris (1702), he trained under a painter of theatrical scenery and under the curator of the Luxembourg Palace, where he studied the works of *Rubens. Despite his early death from tuberculosis, he achieved fame both in Paris and London (which he visited in 1719) with his charming *fêtes galantes* (scenes of gallantry) and paintings of comedians. His best-known works are *L'Embarquement pour l'île de Cythère* and the portrait of the clown *Gilles* (both Louvre).

wattle Any of various Australian □trees and shrubs, especially those of the genus *Acacia*, the stems and branches of which are used for fencing and were formerly employed in the wattle and daub construction of houses. The commonest are the black wattle (*A. binervata*), the golden or green wattle (*A. pycnantha*), and the silver wattle (*A. dealbata*), which has silvery fernlike leaves and fluffy globular heads of tiny yellow flowers and is used by florists under the name of mimosa. Wattles are used as shade trees, ornamentals, and livestock fodder.

wattmeter An instrument for measuring electrical power. The most common type has two conducting coils connected in series, one fixed and one movable. The magnetic forces between them produce a deflection of the movable coil proportional to the square of the current, which is in turn proportional to the power.

Waugh, Evelyn (Arthur St John) (1903–66) British novelist. With *Decline and Fall* (1928) and other novels, including *Vile Bodies* (1930), *A Handful of Dust* (1934), and *The Loved One* (1948), he established his reputation as the most brilliant social satirist of his generation. After his conversion to Roman Catholicism in 1930, religious themes played an increasing part in his novels, especially in *Brideshead Revisited* (1945). Later novels include his war trilogy—*Men at Arms* (1952), *Officers and Gentlemen* (1955), and *Unconditional Surrender* (1961)—and the semiautobiographical *The Ordeal of Gilbert Pinfold* (1957). His elder brother **Alec (Raban) Waugh** (1898–1981), was a novelist and travel writer. Many of his later novels, such as *Island in the Sun* (1956), deal with life in tropical countries. Evelyn's son **Auberon Waugh** (1939–) is a novelist and journalist.

wave Any periodic change in a property of a system that is propagated through a medium (or through space). Waves are classified according to the curve produced when their magnitude is plotted against time on a graph. If the wave is shaped like a sine curve, it is known as a sine (*or* sinusoidal) wave. Examples of sine waves include electromagnetic waves and sound waves. A wave is characterized by three parameters: amplitude, the maximum displacement of the wave; *wavelength; and *frequency. The wave may propagate energy, in which case it is known as a traveling wave, or it may not, when it is known as a standing or stationary wave. For traveling waves the displacement may be either perpendicular to the direction of the propagation of the wave (a transverse wave) or in the direction of propagation (a longitudinal wave). Waves on water and electromagnetic waves are transverse, while sound waves are longitudinal.

waveguide A hollow conductor for transmitting microwaves over short distances. The electromagnetic radiation is guided along the tube, being reflected from the internal walls. The waveguide is usually filled with air but occasionally some other *dielectric is used.

wavelength The distance between successive peaks (or troughs) of a wave. It is equal to the velocity of the wave divided by its frequency. For electromagnetic radiation it is the most commonly used parameter for specifying the part of the *electromagnetic spectrum to which the radiation belongs.

Wavell, Archibald Percival, 1st Earl (1883–1950) British field marshal. After service in World War I he became *Allenby's chief of staff in Palestine. In World War II, as commander in chief in the Middle East, he defeated the Italians in N and East Africa. After the failure of his offensive against Rommel in June, 1941, he was transferred to SE Asia, where he was again replaced after failing to halt the Japanese advance. He was viceroy of India from 1943 to 1947.

wave mechanics A branch of *quantum theory in which elementary particles are treated as *de Broglie waves. Systems of particles are described by a wave equation, known as the *Schrödinger equation. The solutions of this equation give the allowed values of the energy of each particle (eigenvalues) and the associated wave functions (eigenfunctions); the wave functions provide a measure of the probability that each particle will appear at different points in space. The theory, first proposed by de Broglie, was developed by Erwin Schrödinger.

wave number The inverse of *wavelength, i.e. the number of cycles executed by a wave in a unit length.

wave power The use of the energy of wave motion in the sea to generate electricity. Wave-power generators of various types have been developed, the best known being the "nodding-duck" type, which consists of a string of floats that bob up and down in the waves. The bobbing motion turns a generator. However only a fraction of this would become electricity. One of the disadvantages of wave power is that it is variable and unpredictable although, like *wind power, its peak output is likely to coincide with peak demand. Another is that since it is sited off the coast it may be obstructive to shipping and difficult to maintain. In addition, the design and construction of generators and transmission lines to work at sea presents a formidable engineering problem.

wax A smooth substance of low melting point 104–176°F (40–80°C) obtained from plants (e.g. *carnauba wax) or animals (e.g. *beeswax, *lanolin) or made synthetically. They consist of esters of higher fatty acids than are found in fats, usually with monohydric alcohols. Mineral waxes also exist, the most common being paraffin wax, which is a mixture of the higher hydrocarbons obtained from the distillation of petroleum. Waxes are used in making polishes, candles, moldings, etc., and in modeling.

waxbill A bird of the *weaverfinch family having a stout waxy-red conical bill. Most waxbills inhabit open grassy regions of Africa. They are 3–6 in (7.5–15 cm) long and typically gray or brown with red, yellow, or brown markings and fine barring on the wings. Many waxbills rear the nestlings of the *whydahs, which lay their eggs in the waxbills' nests.

wax moth A moth whose caterpillars live in the nests of bees and wasps, where they eat refuse, honeycomb, and young host insects. Some are cannibalistic. The bee moth (*Galleria Mellonella*) is the best-known species, having spread to many parts of the world. Chief genera: *Galleria, Achroea.*

waxplant An evergreen climbing plant, *Hoya carnosa*, native to China and Australia. It produces clusters of large fragrant waxy white flowers with pink centers and is cultivated as an ornamental. Other cultivated species include *H. bella*, a dwarf shrub with crimson- or violet-centered waxy white flowers. Family: *Asclepiadaceae*.

waxwing A broad-billed fruit-eating songbird, *Bombycilla garrulus*, occurring in N coniferous forests and birch woods, sometimes migrating south in hard winters. It has a soft plumage, liver-colored above with a reddish crest, a yellow-banded tail, and a black throat and eyestripe. The red tips of the flight feathers resemble sealing wax. Family: *Bombycillidae* (9 species).

wayfaring tree A deciduous shrub, *Viburnum lantana*, growing in woodlands and hedges over much of Europe. Up to 20 ft (6 m) tall, it has oval to heart-shaped toothed leaves and flat-topped clusters of small creamy-white funnel-shaped flowers. The oval fruits ripen from red to black. Family: *Caprifoliaceae*.

Wayland (*or* Weland) In Teutonic mythology, a skilled smith. He was captured and lamed by a Swedish king, Nidudr, who kept him on an island, where he was forced to practice his metalworking for the king. Wayland secretly murdered the king's sons, made ornaments of their skulls, eyes, and teeth, raped the king's daughter, and then revealed all to Nidudr before escaping.

Wayne, Anthony ("Mad Anthony") (1745–96) American Revolutionary War officer and Indian fighter. Wayne was a surveyor and farmer who was briefly active in politics before being commissioned a colonel and assisting Benedict *Arnold in his retreat from Quebec. He held a variety of increasingly responsible commands during the *American Revolution. He was with *Washington in New Jersey and shared the privations of the winter at Valley Forge (1777–78); in 1779 he took Stony Point, N.Y. Wayne was sent south in 1781 and was trapped by Cornwallis's superior force at Green Spring, Va., but succeeded in escaping with his command intact. He then served under General *Greene in Georgia before retiring to farming and business interests. Recalled by Washington in 1792 (as a major general) to command the Army of the West against the Indians, he was victorious at the Battle of Fallen Timbers (1794), securing a treaty that made possible the settlement of Ohio and Indiana. He built Ft Wayne, Ind., and died in Pennsylvania in 1796 while taking possession of abandoned British forts.

Wayne, John (Marion Michael Morrison; 1907–79) US film actor. Following his success in *Stagecoach* (1939) he played the tough hero of numerous classic Westerns including *Red River* (1948), *She Wore a Yellow Ribbon* (1949), *Rio Bravo* (1959), and *True Grit* (1969). He played similar roles in many war films, from *The Sands of Iwo Jima* (1945) to *The Green Berets* (1968). He was awarded a special Academy Award shortly before his death from cancer.

Waziristan A mountainous area in Pakistan, bordering on Afghanistan. The Waziris, a *Pathan tribe who inhabit the area, are noted for their warlike behavior.

weak interaction One of the four fundamental interactions between elementary particles (*see* particle physics), the others being the *strong, *electromagnetic, and *gravitational interactions. The weak interaction is about 10^{10} times weaker than the electromagnetic interaction. It is believed to be generated by the exchange of *virtual particles known as *intermediate vector bosons.

weasel A small carnivorous mammal, *Mustela nivalis*, of Europe, Asia, and N Africa, recently introduced into New Zealand. Growing to about 10 in (25 cm) long, it is long-bodied and short-legged, bright red-brown above with white underparts. Weasels feed on rats, mice, and voles, hunting along hedgerows and ditches and entering burrows. They swim well but do not climb. Family: *Mustelidae*.

weather. *See* meteorology.

JOHN WAYNE *He is seen here (with Richard Widmark, right) as Davy Crockett, hero of* The Alamo *(1960), which he also directed and produced.*

weathering The physical and chemical disintegration of the rocks of the earth's crust on exposure to the atmosphere. Most rocks were formed under conditions in which temperatures and pressures were higher than those to which they are now exposed; weathering is largely a response to lower temperatures and pressures and the effects of air and water.

weaverbird A small songbird belonging to a mainly tropical Old World family (*Ploceidae*; 132 species) noted for its nest-building activities. Most species build domed nests with long entrance tunnels, often elaborately woven with loops and knots to form a durable structure. Some species build huge communal nests—the nest of the sociable weaver (*Philetairus socius*) reaches about 7 ft (2 m) across and houses 20–30 pairs of birds. Weavers are seed eaters with stout conical bills and variously colored plumage. *See also* sparrow; quelea.

weaverfinch A small finchlike seed-eating songbird belonging to a family (*Estrildidae*; 108 species) occurring in tropical regions of Africa, SE Asia, and Australasia. Weaverfinches have large conical bills and are usually brightly colored. *See* avadavat; grassfinch; mannikin; waxbill; zebra finch.

weaving The process of interlacing two or more *yarns at right angles to produce a fabric. The equipment used is called a loom, which is first set up with a series of longitudinal threads (warp). In plain weave, alternate warp threads are raised and lowered by means of wires or cords (heddles) to allow the crosswire threads (weft), wound onto a bobbin (shuttle), to pass between them. Different kinds of weave, such as *twill and herringbone, are made by altering the pattern of interlacing. Hand looms have been in use all over the world since ancient times. Power looms, in which the shuttle is moved across the warp automatically, were invented by Edmund *Cartwright in 1786; many improvements have since been made to increase the speed of travel of the shuttle and to enable more complicated designs to be woven.

Webb, Sidney (James), Baron Passfield (1859–1947) British economist and socialist. He helped to organize the *Fabian Society in 1884 and was one of the founders of the London School of Economics (1895). He initiated many educational reforms and, after entering Parliament in 1922, held several important government posts. His wife **Beatrice (Potter) Webb** (1858–1943), collaborated with him on a number of books. Their work and writings had a lasting influence on the development of social policies within and outside the Labour party.

WEAVERBIRD *Communal nests of the sociable weaver, seen from below. The birds, which are found in SW Africa, build individual nests close together then cover them with a common roof.*

weber (Wb) The *SI unit of magnetic flux equal to the flux linking a circuit of one turn that produces an electromotive force of one volt when reduced uniformly to zero in one second. Named for Wilhelm Weber (1804–91).

Weber, Carl Maria von (1786–1826) German composer, a pupil of Michael Haydn (1737–1806) and Abbé Vogler (1749–1814). His most successful opera, *Der Freischütz* (1821), based on a German fairy story, was the first opera in the German romantic tradition. The operas *Euryanthe* (1823) and *Oberon* (1826) were less successful. Weber also composed a large number of orchestral works and much piano music.

Weber, Ernst Heinrich (1795–1878) German physiologist, who became professor at Leipzig University in 1818. He is remembered for his discovery that the experience of differences in the intensity of human sensations (pressure, temperature, light, sound) depends on percentage differences in the stimuli rather than absolute differences. This is called the Weber-Fechner Law because Weber's discovery was popularized by Gustav Fechner (1801–87). His brother **Wilhelm Eduard Weber** (1804–91) was professor of physics at Göttingen University. He worked with *Gauss on magnetism and introduced a logical system of electrical units. The SI unit of magnetic flux is named for him.

Weber, Max (1864–1920) German sociologist, who was one of the founding fathers of modern *sociology. His best-known work, *The Protestant Ethic and* *the Spirit of Capitalism* (1904), relates the emergence of a particular type of economic system to the effects of religious values. In attempting to explain why capitalism developed first in Europe, he produced extensive studies in comparative sociology. His *Methodology of the Social Sciences* (1904) remains a major text, as does his account of social and economic organization, *Wirtschaft und Gesellschaft* (1922). Bureaucracy and secularization are also recurrent themes. He was politically active during the last years of his life and served on the committee that drafted the constitution of the *Weimar Republic.

Webern, Anton von (1883–1945) Austrian composer. He studied with Schoenberg and earned his living as a conductor and teacher. Webern adopted the technique of *serialism, as defined by Schoenberg in 1924. His compositions, which are characterized by great brevity, extreme dynamic contrast, and dissonant counterpoint, include *Concerto for Nine Solo Instruments* (1934) and a string quartet (1938). His music has greatly influenced Boulez, Stravinsky, and many other composers.

webspinner A brownish soft-bodied insect, 0.16–0.28 in (4–7 mm) long, belonging to the mainly tropical order *Embioptera* (150 species). Biting jaws are used by the wingless females to feed on dead plant material; the males, which are mostly winged, are carnivores. Webspinners live in communities and make silken webs and tunnels under stones or in soil. The young are cared for by the females.

Webster, Daniel (1782–1852) US statesman and orator. Webster graduated from Dartmouth College in 1801 and was admitted to the bar in 1805. Opposing Jefferson's policies and the War of 1812, he was elected to the House of Representatives in 1812. In 1816 he moved to Boston and gained fame as a brilliant lawyer and orator. He was elected to the House again in 1822 and the Senate in 1827. In his noted reply to Hayne (1830) he defended the Union against states' rights and urged "Liberty *and* Union, now and forever, one and inseparable!" Webster became secretary of state under Harrison and Tyler and was responsible for the Webster-Ashburton Treaty. He left the cabinet (1843), rejoined the Senate (1845), and opposed the acquisition of Texas and war with Mexico. He defended Henry Clay's Compromise of 1850 despite the unpopular Fugitive Slave Act. He was secretary of state again (1850) under Fillmore and died in 1852, having been instrumental in holding the Union together and advancing the ideal of a strong federal government.

Webster, John (c. 1580–c. 1625) English dramatist. Little is known of his life. He collaborated with Thomas Dekker and other dramatists. His own major plays are *The White Devil* (1612) and *The Duchess of Malfi* (c. 1613). Despite their typically Jacobean preoccupation with lust and violence, the plays are distinguished by their poetic intensity and psychological insight.

Webster, Noah (1758–1843) US lexicographer and author of numerous books on English. His *American Dictionary of the English Language* (1828) took over 20 years to compile and was the most influential of all American dictionaries. Webster also did much to standardize American spelling.

Webster-Ashburton Treaty A treaty negotiated in 1842 by Daniel Webster (US) and Lord Ashburton (Britain), which settled the disputed northeastern boundary between Maine and New Brunswick, Canada.

Weddell Sea A large inlet of the S Atlantic Ocean in Antarctica, between the Antarctic Peninsula and Coats Land. Its S section is covered by the Ronne and Filchner Ice Shelves. It is named for the British explorer and seal hunter James Weddell (1787–1834).

Wedekind, Frank (1864–1918) German dramatist. A vivid personality, he was also an actor, singer, poet, and essayist. His tragedy *Frühlings Erwachen* (1891), produced by *Reinhardt (1905), caused a scandal by criticizing the bourgeois attitude to sex. Berg's opera *Lulu* (1937) is based on his plays *Erdgeist* (1895) and *Die Büchse der Pandora* (1904).

Wedgwood, Josiah (1730–95) British potter and industrialist. Trained under his brother Thomas, he was a partner of Thomas Whieldon (1719–95) from 1754 until 1759, when he opened his own factory in Staffordshire, England. In 1769 he opened a new factory where he also built a village for his workmen, displaying his interest in social welfare. Employing leading designers and artists, Wedgwood popularized the neoclassical taste in pottery and was a leading exporter to the Continent.

weed Any plant growing where it is not wanted, especially in areas cultivated or tended by man. Weeds are most important in agriculture, competing with crop plants for space, light, and nutrients, reducing yields, and contaminating the corp. The major weeds of temperate regions include docks, thistles, nettles, shepherd's purse, groundsel, dandelions, couch grass, and wild oats. Some, such as ragwort, may be toxic to grazing livestock. Weeds may also damage paths and buildings and choke waterways.

Weed control has traditionally relied on repeated soil cultivation and crop rotation; modern methods involve use of selective and nonselective *herbicides and, in a few cases, *biological control.

weever A slender carnivorous fish of the genus *Trachinus*, found in sandy bottoms of European coastal waters. Up to 1.8 in (4.6 cm) long, it has an upward slanting mouth, eyes near the top of its head, and venomous spines on the gill covers and first dorsal fin, which can inflict painful wounds. Family: *Trachinidae*; order: *Perciformes*.

weevil A beetle, also called a snout beetle, belonging to the largest family (*Curculionidae*; about 60,000 species) in the animal kingdom, Most weevils are small (less than 0.25 in [6 mm]) and their mouthparts are at the tip of a beaklike rostrum, which can sometimes exceed the body length. Many species are serious pests of gardens, crops, and stored grains and cereals, e.g. the *boll weevil, the grain weevil (*Sitophilus granarius*), and the rice weevil (*S. oryzae*). The larvae are particularly destructive, burrowing or boring into all parts of the plant but especially into wood, fruit, and seeds. *See also* curculio.

Wegener, Alfred Lothar (1880–1930) German geologist, who (in 1912) proposed the theory of *continental drift to account for his observations of the movements of land masses. Wegener also demonstrated how bombardment by meteors could have caused lunar craters. He died while on his fourth expedition to Greenland.

Weigela A genus of E Asian flowering shrubs (12 species), including several ornamentals, often called Japanese honeysuckles. Up to 13 ft (4 m) high, they have simple leaves and small clusters of funnel-shaped white to red flowers, about 1.3 in (3.5 cm) long, with four or five spreading lobes. The fruit is a long narrow seed pod. Family: *Caprifoliaceae*.

weight. *See* mass and weight.

weightlessness The condition in which a body possesses no weight. Such a body still possesses mass but its weight (*see* mass and weight) can become negligible when the gravitational field is extremely weak, as for example in space. It can also be produced artificially by creating a force that is equal and opposite to gravity. The physiological effects of weightlessness are important in long space flights and are countered by pressure suits, exercise routines, and correct control of cabin pressure, temperature, and humidity.

weight lifting A sport in which men and women compete to lift weighted barbells. In the most common form of competition the contestants make three attempts in each of two styles, the snatch and the clean and jerk. The weights, of their own choice, can be increased but not reduced. Power lifting requires different styles—the squat, dead lift, and bench press.

Weil, Simone (1909–43) French mystic and philosopher. An active socialist in the 1930s, she worked briefly in a car factory to gain insight into working-class problems and served in a nonmilitary capacity on the Republican side in the Spanish Civil War. She also taught philosophy at secondary schools until 1938. After a mystical experience she became a convinced Roman Catholic, although she refused baptism. During World War II she worked for the Free French Resistance in London. Her writings on spiritual and social themes, published posthumously, include *Waiting for God* (1951) and *The Need for Roots* (1952).

Weill, Kurt (1900–50) German composer. He studied under Busoni in Berlin. His collaboration with Bertolt *Brecht began with the opera *The Rise and Fall of the City of Mahagonny* (1927), a satirical portrayal of American life. Their most famous work was *The Threepenny Opera* (1928), a modernistic version of *The Beggar's Opera* (*see* Gay, John). The rise of Nazism forced Weill to leave Germany; he settled in the US in 1935 and wrote successfully for Broadway musicals. His wife, the singer Lotte *Lenya, frequently performed in his works.

Weimar 50 59N 11 15E A city in S Germany, on the Ilm River near Erfurt. Weimar has associations with Goethe, Schiller, and Liszt and was the cultural center of Germany in the late 18th and early 19th centuries. It was the capital of the grand duchy of Saxe-Weimar-Eisenach (1815–1918). In 1919 the German National Assembly met in the city and drew up the constitution of the new *Weimar Republic. Population (1990): 80,000.

weimaraner (*or* weimeraner) A breed of dog developed by the nobility of Weimar, Germany, for hunting and retrieving game. It is a lithe dog with drooping ears and a short slender tail. The short sleek coat is silver-gray or mouse-gray. Height: 24–27 in (61–69 cm) (dogs); 22–25 in (56–64 cm) (bitches).

Weimar Republic The government of Germany from 1919 to 1933. Named for the town in which the new German constitution was formulated, the republic faced constant political and economic crises and was finally overthrown by Hitler.

Weismann, August Friedrich Leopold (1834–1914) German biologist, who in 1883 proposed that heredity was based upon the transfer, from generation to generation, of a substance—germ plasm—with a definite molecular constitution. Weismann also predicted that germ plasm must undergo a special nuclear division to produce gametes for the next generation. Weismann's ideas have since been generally accepted and he is regarded as one of the founders of modern genetics.

Weiss, Peter (1916–82) German dramatist and novelist. After leaving Nazi Germany, he settled in Sweden (1939). His plays include the highly successful *Marat/Sade* (short title; 1964), set in a lunatic asylum, and *The Investigation* (1965), recreating the Auschwitz trials.

Weissmuller, Johnny (1904–84) US swimmer, who won five Olympic gold medals (three in 1924 and two in 1928) and set 24 world records. He was the first man to swim 325 ft (100 m) in less than a minute (1922). He later became the first Tarzan of sound films (1932–48) and had a successful television series.

Weizmann, Chaim (Azriel) (1874–1952) Israeli statesman; the first president of Israel (1949–52). Born in Russia, he settled in England in 1904 and worked as a chemist. Leader of the English Zionist movement, his discovery (1916) of a manufacturing process for the production of acetone, which contributed to the British war effort, facilitated the Zionist negotiations with the British Government that led to the *Balfour Declaration (1917). His moderate policies as president (1920–31, 1935–46) of the World Zionist movement brought the hostility of Zionist extremists but he played an important part in the establishment of Israel in 1948.

Weld, Theodore Dwight (1803–95) US abolitionist. Influenced by revivalist preacher Charles G. Finney, he became an evangelist and preached both temperance and the abolition of slavery. He joined the American Anti-Slavery Society and married abolitionist Angelina Grimké. He wrote antislavery tracts, including *American Slavery As It Is* (1839), which influenced Harriet Beecher *Stowe's *Uncle Tom's Cabin*. A moderate, Weld led an antislavery lobby in Washington before retiring to school teaching.

welding A method of joining metals by melting the two parts together, pressing them together, or both (*see also* soldering). In forge welding, which is used to make steel chains, the two parts are heated and then hammered together. Electrical methods use an electric current passed through two metal surfaces in close contact. The temperature rises at the interface because of the high electrical resistance and welds the surfaces together. In spot welding, point contact electrodes press the metal surfaces together. In seam welding, the electrodes are in the form of rollers. Both these methods are used in mass production. Gas welding uses an oxyacetylene flame to heat the metal and a rod of metallic filler material. Molten filler material runs between the two heated edges and solidifies to form the joint. Another method, similar to gas welding, is electric-arc welding. The filler rod forms one electrode and the metal itself another. Current passes by arcing or sparking across the gap between them, melting the rod and the metal edges. Arc welding is generally used for thicker pieces of metal and higher temperatures than gas welding and for small delicate jobs *lasers have been used. A great deal of skill is required to produce a strong reliable weld. The results are often examined by X-rays or other means in, for example, pressure vessels, where reliability is crucial.

Welensky, Sir Roy (1907–91) Rhodesian statesman; prime minister of the Federation of *Rhodesia and Nyasaland (1956–63). A professional boxer, he was chairman (1953–63) of the Railway Workers Union in Northern Rhodesia. Welensky was largely responsible for the creation of the Federation but his aim to establish a harmonious multiracial society was unfulfilled.

welfare state A state that provides a minimum level of well-being for all its members, especially the most vulnerable: the young, the old, the unemployed, and the sick. The UK and the Scandinavian countries are the most advanced in providing these services.

Welkom 27 59S 26 44E A town in South Africa, in N central Orange Free State. It was founded in 1947 and rapidly developed after the discovery of gold. Population (1980 est): 176,608.

Welland Ship Canal A canal in S central Canada, in S Ontario bypassing Niagara Falls. Part of the St Lawrence Seaway, it links Lake Erie to Lake Ontario and has a total lift of 326 ft (99 m). Length: 28 mi (45 km).

Weller, Thomas Huckle (1915–   ) US bacteriologist and virologist. Weller received his medical degree from Harvard Medical School, where he worked with Dr. John Frederick Enders on *in vitro* (test tube) virus cultivation. After service in the Army Medical Corps (1942–46), Weller returned to work with Enders and Dr. Frederick C. Robbins on the tissue culture method whereby the virus for poliomyelitis was developed *in vitro* in non-nerve tissue. For this work, which made possible the development of the polio vaccine, Weller, Enders, and Robbins shared the Nobel Prize in physiology or medicine in 1954.

Welles, (George) Orson (1915–85) US film actor and director. After establishing his reputation as a theater and radio producer he went to Hollywood in 1940. His first film, *Citizen Kane* (1941), became one of the most famous of all time. His other films include *The Magnificent Ambersons* (1942), *Macbeth* (1948), *The Trial* (1962), and *Chimes at Midnight* (1966). As a film actor he is best remembered for the title part in *The Third Man* (1949).

Wellesley, Richard Colley, Marquess. *See* Wellington, Arthur Wellesley, 1st duke of.

Wellesz, Egon (1885–1974) Austrian composer and musicologist. He studied in Vienna under Schoenberg and his complex compositions employed *serialism.

Wellington 41 17S 174 47E The capital of New Zealand, a port in S North Island on Cook Strait. It became the seat of central government in 1865 and is now the commercial and communications center of New Zealand. Notable buildings include the Government Building (1876), one of the world's largest wooden buildings, and Victoria University (1897). A major manufacturing center, it has engineering, food-processing, and textile industries; the chief exports are wool, meat, dairy products, and fruit. Population (1991): 149,598.

Wellington, Arthur Wellesley, 1st duke of (1769–1852) British general and statesman, known as the Iron Duke; prime minister (1828–30). In 1787 he entered the army and in 1799 went to India. In the Napoleonic Wars he was responsible for victory (1814) against the French in the *Peninsular War, for which he was made a duke. He commanded British, German, and Dutch forces at Waterloo (1815), where he and the Prussian general *Blücher finally defeated Napoleon. He represented Britain at the Congresses of *Aix-la-Chapelle (1818) and Verona (1822). As prime minister he came to support *Catholic emancipation. Wellington's opposition to parliamentary reform remained firm and brought about his resignation under pressure. He was commander in chief of the British army from 1827 to 1828 and again from 1842 to 1852.

Wellingtonia. *See* sequoia.

Wells, Henry (1805–78) US businessman, who with **William Fargo** (1818–81) and others founded Wells, Fargo and Co. (1852). An express business, it carried mail to and from the newly developed West. It also controlled banks and later ran a stagecoach service.

Wells, H(erbert) G(eorge) (1866–1946) British novelist. After working as a shopkeeper's apprentice and a teacher, he studied biology with T. H. Huxley. He won literary success with *The Time Machine* (1895) and other science-fiction novels and increased his popularity with a series of comic social novels. A member of the Fabian Society, he engaged in frequent controversy with G. B. Shaw and others concerning social and political issues. He wrote distinguished theoretical works, including *The Outline of History* (1920) and *The Shape of Things to Come* (1933).

wels A large nocturnal predatory *catfish, *Silurus glanis*, also called waller, found in fresh waters of Europe and W Asia. Up to 15 ft (4.5 m) long, it has three pairs of barbels, a long anal fin, and is usually mottled olive-green to blue-black with a paler belly.

HENRY WELLS *Wells, Fargo, and Co. ran a perilous mail and stagecoach service across the US.*

Wels 48 10N 14 02E A city in N central Austria, in Upper Austria. It has a castle in which Emperor Maximilian I died. Industries include agricultural machinery, textiles, and food processing. Population (1981): 51,033.

Welsh literature The most important literature written in the Welsh language is poetry belonging to the early and medieval periods prior to the anglicization that began in the 16th century. Much of the poetry of the *Cynfeirdd*, or early poets of the 6th century, is anonymous. The works of the period are preserved in the "Four Ancient Books of Wales," manuscripts dating from the 12th, 13th and 14th centuries. The *Gogynfeirdd*, or medieval poets, belong to the Norman period (up to the loss of independence in 1282). These poets were *bards, who held important offices in the courts of Welsh princes; Cynddelw (12th century) is regarded as the greatest of them. The 14th century was dominated by Wales's greatest poet, *Dafydd ap Gwilym, who introduced techniques and a sensuous richness of metaphor that influenced all subsequent Welsh poetry. The first record of an *eisteddfod dates from the 15th century, although it is believed that such bardic contests must date from a much earlier period. The 16th century marks the beginning of a decline in the use of Welsh, although the language has recently been revived and continues to be used as a literary medium.

Welsh pony One of two breeds of pony originating in Wales. The Welsh mountain pony, used for riding, has a compact muscular body with short strong legs and a profuse mane and tail. It has been used to develop the larger Welsh riding pony, which is a popular children's mount. Both may be any solid color. Height: Mountain pony: up to 12 hands (4 ft; 1.22 m); riding pony: up to 13.5 hands (4.5 ft; 1.37 m).

Welsh poppy A perennial herbaceous plant, *Mecanopsis cambrica*, up to 15 in (38 cm) tall and found in damp regions of W Europe. It has fernlike deeply lobed leaves and bears solitary yellow flowers, up to 3 in (7.5 cm) across. Cultivated ornamental forms may have either single or double orange or yellow flowers.

Welty, Eudora (1909–) US author. Acclaimed author of short stories and novels, Welty received six O. Henry awards and won the Pulitzer Prize in 1973 for *The Optimist's Daughter* (1972). Other works include *Delta Wedding* (1946), *The Golden Apples* (1949), *The Ponder Heart* (1954), *The Shoe Bird* (1964), and *Losing Battles* (1970). Her autobiography, *One Writer's Beginnings*, appeared in 1984.

welwitschia An unusual *gymnosperm plant, *Welwitschia mirabilis*, confined to the deserts of SW Africa. The very short stem bears two strap-shaped waxy leaves, which grow continuously and are up to 40 in (1 m) long. The long taproot absorbs water from the desert subsoil, and small conelike flowers produce winged seeds, which are dispersed by the wind. Individual plants may live for more than a hundred years. Order: *Gnetales*.

Wenceslas (1361–1419) King of Bohemia (1363–1402, 1404–19) and German king and Holy Roman Emperor (1376–1400). An extremely weak king, in Bohemia he was twice imprisoned by rebellious nobles (1393–94, 1402) and briefly deposed. In Germany, princes deposed him in 1400 but he retained the title of king until his death.

Wenceslas, St (d. 929 AD) Duke of Bohemia (?924–29), famous for his piety. Wenceslas's unpopular submission to the German king Henry the Fowler gave rise to a conspiracy of nobles, who incited Wenceslas's brother to assassinate him. He became Bohemia's patron saint.

Wenchow. *See* Wenzhou.

wentletrap A *gastropod mollusk of the worldwide family *Epitoniidae* (about 200 species), often found in association with sea anemones and corals; 0.8–4 in (2–10 cm) long, wentletraps have □shells with long spires, usually white but sometimes tinged with brown (that of the precious wentletrap [*Epitonium scalare*] has long been prized by collectors). They can produce a purple substance used as a dye.

Wentworth, Thomas. *See* Strafford, Thomas Wentworth, 1st Earl of.

Wenzhou (Wen-chou *or* Wenchow) 28 02N 120 40E A port in SE China, in Zhejiang province on the Ou Jiang (River). It is the site of many historic buildings. A trading center, it has processed food, paper, and handicraft industries. Population (1991 est): 402,000.

werewolf In folklore, a man who becomes a wolf by night and preys on humans. Some werewolves, who have no power over their condition because it is hereditary or the result of a spell or another werewolf's bite, only change form during a full moon, a transformation known as lycanthropy. Belief in werewolves is worldwide and of ancient origin. In countries where wolves are rare, some men are believed to turn into other fierce animals.

Werfel, Franz (1890–1945) Austrian Jewish poet, dramatist, and novelist. A leading expressionist, his pacifism and desire for human brotherhood are reflected in his poetry and plays, including *Der Spiegelmensch* (1920). His later novels include *The Song of Bernadette* (1941).

Wergeland, Henrik Arnold (1808–45) Norwegian poet, known as the "uncrowned king" of Norway because of his involvement in nationalist politics. He is best known for his lyric poetry and for an epic on the Creation, entitled *Skabelsen, Mennesket, og Messias* (*Creation, Humanity, and Messiah*; 1830).

wergild The sum payable as compensation in Anglo-Saxon England to the family of a slain man by his assassin or the latter's kin. The amount was regulated by law according to the status and nationality of the victim and varied in different regions.

Weser River A river in NW Germany. It flows NW from Münden, through Bremen, to the North Sea at Bremerhaven. The Mitelland Canal connects it to the Rhine and Elbe rivers. Length: 296 mi (477 km).

WEREWOLF *Reports of werewolves were particularly common in 16th-century France. The illustration claims to be an exact representation of one.*

Wesley, John (1703–91) British religious leader, founder of *Methodism. As a student at Oxford and later, Wesley was one of a group nicknamed "Methodists," who sought to live disciplined religious lives. His younger brother **Charles Wesley** (1707–88) was also a member. The brothers, both ordained, sailed to Georgia as missionaries in 1735, but returned disillusioned in 1738. In the same year both experienced a spiritual awakening while attending meetings of the *Moravians as a result of which they toured the country preaching a message of repentance, faith, and love. Anglican opposition forced them out of the churches into open-air meetings; they were also obliged to organize societies for their many working-class converts. They did not intend to form a new denomination, the Wesleyan Methodist Church being organized only after their death. John was a tireless writer and administrator, while Charles was the author of many well-known hymns.

Wessex The kingdom of the West *Saxons, under which Anglo-Saxon England was united in the 9th century. Wessex centered on the upper Thames basin and from the late 6th century expanded southwestward. Its expansion northward was frustrated by the power of Mercia, which was supreme until Egbert, king of Wessex (802–39), destroyed Mercian ascendancy in 825 and made possible the subsequent union of England under the leadership of the Wessex king, Alfred the Great.

West, Benjamin (1738–1820) US painter. After achieving acclaim as a portraitist in New York, he visited Italy (1760–63), where he was influenced by *neoclassicism, before settling permanently in England. There, patronized by George III and exhibiting at the Royal Academy, of which he became president in 1792, he made his name as a history painter, particularly with his controversially realistic *Death of General Wolfe*.

West, Mae (1892–1980) US actress. Her unashamedly sensual performances in vaudeville, the theater, and films established her as an international sex symbol during the 1930s, although she is perhaps best known for her comic talent. Her early stage successes included *Sex* (1926) and *Diamond Lil* (1928). Her films, many of which she wrote, included *She Done Him Wrong* (1933), *I'm No Angel* (1933), and *My Little Chickadee* (1939).

West, Nathaniel (Nathan Weinstein; 1903–40) US novelist. The best known of his four short novels are *Miss Lonely-hearts* (1933), about an advice columnist, and *The Day of the Locust* (1939), a satire of the grotesque world of Hollywood, where he worked as a scriptwriter. He was killed in an automobile accident.

West, Dame Rebecca (Cicely Isabel Fairfield, 1892–1983) British novelist and journalist. She was the author of several novels, including *The Thinking Reed* (1936) and *The Birds Fall Down* (1966). Among a number of books of political journalism are *The Meaning of Treason* (1949) and *A Train of Powder* (1955), which includes her reports on the Nuremberg trials.

West Atlantic languages A subgroup of the *Niger-Congo family, spoken in Guinea and Senegal. It includes the languages Wolof and *Fulani, and, despite being a small group, is found over a wide area since the speakers of West Atlantic languages are mainly nomadic.

West Bank A territory in the Middle East, on the W bank of the Jordan River. It comprises the hills of Judea and Samaria (which Israel considers to be of crucial strategic importance with regard to the security of its coastal settlements) and part of the city of *Jerusalem. Formerly part of *Palestine, it was left in Arab hands after partition (1948), became part of Jordan following the ceasefire of 1949, and was occupied by Israeli forces in 1967. Israel has since been under pressure from the Arabs, especially the *Palestine Liberation Organization, to withdraw from the territory and allow an autonomous Palestinian state to be set up. In the Camp David agreement (1978) proposals were put forward for future negotiations leading to the establishment of a self-governing authority in the West Bank. Area: about 2320 sq mi (6000 sq km).

West Bengal A state in NE India, stretching along the Bangladeshi W border from the Ganges delta N into the Himalayan foothills. Rice, jute, tea, and other crops are farmed. Fishing, forestry, and mining are also important, as well as industry (especially engineering, steel, chemicals, and motor cars). Bengali cul-

West Highland white terrier

ture remains very strong. Area: 33,911 sq mi (87,853 sq km). Population (1991): 67,982,732. Capital: Calcutta. *See also* Bengal.

West Bromwich 52 31N 1 59W An industrial city in central England, in the West Midlands. Metal goods (kitchen utensils, springs, nails, scales) are manufactured, as well as chemical and paint. Population (1981): 154,930.

westerlies The chief winds blowing between 30° and 70° latitude. Their name derives from the prevailing wind direction; in the N hemisphere winds blow mainly from the SW and in the S hemisphere, from the NW.

Western Australia The largest state of Australia, bordering on the Indian Ocean, Timor Sea, and Great Australian Bight. It is mainly an arid undulating plateau with the Great Sandy Desert, the Gibson Desert, and the Great Victoria Desert in the interior. In the SW is the Darling Range, a scarp behind the city of Perth (where most of the population is concentrated). In the N the broken edge of the plateau is marked by the Kimberleys. Agricultural activities include dairy farming, lumbering, and the cultivation of citrus fruits, wheat, and wine grapes in the extreme SW. Western Australia is rich in mineral resources; bauxite in the Darling Range, nickel in the S central part, oil near Barrow Island off the NW coast, and gold in the SW around Kalgoorlie. Probably the most important discoveries have been the huge deposits of ferrous minerals in the NW. Industry is located chiefly around Perth and includes the manufacture of iron and steel, chemicals, textiles, and oil refining. Area: 975,920 sq mi (2,527 sq km). Population (1992 est): 1,666,700. Capital: Perth.

Western European Union An organization formed in 1955 by the UK, Belgium, France, Italy, Luxembourg, the Netherlands, and West Germany to coordinate defense policy and equipment and to cooperate in political and other spheres. It succeeded the *European Defense Community and collaborates closely with the *North Atlantic Treaty Organization.

Westerns A US genre of popular novels and films set in the American West during that region's development in the 19th century. Its rigid conventions of plot and character invested the struggles of pioneers and the battles between lawmen and outlaws with mythical significance. Notable writers include Owen *Wister, the prolific Zane *Grey, and Louis L'Amour (1908–88). The first film Western was *The Great Train Robbery* (1903). Other notable films include *Stagecoach* (1939), *Red River* (1948), and *High Noon* (1952); directors who have specialized in this genre include John *Ford and Howard *Hawks.

Western Sahara (name until 1975: Spanish Sahara) A territory in NW Africa, bordering on the Atlantic Ocean, Mauritania, and Morocco. It consists chiefly of desert and has phosphate deposits (the chief export) SE of El Aaiún. *History*: in 1884 Spain claimed a protectorate over the S coastal zone of Río de Oro and in 1958 Spanish Sahara became a province of Spain with its capital at El Aaiún. In 1976 Spain withdrew from the province and it was partitioned between Mauritania and Morocco. Since then the Polisario Front, an organization engaged in guerrilla activities to establish Western Sahara as the independent Saharan Arab Democratic Republic, has been supported by Algeria. Mauritania withdrew from the S part of Western Sahara in 1979 and it came under Moroccan occupation with active opposition from the Polisario Front and Algeria. Area: 102,680 sq mi (226,000 sq km). Population (1992 est): 209,000.

West Germany. *See* Germany.

West Highland white terrier A breed of dog thought to have originated in Argyll, Scotland. Known affectionately as the westie, it is compact and alert-looking with short legs and a long double-layered pure white coat. Height: about 11 in (28 cm).

West Indies An archipelago extending in a curved chain for over 1500 mi (2400 km) from the Florida peninsula in North America to the coast of Venezuela enclosing the Caribbean Sea. It is often subdivided into the *Greater Antilles, the *Lesser Antilles, and the *Bahamas. The islands are chiefly of volcanic origin but some, including the Bahamas and Antigua, are composed largely of coral. Hurricanes occur frequently, often causing serious damage. The West Indian people are of mixed origin but the descendants of African slaves form the largest group. The original Arawak and Carib Indians have virtually disappeared, although some Caribs remain on Dominica. *Economy*: sugarcane cultivation has been of importance throughout the West Indies since the beginning of colonization. Many islands also grow a major subsidiary crop, such as tobacco, bananas, spices, or coffee. The few mineral deposits include asphalt from Trinidad's unique Pitch Lake and bauxite from Hispaniola and Jamaica. *History*: Columbus discovered the archipelago in 1492 and named it in the belief that he had found the western route to India. The Spanish, who were the first Europeans to settle, introduced the cultivation of sugar and imported African slaves to work the plantations. The slave trade was maintained until its abolition during the 19th century. In 1958 the Federation of the West Indies was created, comprising Antigua, Dominica, Grenada, Jamaica, Montserrat, St Kitts and Nevis and Anguilla, St Lucia, St Vincent, and Trinidad and Tobago. The federal parliament was situated at Port-of-Spain, Trinidad, but following the withdrawal of Jamaica and then Trinidad and Tobago the Federation was dissolved in 1962. However, further attempts were made at regional economic integration by what became the *Caribbean Community. In 1967 the noncolonial status of associated state was adopted by Antigua, Dominica, Grenada, St Kitts-Nevis-Anguilla, St Lucia, and by St Vincent in 1969. Grenada became independent in 1974, Dominica in 1978, St Lucia and St Vincent in 1979, and St Kitts-Nevis in 1983. Area: over 91,000 sq mi (235,000 sq km).

Westinghouse, George (1846–1914) US mechanical engineer, inventor, and manufacturer. After training in his father's machine shop and serving in the Civil War, Westinghouse settled in Pittsburgh and invented (1869) the air brake for railroad cars, which made high-speed railroad travel safe. On the basis of this success, he organized the Westinghouse Air Brake Company and developed railroad switching and signaling systems. He developed a safe system for transporting natural gas, and a system for using alternating current for electrical power. To promote the latter he formed Westinghouse Electric Company, which grew to be a leading manufacturer of electrical equipment.

West Irian (Indonesian name: Irian Jaya) A province in E Indonesia comprising W *New Guinea. Mountainous and densely forested with coastal swamps, it is largely undeveloped although it possesses important mineral resources including oil, nickel, and copper. Formerly under Dutch rule, it was transferred to Indonesia in 1963. Area: 161,000 sq mi (416,990 sq km). Population (1990): 1,641,000. Capital: Jajapura.

West Jersey Name given to the W part of the New Jersey colony under the Quintipartite Deed of 1676. The colony had been settled by the Swedes and the Dutch before the English took control and divided it into the two proprietorships. West Jersey was granted to Lord John Berkeley, who sold out to Edward Byllinge, who in turn sold most of West Jersey to a Quaker group. In 1702, East and West Jersey were combined into the Province of New Jersey.

Westmeath (Irish name: Contae Na Hiarmhidhe) A country in the central Republic of Ireland, in Leinster. Predominantly low lying with areas of bog, much of the land is under pasture. Agriculture consists chiefly of cattle fattening and dairy farming. Area: 681 sq mi (1764 sq km). Population: 59,885. County town: Millingar.

Westminster Abbey A historic abbey church in the city of Westminster in greater London, England. The present building was begun in 1245 and since William I, every English monarch (with two exceptions—Edward V and Edward VIII) has been crowned in Westminster Abbey and many are buried there. The Coronation Chair, first used in 1307, stands there upon the Stone of Scone, captured by Edward I from the Scots in 1296. Other notable features include Poets' Corner, where Chaucer, Spenser, Dryden, Tennyson, Dickens, Browning, Kipling, and many others are buried or have memorials.

WESTMINSTER ABBEY

Weston-super-Mare 51 21N 2 59W A resort in SW England, on the Bristol Channel. Originally a fishing village, it developed as a resort in the 19th century. Population (1981): 57,980.

Westphalia A region of NW Germany, approximating present-day Nordrhein-Westfalen. By the 12th century Westphalia comprised many small principalities and in the 18th century came largely under Prussian control. During the period 1807–13 Prussian Westphalian territories became the kingdom of Westphalia, which Napoleon placed under the rule of his brother Jérôme Bonaparte. The Congress of Vienna (1815) dissolved the kingdom and restored most of Westphalia to Prussia.

Westphalia, Peace of (1648) The agreements, negotiated in Osnabrück and Münster (Westphalia), that ended the *Thirty Years' War. The peace marked the end of the supremacy in Europe of the Holy Roman Empire and the emergence of France (which gained the bishoprics of Metz, Toul, and Verdun and also Alsace) as a dominant power (*see also* Pyrenees, Treaty of). It recognized the sovereignty of the German states, the Swiss Confederation, and the Netherlands, previously subject to the Empire, and granted W Pomerania to Sweden. Lutherans, Calvinists, and Roman Catholics were given equal rights.

West Point 41 23N 73 58W A military reservation in New York state. It is the site of the *United States Military Academy (1802).

West Virginia A state in the E central US, bordered by Kentucky and Ohio (W and NW), Pennsylvania and Maryland (NE), and Virginia (E and S). It consists of a ridge and valley region (the Great Appalachian Valley) in the E and the rugged Appalachian Plateau, which constitutes the remaining two-thirds of the state. Most of the larger cities lie on the Ohio River in the W. Although predominantly a rural state, manufacturing and mining (the state is the foremost US producer of bituminous coal) are important. The principal manufactures are chemicals, primary metals, and stone and clay products. The state's farmers concentrate on livestock products. A growing tourist industry is based upon the state's spectacular scenery and varied recreational facilities. *History*: first inhabited by the Mound Builders, the area was sparsely populated when European traders and explorers penetrated it in the late 1600s. German and Scots-Irish settlers fought for land with the Indians and the French. After the Revolution, the area became part of Virginia; it refused to secede with the state, and became West Virginia on joining the Union as a separate state in 1863. Area: 24,181 sq mi (62,628 sq km). Population (1990): 1,793,477. Capital: Charleston.

wet rot The decay that affects timber with a relatively high moisture content, caused by the cellar fungus (*Coniophora cerebella*) and characterized by the formation of a dark surface mass. Treatment is by drying affected timbers, and wet rot is prevented by the application of tar-based preservatives, such as creosote. *Compare* dry rot.

Wexford (Irish name: Contae Loch Garman) A county in the SE Republic of Ireland, in Leinster bordering on the Irish Sea. It was the first Irish county to be colonized from England (1169). Consisting chiefly of lowlands, it rises to mountains in the W. Cattle rearing is the main agricultural occupation. Area: 908 sq mi (2352 sq km). Population (1991): 102,045. County town: Wexford.

Weyden, Rogier van der (c. 1400–64) Flemish painter of portraits and religious altarpieces. Almost nothing is known of his early life, but he was probably the pupil of the Master of *Flémalle, whose influence is evident in *The Deposition*. From 1436 until his death he was city painter of Brussels and frequently worked for the Burgundian court. In 1450 he visited Italy and paintings from this period, for example the *Entombment*, show Italian influences. His work became widely known in Europe during his lifetime.

whale A large marine mammal belonging to the order *Cetacea*. Whales have no hind limbs; tneir forelimbs are flippers and their tails are horizontally flattened to form a pair of flukes. They breath through a blowhole on top of the head, which is closed when they are submerged. Whales are virtually hairless and insulated by a thick layer of blubber under the skin. They bear their young and suckle them at sea.

There are two suborders. The whalebone whales (*Mysticetae*; 12 species)—including the *rorquals, *blue whale, and *right whales—are large and slow-moving and feed on krill, which they filter from the water using a sieve of whalebone (*see* baleen) plates. They have a double blowhole. Toothed whales (*Odontocetae*; 80 species)—including the *dolphins, *narwhal, and *sperm whale—are smaller and more agile. They feed on fish and squid and are often gregarious, communicating by underwater sounds. *See also* whaling.

whalebone. *See* baleen.

whale shark A gigantic but harmless *shark, *Rhincodon typus*, that has a gray or brown spotted body with pale undersides, ridges along its sides, and a terminal mouth. Up to 60 ft (18 m) long, it swims slowly, mainly in tropical waters, and feeds near the surface on small fish, invertebrates, and plankton. Family: *Rhincodontidae*.

whaling The hunting and slaughter of whales for their carcasses. Traditionally, whales were hunted offshore and processed on land, but modern commercial whaling fleets comprise a mother factory ship for processing the carcasses at sea and a fleet of small hunter vessels equipped with harpoon guns and winches. The carcasses are a source of meat, fats, oils, and other chemicals used in many industries. Whaling has depleted whale populations to the point that some species, such as the blue whale and bowhead whale, are in danger of extinction. Many conservationists are campaigning for a complete ban on whaling, especially since substitutes for most whale products are available. Catch quotas for whaling nations, such as Russia and Japan, are set annually by the International Whaling Commission.

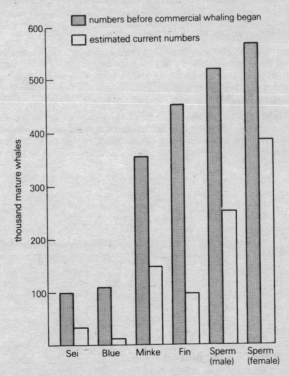

WHALING *Effects of whaling on populations of various whale species.*

whangee A hard white-skinned tropical *bamboo of the genus *Phyllostachys*, from SE Asia, the stems of which are used as canes or walking sticks. The woody jointed stems arise from a creeping underground stem; whorls of slender shoots with narrow leaves are produced from each joint.

Wharton, Edith (Newbold) (1862–1937) US novelist. Her novels about New York society, such as *The House of Mirth* (1905) and *The Age of Innocence* (1920), which won a Pulitzer Prize, were influenced by her friend Henry *James. From 1907 she lived in Paris, and France during World War I was the subject of *The Marne* (1918) and *Son at the Front* (1923). Her short fiction was printed in *Collected Short Stories* (2 vols, 1968). Her later work includes *Hudson River Bracketed* (1929), *The Gods Arrive* (1932) and her autobiography, *A Backward Glance* (1934). *Ethan Frome* (1911), a short tragic novel set in New England, remains her best-known work.

wheat A cereal *grass belonging to the genus *Triticum*, native to W Asia but widely cultivated in subtropical and temperate regions. With the exception of einkorn (*T. monococcum*), most commercial wheats are hybrids with the genus *Aegilops*. Many different varieties have been developed; winter wheats, sown in autumn, are hardier than spring wheats. The stems, up to 40 in (1 m) high, each bear a cylindrical head of up to a hundred flower clusters, grouped in vertical rows and sometimes bearing bristles (awns) up to 4 in (10 cm) long. The grain of bread wheat (*T. aestivum*) is milled to produce flour for bread, cakes, biscuits, etc. Hard or durum wheat (*T. durum*) is used to make pasta and semolina. Surplus grain, bran, etc., is fed to livestock. Wheat is also a commercial source of alcohol, dextrose, gluten, malt, and starch.

wheatear A migratory songbird, *Oenanthe oenanthe*, that winters in tropical Africa and Eurasia, and breeds in N tundra regions, nesting in holes in the ground. It is about 8 in (15 cm) long and in summer the male has a blue-gray back, white rump, and a black mask and wings. In winter, males resemble females, having a brown mask, back, and wings. Family: *Turdidae* (thrushes).

Wheatstone, Sir Charles (1802–75) British physicist. He was the first to patent the electrical telegraph and recognized the value of the network used to measure resistances now called the *Wheatstone bridge (invented by Samuel Hunter Christie; 1784–1865).

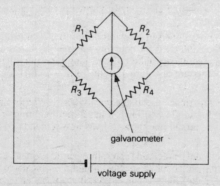

galvanometer

voltage supply

WHEATSTONE BRIDGE

Wheatstone bridge An arrangement of four resistances used to measure the value of one of the resistances when the other three are known. The resistances are arranged to form a square with a voltage applied across two opposite junctions and a galvanometer connected across the other two opposite junctions. When the galvanometer indicates that no current is flowing the bridge is balanced and $R_1/R_2 = R_3/R_4$.

wheel animalcule. *See* rotifer.

Wheeler, Sir (Robert Eric) Mortimer (1890–1976) British archeologist. Wheeler's skill in excavating, recording, and interpreting archeological strata was renowned. He excavated Romano-British sites (e.g. *Maiden Castle) and was influential as director of the Archaeological Survey of India (1944–48).

wheel of life. *See* Bhavachakra.

whelk A *gastropod mollusk of the family *Buccinidae* (over 400 species), of warm and cold seas; 1.6–4.7 in (4–12 cm) long, whelks feed on mollusks and worms. The common northern whelk (*Buccinum undatum*), 2 in (5 cm) long, has a drab yellow-brown shell and edible flesh. Tropical species are more colorful.

whidah. *See* whydah.

Whigs Members of a British political group that became the *Liberal party after about 1868. The Whigs dominated politics in the first half of the 18th century, forming rival aristocratic groups. When in the late 18th century the Tories reemerged, the Whigs formed a more united group under Charles James *Fox. Identifying with industrialist, Nonconformist, and reforming interests, they became the Liberal party under *Gladstone.

whimbrel A *curlew, *Numenius phaeopus*, that breeds on Arctic tundra and winters in Africa, South America, and S Asia; 16 in (40 cm) long, it has a streaked brown plumage and a dark crown with a pale central stripe. It feeds on insects, spiders, worms, and snails.

whinchat A migratory *chat, *Saxicola rubetra*, common on open farmland. It winters in Africa and breeds in Eurasia, nesting in rough vegetation and feeding on flies and moths. The male has a streaked brown plumage, pale chestnut breast, white wingbars, and a white eyestripe; the female is duller.

whipbird A shy songbird belonging to the Australian genus *Psophodes* (2 species). They are about 10 in (25 cm) long with a dark-green plumage, and feed on insects among scrub and undergrowth. The eastern whipbird (*P. olivaceus*) has a long whistling call ended by a whipcrack sound. Family: *Muscicapidae*.

whippet A breed of dog developed in England during the 19th century from terrier and greyhound stock and used for coursing and racing. It has a slender streamlined build with a smooth whiplike tail and long tapering muzzle. The fine short coat can be any mixture of colors. Height: 18 in (46 cm) (dogs); 17 in (43 cm) (bitches).

whippoorwill A North American *nightjar, *Caprimulgus vociferus*, named for its distinctive call. About 9.4 in (24 cm) long, it has a mottled brown plumage; the male has a white collar and tail markings. It lives in woodland and feeds on insects.

whip scorpion A nocturnal *arachnid, sometimes called vinegarroon, belonging to a suborder (*Uropygi*; about 75 species) found in tropical and subtropical regions. Up to 5 in (13 cm) long, it has large spiny pincers and a whiplike tail and it secretes acetic acid for defense. Order: *Pedipalpi*.

whip snake A slender arboreal snake belonging to the genus *Zamenis* (5 species). The common European speckled gray whip snake (*Z. gemonensis*) reaches a length of 6 ft (1.8 m) and feeds on other snakes and lizards. The pencil-thin green whip snakes (genus *Dryophis*; 8 species) occur in tropical Asia and Australasia and grow to a length of 40 in (1 m). Family: *Colubridae*.

whirligig A dark shiny *water beetle belonging to the widely distributed family *Gyrinidae* (about 700 species). It spins around on the surface of still or slow-moving fresh water, feeding on insects or other small animals that have fallen in. The aquatic larvae prey on mayfly or dragonfly nymphs. If disturbed, whirligig beetles dive from the surface and exude a foul-smelling milky liquid.

whirlpool A violent circular eddy in the sea or a large river, caused by opposing currents or winds or where a strong current is impeded by some obstacle. Large-scale whirlpools are rare. *See also* maelstrom.

whirlwind A small revolving column of air, which whirls around a low-pressure center produced by local heating and convectional uprising. It may pick up small pieces of debris and dust and in desert areas may cause *sandstorms.

whiskey A *liquor distilled from malted grain. The word comes from the Gaelic *uisgebeatha*, water of life. The milled grain is mixed with water to form a mash, which must be converted to sugar before fermentation; the resulting alcoholic liquid is distilled and then aged in the cask for at least three years (generally for much longer). Whiskey is classified according to where it is produced, e.g. scotch whisky (distilled from barley and spelled without an *e*), Irish whiskey or, as in the US, by type. Most US whiskey is either rye or bourbon (named for the county in Kentucky where it was first produced).

Whiskey Rebellion (1794) An uprising in protest against a federal excise tax on whiskey. Farmers in W Pennsylvania usually made whiskey from excess grain and traded it. They gathered in armed groups and terrorized some federal officials, but the rebellion was easily ended when George Washington, on the advice of Secretary of State Alexander Hamilton, called out the federal militia. All the participants who were tried were acquitted or pardoned, but the incident served as a demonstration of federal strength.

whist A card game for two pairs of partners; it originated in the 17th century and was popularized by *Hoyle. A pack of 52 cards is dealt out, the last card determining the trump suit. The object of the game is to win the highest number of tricks by playing the highest card of a suit (the cards ranking from ace high) or by trumping (one may also discard a nontrump when one cannot follow suit). The winner of a trick leads the next card. Each trick over the first six (the "book") scores a point to the partners; five or (in long whist) 10 points make a game and two out of three games win the rubber. There are a number of variations. *See also* bridge.

Whistler, James (Abbott) McNeill (1834–1903) US painter and etcher. After briefly attending West Point, from which he was dismissed, he settled in Paris (1855), where he was particularly influenced by Oriental art, especially Japanese prints. Moving to England (1859), he specialized in portraits and landscapes dominated by one or two colors, the best known being a portrait of his mother, *Arrangement in Gray and Black* (1872) and *Old Battersea Bridge* (1872–73). In 1877 *Ruskin described one of Whistler's works as "flinging a pot of paint in the public's face" and was sued for libel (1878); although Whistler won the case his legal costs ruined him. Whistler was also famous as a wit and as the author of *The Gentle Art of Making Enemies* (1890).

whistling duck A long-legged long-necked *duck belonging to a tribe (*Dendrocygnini*; 8 species), also called tree duck, ranging throughout tropical regions. They have a distinctive whistling cry. The fulvous tree duck (*Dendrocygnus bicolor*) is 22 in (55 cm) long and has a red-brown plumage with cream stripes on the flanks.

Whitby, Synod of (663 AD) A council convened at Whitby (England) by King Oswy of Northumbria to decide whether to adopt Roman or Celtic Church usages in Britain. The major source of controversy was the dating of Easter. The Roman view triumphed, with the result that the English Church was brought into line with the Continent.

White, Byron Raymond (1917–   ) US jurist; associate justice of the Supreme Court (1972–93). He gained his nickname of "Whizzer White" while an outstanding student and football player at the University of Colorado. He played professional football (1938–39) before leaving for England as a Rhodes scholar in 1939. With the outbreak of World War II, White returned to the US and attended Yale Law School while again playing football (1940–41). When the US entered the war, he joined the navy and served in the South Pacific. In 1946 he received his law degree from Yale; from 1947–61 he practiced corporate law with a Denver firm. In 1961 he was named deputy US attorney general, and in 1962 he became President Kennedy's first appointee to the Supreme Court. After his retirement, his seat was filled by Ruth Bader Ginsburg.

White, Edward Douglass (1845–1921) US jurist; associate (1894–1910) and chief justice (1910–21) of the US Supreme Court. He served in the Confederate army and was admitted to the bar in 1868. White was a Louisiana state senator in 1874, a Louisiana supreme court judge (1879–80), and was elected to the US Senate in 1890. In 1894, White was appointed to the Supreme Court by Pres. Grover Cleveland; he served as an associate justice until 1910, when Pres. William Taft appointed him chief justice, a post he held until his death. A moderate, he is particularly known for his "rule of reason" interpretation of antitrust laws and his support of an 8-hour work day for railroad workers.

White, E(lwyn) B(rooks) (1899–1985) US poet, essayist, and author. After graduating from Cornell University, he was variously a reporter for the Seattle *Times*, a ship's messboy, an advertising copywriter in New York City, and a staff writer for the *New Yorker* (1926–38) with his column "Talk of the Town." In 1937 he moved to a farm in Maine and had a monthly column (1938–43) "One Man's Meat" in *Harper's* magazine. Among his many works are *The Lady is Cold* (1929), a collection of poems; *Is Sex Necessary* (1929), satire written with James Thurber; *Quo Vadimus?* (1939), *The Wild Flag* (1946), *The Second Tree From the Corner* (1954), *The Points of My Compass* (1962), and *Essays of E. B. White* (1977), all collections of essays; and his children's stories *Stuart Little* (1945), *Charlotte's Web* (1952), and *Trumpet of the Swan* (1970). He is also noted for his best-selling revision of William Strunk Jr.'s *The Elements of Style* (1959). Among his many awards are the Laura Ingalls Wilder Medal for contributions to children's literature (1970) and a special Pulitzer Prize recognizing the full body of his work (1978).

White, Patrick (1912–90) Australian novelist. Born in England and educated at Cambridge University, he settled in Australia after World War II and explored the national consciousness in his epic novels *The Tree of Man* (1955) and *Voss* (1957). His other works include *Riders in the Chariot* (1961), *The Solid Mandala* (1966), *The Eye of the Storm* (1974), *The Vivisector* (1970), *A Fringe of Leaves* (1976), *The Twyborn Affair* (1980), and *Flaws in the Glass* (1982). He won the Nobel Prize in 1973.

White, T(erence) H(anbury) (1906–64) British novelist. He lived for long periods as a recluse in Ireland and in the Channel Isles. His books include a retelling of the Arthurian legends, *The Once and Future King* (1958), and several works of social history.

whitebeam A tree, *Sorbus aria*, up to 50 ft (15 m) tall and found mainly in S and central Europe. The young leaves are covered with fine white down, which persists on the undersurface. The creamy-white five-petaled flowers are borne in branched clusters and produce red berries. Swedish whitebeam (*S. × intermedia*), a hybrid between whitebeam and *mountain ash, is often planted in parks. Family: *Rosaceae*.

white dwarf A very small faint low-mass star (less than 1.44 solar masses) that has undergone *gravitational collapse following exhaustion of its nuclear fuel. Electrons are stripped from the constituent atoms, and it is the pressure exerted by these densely packed electrons that eventually halts the star's contraction. The density is then 10^7–10^{11} kg m^{-3}. As they cool, their colors change from white (for the brightest) through yellow and red until they become cold black objects.

white-eye A small long-tailed songbird belonging to a family (*Zosteropidae*; 85 species) occurring in Old World tropical regions. White-eyes are less than 6 in (15 cm) long, typically yellow-green with white underparts, and have characteristic white rings around the eyes. They are arboreal and have brush-tipped tongues for feeding on nectar; they also eat insects and sweet fruits, sometimes damaging cultivated fruit crops.

Whitefield, George (1714–70) British Methodist preacher. Ordained an Anglican minister, he was not allowed to preach in Anglican churches, where his evangelism was considered extreme. An associate of the Wesleys at Oxford, Whitefield began open-air preaching in England in 1739 and in 1740, during one of his seven visits to America, he became associated with the *Great Awakening in New England. His preaching was strongly Calvinist, in contrast to the Wesleys' Arminianism.

whitefish A slender fish, belonging to a genus (*Coregonus*) related to trout, that occurs mainly in deep northern lakes and rivers of Europe, Asia, and North America. It has a small mouth, minute teeth, and a covering of large silvery scales. Whitefish feed on insects and other small animals and most are food and game fish.

white fly A small winged insect of the mainly tropical family *Aleyrodidae*; 0.08–0.12 in (2–3 mm) long, it is covered with a mealy white powder and resembles a minute moth. White flies suck plant juices and exude honeydew on which a sooty black mold grows, often damaging crops. The larvae go through a sedentary stage, in which they are scalelike and covered with a cottony wax. Suborder: *Homoptera*; order: *Hemiptera*.

Whitehead, A(lfred) N(orth) (1861–1947) British philosopher and mathematician. Whitehead's first major work, the *Principia Mathematica* (1910–13), was written in collaboration with Bertrand *Russell. In later books, such as the *Principles of Natural Knowledge* (1919) and *The Concepts of Nature* (1920), he explored the relationships that exist between concepts and sense perception. Thereafter, his philosophy became more metaphysical.

Whitehorse 60 40N 135 08W A city in NW Canada, the capital of the *Yukon. Founded in 1900, at the time of the Klondike gold rush, it is now a center for distribution, administration, and tourism. Population (1986): 16,000.

White House The official residence of the president of the US. In Washington, D.C., on Pennsylvania Avenue, the building was designed by James Hoban (c. 1762–1831) in 1792. It was burned (1814) by the British during the *War of 1812 but was subsequently restored under Hoban's supervision, being painted white to hide the smoke stains (its name, however, had been adopted earlier). It was partly rebuilt between 1949 and 1952.

WHITE HOUSE *The colonnaded north portico was added in the 1820s.*

White Mountains A mountain range in N central New Hampshire and W central Maine, part of the Appalachian Mountains. The highest point is Mt Washington (6288 ft; 1917 m) in the Presidential Range in E New Hampshire. Franconia Notch is typical of the many glacier-carved passes here. The Androscoggin, Saco, and Pemigewasset rivers rise in the White Mountains. The area has long been popular with summer and winter vacationers.

white rhinoceros The largest species of *rhinoceros, *Diceros simus*, of South Africa. It is grayish brown and has a broad square upper lip. Up to 7 ft (2 m) high at the shoulder and weighing up to 3.5 tons, white rhinos are now very rare.

White Russia. *See* Belarus.

White Russians The Russians who fought against the Soviet Red Army in the civil war (1917–21) that followed the *Russian Revolution. The name derives from that of the royalist opponents to the French Revolution, called Whites because they adopted the white flag of the Bourbon dynasty.

White Sea (Russian name: Beloye More) A gulf of the Arctic Ocean in NW Russia, to the S and E of the Kola Peninsula. It gives access to Archangel and the fishing port and aluminum works of Kandalaksha and is connected by inland waterways to the Gulf of Finland.

white shark A dangerous man-eating *mackerel shark, *Carcharodon carcharias*, that occurs singly or in groups, mainly in tropical and temperate seas. Its heavy body, up to 36 ft (11 m) long, is gray-brown to slate-blue with light-gray undersides and it feeds voraciously on fish, turtles, seals, etc.

whitethroat An Old World *warbler, *Sylvia communis*, that breeds in N Eurasia and winters in central Africa. It is about 5.5 in (14 cm) long including its long slender tail. The male is russet brown with a grayish head and white throat and performs a tumbling courtship display in flight. The female is a duller brown.

white whale A small Arctic toothed *whale, *Delphinapterus leucas*, also called beluga. Young white whales are blue-gray, but change to white as they mature. About 15 ft (4.5 m) long, with a rounded head and large flukes and flippers, they feed mainly on fish. Family: *Monodontidae*.

whiting A marine food and game fish belonging to the genus *Gadus* (or *Merlangius*) related to cod, especially *M. merlangus* found in shallow European waters, down to 650 ft (200 m). It has a slender body, up to 27.5 in (70 cm) long, which is olive, sandy, or bluish above and silvery white below, a black blotch on each pectoral fin, and three dorsal and two anal fins.

Whitlam, (Edward) Gough (1916–   ) Australian statesman; Labor prime minister (1972–75). He became Labor leader in 1967. As prime minister he ended conscription, relaxed rules on nonwhite immigration, and tried to lessen US influence in Australia. In 1975, during a budget crisis, Whitlam was dismissed by the governor, an unprecedented step in the history of Australian politics. Whitlam resigned the Labor leadership in 1977.

WALT WHITMAN *Poet who described America and its spirit in his works, the best known of which are collected in* Leaves of Grass.

Whitman, Walt (1819–92) US poet. As a young man he worked as a printer, teacher, journalist, and property speculator and contributed unoriginal poems to various magazines. He expressed his democratic idealism and passionate love of life in the revolutionary free-verse poems of *Leaves of Grass* (1855), which was revised and enlarged in nine editions during his lifetime. Its publication marked the beginning of his career as a poet, helping to earn him the distinction of being one of the principal 19th-century American poets. During the Civil War he nursed wounded soldiers, and subsequently suffered from illness himself. His later works include the prose *Democratic Vistas* (1871).

Whitney, Eli (1765–1825) American inventor, best known for his invention of the cotton gin, a machine that separated cotton fiber from the seeds. The device, patented in 1793, greatly stimulated cotton growing in the southern states. Whitney subsequently turned to firearms manufacture, into which he introduced the concept of interchangeable parts.

Whitney, Mount A mountain in Sequoia National Park, in W central California in the Sierra Nevada. It is the highest point in the contiguous United States, rising to 14,494 ft (4418 m). First measured in 1864 by Josiah Dwight Whitney, it was not scaled until 1873. Owens Valley is on the E side of the mountain, and the valley of the Kern River is on the W.

Whittier, John Greenleaf (1807–92) US poet. An active Quaker and humanitarian, he championed the antislavery cause in both his journalism and his early poetry. His later and better-known poetry includes "Maude Miller" (1854), "The Barefoot Boy" (1855), "Barbara Frietchie" (1863), and *Snowbound* (1866).

Whittington, Dick (Richard W.; d. 1423) English merchant, who was three times lord mayor of London (1397–98, 1406–07, 1419–20). He traded with, and made loans to, both Henry IV and Henry V. The legend of Whittington and his cat dates from the early 17th century.

WHO. *See* World Health Organization.

whooping cough (pertussis) A respiratory infection of children caused by the bacterium *Bordetella pertussis*. After an incubation period of 7–14 days, the child develops a cough, a nasal discharge, and low fever, followed a week or two later by paroxysms of coughing accompanied by a characteristic whooping sound. The disease may persist for months and it may be complicated by pneumonia or convulsions. A vaccine is now available.

whooping crane A rare bird, *Grus americana*, that breeds in the marshlands of NW Canada and winters in the swamps of SE Texas: 60 in (150 cm) tall with a wingspan of 7 ft (210 cm), it has a white plumage with black-tipped wings, black legs, and a bare red face and has a loud whooping call. Captive breeding programs may prevent its extinction. Family: *Gruidae* (cranes).

Whorf, Benjamin Lee (1897–1941) US linguist, who studied American Indian and other languages as a hobby. In *Language, Thought, and Reality* (1956) he argued that human conceptual systems are dependent upon individual languages and that comparison of different languages reveals that different peoples analyze the world in very different ways. This controversial form of linguistic relativism was also argued by *Sapir and has been influential in psycholinguistics (*see* linguistics).

whydah (*or* widah) A small *weaverbird belonging to the genus *Vidua* (11 species), also called widowbird and occurring in open grassy regions of Africa. The males have long ornamental tail feathers used in courtship display and the females lay their eggs in the nests of closely related *waxbills, which rear their young. The young whydals closely resemble the offspring of their host species although the adults are very different in appearance.

Whymper, Edward (1840–1911) British mountaineer, explorer, artist, and author. He led the first ascent of the Matterhorn (1865), in which four members of the team died on the descent. He also visited Greenland, the Andes, and Canada on explorations.

Wichita 37 43N 97 20W A city in Kansas, on the Arkansas River. Founded in 1864, it had developed into an important agricultural trading center by the late 19th century. Today Wichita is the state's largest city and the principal commercial and industrial center of S Kansas with railroad workshops, oil refineries, and an aircraft industry. It is the site of two universities, including Wichita State University (1895). Population (1990): 304,011.

Wicklow (Irish name: Contae Chill Mhantáin) A county in the E Republic of Ireland, in Leinster bordering on the Irish Sea. Fertile lowlands rise to the central Wicklow Mountains. Agriculture is the chief occupation; along the coast are several resorts, notably Bray. Area: 782 sq mi (2025 sq km). Population (1991): 97,293. County town: Wicklow.

Widor, Charles Marie (1844–1937) French organist and composer. He was organist of Saint-Sulpice in Paris for over 60 years. His compositions include eight symphonies for the organ, concertos, chamber music, and choral music.

Wieland, Christoph Martin (1733–1813) German novelist and poet. His first distinguished work is the romance *Agathon* (1766–67), while his translations of Shakespeare later influenced the *Sturm und Drang* movement. The verse epic *Oberon* (1780) introduced exotic Middle Eastern matter into European literature.

Wiener, Norbert (1894–1964) US mathematician. During World War II he worked on the problem of aiming an antiaircraft gun by computing such factors as the speed and direction of the aircraft, wind speed, etc. He thus developed an interest in the mathematics of information and communication, which he called *cybernetics. After the war Weiner, refusing to do any more military research, spent the rest of his life writing about the social problems resulting from automation.

Wiesbaden 50 05N 8 15E A spa city in SW Germany, the capital of Hesse on the Rhine River. Its hot saline springs have made it a popular resort since Roman times. A center of the wine industry, its manufactures include chemicals and plastics. Population (1991 est): 257,000.

Wiesel, Elie(zer) (1928–) US author, winner of the Nobel Peace Prize (1986). He survived the concentration camps during World War II, became a US citizen (1963), and taught at college. As chairman of the US President's Commission on the Holocaust he received a Congressional Medal of Achievement in 1985. His works, which attest to the horrors of the Holocaust, include *Night* (1960), *Dawn* (1961), *The Jews of Silence* (1966), *A Beggar in Jerusalem* (1970), *The Oath* (1973), *A Jew Today* (1978), *The Testament* (1980), and *The Fifth Son* (1984).

wigeon A fast-flying *duck, *Anas penelope*, that breeds on tundra and moorland of N Eurasia and winters on mudflats, estuaries, and lakes as far south as Africa and S Asia; 18 in (45 cm) long, it has a pale-gray black-tipped bill; males have a chestnut head with a yellowish crown and gray back, while females are brown with a white belly and white shoulders.

Wight, Isle of (Latin name: Vectis) 50 40N 1 15W An island and county in S England, separated from the mainland by the Solent and Spithead. It consists chiefly of undulating chalk downs. Tourism is important, especially in the coastal resorts; yachting is an added attraction. Other occupations include agriculture and ship building. Area: 147 sq mi (380 sq km). Population (1981): 118,192. Administrative center: Newport.

Wigner, Eugene Paul (1902–) US physicist, born in Hungary, who worked out the theory of neutron absorption by nuclei and discovered that solids change their size under radiation (Wigner effect). Wigner helped *Szilard and *Teller persuade *Einstein to warn Roosevelt of the dangers of an atomic bomb being made by the Germans, and he worked with Fermi on the first atomic pile. He won a share of the Nobel Prize (1963) for his work on nuclear physics.

WIGEON *Drakes, seen here preening and sleeping, have a high whistling note. Females make a lower purring noise.*

wigwam 1. Strictly, a square dome-roofed hut made of saplings covered with bark or rush matting used by some North American Indian peoples. **2.** (*or* tepee) A conical tent made of a framework of poles tied together at the top and covered with decorated buffalo skins, used by the Plains tribes.

Wilberforce, William (1759–1833) British philanthropist, who played a major part in the antislavery movement. As a member of Parliament (1780–1825) he led the parliamentary campaign to abolish the slave trade (achieved in 1807) and then to emancipate existing slaves (achieved a month after his death). He was a founder of the Society for the Abolition of the Slave Trade (1787) and of the Antislavery Society (1823).

wildcat A *cat, *Felis sylvestris*, of Europe and W Asia. About 30 in (75 cm) long, it has a bushy rounded tail and thick striped coat. Wildcats inhabit dense woodland and breed once a year, in a den in a hollow log or tree. They may interbreed with domestic cats.

Wilde, Oscar (Fingal O'Flahertie Wills W.; 1854–1900) British dramatist and poet, born in Dublin. He dazzled London literary society with his charm and wit and became a leading figure of the *aesthetic movement. His works include *Poems* (1881), a novel, *The Picture of Dorian Gray* (1891), and a series of brilliant social comedies: *Lady Windermere's Fan* (1892), *A Woman of No Importance* (1893), *An Ideal Husband* (1895), and *The Importance of Being Earnest* (1895). Socially and financially ruined by a trial in 1895 arising from his homosexual relationship with Lord Alfred Douglas (1870–1945), he was imprisoned for two years and lived in exile in France from 1897. While in prison he wrote a long letter on his relationship with Douglas, passages of which were published as *De profundis* (1905). In exile he produced his last and best-known poem, *The Ballad of Reading Gaol* (1898).

wildebeest. *See* gnu.

Wilder, Billy (Samuel W.; 1906–) US film director, born in Austria. He went to Hollywood in 1934. His films are characterized by his acerbic humor and his unconventional choice of subject matter. They include *The Lost Weekend* (1945), *Sunset Boulevard* (1950), and *Some Like It Hot* (1959).

Wilder, Laura Ingalls (1867–1957) US author. At the age of 65, Wilder began her series of children's stories at the urging of her daughter. Based on her early life as a pioneer, the series includes *Little House in the Big Woods* (1932), *Little House on the Prairie* (1935), and *Little Town on the Prairie* (1941), among others. In 1954 the American Library Association established its Laura Ingalls Wilder Award for lasting contributions to children's literature. Wilder's stories formed the basis for a successful television series.

Wilder, Thornton (1897–1975) US novelist and dramatist. His best-known plays are *Our Town* (1938) and *The Skin of Our Teeth* (1942), and his novels include *The Bridge of San Luis Rey* (1927). He was a skilled literary craftsman who enjoyed great popular success.

Wilderness, Battle of the (May 5–6, 1864) Civil War battle. Gen. Ulysses S. *Grant, newly appointed as commander of the Union forces, joined Gen. George C. Meade's Army of the Potomac (with more than 100,000 men) in Virginia. Gen. Robert E. *Lee's Confederate Army of Northern Virginia (with just over 60,000 men) held the forested area on the south bank of the Rapidan River. The two-day battle was bloody and indecisive; although the Union forces lost at least twice as many men (about 18,000) as Lee, the Confederates had fewer reserves to draw upon. This battle opened two months of warfare and led to Grant's siege of Petersburg and Richmond.

Wilderness Road A trail that led settlers from SW Virginia W through the Appalachian Mountains and the Cumberland Gap to Louisville, Ky. Branches led to Boonesboro on the Kentucky River and Nashville, Tenn. Blazed by Daniel Boone in 1775 from an old Indian route, the overland trail opened up lands further W; it was the main road westward until the early 1800s when the National Road was built further north. It is now part of the Dixie Highway.

wildfowl Waterbirds, usually ones that are shot for sport, especially ducks and geese but sometimes also coots, rails, and grebes.

Wilkes, John (1725–97) British journalist and politician. In 1757 he became a member of Parliament and in 1762 founded the weekly *North Briton*, in which he attacked George III's ministers and accused the government of lying. Wilkes was arrested for libel. In 1764 while in Paris he was expelled from the House of Commons and outlawed. In 1768 he returned to England and was twice elected to Parliament and twice expelled. After serving as lord mayor of London (1774) he was reelected to Parliament and at last permitted to take his seat (1774–90).

Wilkins, Maurice Hugh Frederick (1916–) New Zealand physicist, who worked in California on the atom bomb during World War II. After the war, uneasy about nuclear weapons, he turned to life sciences and developed a method of using X-ray diffraction, which assisted James *Watson and Francis *Crick in determining the structure of DNA. These three scientists were awarded the 1962 Nobel Prize for this work.

Wilkins, Roy (1901–81) US civil rights leader. A graduate of the University of Minnesota, he was a journalist for the Kansas City (Mo.) *Call*, an African-American weekly, before joining the National Association for the Advancement of Colored People (NAACP) in 1931, as assistant executive secretary. He edited *Crisis*, the official organ of the NAACP, from 1934 to 1949. He was named administrator of internal affairs in 1950, and he led the organization as executive secretary (1955) and executive director (1964) until his retirement in 1977. Wilkins urged economic and civil rights in a moderate fashion and was instrumental in preparing the legal challenge that led to school desegregation in 1954.

Wilkinson, James (1757–1825) US army officer. Wilkinson served in the Revolutionary War and became a brigadier general in 1777, but was forced to resign after taking part in an effort to replace George Washington as commander in chief. Wilkinson moved to Kentucky and entered into an agreement with the Spanish governor of Louisiana to help Spain gain control of the Kentucky region in exchange for money and trade concessions for himself. While still in Spain's pay, he served under Gen. Anthony *Wayne in the Indian wars in Ohio and became commander in chief of the army after Wayne's death (1796). Wilkinson officiated at the transfer of Louisiana to the US in 1803 and was governor of the territory (1805–06). He was accused of conspiring with Aaron *Burr to form a separate republic under Burr in the Southwest (including Louisiana), and testified for the prosecution at Burr's trial. Both Burr and Wilkinson (who was also tried) were acquitted. Wilkinson served as a major general in the War of 1812, and was tried for negligence in the campaign against Montreal. He was acquitted. Honorably discharged from the army in 1815, he died in Mexico in 1825.

will In law, the written declaration of a person's intentions in relation to the disposal of his property after his death. By its own nature, a will is ambulatory and revocable during his lifetime. Two witnesses are required to authenticate the will. Dependents of the deceased inadequately provided for may challenge the will, the provisions of which are carried out by one or more executors.

Willemstad 12 12N 68 56W The capital and main port of the *Netherlands Antilles, on the SE coast of Curaçao. It is an important free port and a refining center for Venezuelan oil. Population: 234,374.

William (I) the Bad (1120–66) Norman king of Sicily (1154–66). In 1155 he reconquered Apulia from the Byzantines and in 1156 (the Concordat of Benevento) gained papal acknowledgement of his possessions. His attempts to reduce the power of the barons incited a revolt, which he was able to suppress. An outstanding patron of learning, he welcomed many Muslim scholars to his court.

William (I) the Conqueror (c. 1028–1087) Duke of Normandy (1035–87) and the first Norman king of England (1066–87). He claimed to have been named by Edward the Confessor as heir to the English throne. When Harold II succeeded Edward, William invaded England, defeated and killed his rival at the battle of Hastings, and became king. The *Norman conquest of England was completed by 1072, aided by the establishment of *feudalism, under which his followers were granted land in return for pledges of service and loyalty. As king, William was noted for his efficient, if harsh, rule. His administration relied upon Norman and other foreign personnel, especially *Lanfranc, archbishop of Canterbury. In 1085 William initiated the compilation of *Domesday Book.

William (I) the Lion (1143–1214) King of the Scots (1165–1214). After his capture in a revolt against *Henry II of England in 1174, he became a vassal of the English throne. On Henry's death in 1189 he regained independence for his kingdom in return for a payment to Richard I.

William (I) the Silent (1533–84) The leader of the *Revolt of the Netherlands against Spanish rule. He was the son of the Count of Nassau and in 1544 became prince of Orange. Appointed to the Council of State in 1555, he became governor of Holland, Zeeland, and Utrecht in 1559. He opposed the autocracy of the Spanish Government and its persecution of Protestants (he himself became a Protestant in 1573), withdrawing with Egmont and Horn from the Council of State in 1563. When open revolt broke out in 1568, William soon emerged as its leader and in 1576 succeeded in uniting the Roman Catholic provinces in the south with the Protestant north. This union was short lived, however, and in 1579 the northern provinces declared their independence of Spain, with William as their first stadtholder (chief magistrate). He was assassinated by a Spanish agent.

William I (1772–1843) King of the Netherlands (1815–40). Following Napoleon's conquest of the Netherlands (1795), he lived in exile until Napoleon's defeat (1813), becoming king of the United Netherlands, which included Belgium and Luxembourg. He fostered the Netherlands' economic recovery but antagonized the Belgians, who achieved independence (1831) by revolt. William abdicated in favor of his son William II.

William I (1797–1888) King of Prussia (1861–88) and German emperor (1871–88). His advocacy of using arms against the Revolution of 1848 brought him the nickname Prince of Grapeshot and he was forced into exile (1848–49). He became regent for his brother Frederick William IV in 1858. His reign was dominated by *Bismarck, who achieved German unification under Prussian leadership in 1871, when William was proclaimed German emperor.

William II Rufus (c. 1056–1100) King of England (1087–1100), succeeding his father William the Conqueror. His harsh rule aroused baronial and ecclesiastical opposition, notably from *Anselm, archbishop of Canterbury. He made several attempts to recover Normandy from his elder brother Robert (d. 1134) and was killed by an arrow while hunting in the New Forest. He may have been assassinated by order of his younger brother, who became Henry I.

William (II) the Good (1154–89) The last Norman king of Sicily (1166–89). He ruled in person from 1171, engaging in intermittent war against the Byzantine Empire until final defeat near Constantinople in 1185. In 1177 he married Joan (1165–99), the daughter of Henry II of England.

William II (1792–1849) King of the Netherlands (1840–49), following the abdication of his father William I. His authorization of a liberal constitution (1848) prevented the spread of the *Revolutions of 1848 to the Netherlands.

William II (1859–1941) German emperor (1888–1918); grandson of Britain's Queen Victoria. After securing □Bismarck's resignation as chancellor, William encouraged policies that were regarded abroad as warmongering. The German navy was built up, friendly overtures were made to Turkey and to the Transvaal, and Germany interfered against France in the Morocco crises (1905, 1911). William supported Austria-Hungary's ultimatum to Serbia and then tried in vain to prevent the conflict from escalating into a world war. Following Germany's defeat, he was forced to abdicate.

William III (1650–1702) King of England (1689–1702) and stadtholder (chief magistrate) of the United Provinces (1672–1702), known as William of Orange. Grandson of Charles I of England and son of William II, prince of Orange (1626–50), in 1677 he married James II of England's daughter Mary. In 1688 he was invited by the opposition to his father-in-law to invade England and in 1689 was proclaimed joint sovereign with his wife, Mary II (*see* Glorious Revolution). William defeated the former king at the *Boyne in Ireland in 1690. On the

Continent he was successful in the War of the *Grand Alliance (1689–97) against Louis XIV of France, leaving a strong army that, under the duke of Marlborough, was to crush France after his death.

William IV (1765–1837) King of England and Hanover (1830–37), known as the Sailor King or Silly Billy. He served in the Royal Navy from 1778 to 1790. He had 10 illegitimate children by the Irish actress Dorothea Jordan before marrying (1818) Adelaide of Saxe-Meiningen (1792–1849). Their two daughters died in infancy and William was succeeded in England by his niece Victoria and in Hanover by his brother Ernest Augustus (1771–1851).

William and Mary style An English derivative (1689–1702) of the *Louis XIV style of furniture. The Huguenot artisans patronized by William III were trained in France and their tastes and techniques predominated. The cabriole leg was a typical innovation replacing the preceding twist-turned legs. Rich gilding was common and some important furniture was made of cast silver. Cabinet furniture was finely veneered with *marquetry or lacquered and gilded.

William of Ockham (c. 1285–1349) English scholastic philosopher (*see* scholasticism). A pupil of *Duns Scotus and later his rival, Ockham is best known for his revival of *nominalism. He systematized the theories on the meaning of universals and linked them with logical principles. *See also* Ockham's Razor.

William of Orange *See* William III.

Williams, Robin (1952–) US comedian and actor. He first achieved fame in 1978 with the television series "Mork and Mindy," playing a space alien, and subsequently made many television specials. His movie successes included both comedic and dramatic roles in such films as *The World According to Garp* (1982), *Good Morning, Vietnam* (1987), *Dead Poets Society* (1989), *Cadillac Man* (1990), *The Fisher King* (1991), and *Mrs. Doubtfire* (1993).

Williams, Roger (c. 1604–83) English colonizer, who founded the colony of Rhode Island. A Puritan, Williams settled in Boston in 1631 but was banished in 1635 because he disagreed with the theocratic government of Massachusetts, advocating the separation of church and state. He founded a new settlement (1636) at Providence, R.I., the patent of which allowed full religious freedom. There he established the first Baptist Church in America.

Williams, Tennessee (1911–83) US dramatist. *The Glass Menagerie* (1945), his first major success, was partly autobiographical and introduced his recurrent themes of family tensions and sexual frustration, which were treated with increasing violence in *A Streetcar Named Desire* (1947) and *Cat on a Hot Tin Roof* (1955), both set in the South. After recovering from a mental and physical breakdown, he continued to write plays, including *Vieux Carré* (1978).

Williams, William Carlos (1883–1963) US poet. The influences of *imagism and of Ezra *Pound, whom he met while studying medicine at the University of Pennsylvania, are apparent in his early poetry, and he continued to develop a style noted for its clarity, directness, and use of natural speech rhythms. His volumes of poetry include *Collected Poems* (1934) and *Pictures from Brueghel* (1963), which won a Pulitzer Prize. *Paterson* (5 vols, 1946–58) is an ambitious epic poem employing various experimental techniques.

Williamsburg 37 17N 76 43W A city in Virginia. Once the state capital (1699–1779), many of its colonial buildings have been renovated or completely rebuilt, attracting many tourists to the city. One of the country's oldest colleges, the College of William and Mary (1693), is also situated there. Population (1990): 11,530.

willow A tree or shrub of the genus *Salix* (about 300 species), native to temperate and arctic regions. Most willows have long narrow leaves (an exception is the Eurasian goat willow [*S. caprea*], also called sallow and pussy willow, which has oval pointed leaves). Male and female catkins are borne on separate trees and open before the leaves; the seeds have long silky hairs. Willows are common in wet places and along stream banks and some are grown as ornamentals, especially the weeping willow (*S. babylonica*), with its slender drooping branches, and the bay willow (*S. pentandra*). Cricket bats are made from the wood of the cricket bat willow (*S. alba* var. *coerulea*). Family: *Salicaceae*. *See also* osier.

willowherb A perennial herb of either of the genera *Epilobium* (160 species) or *Chamaenerion* (about 8 species), of temperate and arctic regions. Rosebay willowherb, or fireweed (*E. angustifolium*), 12–48 in (30–120 cm) high, is a common and fast-growing weed on waste ground in woodland clearings and gardens, etc. It has showy spikes of purple flowers and white fluffy seeds. Family: *Onagraceae*.

willow pattern A *chinoiserie pattern attributed to Thomas Minton (*see* Minton ware) and introduced about 1780. It was extensively used on 19th-century English ceramics. The elements are a willow tree, pagoda, figures on a river bridge, and two flying birds in an elaborate border.

Willow South A city in S Alaska situated about 70 mi (113 km) NW of Anchorage. In 1976 it was chosen as the site of the new state capital, planned to replace Juneau.

Wills (Moody), Helen (1905–) US tennis player, who won the singles title at Wimbledon a record eight times between 1927 and 1938. She also won between 1923 and 1938 the US singles title seven times and the French title four times.

Wilmington 39 46N 75 31W A city in North Carolina, on the Cape Fear River. The first armed resistance against the Stamp Act occurred here in November 1765. The state's chief seaport, Wilmington is also a resort and has varied manufactures. Population (1990): 55,530.

Wilmot Proviso (1846) Proposed constitutional amendment. Following the Mexican War, an appropriations bill was introduced to provide funds for territorial negotiations in the settlement of the US-Mexican boundary. David Wilmot (Democrat, Pa.) proposed an amendment, called the Wilmot Proviso, which provided that "neither slavery nor involuntary servitude shall ever exist in any part of said territory." The bill, which provoked bitter controversy and exacerbated North-South differences, passed in the House of Representatives twice (1846, 1947) but did not pass in the Senate. The new Republican party later adopted the provision as part of its platform.

Wilson, Sir Angus (1913–91) British novelist. His satirical novels and collections of short stories include *Hemlock and After* (1952), *Anglo-Saxon Attitudes* (1956), *No Laughing Matter* (1967), *As If By Magic* (1973), and *Setting the World on Fire* (1980). He has also published several works of criticism.

Wilson, Charles Thomson Rees (1869–1959) British physicist, who won the Nobel Prize (1927) for his invention of the Wilson *cloud chamber. During the 1890s Wilson was experimenting on cloud formation and supersaturated air. He discovered that moisture condensed in the presence of ions and, when X-rays and radioactivity were discovered, applied his discoveries to invent the cloud chamber for detecting ionizing radiation. It was perfected in 1911.

Wilson, Edmund (1895–1972) US critic and essayist. He gave valuable encouragement to young writers in his journalism from the 1920s to the 1940s. His books include *Axel's Castle* (1931), a study of symbolist writers, *To the Finland Station* (1940), on the origins of the Russian Revolution, *The Scrolls from the Dead Sea* (1955), *The American Earthquake* (1958), and *Patriotic Gore* (1962).

Wilson, Edmund Beecher (1856–1939) US biologist, who proposed that sex is determined by the presence or absence of certain chromosomes. Wilson's research and his *Cell in Development and Inheritance* (1896) were a major influence in genetics.

Wilson, (James) Harold, Baron (1916–) British statesman; Labour prime minister (1964–70, 1974–76). An economist, after World War II he became a member of Parliament (1945). As Labour leader after 1963 he achieved electoral victory in 1964, but lost the 1970 election. His second ministry saw the renegotiation of the UK's terms of membership to the EEC, which was confirmed by a referendum in 1975. In 1976 Wilson unexpectedly resigned. His publications include *The Labour Government* (1964–70) and *The Governance of Britain* (1976). He was made a life peer in 1983.

Wilson, Richard (1714–82) British landscape painter. He worked as a portraitist in London before visiting Italy (1750–c. 1757), where he gave up portraiture for landscape painting. After his return to England, he continued to paint Italian scenes as well as English country houses and their parks and scenes of the Welsh mountains. In their feeling for atmosphere and light these paintings established him as the first great British landscapist.

Wilson, (Thomas) Woodrow (1856–1924) US statesman; 28th president of the United States (1913–21). A nationally recognized scholar of political economics, Wilson was a professor (1890–1902) and president (1902–10) of Princeton University, before beginning his political career. In 1910 he was elected governor of New Jersey as the Democratic Reform candidate and during his two-year term in that office he succeeded in reorganizing the state government. Wilson received the Democratic presidential nomination in 1912, and because of a bitter split in the Republican party between the supporters of Pres. William H. *Taft and former Pres. Theodore *Roosevelt, Wilson won the election with a plurality of the popular vote.

True to his progressive ideals, Wilson introduced several reform proposals during his first term. These included the enactment of the Underwood Tariff (1913), which lowered the duties on imported goods; the Federal Reserve Act (1913), which established the *Federal Reserve System; the *Federal Trade Commission Act (1914); and the *Clayton Anti-Trust Act (1914), which extended and strengthened many of the provisions of the earlier *Sherman Anti-Trust Act. Although Wilson pledged to maintain American neutrality after the outbreak of World War I in 1914 in Europe and was reelected in 1916 with the slogan "he kept us out of war," he was forced to change his policy in the spring of 1917. With the resumption of unrestricted German submarine warfare in the Atlantic, the US officially entered the war. Shortly before the 1918 armistice, Wilson proposed his *Fourteen Points, which he hoped could serve as the basis for the rebuilding of the postwar world. One of the most important of these proposals was the establishment of a *League of Nations, an idea incorporated into the Treaty of *Versailles (1919). Despite Wilson's personal campaign for the League of Nations in the US, conservative opponents in the Senate prevented the entry of the US into that international body. Wilson suffered a stroke while touring the country to gain support for the League of Nations and retired from public life in 1921.

WOODROW WILSON *President whose Fourteen Points were incorporated into the Treaty of Versailles, ending World War I.*

Wiltshire A county of S England. It consists of a rolling chalk plateau, which includes the Marlborough Downs and Salisbury Plain, bordered by lowlands in the NW and SE. It is predominantly agricultural; the chief crops are wheat, oats, and barley, and pig and sheep farming are important. There are many remaining features of prehistoric times, notably the Neolithic *Stonehenge and *Avebury. Area: 1344 sq mi (3481 sq km). Population (1981): 518,167. Administrative center: Trowbridge.

Winchester 51 04N 1 19W A city in S England, the administrative center of Hampshire. As capital of Saxon Wessex and residence of the Saxon kings, it rivaled the supremacy of London. The cathedral, built in the 11th century on earlier Saxon foundations, is the longest in England and contains many royal tombs. Winchester College (1382), is England's oldest private secondary school. Population (1981): 30,642.

Winckelmann, Johann Joachim (1717–68) German art historian, who worked mainly in Rome. His promotion of the critical study of Greek and Roman art was encouraged by contemporary discoveries at *Pompeii and *Herculaneum. His *History of Ancient Art* (1764), which exalted Greek art of the 5th and 4th centuries BC and denigrated Roman art in comparison, pioneered modern art historiography.

wind The horizontal movement of air over the earth's surface and one of the basic elements of weather. Thermal differences throughout the world produce variations in air pressure and air will flow generally from high-pressure to low-pressure areas. A wind is classified according to the direction from which it blows, i.e. a wind blowing from the S is a southerly wind. Its speed is usually measured in knots or in meters per second, actual velocities being measured by an anemometer, and it may be classified according to the *Beaufort scale. The major wind systems in the world include the trade winds and *westerlies. □trade winds; □meteorology.

Wind Cave National Park A national park in SW South Dakota, in the S Black Hills, SW of Rapid City. The main feature of the park, established in 1903, is Wind Cave, a limestone cave with a small natural opening, through which a wind blows in and out. The maze of chambers and hallways within the cave are lined with honeycomb-patterned boxwork and frosted deposits of calcite crystals. The park is also a game preserve and is home to prairie dogs, bison, and other wildlife. Area: 44 sq mi (114 sq km).

Windhoek 22 34S 17 06E The capital of Namibia. It is the center of the world's karakul (Persian lamb) skin industry; other industries include meat canning and bone-meal production. Population (1990 est): 115,000.

wind instruments Musical instruments in which notes are produced by a vibrating column of air. *Brass instruments are activated by lip pressure; *reed instruments employ double or single reed mouthpieces; the *flute is side blown; the *recorder has a mouthpiece and fipple (whistle hole); *organ pipes have air blown into them by mechanically activated bellows. *Compare* drums; percussion instruments; stringed instruments.

windmills Machines that enable useful work to be obtained from wind power. The principle is that the energy of the wind turns a set of vanes or sails mounted on a horizontal shaft, the rotation of which is transmitted by gearing to working machinery. Windmills had appeared by 1150 in NE Europe and were used for grinding corn, pumping water, and powering light industry, until they were superseded by steam engines in the 19th century. Two common designs were the Dutch mill, in which only the sails and the conical roof moved to catch the wind, and the German post mill, in which the whole millhouse with sails attached rotated around a central supporting pole. The modern metal windmill with multiple-bladed sails is found all over the world in rural areas, pumping water or powering small electric generators. The use of windmills for electricity generation on a large scale has long been considered and is now technically feasible (*see* wind power).

windpipe. *See* trachea.

wind power The use of wind energy to generate electricity. Because of the world shortage of conventional energy resources, wind-power generators, like other *alternative energy sources, have now become more attractive economically. Some advantages of wind power are that it is free from pollution, uses no fuel, and the times of peak output are likely to coincide with peak demand (i.e. cold windy days). Among the disadvantages are that it must be supplemented by other means, ideally including electricity storage, since it is not sufficiently predictable. It takes up a great deal of space and the best sites are on open ground rather than in the cities, where most power is needed.

There are several different designs of wind-power generators: some with a horizontal axis and blades like the familiar *windmill; some with specially shaped blades rotating on a vertical axis. Larger generators, producing about 1–45 megawatts, are being considered for supplying electricity by some utility companies. Smaller units may be useful for supplying one or two houses in a local community.

Windsor 42 18N 83 00W A city and port in E Canada, in SW Ontario on the Detroit River opposite *Detroit. Settled in the 18th century by French colonists, it is a transportation and manufacturing center, producing motor vehicles, foods, pharmaceuticals, machinery, and metals. Windsor is the center of a rich farming district. The University of Windsor (1963) is situated there. Population (1991): 191,435.

Windsor, House of The name of Britain's royal family from 1917, when it replaced that of House of Saxe-Coburg-Gotha, of which Prince *Albert had been a member. In 1960 Elizabeth II declared that those of her descendants in the male line who were not princes or princesses would take the surname Mountbatten-Windsor, Mountbatten being Prince *Philip's surname.

Windsor Castle A royal residence in Windsor, begun by William the Conqueror. Many additions were made, notably the keep by Henry III, St George's Chapel by Edward IV, and the Albert Memorial Chapel (so called by Queen Victoria) by Henry VII. Many British rulers are buried in these chapels. In the 16th and 17th centuries it began to be altered from a fortress to a palace with substantial rebuilding being carried into the 19th century.

wind tunnel A device for testing the flow of air around an object, for example an airfoil or aircraft, with a view to studying the lift, drag, streamlining, onset of *turbulence, etc. It consists of a duct with an electrically driven fan, usually with water-cooling systems to maintain the air at the correct temperature. *See also* aerodynamics; aeronautics.

Windward Islands (Spanish name: Islas de Barlovento) A West-Indian group of islands forming part of the S Lesser Antilles. They comprise the islands of Martinique, St Lucia, St Vincent, the N Grenadines, and Grenada.

wine An alcoholic drink made from fermented grape juice. The grapes are first crushed, traditionally by treading, now generally by machine. This process brings the yeast on the grapeskins, visible as the "bloom," into contact with the sugar in the juice, which it then converts into ethanol (ethyl alcohol). Depending upon whether the fermentation is stopped when all, part, or only a little of the sugar has been converted, the resulting wine is dry, medium, or sweet. Table wines contain about 9–13% alcohol. Fortified wines (e.g. *port, *sherry), to which a liquor is added at some stage in production, contain about 16–23% alcohol. The bubbles in sparkling wines are caused by a secondary fermentation in the bottle (*see also* champagne).

Wines may be red, white, or rosé. Red wines are made from whole grapes; for white wines the grapeskins are removed at an early stage in production. True rosé wines are made from the grenache grape, from which the skins are removed before the juice is deeply stained by them. Favored varieties of wine grapes include Pinot, Cabernet, Hermitage, Riesling, and Sylvaner. The variety of grape, the soil of the vineyard, and the local climate govern a wine's quality. The appellation "vintage" is now used by wine producers under strictly regulated conditions to designate a wine of a particular year that shows outstanding quality.

French wines are famous for their quality and diversity, especially those produced in Burgundy and the chateaux of the Bordeaux area (the red varieties of which are called clarets). Germany produces fine white wines (hocks). Italian wines are very diverse, including red Lambrusco, red or white Chianti, red Valpolicella, and sweet Marsala. Spain and other European countries produce notable wines. In the US, where the first vineyards date from the 18th century, the best commercial wines are produced in California and New York. Local traditions of wine making are also well established in South Africa, Australia, Chile, and several other countries.

Wingate, Orde Charles (1903–44) British soldier, who organized the *Chindits in Burma in World War II. A Zionist, he organized Jewish guerrillas in Palestine (1936–39). In World War II, after taking Addis Ababa from the Italians (1941), he organized the Chindits to disrupt communications behind the Japanese lines in Burma. He was killed in an airplane crash.

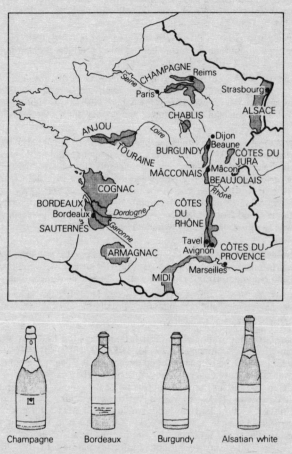

WINE *The major French wine-producing regions and some standard bottle shapes.*

Winnipeg 49 53N 97 10W A city in W Canada, capital of Manitoba at the junction of the Assiniboine and Red rivers. Established as a fur-trading post (1806), it expanded with the growth of farming and the arrival of the railroad (1881) from E Canada. It is the distribution, wholesaling, financial, and manufacturing center of the Canadian prairies and a major transportation junction. Winnipeg is the site of the University of Manitoba and the Royal Winnipeg Ballet. Population (1991): 616,790.

Winnipeg, Lake A lake in W Canada, in S Manitoba. Emptying via the Nebon Rivers into Hudson Bay, it drains much of the Canadian prairies. It is exploited for tourism, fishing, and shipping. Area: 9465 sq mi (24,514 sq km).

Winnipesaukee, Lake A lake in E central New Hampshire, in the White Mountain foothills. The largest lake (25 mi long, 12 mi wide; 40 km long, 19 km wide) in New Hampshire, it is a popular resort area. A western outlet, the Winnipesaukee River, flows SW into the Merrimack River at Franklin. Area: 71 sq mi (184 sq km).

Winston Salem 36 05N 80 18W A city and port in North Carolina. A major tobacco-growing and manufacturing center, other products include textiles and furniture. Population (1990): 143,485.

winter aconite An early-flowering perennial herb of the genus *Eranthis* (7 species), native to temperate Europe, especially *E. hyemalis*, which is often grown in gardens. The flowers are cup-shaped, with six golden-yellow petals surrounded by larger leaflike structures, and appear before the leaves. Family: *Ranunculaceae*.

wintergreen An evergreen creeping perennial herb or small shrub of the family *Pyrolaceae* (about 35 species), found in N temperate and arctic regions. The leaves are simple and the flowers are borne singly or in a terminal spike. They are white or pale-pink with five petals and the fruit is a capsule. Oil of wintergreen comes from the leaves of the winterberry (*Gaultheria procumbens*), a North American shrub, whereas the common wintergreen (*Pyrola minor*) is an herb of Eurasia and North America. Also in the family are the North American pipsissewas (genus *Chimaphila*), woodland herbs with leathery leaves and fragrant flowers.

Winterhalter, Franz Xavier (1806–73) German painter and lithographer, famous for his portraits of European royalty. His sitters included King Louis Philippe and Napoleon III of France as well as Queen Victoria and her family.

Winterthur 47 30N 8 45E A city in N Switzerland. It is an industrial center with heavy engineering and cotton textiles. Population (1987): 108,000.

Winter War. *See* Russo-Finnish War.

Winthrop, John (1588–1649) English colonizer; the first governor of the *Massachusetts Bay Company (1629–33, 1637–39, 1642–43, 1646–48). Leaving England in 1630, he helped to found the colony at Boston. He led the colony as governor and deputy governor for two decades. His *History of New England from 1630 to 1649* is an important chronicle of the colony's development. His son **John Winthrop** (1606–76) was an American colonial governor. Educated at Trinity College, Dublin, he followed his father to the Massachusetts Colony. In 1633, he settled Ipswich, Mass. He returned to London in 1634, but was commissioned to return to Massachusetts and begin a new settlement on the Connecticut River, called Saybrook, named after his patrons. In 1657 he became governor of the Connecticut colony, a position he held until his death. In 1662 he secured a charter from Charles II, which united the colonies of Connecticut and New Haven. He was an enthusiastic amateur chemist, physician, astronomer, and economist, the first American to become a member of the British Royal Society.

wirehaired pointing griffon A breed of hunting dog developed in France during the late 19th century. It is strongly built with a short tail and a longish square muzzle. The harsh bristly coat is a mixture of gray, white, and brown. Height: 21–23 in (54–59 cm) (dogs); 19–21 in (49–54 cm) (bitches).

wireworm. *See* click beetle.

Wisconsin A state in the N central US, situated between the Mississippi River in the W, Lake Michigan in the E, and Lake Superior in the N. It is bordered by Iowa and Minnesota (SW and W), Michigan (NE), and Illinois (S). The Central

Lowlands, which cover the lower two-thirds of the state, give way in the N to the Superior Upland, which is part of the Canadian Shield and contains many forests and lakes. Manufacturing is the state's major economic activity and its industrial belt in the SE links Milwaukee to the Chicago area. The state has 14 ports on the Great Lakes. Leading products include metal goods, lumber, machinery, paper products, and electrical and transport equipment. The state is famous for its dairy products and livestock; it is among the highest producers of hay, alfalfa, and corn, and food processing is a major industry. Tourism is growing, attracted by numerous state parks and forests and developing recreational facilities. *History*: the first European fur traders, explorers, and missionaries entered the area in the 1630s, followed by major tribal shifting among Indian peoples driven westward. The French lost their control of the area to the British at the end of the *French and Indian Wars (1763). Ceded to the US by the British in 1783, large-scale immigration in the 1820s led to its organization as a territory (1836) and it became a state in 1848. During and after the Civil War the area was enormously productive in industry and agriculture. World War II ship building increased the state's prosperity, and the state remains a great industrial center. Area: 56,154 sq mi (145,438 sq km). Population (1990): 4,891,769. Capital: Madison.

Wisdom of Solomon Book of the *Apocrypha, an important example of Jewish "wisdom literature," which also includes the books of Proverbs, Job, Ecclesiastes, and Ecclesiasticus. It was originally written in Greek, probably by a Hellenized Jew of Alexandria in the 2nd century BC. In encouraging a search for wisdom, it describes its benefits, praises its divine source, which is God, and traces how wisdom has helped the Jews and confounded their enemies.

Wise, Isaac Mayer (1819–1900) US rabbi, born in Bohemia. Wise had congregations in Albany, N.Y., and Cincinnati, Ohio, where the changes he urged led to his becoming a leader of Reformed Judaism in the US. He founded the Union of American Hebrew Congregations (1873), the Hebrew Union College (1875), of which he was president for 25 years, and the Central Conference of American Rabbis (1889).

Wise, Stephen Samuel (1874–1949) US rabbi, born in Hungary. Wise received his doctorate from Columbia University in 1901 and founded the Free Synagogue in New York City in 1907. An ardent Zionist, he founded the American and the World Jewish Conferences, and the Jewish Institute of Religion, which later united with the Hebrew Union College. Wise was involved in political struggles for better government and social legislation.

Wissler, Clark (1870–1947) US anthropologist. Professor of anthropology at Yale University (1924–40), Wissler was famous for his research on the geographical and regional aspects of race and culture. His best-known book is *The American Indian* (1917).

Wister, Owen (1860–1938) US novelist. A graduate of Harvard (1882), he studied music in Paris before returning to Harvard for a law degree. He spent his summers in Wyoming and made the West the topic of most of his fiction: the collections *Red Men and White* (1896), *Lin McLean* (1898), and *The Jimmyjohn Boss and Other Stories* (1900). His best-known work, a novel entitled *The Virginian* (1902), became a best-seller with a play, three films, and a television series based on it. The title character, strong and taciturn, became a model for the Western hero. Wister also wrote biographies of Ulysses S. Grant, George Washington, and Theodore Roosevelt.

Wisteria A genus of twining, usually woody vines (10 species), native to E Asia and North America and grown as ornamentals, especially *W. floribunda* from Japan, which may reach a height of 100 ft (30 m). The compound leaves have paired pointed leaflets and the flowers, usually purple, are borne in large hanging clusters, up to 35 in (90 cm) long. Family: *Leguminosae*.

witan A body of 30 to 40 high-ranking laymen and ecclesiastics, which advised Anglo-Saxon kings on such major policy matters as foreign policy and taxation. It met only at the king's will and had no fixed procedure. As a court, it decided on cases affecting the king and other important persons.

witchcraft The supposed manipulation of natural events by persons using supernatural means to harmful ends. In Europe the biblical injunction "Thou shalt not suffer a witch to live" (Exodus 22.18) sanctioned widespread persecution. Social and religious upheavals in the 16th and 17th centuries brought an upsurge in witch-hunts; the famous outbreak at Salem, Mass. (1692), is a case of witch hysteria. Witches were accused of worshiping the devil at nocturnal orgies (sabbaths), of keeping evil spirits (familiars), and of killing livestock, wrecking crops, and causing barrenness, impotence, and fits. Many traditional African communities hold witchcraft accountable for a similar range of inexplicable misfortunes. It is countered by witch-doctors who identify witches and suggest means of neutralizing their malign psychic powers.

witch hazel A shrub or small tree of the genus *Hamamelis* (6 species), native to E Asia and North America, especially the American *H. virginiana*, which is the source of witch-hazel lotion used in pharmacy. This and several other species are often grown as ornamentals, having small clusters of attractive yellow flowers, each with four strap-shaped petals. The fruit is a woody capsule surrounded by a yellow cuplike calyx. Family: *Hamamelidaceae*.

witchweed A parasitic herb of the genus *Striga* (about 10 species), native to the Old World tropics. Up to 30 in (75 cm) tall, it has rough narrow sometimes scalelike leaves and solitary blue, purple, red, yellow, or white two-lipped flowers. The roots derive nutrients from the roots of other plants, including many crops. Family: *Scrophulariaceae*.

Witte, Sergei Yulievich (1849–1915) Russian statesman. As finance minister (1892–1903) Witte initiated the Russian industrial revolution, making capital available to industry and obtaining foreign loans. He greatly encouraged railroad construction. As prime minister (1905–06), he was instrumental in founding the *Duma following the Revolution of 1905.

Wittelsbach The ruling dynasty of Bavaria and the Rhine Palatinate. Wittelsbachs ruled these German states from the late 12th century until deposed in 1918 in a republican coup.

Wittenberg 53 00N 11 41E A city in E Germany, on the *Elbe River. The Reformation began here on Oct 31, 1517, when Martin Luther nailed his 95 theses to the door of All Saints Church. The town is an important industrial center. Population (1981): 54,000.

Wittgenstein, Ludwig (1889–1951) Austrian philosopher. After studying engineering in Vienna he turned to philosophy, studying under Bertrand *Russell at Cambridge (1912–13), where he eventually succeeded G. E. *Moore as professor. His two major works are the *Tractatus Logico-philosophicus* (1921) and the posthumously published *Philosophical Investigations* (1953). Wittgenstein's abiding preoccupation was with language, particularly with the problems that language's relationship to things pose for the philosopher. In his earlier work he developed the "picture theory" of language—words represent things by established conventions—but later he developed the more sophisticated "game" or "toolkit" models, in which actual usage is more important than set convention.

This approach to language as a predominantly social phenomenon has been enormously influential among English-speaking philosophers.

Witwatersrand (*or* the Rand) A ridge of hills in NE South Africa. It extends about 100 mi (160 km) chiefly W of Johannesburg, forming the watershed between the Limpopo and Orange river systems. It has been worked for gold since the 1880s and now produces about one-third of the world's gold output.

woad A branching perennial or biennial herb, *Isatis tinctoria*, native to central and S Europe. Formerly cultivated for the blue dye extracted from its crushed leaves, it is now rare. Up to 48 in (120 cm) tall, it has narrow leaves and terminal branching clusters of tiny four-petaled yellow flowers. Family: **Cruciferae*.

Wodehouse, Sir P(elham) G(renville) (1881–1975) US humorous writer, born in Britain. After 1909 he lived mostly abroad and became a US citizen in 1955. In his many comic novels featuring Bertie Wooster and his manservant Jeeves, including *The Inimitable Jeeves* (1923) and *The Code of the Woosters* (1938), he portrayed an English upper-class society fixed forever in the 1920s.

Woden. *See* Odin.

Wöhler, Friedrich (1800–82) German chemist, who, while professor of chemistry at Göttingen University, synthesized urea from ammonium cyanate (1828). This was the first organic compound to have been derived from an inorganic compound, providing evidence against the theory that organic compounds contained a "vital force" absent in inorganic compounds. He also succeeded in isolating the elements aluminum, beryllium, and titanium.

wolf A wild *dog, *Canis lupus*, of Eurasia and North America. Wolves are 55–75 in (140–190 cm) long including the tail (12–22 in; 30–55 cm). They live in packs of 5–30 animals, which patrol their own territories, and feed mainly on mice, fish, and carrion but also attack deer. Mating is often for life and both parents may share in rearing the pups.

Wolves in colder climate are generally larger and shaggier and form bigger packs. There is an almost white N Siberian race, while the Indian pale-footed wolf is small and gray. *See also* timber wolf. □mammal.

Wolf, Hugo (1860–1903) Austrian composer. He studied briefly at the Vienna conservatory and earned his living as a teacher, conductor, and critic. He died insane in an asylum. He wrote 300 *Lieder* (many of which were settings of poems by Goethe and Mörike), the opera *Der Corregidor* (1895), and an *Italian Serenade* for string quartet.

Wolfe, James (1727–59) British soldier. After the outbreak of the Seven Years' War he was sent to Canada. He excelled, under *Amherst, in the capture of Louisburg from the French (1758) and in the following year he besieged *Montcalm in Quebec. His forces scaled the undefended Heights of Abraham from the St Lawrence and a pitched battle ensued in which both commanders were killed. The British victory established their supremacy in Canada.

Wolfe, Thomas (1900–38) US novelist. After abandoning his studies at Harvard University, where he had hoped to become a playwright, Wolfe taught literature at New York University (1924–30) before receiving national attention with the publication of his massive first novel, *Look Homeward, Angel* (1929). His later novels, based for the most part on autobiographical material and set in his native North Carolina, include *Of Time and the River* (1935), *The Web and the Rock* (1939), and *You Can't Go Home Again* (1940). The final two works were published posthumously.

Wolf-Ferrari, Ermanno (1876–1948) Italian composer of German-Italian parentage. He spent most of his life in Venice, composing such operas as *The School for Fathers* (1906) and *Susanna's Secret* (1909).

wolf fish A slender marine fish, *Anarhichas lupus*, also called catfish, found in the N Atlantic and North Sea, down to 1000 ft (300 m). It has a blue-green or greenish body up to 47 in (120 cm) long, with dark vertical bars, a long blunt head, doglike teeth, long dorsal and anal fins, and no pelvic fins. It feeds on bottom-dwelling hard-shelled animals. Family: *Anarhichadidae*; order: *Perciformes*.

Wölfflin, Heinrich (1864–1945) Swiss art historian. A pupil of Jakob Burckhardt (1818–97), Wölfflin wrote chiefly on baroque and classical art. He was the principal exponent of the formal school of art historians, which analyzes style by changes of form in art.

wolfhound. *See* borzoi; Irish wolfhound.

wolframite The principal ore of tungsten, consisting of ferrous tungstate, (Fe,Mn)WO$_4$. It is brown, black, gray, or reddish in color and is found particularly in quartz veins associated with granitic rocks. *See also* scheelite.

Wolfram von Eschenbach (c. 1170–c. 1220) German poet. A knight, he served at several courts. His great romance, *Parzifal* (c. 1212), is the first German work to use the story of the Holy Grail and is the basis of Wagner's opera. Allegorizing man's spiritual development, it tells how the innocent fool becomes the wise keeper of the Grail.

wolfsbane. *See* aconite.

Wolfsburg 52 27N 10 49E A city in N Germany, in Lower Saxony on the Mittelland Canal. Founded in 1938, it grew around the Volkswagen car factory. Population (1991 est): 127,000.

wolf spider A *spider, also called hunting spider, belonging to a widespread family (*Lycosidae*; over 175 species). Wolf spiders, up to 1 in (25 mm) long, are dark brown with long stout legs and live on or in the ground, often in specially constructed tubes. They are usually active at night, hunting prey rather than trapping it in webs. The female carries the eggs and young.

Wollstonecraft, Mary (1759–97) British writer. She was a member of a group of political radicals that included Tom Paine and her husband, the social philosopher William *Godwin. Her best-known work is *A Vindication of the Rights of Women* (1792), which argued for equal opportunities for all in education. She died in giving birth to her daughter, who became Mary *Shelley.

Wolsey, Thomas, Cardinal (c. 1475–1530) English churchman and statesman; lord chancellor (1515–29) under Henry VIII. He entered Henry's service in 1509 and became archbishop of York and (1515) a cardinal. He used his position to amass a huge personal fortune that did much on the eve of the Reformation to bring the Church into disrepute. Wolsey's attempts to raise taxes to pay for his foreign policy encountered violent opposition. He fell from power after failing to persuade the pope to permit Henry to divorce Catherine of Aragon and died on his way to face trial in London.

Wolverhampton 52 36N 2 08W A city in central England. Metalworking and engineering are the principal industries. Traditionally known for locks and keys, it also produces bicycles, tools, hardware, and chemicals. Population (1984): 254,000.

wolverine A carnivorous mammal, *Gulo gulo*, also called glutton, inhabiting northern evergreen forests of Europe, Asia, and America. It is heavily built, about 40 in (1 m) long and weighing about 55 lb (25 kg), and hunts alone, typically ambushing lemmings and rabbits (although it can overcome an old or unfit deer). Family: *Mustelidae.*

Woman's Christian Temperance Union (WCTU) Organization founded in 1874 in Cleveland, Ohio, to work for the abolition of liquor traffic. Now an international organization with over 300,000 members, the WCTU is fighting liquor and narcotics as well as concerning itself with civil and philanthropic works. It publishes the *Union Signal* and the *Young Crusader* and sponsors the Youth Temperance Council (ages 13–29) and the Loyal Temperance Legion (ages 6–12).

womb. *See* uterus.

wombat A bearlike *marsupial belonging to the family *Phascolomidae* (2–3 species), of Australia (including Tasmania). The coarse-haired wombat (*Phascolomis ursinus*) is about 40 in (1 m) long and has short powerful legs with strong claws, which it uses for tunneling underground. It feeds on grass, roots, and tree bark.

Women's Liberation Movement The movement for female equality, which underwent a resurgence in the 1960s and now embraces many different political and social goals. Among the rights feminists demand are: equal pay for equal work, equal educational and job opportunities, the right of the individual to control her own reproductive choices (contraceptives and abortion), the end to segregated clubs or professional organizations, affordable child care, and the passage of the ERA (Equal Rights Amendment). Additionally, adherents believe that attitudes and social customs must be changed if women are to be "liberated." The portrayal of women in the media, a double standard of sexual behavior, and views of women as primarily childbearers or housekeepers, are some of the areas where change is mandated, feminists believe. One of the leading advocates of women's liberation is NOW (*National Organization for Women), founded in 1966 by Betty *Friedan. This and many other organizations continue to work toward the goals of women's liberation.

Women's Rights Movement The movement for women's rights was originally concerned with the issue of female suffrage. In the US, the *Seneca Falls Convention in 1848, organized by Elizabeth Cady *Stanton and Lucretia *Mott, began the movement. In 1869 the *National Woman Suffrage Association, led by Susan B. *Anthony and Stanton, and the *National American Woman Suffrage Association, led by Lucy *Stone, were established. The two groups merged in 1890, but it was not until the passage of the 16th Amendment in 1920 that women gained the right to vote. The movement faded for a time, but has worked in recent decades for equal pay, educational and employment opportunities, liberal abortion laws, child care, and the ERA (*Equal Rights Amendment). While the women's rights and the *women's liberation movements share many of the same goals, both are general designations that include different activities undertaken by different groups at various times and places.

Wŏnsan 39 20N 127 25E A port in SE North Korea, on the Sea of Japan. Badly damaged during the Korean War (1950–53), its industries have since been rebuilt and include oil refining, ship building, railroad engineering, and chemicals. Population (1967 est): 215,000.

wood The hard tissue of the stems and branches of trees and shrubs, beneath the bark, consisting of *xylem cells strengthened with deposits of lignin. The newest xylem—sapwood—is essential for transport of water and nutrients up the tree. As the xylem ages lignin is deposited within the cells, which eventually die. The central part of the trunk—heartwood—consists of dead xylem, which is darker than sapwood due to deposits of tannins and resins. Conifers are referred to as softwoods because the xylem is porous; broad-leaved (angiosperm) trees, which are called hardwoods, contain more fibers and are therefore stronger (*see* timber). □plant.

Wood, Grant (1891–1942) US artist. Wood studied at the Art Institute of Chicago, served with the army in World War I, and studied in Paris in 1923. In 1927 he went to Germany and was influenced both by the "new realism" and by German and Flemish artists of the 15th and 16th centuries. His best subjects were the simple, sturdy, rural folk of his native Iowa, and his most famous work, *American Gothic* (1930), depicts such a couple. His style, known as American regionalism, gives great attention to realism and detail, but with satiric overtones. Other works include *Daughters of Revolution* (1932) and *Parson Weems' Fable* (1939).

woodbine. *See* honeysuckle; Virginia creeper.

wood carving The art of carving sculptures or architectural and furniture decoration in wood. It has been practiced universally since ancient times. *African art principally consists of wood carving. In Europe some of the finest decorative wood carving was achieved in medieval churches. In the 20th century sculptors such as *Brancusi and Henry *Moore have exploited the special characteristics of wood—its vertical graining and organic nature—in the trend toward retaining the inherent characteristics of materials in finished sculptures.

woodchat A small *shrike, *Lanius senator*, occurring in wooded Mediterranean regions. The male has dark wings, back, and tail patches, white underparts, a chestnut neck and cap, and a broad black band across the forehead; the female is duller.

woodchuck. *See* marmot.

woodcock Two species of gamebird, *Scolopax rusticola*, occurring in freshwater marshes and dense damp woodland and generally active at night. They have long bills and feed on worms and insect larvae. Males perform a slow display flight (called roding) during courtship. The American woodcock (*Philohela minor*) is brownish red underneath with a "dead-leaf" pattern above. About 11 in (28 cm) long, it is very stocky with almost no neck. The Eurasian woodcock has a stocky body, 13 in (34 cm) long, and a russet plumage with a dark-barred head and underparts and a white-tipped tail. Family: *Scolopacidae* (sandpipers, snipe).

woodcreeper An arboreal passerine bird belonging to a family (*Dendrocolaptidae*; 48 species) ranging through Central and South America. Woodcreepers are typically 8–12 in (20–30 cm) long and have stout bills, powerful feet with long claws, and an olive-brown plumage with pale stripes on the head and underparts. The tail is stiff, providing support when it climbs spirally up trees, prising off bark and probing in crevices for insects and spiders.

woodcut A relief *printing technique. The design is drawn on the surface of a block of wood, all the undrawn parts being cut away to produce the white areas of the print. The design is then transferred to paper by pressing the inked block onto the paper. The woodcut was used in China (c. 5th century AD) for textile design but its history in Europe dates from the 14th century and is closely connected with the early printed book. Its special qualities—cheapness, boldness, and simplicity—made it particularly suitable for popular book illustration. Leading 16th-century German artists, such as *Dürer and *Holbein, used the medium to supreme effect. Although subsequently used for book illustration, it was only revived as an art form in the late 19th century by *Gauguin and *Munch.

wood engraving A technique of printing images, refined in the 18th century by Thomas Bewick and used extensively during the 19th century for reproductive engraving. The surface of the woodblock is cut away to leave raised areas which, when treated with ink, will appear dark when printed, in contrast to the white line of the incised areas. Boxwood is used for its fine grain, the block being cut transversely. Wood engraving produces a more subtle effect than *woodcut.

woodlouse A terrestrial crustacean of the suborder *Oniscoidea*, found in damp shady places under stones, logs, etc. Woodlice have a body covering of armorlike plates: they can breathe air (through specially modified gills) but require damp surroundings to avoid desiccation. A common species is the pill bug or woodlouse (*Armadillidium vulgare*), about 0.66 in (17 mm) long, which rolls into a ball when disturbed. It has spread from Europe to occur in leaf litter in wooded areas all over the world. Common genera: *Oniscus, Porcellio*; order: *Isopoda.

woodpecker A bird belonging to a family (*Picidae*; about 220 species) occurring worldwide except Madagascar, Australia, and New Zealand; 3.5–22 in (9–57 cm) long, woodpeckers have multicolored plumage, often barred or spotted. Most are exclusively arboreal, chiseling through bark with their long straight bills in search of insects, which are extracted with a long sticky protrusible tongue. Their short strong feet with large claws and the stiff wedge-shaped tail are adaptations for climbing. *See also* ivory-billed woodpecker; wryneck.

WOODPECKER *The European green woodpecker* (Picus viridis) *bringing food to its young, which are housed in a tree hole.*

wood pigeon A large Eurasian *pigeon, *Columba palumbus*, which is a serious pest on farmland, eating grain and other crops; 16 in (40 cm) long, it has a predominantly gray plumage with a black-tipped tail, brownish back and wings, white wing patches, and a green, purple, and white neck patch.

woodrush A grasslike perennial plant of the genus *Luzula* (about 80 species), occurring chiefly in cold N temperate regions. The Eurasian great woodrush (*L. sylvatica*) has leaves up to 12 in (30 cm) long and 0.8 in (2 cm) wide, which are fringed with colorless hairs. Family: *Juncaceae* (rush family).

wood sorrel A herbaceous plant of the genus *Oxalis* (about 800 species), of temperate and tropical regions, especially *O. acetosella*, of Europe. This species has compound three-part leaves (made up of heart-shaped leaflets) and solitary white five-petaled flowers. Many species are ornamentals and some, including the vegetable oca (*O. tuberosa*), have edible tubers. Family: *Oxalidaceae*.

Woodville, Elizabeth (c. 1437–92) The wife from 1464 of Edward IV of England. Royal patronage of her family caused dissensions among Edward's Yorkist supporters and on his death (1483) the power of the Woodvilles was undermined by the duke of Gloucester, who deposed Elizabeth's son Edward V and became Richard III. Elizabeth was retired to a convent.

Woodward, Robert Burns (1917–) US chemist, who, while working at Harvard, won the 1965 Nobel Prize for his syntheses of a number of organic compounds. His first success was his synthesis of quinine in 1944. He then went on to synthesize strychnine, cortisone, cholesterol, and chlorophyll as well as an antibiotic.

woodwasp A *sawfly belonging to the families *Xiphydriidae* (Europe and North America), *Sytexidae* (North America), or *Orussidae* (worldwide). *Xiphydriidae* larvae bore into deciduous trees, such as alder, birch, and maple. *Sytexidae* are restricted to the incense cedar tree. *Orussidae* larvae are external parasites on wood-dwelling beetle larvae. *See also* horntail.

woodwind instruments Blown musical instruments in which a column of air is made to vibrate either by blowing across a mouth hole, as in the flute, or by making a single or a double reed vibrate, as in the oboe, bassoon, clarinet, and saxophone. The length of the vibrating column is varied by opening and closing holes, either with the finger or by means of keys.

woodworm A wood-boring beetle of the genus *Anobium*, especially the furniture beetle (*A. punctatum*), 0.20 in (5 mm) long, which damages furniture and old buildings. The larvae bore into wood and emerge when adult, leaving large numbers of holes. In time, the wood is reduced to dust. Family: *Anobiidae*.

wool Fibers obtained from the coats or fleeces of domestic sheep. Elastic, resilient, and absorbent, it is also an excellent insulator because of its bulk, the result of its curliness (crimp). The fleeces of different breeds vary widely. *Merino wool is the best in quality; it is short, fine, soft, and the most crimpy. It now comes chiefly from Australia, South Africa, South America, and the US. Since World War II synthetic fibers have been mixed with wool.

Woolf, (Adeline) Virginia (*born* Stephen; 1882–1941 British novelist. A central figure of the *Bloomsbury group, she developed an impressionistic style in which she attempted to express the essential fluidity of existence. Her novels include *Mrs. Dalloway* (1925), *To the Lighthouse* (1927), and *The Waves* (1931). She also wrote biographies and criticism, including a series of essays entitled *The Common Reader* (1925–32). She committed suicide by drowning after the recurrence of a mental illness. Her husband **Leonard (Sidney) Woolf** (1880–1969), whom she married in 1912 and with whom she founded the Hogarth Press in 1917, was literary editor of the *Nation* (1923–30) and wrote five volumes of autobiography (1960–69).

Woollcott, Alexander Humphreys (1887–1943) US journalist and critic. He worked as drama critic for the *New York Times* before serving on the army newspaper *Stars and Stripes* during World War I. He returned as drama critic for the *Times* until 1922, then reviewed for the *Herald* (1922–25) and the *World* (1925–28). Known for his acid wit and theater gossip, he had a successful radio program, "The Town Crier." Among his collected writings are *Shouts and Murmurs* (1922), *Enchanted Isles* (1924), *While Rome Burns* (1934), and *Long, Long Ago* (1943). Woollcott had some acting roles and performed in *The Man Who Came to Dinner* as a character George S. Kaufman and Moss Hart modeled on Woollcott himself.

Woolley, Sir Leonard (1880–1960) British archeologist. He worked at *Carchemish and *Tell el-Amarna but is famous chiefly for his brilliant excavations at *Ur (1922–34), his popular accounts of which stimulated widespread interest in the archeology of the biblical lands.

woolly bear. *See* tiger moth.

woolly monkey A large long-tailed monkey belonging to the genus *Lagothrix* (3 species), of South America. The smoky woolly monkey (*L. cana*) has short pale hair and dark head, arms, legs, and tail. Males may grow to 48 in (120 cm) long including the tail (24–27.5 in; 60–70 cm). They have strong teeth and jaws and feed on fruit, leaves and unripe nuts. Family: *Cebidae.*

woolly rhinoceros A rhinoceros belonging to the extinct genus *Coelodonta*, which inhabited Eurasia and North Africa during the Pleistocene epoch (2.5 million to 10,000 years ago). Well-preserved specimens found in ice and oil deposits show that it was a large shaggy-coated animal with two horns, the front one very long and sharp.

woolly spider monkey A rare monkey, *Brachyteles arachnoides*, of SE Brazil. It has long legs, short woolly fur, and a prehensile tail and is thought to be arboreal and vegetarian. Family: *Cebidae.*

Woolworth, F(rank) W(infield) (1852–1919) US businessman, who created a chain of over a thousand shops across the US selling low-priced goods. The first was opened in 1879 in Utica, N.Y. He also opened stores in many other countries. The Woolworth Building in New York City, which he commissioned, was the world's tallest building (1913–30).

Worcester 42 17N 71 48W A city in Massachusetts on the Blackstone River. Settled in 1673, textile manufacturing began in 1789 and the country's first corduroy cloth was produced there. The Free-Soil party, which opposed the extension of slavery, developed from a meeting held there in 1848. A cultural and educational center, it is the site of Clark University (1887) and several other colleges and universities. Manufactures include precision instruments and chemicals. Population (1990): 169,759.

Worcester 52 11N 2 13W A city in W central England, on the Severn River. The cathedral, begun in 1084, is mainly 14th-century. At the battle of Worcester (1651) Charles II was defeated by Cromwell. Worcester is famous for its porcelain. Population (1981): 74,247.

Wordsworth, William (1770–1850) British poet. He became an enthusiastic republican during a visit to Revolutionary France (1791–92). In 1795 he met S. T. *Coleridge, with whom he collaborated on *Lyrical Ballads* (1798), a seminal work of the romantic movement. In 1799 he settled in the Lake District of England, where, cared for devotedly by his wife Mary and his sister Dorothy, he wrote what is usually considered his masterpiece, a verse autobiography entitled *The Prelude* (completed 1805; published 1850). In this and other poems he described his feelings of mystical union with nature.

WILLIAM WORDSWORTH *A profile of Wordsworth drawn in 1807.*

work The product of a force and the distance through which it causes a body to move in the direction of the force. Work, like energy, is measured in *joules.

work hardening The strengthening of metal by hammering or rolling it without heating. Metal consists of small crystals (grains). Softness or ductility is caused by irregularities (dislocations) in the grains that are able to move and change the crystal shape under stress. Movement of dislocations is blocked at the boundaries between grains. Continued working makes the dislocations collect at the grain boundaries, thus making the metal harder. *See also* heat treatment.

workhouses Institutions set up in the 17th century in Europe, primarily Britain, to provide employment and shelter for paupers. An 1834 British law made it necessary for anyone seeking assistance to enter a workhouse, which because of their inhuman rules and severe discipline soon became dreaded places.

Works Progress Administration (WPA) A federal agency created in 1935 as part of Pres. Franklin D. Roosevelt's *New Deal program. It was renamed the Works Projects Administration in 1939. Its purpose was to provide employment during the *Depression, and during the years 1935–43 it employed 8.5 million people at a cost of nearly $11 billion. The WPA sponsored a construction program that built roads, buildings, bridges, and airports, and an arts program that employed artists, musicians, sculptors, and writers, as well as the National Youth Administration, which found part-time work for young people. The agency was disbanded in 1943 in the wake of the increased prosperity that accompanied World War II.

World Bank. *See* International Bank for Reconstruction and Development.

World Council of Churches An organization of more than 200 Protestant and Orthodox churches. One of the principal results of the *ecumenical movement of the first half of the 20th century, it was founded at Amsterdam in 1948, with headquarters at Geneva. Its membership includes almost all major Christian Churches except the Roman Catholic, which sends observers and cooperates closely with it.

World Cup An international soccer competition first held in 1930 and thereafter every four years, except during World War II. It is organized by the *Fédération internationale de Football association.

World Federation of Trade Unions An international association of national federations of labor unions, founded in 1945. A number of Western labor-union federations withdrew in 1949 to establish the *International Confederation of Free Trade Unions.

World Health Organization (WHO) A specialized agency of the *United Nations established in 1948 to facilitate "the attainment by all peoples of the highest possible level of health." WHO supports programs to eradicate diseases (in 1979 WHO was able to report that smallpox had ceased to exist), carries out and finances epidemiological research, trains health workers, strengthens national health services, and has established international health regulations; it also provides aid in emergencies and disasters. Its headquarters are in Geneva.

World Meteorological Organization (WMO) A specialized agency of the *United Nations established in 1951 with the aim of standardizing international meteorological observations and improving the exchange of weather information. Its chief activities are the World Weather Watch program, which coordinates facilities and services provided by member states, and a research and development program that aims to extend knowledge of the natural and human-induced variability of climate. Its headquarters are in Geneva.

World War I (1914–18) The Great War between the *Allied Powers, including the UK, with countries of the British Empire, France, Russia, Belgium, Japan, Serbia, Italy (from May 1915), Portugal (from March 1916), Romania (from August 1916), the US (from April 1917), and Greece (from July 1917) on one side, and the *Central Powers, including Germany, Austria-Hungary, Turkey (from November 1914), and Bulgaria (from October 1915) on the other. Its causes included fear of the German Empire's European and colonial ambitions since its defeat of France in the Franco-Prussian War (1870–71). Tensions among European powers were expressed by the formation of the *Triple Alliance of Germany and Austria-Hungary (1879) and Italy (1882) and of the *Triple Entente between France and Russia (1893) and France and the UK (1904; *see* Entente Cordiale). Rivalries surfaced in the crises in Morocco in 1905–06 and 1911 and in Bosnia in 1909; the immediate cause of the war lay in the conflict of interests between Russia and Austria-Hungary in the Balkans. On June 28, 1914, the heir to the Austro-Hungarian throne, Archduke Francis Ferdinand, was assassinated at Sarajevo in Bosnia by a Serbian nationalist and on July 28 Austria-Hungary, with German support, declared war on Serbia. On July 29 Russia mobilized its forces in support of Serbia; on Aug 1 Germany declared war on Russia and on Aug 3, upon France. Germany's invasion of Belgium brought the UK into the war at midnight on Aug 4. The main theaters of war were the Western and Eastern Fronts, the Middle East, Italy, and the German colonies in Africa and the Pacific.

Western Front: German strategy at the start of the war was based on the *Schlieffen plan, which envisaged a rapid flanking movement through the Low Countries. The German forces under von Moltke advanced rapidly through Belgium until they were forced by the British Expeditionary Force (BEF) and the French under Joffre, at the first battle of the Marne (Sept 5–9), to retreat across the River Aisne. Germany's effort to reach the Channel was thwarted at the first battle of Ypres (Oct 12–Nov 11) and the combatants settled, on either side of a line from Ostend to Switzerland, to the futile trench warfare for which World War I is notorious. The year 1915 saw a series of inconclusive battles with huge loss of life—at Neuve-Chapelle (March), again at Ypres (April–May), where the Germans used poison gas for the first time, and at Loos (Sept). On Feb 21, 1916, the Germans launched a crippling attack on the French at Verdun but on July 1 Haig, who had succeeded Sir John French as commander of the BEF, opened the crucial battle of the Somme, during which *tanks were used (by the British) for the first time and where the Allies lost some 600,000 men and the Germans, about 650,000. In early 1917 the Germans under Ludendorff withdrew behind the *Hindenburg line; in April, Haig took Vimy Ridge (with the loss of 132,000 men); but the French campaign in Champagne was disastrous and in mid-May Gen. R. G. Nivelle (1856–1924) was replaced by Pétain. With the US (incensed by German *submarine warfare) now participating, on July 31 Britain launched the third battle of Ypres and by Nov 6 had taken Passchendaele. In the spring of 1918 Germany thrust a bulge in the Allied line, which Foch was able to wipe out at the second battle of the Marne. Ludendorff was forced back to the Hindenburg line, which in September was broken between Saint Quentin and Cambrai. By October Germany was suing for peace.

Eastern Front: in August 1914 the Russians advanced into E Prussia but were defeated at *Tannenburg. When late in 1914 Turkey attacked Russia in the Caucasus Mountains, the Allies launched the **Gallipoli campaign**, at first a naval (Feb–March) and then a military operation fought mainly by Australian and New Zealand forces (*see* ANZAC). It failed to break through the Dardanelles and by January 1916, the Allies had withdrawn. Germany's offensive on the Eastern Front in the summer of 1915 forced Russia back and after the Central Powers had overcome Poland, most of Lithuania, and Serbia the Allies landed at Salonika; the ensuing **Macedonian campaign** continued without progress until Bulgaria at last capitulated in September 1918. The failure of the Allies to relieve Russia led to its collapse following the outbreak of the Russian Revolution (March 1917).

Middle East: the **Mesopotamian campaign**, intended to protect oil installations, was launched with the landing of an Indian force at Abadan on Nov 6, 1914. Early advances were halted when the Allies failed to take Baghdad (November 1915) and in April 1916, they lost Kut al-Amara to the Turks. In February 1917, it was retaken and, in March, Baghdad fell. Meanwhile the Allies had invaded Palestine and, aided by the Arab revolt, Allenby took Jerusalem in December 1917; his victory at Megiddo (September 1918) and capture of Damascus and Aleppo finally crushed the Turks.

Italy: the Italian front was maintained along the River Isonzo through 11 battles until 1917, when the Italians were forced by Austria-Hungary to retreat from Caporetto (Oct–Nov) in an overwhelming defeat. In October 1918, however, Austria-Hungary was defeated at Vittorio-Veneto and in November finally capitulated.

War at sea and in the air: at **sea** the superior British navy was dominant until shaken by the battle of *Jutland in May 1916. Although defeated off Coronel in November 1914, victory in December off the Falkland Islands enabled Britain, with Australia, New Zealand, and Japan, to take the German colonies in Africa and the Pacific by September 1916. The real threat to the Allies at sea came from the German U-boats, which sunk some 6000 ships, including the *Lusita-

nia, in the course of the war. At their most active in 1917, their effectiveness was reduced following the introduction of the convoy system. World War I was the first war in which **aircraft** were used: in 1915 the German Zeppelins began to attack British cities and in 1917 German aircraft were also introduced. Some air combat took place on the Western and Eastern Fronts and toward the end of the war the Allies were bombing German cities.

WORLD WAR I *The Eastern Front.*

Conclusion: with the defeat of the Turks and Bulgarians in September 1918, and of Germany on the Western Front and Austria-Hungary in Italy in October, revolt broke out in Germany. On Nov 9 the German emperor, William II, fled and on Nov 11 Germany signed the armistice. On Jan 18, 1919, the Allies met at the *Paris Peace Conference to determine the peace settlement, which was signed by Germany (the Treaty of Versailles) on June 28. The Allies lost some 5 million lives (of which 3 million were French and Russian) in the war and the Central Powers, some 3.5 million (of which 3 million were German and Austro-Hungarian). A further 21 million combatants were wounded.

World War II (1939–45) The war between the Allied forces, including the UK and countries of the Commonwealth, France (until June 1940; thereafter the

Free French), the Soviet Union (from June 1941), the US (from December 1941), and China (from December 1941) on one side, and the *Axis powers, including Germany, Italy (from June 1940), and Japan (from December 1941) on the other. The war was caused by the failure of the *Paris Peace Conference to provide for the maintenance of international security after World War I and by the territorial ambitions of Nazi Germany under Adolf Hitler. In March 1938, Germany annexed Austria (*see* Anschluss) and in September, following the *Munich Agreement, the *Sudetenland. In March 1939, Hitler occupied the rest of Czechoslovakia, and Britain and France guaranteed to support Poland—Hitler's next objective—against German aggression. On May 23 Hitler came to an agreement with Mussolini's Italy, which in April had conquered Albania. Hitler's and Stalin's nonaggression pact followed on Aug 23 and Britain, France, and Poland made an agreement of mutual assistance on Aug 25. On Sept 1 Germany invaded Poland and two days later Britain and France declared war.

Western Europe (1939–41): by Sept 27 Poland had succumbed to the German *Blitzkreig. The Soviet invasion of Finland (*see* Russo-Finnish War) brought Finnish capitulation by March 1940, and in April Germany invaded Denmark and Norway. The Allied failure in Scandinavia led to Neville Chamberlain's resignation and on May 10, the day that Germany invaded Belgium and the Netherlands, Churchill became Britain's prime minister. The German advance across the Meuse River to the coast outflanked the *Maginot line and separated the main French force from the French First Army, the Belgian army, and the British Expeditionary Force; on May 26 an Allied evacuation from the Continent was ordered. Between May 29 and June 4, some 338,226 Allied troops were rescued from Dunkirk by the British navy and a fleet of small private boats. On June 22 Pétain signed the French armistice with Germany, following which French resistance to the Axis powers was directed by de Gaulle from London, where he organized the *Free French (*see also* Maquis).

Britain now faced an imminent German invasion. In August and September 1940, the German *Luftwaffe attacked SE England and then London in a series of daytime raids. In October, German bombing was carried out at night and extended to other British cities in the following months. The Luftwaffe failed to cripple the RAF or to terrorize the British people and by the end of October the so-called Battle of Britain had been won by the RAF. The RAF lost 915 aircraft in the conflict and the Luftwaffe some 1733.

Africa and the Middle East (1940–43): in September 1940, Italy advanced from Libya into Egypt but the Italians were forced to retreat by British troops. By Feb 6, 1941, the Allies had captured 113,000 Italian soldiers but their success was undermined by the arrival in N Africa of Rommel and the German Afrika Corps. In March the British force was weakened by the dispatch of troops to aid Greece against an imminent German invasion (Yugoslavia and Greece were to fall in April and Crete in May) and Rommel was able to force an Allied retreat to the Egyptian border.

In November the Allies launched an offensive against Rommel but by January 1942, had again been forced to withdraw, taking up a defensive position at El-Alamein, inside the Egyptian frontier. In the decisive battle of Alamein (Oct 23–Nov 4) Britain's Montgomery defeated Rommel, forcing his retreat along the N African coast. On Nov 8 an Anglo-US force under Eisenhower landed on the coast of French N Africa. The French under Darlan surrendered and the Allies advanced through Tunisia to make contact (Apr 7, 1943) with Montgomery's Eighth Army, which was moving N from Alamein. On May 7 the Allies took Bizerte and Tunis and on May 13 the Axis forces surrendered; some 248,000 German and Italian troops were captured.

WORLD WAR II

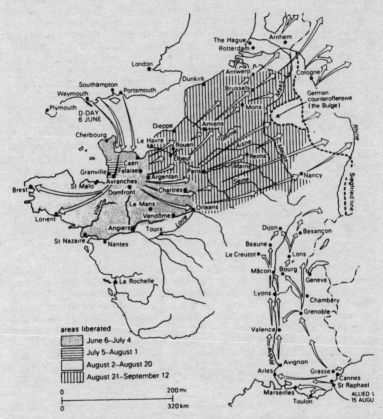

The development of the Western Front after the Allied D-Day invasion of Normandy.

In **East Africa**, the British had taken Addis Ababa from the Italians in April 1941, and were in control of Ethiopia, as well as British Somaliland (captured by Italy in August 1940), by May. In the **Middle East**, in April, Britain occupied Iraq, by June Lebanon and Syria were in Allied hands, and in August the Allies gained control of Iran.

Italy (1943–45): on July 10, 1943, the Allies landed in Sicily. On July 25 Mussolini fell and on Sept 3 the Italian armistice was signed and the Allies landed on the Italian mainland. The Germans held back the Allies at the Ortona-Garigliano line until an Allied offensive, launched on May 12, 1944, succeeded in breaking through to Rome (June 4). In the following months the Allied forces made their way northward; Bologna and then Milan were taken in April 1945, and on May 2, shortly before the final German collapse, Trieste fell.

Eastern Front (1941–45): Germany, with Finland, Hungary, and Romania, invaded the Soviet Union on June 22, 1941. The Axis forces took the Crimea and the Ukraine in the S, besieged Leningrad in the N, and by November were in sight of Moscow. The Soviets staged an effective counterattack in the winter of 1941–42 but Germany retaliated in June with a new offensive and by August the famous battle of *Stalingrad had begun. This heroic Soviet victory resulted in a decimated German Sixth Army and the capture (January 1943) of its commander Paulus. The Germans launched a new offensive in July but were gradually forced back until expelled from Soviet soil in August 1944. On Aug 23 the Soviet Union secured a Romanian armistice and on Sept 19, a Finnish armistice. Also in September, Bulgaria declared war on Germany and the Germans evacuated Greece. On Oct 5 Belgrade fell following collaboration between the Red Army and Tito's Partisans. In October, Soviet troops invaded Germany and in January 1945, launched a final offensive, taking Poland, Austria, and Hungary and entering Czechoslovakia. Berlin fell on May 2, shortly after Hitler's suicide.

Western Front (1944–45): on June 6, 1944, D-Day, the Allied invasion of Normandy began under the supreme command of Eisenhower. Allied bombers had prepared the way with an operation of strategic bombing in place of the relatively ineffective (although destructive of life) bombing of German cities that had reached its peak early in 1944. By July 2 one million US and British troops had landed in Normandy. The British took Caen and US troops, after capturing St Lô (July), invaded Brittany. The Canadians took Falaise on Aug 17, shortly after US and French troops had landed in the south of France from the Mediterranean. On Aug 25 Paris fell to the Allies, who now pursued Montgomery's plan for advancing into the Ruhr from Belgium and the Zuider Zee.

At the battle of Arnhem in September airborne troops were dropped to secure bridges but were withdrawn after ground forces were delayed in breaking through the German defense. In December the Germans launched a counteroffensive (the Battle of the Bulge), driving a bulge, or salient, into Allied lines in the Ardennes region of S Belgium. US troops forced the Germans to retreat in January 1945, and the final Allied offensive was launched. The Rhine was crossed, with air support, in March and by Apr 1 the Ruhr was encircled. On May 4, two days after the fall of Berlin to Soviet troops, German forces surrendered in NW Germany, Holland, and Denmark at Lüneburg Heath. On May 7 the Germans signed a general surrender at Reims, which was ratified two days later in Berlin.

War at sea: The battle for control of the sea routes, known as the **Battle of the Atlantic**, was fought from December 1939, when the German *Graf Spee* inflicted considerable damage on HMS *Exeter* in the battle of the Río de la Plata in the S Atlantic. In November 1940, a successful naval air attack was launched on Taranto and in March 1941, at Cape Matapan the British Mediterranean fleet thwarted an Italian attempt to prevent the transfer of British troops from Egypt to Greece. In May occurred the famous sinking of the *Hood* by the *Bismarck* and, three days later, of the *Bismarck* by the *Dorsetshire*. However, as in World War I, the major threat to Allied naval supremacy in western waters was posed by the German U-boats. These reached their height of effectiveness early in 1943 but by the summer, partly owing to the introduction of Allied escort carriers, 37 U-boats had been sunk and the battle of the Atlantic was over.

Asia (1941–45): the Japanese attack on US military installations at Pearl Harbor, Hawaii, on Dec 7, 1941, initiated a truly "world" war. The US immediately declared war on Japan and the other Axis powers. On Dec 10 Germany and Italy declared war on the US and the second *Sino-Japanese War now became part of the wider conflict.

Japan invaded Malaya on Dec 8 and captured Hong Kong (Dec 25), Manila (Jan 3, 1942), and Singapore (Feb 15) together with 90,000 British and Commonwealth troops. The Dutch East Indies (Sumatra, Java, and parts of New Guinea) fell on March 10, and the Philippines and Burma in May. The Japanese seemed within reach of India and Australia when the US naval and air victories of the *Coral Sea (May 4–8), *Midway Island (June 4–6), and *Guadalcanal (August) halted Japan's eastward expansion. In October 1944, the Japanese fleet was decisively defeated at *Leyte Gulf and the Allied conquest of Manila (February 1945), the Philippines (June), and Borneo (May–June) followed. Burma was reconquered between January and May 1945. Japanese resistance was finally ended by the atomic bombing on Aug 6 and 9 respectively of Hiroshima and Nagasaki, and Japan formally surrendered on Aug 14.

Conclusion: in May 1945, with the fall of Berlin and the German collapse in Italy and on the Western Front, the war in Europe was over. The postwar settlement was decided upon at the *Potsdam Conference, held near ruined Berlin, in July and August (*see also* Tehran Conference; Yalta Conference).

In the course of the war Germany lost some 3.5 million combatants and 780,000 civilians. In contrast the Soviet Union lost 11 million combatants and 7 million civilians; the Japanese 1.3 million and 672,000, respectively; the US, 292,131 and 6000 and the UK 264,443 and 92,673. In addition some 5.7 million Jews died in Nazi *concentration camps; of these 3.2 million were Poles.

World's Columbia Exposition (May 5–Oct 30, 1893) International exposition, or world's fair, held in Chicago to celebrate the 400th anniversary of Christopher Columbus's discovery of America. Covering 666 acres (270 hectares) in Jackson Park, on the shores of Lake Michigan, the fair boasted 150 buildings known as the "White City" because of their white plaster facades. Their style influenced American architecture greatly in the following century. Total attendance was 27 million people; the fair cost $31 million and showed a profit of $1.85 million. It was the first exposition to include a separate "midway," or amusement area.

worm A soft-bodied elongated invertebrate. The term is applied to members of several different groups, especially *earthworms and various parasitic species, and sometimes the larvae of insects. *See also* annelidworm; beardworm; flatworm; nematode; ribbon worm.

worm lizard. *See* amphisbaena.

Worms 49 38N 8 23E A city in SW Germany, in Rhineland-Palatinate on the Rhine River. Heavily bombed during World War II, it has an 11th-century cathedral and a romanesque-gothic synagogue (1034). It is an industrial center and is famed for its local wine, *Liebfraumilch*. *History*: in the 5th century AD it was the capital of the kingdom of Burgundy. Among the imperial diets (assemblies) held there was that of 1521 at which Luther refused to recant. It was annexed by France in 1797 and passed to Hesse-Darmstadt in 1815. Population (1984): 73,000.

wormwood An aromatic herb or shrub of the worldwide genus *Artemisia* (about 200 species), especially *A. absinthium*, which is found chiefly in grasslands of the N hemisphere and is the source of *absinthe. Up to 31 in (80 cm) high, it has deeply divided leaves and small yellow flowers grouped into long loose spikes. Family: *Compositae*.

Wouk, Herman (1915–   ) US novelist. He wrote radio scripts before starting his first novel while in the US Navy during World War II. Among his works are *Aurora Dawn* (1947), *City Boy* (1948), *The Caine Mutiny* (1951), for which he won the Pulitzer Prize, *Marjorie Morningstar* (1955), *Youngblood Hawke* (1962), *The Winds of War* (1971), *War and Remembrance* (1978), *Inside, Out-*

side (1985), and *The Hope* (1994). Several of Wouk's works have been adapted as movies or television miniseries.

Wounded Knee The site in SW South Dakota of the last confrontation (Dec 29, 1890) between the Indians and US troops. Fearing that the anti-white Ghost Dance cult (the popularity of which was in part a response to the wretchedness of life on reservations) would cause an uprising among the discontented Sioux, troops killed more than 200 men, women, and children at Wounded Knee creek. In 1973 some 200 members of the American Indian movement occupied the village of Wounded Knee in protest against government Indian policies. After a 69-day siege, in which two Indians were killed, they were forced to surrender.

woundwort An annual or perennial herb of the widely distributed genus *Stachys* (some 200 species). It has square stems and lance-shaped or heart-shaped toothed leaves. Whorls of two-lipped tubular flowers, yellowish-white, pink, deep-red, or purple, are borne in the leaf axils and the fruit is a small nutlet. Family: **Labiatae.*

Wouwerman, Philips (1619–68) Dutch painter, born in Haarlem. Influenced by the Dutch painter Bamboccio (Pieter van Laer; c. 1592–1642), he specialized in camp and battle scenes, particularly studies of horses. Some of his prolific output is attributed to his brothers **Pieter Wouwerman** (1623–82) and **Jan Wouwerman** (1629–66).

wrack A large brown **seaweed of the order *Fucales*, found almost worldwide on rocky shores and particularly prominent in colder regions. Leathery straplike branching fronds arise from a circular rootlike anchor (holdfast), often bearing numerous air bladders to aid flotation. Examples are bladderwrack (*Fucus vesiculosus*) and serrated wrack (*F. serratus*).

Wrangel, Ferdinand Petrovich, Baron von (1794–1870) Russian explorer. He led a Russian naval expedition to the Arctic (1820–24). Both the Wrangell Mountains and Wrangel Island are named for him. As governor of Russian territories in Alaska (1829–35), he opposed its sale to the US.

Wrangel, Peter Nikolaievich, Baron (1878–1928) Russian general. A divisional commander in World War I, following the Russian Revolution he joined the White armies against the Bolsheviks, distinguishing himself at Tsaritsyn (now Volgograd; 1919). Succeeding **Denikin as commander, he lost Sevastopol and was forced to evacuate his armies from the Crimea (1920).

Wrangel Island (Russian name: Ostrov Vrangelya) A Russian island in the Arctic Ocean, between the East Siberian Sea and the Chukchi Sea. Since 1926 there has been a small Chukchi and Eskimo population. Area: about 2818 sq mi (7300 sq km).

wrasse A fish of the family *Labridae* (300 species) found near rocks or coral reefs in shallow tropical and temperate seas. It has a slender often brilliantly colored body, 2–79 in (5–200 cm) long, long dorsal and anal fins, and thick lips. They are known for their elaborate courtship and nesting behavior and many species can change their sex and coloring. They feed on marine invertebrates and the external parasites of other fish. Order: *Perciformes. See also* hogfish.

wreckfish A carnivorous fish, *Polyprion americanus*, also called stone bass, found in Mediterranean and Atlantic offshore waters, often associated with floating wreckage and seaweed. It has a deep heavy body, up to 7 ft (2 m) long, dark brown above and yellowish below, a large head, and a jutting lower jaw. Family: *Serranidae*; order: *Perciformes.*

wren A small brown bird belonging to a family (*Troglodytidae*; 63 species) found in North and South America. Wrens are 3.5–9 in (9–22 cm) long with sharp slender bills and short cocked tails. The only Eurasian species, *Troglodytes troglodytes*, is about 4 in (10 cm) long and has a reddish-brown plumage with barring on the wings and tail. It lives mainly in undergrowth, feeding on small insects and spiders.

The name is also given to small songbirds of the families *Maluridae* (Australian wrens, e.g. the *emu wren) and *Xenicidae* (New Zealand wrens, e.g. the rifleman).

Wren, Sir Christopher (1632–1723) English architect and scientist. He was a founder member of Britain's Royal Society and later its president (1680–82). His first architectural designs were for Pembroke College chapel, Cambridge (1663), and the Sheldonian Theater, Oxford (1664). A short trip to Paris (1665–66) led him to adopt his typically baroque style. Within days of the Fire of London in 1666, Wren produced a new plan for the whole city, incorporating spacious avenues and piazzas. The plan was rejected but Wren was commissioned to rebuild 51 city churches and some 36 company halls. Basing many of his designs for the churches on *Vitruvius's Roman basilica, Wren showed enormous ingenuity in fitting his buildings into the old irregular sites. His design for St Paul's Cathedral was accepted, after many modifications, in 1675. His later buildings include the Greenwich Hospital (begun in 1694) and additions to Hampton Court (1698).

Wren, P(ercival) C(hristopher) (1885–1941) British novelist. He spent his early life wandering the world, working mostly as a soldier. The best known of his many popular adventure novels are those concerning the French Foreign Legion, especially *Beau Geste* (1924).

wren babbler. An insect-eating bird belonging to one of several genera of the family *Timaliidae* (*see* babbler), occurring chiefly in S Asia; 4–6 in (10–15 cm) long, wren babblers have a shortish upturned tail and short straight bill. They usually live on the ground, feeding in small flocks beneath bushes and forest undergrowth.

wrestling A form of unarmed combat, one of the most ancient sports, in which two people attempt to throw and hold each other down. It first became an Olympic sport in 704 BC. Modern wrestling became an organized sport in the 18th century. There are two main international styles. **Graeco-Roman wrestling** is the most popular style on the European continent; holds on the body below the waist and the use of legs to hold or trip are not allowed. They are, however, allowed in **freestyle wrestling** (which developed from the Anglo-American **catch-as-catch-can** form). In both styles a wrestler wins a match by securing a fall (throwing his opponent onto his back and pinning both shoulders to the mat for one second) or by accumulating the most points according to a complex scoring system. If neither wrestler achieves a fall or is disqualified the bout lasts for three three-minute rounds. There are 10 weight categories. **Sambo wrestling** is the third recognized international style, originating from styles found in the Soviet Union. **Sumo** is the highly popular Japanese style in which the wrestlers, usually weighing around 285 lb (130 kg), attempt to force each other out of the ring. The international governing body is the Fédération internationale des Luttes amateurs. *See also* judo.

Wright, Frank Lloyd (1869–1959) US architect of international fame, whose style was among the most individual of the modern movement. A pupil of Louis *Sullivan from 1888 to 1893, he first demonstrated his originality in a series of Chicago houses between 1900 and 1909, the most famous being the Robie house (1909). These long low spacious designs have proved very influential.

Later buildings include Falling Water in Bear Run, Pa. (1936), the Johnson Wax factory at Racine, Wisc. (1936–39), Taliesin West (1938), his winter home in the Arizona desert, where he established an architectural community, and the Guggenheim Museum (1959) in New York City. □architecture.

Wright, Orville (1871–1948) US aviator, who with his brother **Wilbur Wright** (1867–1912) made the first powered and controlled flights on Dec 17, 1903. They took place near Kitty Hawk, N.C., and in the second, lasting about a minute, the aircraft covered a distance of 820 ft (250 meters). The flight failed to interest either the US public or the government but the brothers continued to make improvements to their machine, eventually succeeding in staying airborne for an hour. In 1908 Wilbur Wright shipped the aircraft to France, where it was enthusiastically received, and in 1909 Orville secured a US army contract. □aircraft.

Wright, Richard (1908–60) US novelist and critic. He was born into a poor family. His works include *Native Son* (1940), a seminal novel of social protest, the autobiographical *Black Boy* (1945) and its sequel *American Hunger* (1977), *The Outsider* (1953), *Black Power* (1954), and *White Man, Listen!* (1957). From 1946 he lived in Paris.

writing systems The recording of human communication using signs or symbols to represent spoken words or concepts. The earliest known writing systems were all originally *pictographic; if they survived at all they developed into *ideographic systems (*see also* Chinese). True alphabetic writing developed around the E Mediterranean about 2000 BC (*see* Semitic alphabets). An intermediate stage is the use of *syllabaries.

Wrocław (German name: Breslau) 51 05N 17 00E A city in SW Poland, on the Oder River. Founded during the 10th century, it developed as an important center on the amber trade route between the Roman Empire and the Baltic Sea. During World War II it suffered severe damage under siege from the Soviet armies (1945). Old buildings that have been reconstructed include the 13th-century cathedral. Its university was founded in 1945. It is now an important industrial and communications center; industries include electronics, engineering, and food processing. Population (1992 est): 643,100.

wrought iron An almost pure form of iron, often with less than 0.1% carbon. It was originally produced by a laborious process of repeatedly hammering and folding hot *pig iron to squeeze out the impurities. The *puddling process has now superseded hand working.

wrybill A New Zealand *plover, *Anarhynchus frontalis*; 6 in (15 cm) long, it has a gray plumage with white underparts and a black breast band. The bill, which is curved to the right, is used to probe for insects under stones and in muddy shallow water.

wryneck A small *woodpecker belonging to a subfamily (*Jynginae*; 2 species) occurring in Eurasia; 6 in (16 cm) long, wrynecks have a gray-brown mottled plumage and a small bill. They do not drill holes but feed mostly on ants and pupae and nest in empty holes.

Wuchow. *See* Wuzhou.

Wuhan 30 35N 114 19E A port in E central China, the capital of Hubei province at the confluence of the Yangtze and Han rivers. Formed by the amalgamation (1950) of the ancient cities of Hankou (*or* Hankow), Hanyang, and Wuchang, it is the commercial and industrial center of central China. The university was established in 1913. It was a center of both the Taiping Rebellion (1851–64) and the 1911 revolution. Its chief industry is iron and steel. Population (1990): 3,284,229.

Wu Hou (625–705 AD) A Chinese empress of the Tang dynasty. Following the death of her husband, the emperor, she ruled through two puppet emperors until 690 when she seized the throne and the imperial title. Although a capable ruler, she was forced to relinquish the throne shortly before her death.

Wu-hsi. *See* Wuxi.

Wu-hsing. *See* Wuxing.

Wundt, Wilhelm (1832–1920) German physiologist and pioneer of modern experimental psychology. His *Principles of Physiological Psychology* (2 vols, 1873–74) was one of the first scientific approaches to the study of the conscious mind. Wundt also wrote works on human physiology and perception.

Wuppertal 51 05N 7 10E A city in NW Germany, in North Rhine-Westphalia in the *Ruhr. It was formed in 1929 from six towns, including Elberfeld, and was heavily bombed in World War II. It is a textile-producing center. Population (1991 est): 378,000.

Württemberg A former kingdom in W Europe. It became a duchy in 1495 and a kingdom in 1806. Divided into two West German *Länder* following World War II, these became part of the *Land* of *Baden-Württemberg (1952).

Würzberg 49 48N 9 57E A city in S Germany, in Bavaria on the Main River. The former episcopal residence (1720–44), containing frescoes by Tiepolo, was damaged in the bombing of World War II but later restored, as was the cathedral (1034). Roentgen taught at the university (founded 1582). A wine-producing center, its manufactures include machine tools and chemicals. Population (1991 est): 126,000.

Wuxi (*or* Wu-hsi) 31 35N 120 19E A city in E China, in Jiangsu province on the *Grand Canal. A major grain market since the 7th century AD, it is also an industrial center. Population (1990): 826,833.

Wyatt, Sir Thomas (1503–42) English poet. A member of the court of Henry VIII, he served on various foreign diplomatic missions. He was one of those responsible for introducing Italian verse forms and meters, notably the Petrarchan sonnet, into English poetry. Ninety-six of his poems were included in the influential collection known as *Tottel's Miscellany* (1557).

Wycliffe, John (c. 1329–84) English religious reformer. Wycliffe spent most of his life at Oxford, first as a student and then as lecturer in philosophy. Although initially protected by friends at court, he made increasingly radical criticisms of the Church, resulting in his enforced retirement to Lutterworth and his condemnation as a heretic. He attacked the doctrine of transubstantiation and emphasized the importance of the Bible, of which he supervised the first English translation from the Latin. Wycliffe's adherents, the *Lollards, were forerunners of English Protestantism.

Wye River A river in E Wales and W England. Flowing mainly SE from Plynlimmon through Builth Wells and Monmouth, it joins the Severn River near Chepstow. It is noted for its beautiful scenery and has valuable salmon fisheries. Length: 130 mi (210 km).

Wyeth, Andrew (Newell) (1917–) US painter; the son and pupil of artist/illustrator **N(ewell) C(onvers) Wyeth** (1882–1945). One of the best-known 20th century American artists, his most famous work is *Christina's World* (1948). Wyeth's realistic style is spare and somber, as he uses watercolor and tempera to record scenes of everyday life in rural America with meticulous detail. His son **Andrew Wyeth** (1946–) is a well-known painter with many of the artistic characteristics of his father.

Wylie, Philip Gordon (1902–71) US author. His works include *Heavy Laden* (1928) and *Opus 21* (1949), as well as some science fiction and the essays *A Generation of Vipers* (1942) and *Essay on Morals* (1947). He combined an interest in Jungian psychology with a critical view of such aspects of American society as women's influence over men ("momism"), religion, attitudes toward sex, conservation, and ecology.

Wyoming One of the mountain states in the NW US, bordered by Idaho (W), Montana (N), South Dakota and Nebraska (E), and Colorado and Utah (S and SW). The topography is one of forested mountains (the state is crossed diagonally from the NW by the Rocky Mountains) and grassy plains. Its economy is based on natural resources, especially oil; other important minerals are natural gas, uranium, coal, trona, bentonite clay, and iron ore. Livestock production, principally cattle, dominates farming. There is very little manufacturing; the main activities are oil refining, food processing, printing, and publishing. Tourism is significant with visitors attracted to the superb scenery of Grand Teton and Yellowstone national parks. *History*: part of the territory acquired from France by the Louisiana Purchase (1803), the area became a major crossing in the expansion westward; the arrival of the Union Pacific Railroad (1867–69) brought settlement in the S and the area became a state in 1890. Agrarian development has been encouraged by liberal legislation and progressive conservation policies. Area: 97,914 sq mi (253,596 sq km). Population (1990): 453,588. Capital: Cheyenne.

Wyss, Johann Rudolph (1782–1830) Swiss writer. A professor of philosophy, he collected and published Swiss folk tales and folklore. He also completed his father's manuscript of the successful novel *The Swiss Family Robinson* (1812–27) and wrote the Swiss national anthem.

Wyszyński, Stefan, Cardinal (1901–81) Polish Roman Catholic churchman. Ordained in 1924, he became bishop of Lublin in 1946, and archbishop of Gniezno and Warsaw and Primate of Poland in 1949. He was imprisoned in 1953 for condemning Communist opposition to the Church. On release (1956) he enjoyed considerable pastoral liberty, serving as president of the Second Vatican Council in 1962.

X

Xanthus A city of ancient Lycia in Asia Minor famous for its heroic resistance to the Persians about 540 BC and to Brutus's Roman forces in about 43 BC.

Xenakis, Yannis (1922–) Greek composer, who studied engineering and architecture before turning to music. He developed a method of composition based on mathematical studies of probability. His compositions include *Duel* (for 54 instruments and 2 conductors; 1959).

xenon (Xe) A noble gas, present in the atmosphere and discovered in 1898 by Sir William Ramsay and M. W. Travers (1872–1961), in the residue of distilled liquid air. The first noble gas compounds were discovered by N. Bartlett (1932–), by reacting xenon with dioxygenyl platinum hexafluoride ($O^+_2PtF^{-6}$) to form Xe^+PtF^{-6}, which is a white solid. Several compounds are now known. Xenon is used in special lamps and the radioactive isotope ^{133}Xe is produced in nuclear reactors. It is a "poison," i.e. a neutron absorber, and is a crucial factor in the control of the chain reaction (*see* nuclear energy), building up to a constant level during steady operation and decaying with a half-life of a few days on shutdown. At no 54; at wt 131.3; mp −170°F (−111.9°C); bp −161°F (−107°C).

Xenophanes (6th century BC) Greek poet. Born in Ionia, he traveled extensively in the Mediterranean countries and lived mostly in Sicily and S Italy. Only a few fragments survive of a philosophical poem on nature and of some elegies. He was a monotheist, rejecting Homeric mythology and traditional Greek religious beliefs.

Xenophon (c. 430–c. 354 BC) Greek historian and soldier. He was born in Athens and, although he had little talent for philosophy, made the acquaintance of Socrates and became his devoted disciple. In 410 he joined a group of Greek mercenaries serving under the Persian prince Cyrus, who was leading an expedition against his brother, Artaxerxes II, king of Persia. Cyrus was killed in battle, the Asiatic army fled, and the force of 10,000 Greeks was left isolated. Xenophon as commander successfully led the mercenaries in a heroic retreat through the hostile Persian Empire to the Black Sea, a feat that formed the subject of his best-known work, the *Anabasis*. He later served in the Spartan army under King Aegesilaus. He wrote numerous other works, including *Memorabilia, Apology*, and *Symposium*, which deal with Socrates.

Xenopus. *See* clawed frog.

Xerography. *See* photocopying machine.

xerophyte A plant that lives in a hot dry climate, such as a desert, and is adapted for conserving water. Cacti, for example, often have spiny leaves (to prevent water loss) and green succulent stems (in which water is stored). A **xeromorph** is a plant that shows some of the features of xerophytes but may not live in desert areas.

Xerxes I (d. 465 BC) King of Persia (486–465). Having brutally repressed revolts in Egypt, he invaded Greece (*see* Greek-Persian Wars) with huge forces (480), at first successfully. However, defeat at *Salamis (480), *Plataea and Mycale (479), and the consequent revolt of the Asiatic Greeks forced him to withdraw. This tyrannous ruler and compulsive builder was assassinated in a court intrigue.

Xhosa A Bantu people of the *Transkei (South Africa). They are primarily cultivators, with some cattle. Today many Xhosa are migrant laborers in other areas of South Africa. Their language employs click sounds borrowed from the *Khoisan languages.

Xia Gui (*or* Hsia Knei; c. 1180–c. 1230) Chinese landscape painter, who worked for the Song emperors. His lyrical and mystical interpretations of landscape, in which human figures are dwarfed by mist-swathed mountains and dramatically poised trees, influenced later Chinese and Japanese artists.

Xiamen (Hsia-men *or* Amoy) 24 26N 118 07E A city in SE China on the island of Xiamen, in Fujian province, situated on Taiwan Strait. It is linked to the mainland by a causeway. The university was established in 1921. Industries include ship building, engineering, fishing, and food processing. *History*: Xiamen has traded intermittently with Europeans since 1544. After its capture by the British during the Opium War (1841) it became a major tea-exporting port, through which many Chinese emigrants passed. Population (1990): 368,786.

Xi An (Hsi-an *or* Sian) 34 16N 108 54E A city in central China, the capital of Shenxi province on the Wei Ho (River). It contains many Tang pagodas and a noted museum. An important industrial center, its industries include steel, chemicals, textiles, and electronics. *History*: as a Tang capital (618–906 AD) it attracted many Buddhist, Muslim, and Christian missionaries. After 1935 it was a Guomindang (Nationalist) base (*see* Xi An incident). Population (1990): 1,959,044.

Xiangtan (*or* Hsiang-t'an) 27 55N 112 47E A port in SE China, in Hunan province on the Xiang Jiang (River; *or* Hsiang Chiang). The commercial center of an agricultural area, its products include textiles, iron and steel, and pig bristles. Population (1953): 183,600.

Xi An Incident (1936) The kidnapping of Chiang Kai-shek by his mutinous army in Manchuria. Chiang was captured by two young marshals, who demanded an end to fighting between Chinese Nationalists (Guomindang) and Communists in the face of the Japanese invasion. Chiang was released when the Communists announced that they would cooperate with the Guomindang in opposing Japan (*see* United Fronts).

Xi Jiang (*or* Hsi Chiang) The most important river in S China, rising in Yunnan province and flowing E to form the densely populated Canton delta and the *Zhu Jiang. Most of its length is navigable by large ships. Length: about 1200 mi (1900 km).

Xingu River A river in central Brazil, rising on the Mato Grosso plateau and flowing generally N to enter the Amazon delta. Length: 1200 mi (1932 km).

Xining (*or* Hsi-ning) 36 35N 101 55E A city in N central China, the capital of Qinghai province. Formerly on the W Chinese border, it was strategically important. Industries include chemicals, metals, wool, and leather. Population (1990): 551,776.

Xinjiang Uygur Autonomous Region (*or* Sinkiang Uigur AR) An administrative region in NW China, the largest, covering one-sixth of the country. It borders on Kazakhstan, Mongolia, Kashmir, and Tibet. Very dry with extreme temperatures, it consists of mountains in the center with the Junggar Pendi in the N and the mainly desert Tarim Basin in the S. The Muslim Uigurs and the Chinese are the largest ethnic groups. Nomads in the N herd livestock, and wheat, cotton, and fruit are grown in oases and valleys. Oil and minerals are produced. *History*: from 206 BC to 1756 AD, Chinese rule alternated with rule by Uigurs, Tibetans, and Mongols, and rebellions against Chinese government continued until 1949. It has recently been greatly developed by the central government. The scene of border clashes with the Soviet Union in 1969, it has great strategic importance. Area: 635,829 sq mi (1,646,799 sq km). Population (1990): 15,155,778. Capital: Ürümqi.

Xiong Nu (*or* Hsiung-nu) Turkish and Mongol tribes on the N and NW borders of China, which threatened Chinese security from about 500 BC. They depended on herding animals for their livelihood and, skilled horseback warriors, conducted raids in times of hardship to plunder the settled Chinese farming communities. The Chinese attempted to control the Xiong Nu by building the frontier walls that eventually became the Great Wall of China, marrying their daughters to Xiong Nu leaders, and trading with them.

Xochimilco 19 08N 99 09W A town in central Mexico, on Lake Xochimilco. It is famous for its *chinamoas* (floating gardens), which originated as soil covered rafts on which fruit and vegetables were grown and have since become islands.

X-ray diffraction The *diffraction of *X-rays when they strike a crystal. The angle through which the X-rays are diffracted depends on the spacing between the different planes in the crystal in a manner given by *Bragg's law. The technique is used in studying crystal structure.

X-rays Electromagnetic radiation lying between ultraviolet radiation and gamma rays in the *electromagnetic spectrum. X-rays may have wavelengths between 10^{-9} meter and 10^{-11} meter, the shorter wavelengths being known as hard X-rays and the longer wavelengths as soft X-rays. Discovered by Wilhelm *Roentgen (and formerly called Roentgen rays) in 1895, they are produced when heavy metal atoms (usually tungsten) are struck by sufficiently energetic electrons, as in an **X-ray tube**. The electrons in an X-ray tube are produced by a heated cathode in an evacuated tube and accelerated to the heavy-metal anode by an electric field. The collisions knock inner electrons from the atoms, X-rays being emitted when the vacancy is filled by outer electrons. X-rays cause ionization in gases and penetrate matter. X-rays have many uses including the examination of internal organs and structures in medical diagnosis, the killing of cancer cells in *radiotherapy, investigating structures for flaws, and in *X-ray diffraction by crystals in order to study their structure.

Xuan Cang (*or* Hsuan-tsang; 602–64 AD) Chinese Buddhist monk. He traveled alone to India and after studying there for about 10 years returned with Buddhist texts, 75 of which he translated. He also left a record of his travels, of great historical value.

xylem A plant tissue specialized for the transport of water and salts. The main cells are tubelike, with their walls strengthened by deposits of *lignin in a spinal arrangement, which aids upward movement of materials by capillary action. In trees and shrubs the lignin deposits eventually block the tubes completely: this tissue forms *wood, and new secondary xylem is produced to transport water.

xylene (*or* dimethyl benzene; $C_6H_4(CH_3)_2$) A colorless toxic flammable liquid consisting of a mixture of three isomers. It is obtained by fractional distillation of petroleum and is used as an aviation fuel and as a solvent.

xylophone A pitched percussion instrument, consisting of a frame on which wooden bars in the pattern of a keyboard are fixed, each with a tubular metal resonator beneath it. It is played with two sticks. Orchestral xylophones usually have a compass of three octaves. *See also* vibraphone.

XYZ Affair (c. 1796–1800) A controversy between the US and France. France expressed its dissatisfaction with the US-British accord of 1794 (Jay's Treaty) by interfering with American shipping. President *Washington's emissary, Charles Pinckney, was insulted by the French in 1796 but returned to France the next year, together with John Marshall and Eldridge Gerry, at Pres. John *Adams's request. After many delays by French officials, the Americans were approached by three unofficial agents (the so-called X, Y, and Z of President Adams's later report to Congress), who volunteered to arrange negotiations in return for a bribe of $250,000 to French foreign minister Talleyrand, loans, and other US concessions. The Americans refused, the proceedings were made public, and outraged Americans threatened war. However, Adams appointed another three-man commission, which arranged the Treaty of Mortefontaine (Convention of 1800) with France.

Y

Yahweh The conjectural pronunciation of one of the Hebrew names of God. The name YHWH (the Tetragrammaton or "four-letter" name) occurs very frequently in the Bible; out of reverence it was traditionally not pronounced, but replaced by *Adonai* (Lord) or *Hashem* (the Name), except by the *high priest when he entered the *Holy of Holies. "Jehovah" represents another attempt to pronounce this name.

yak A shaggy-coated wild ox, *Bos grunniens*, inhabiting mountain pastures of central Asia. Yaks have long been domesticated for draft purposes and milk; their dung is used as fuel. Wild yaks, up to 7 ft (2 m) high at the shoulder with long upward-curving horns, are larger than domestic yaks and are always black; they live in large herds, feeding on coarse grasses, and are expert climbers.

Yakut Autonomous Republic (*or* Yakutia) An administrative division in Russia. The Yakuts, a Mongoloid people, are traditionally nomadic herdsmen but have become sedentary. In NE Siberia, Yakutia (an autonomous republic since 1922) is one of the world's coldest inhabited regions, and agriculture is only possible in the S. Mining for diamonds, gold, tin, and coal is the main occupation, and trapping and breeding of sable, squirrel, and silver fox are also important. Area: 1,197,760 sq mi (3,103,000 sq km). Population (1986): 1,009,000. Capital: Yakutsk.

Yale University One of the oldest universities in the US (founded 1701), situated at New Haven, Conn. It is named for Elihu Yale (1648–1721), who donated his books to the college.

Yalow, Rosalyn S(ussman) (1921–   ) US medical physicist who won the Nobel Prize in medicine (1977). Her research with Dr. Solomon A. Berson led to their development of the radioimmunoassay (RIA) test, which measures minute concentrations of biologically active substances (such as hormones, enzymes, and proteins) in the blood or other body fluids.

Yalta 44 30N 34 09E A port in S Ukraine, on the Black Sea. It is the Crimea's largest seaside resort and was the site of the Allied *Yalta Conference in 1945. Population: 80,000.

Yalta Conference (1945) The conference toward the end of World War II attended by Franklin D. Roosevelt (US), Stalin (Soviet Union), and Churchill (UK). They agreed upon the postwar occupation of Germany by the US, Soviet Union, UK, and France and decided that German surrender must be unconditional.

yam A twining herbaceous plant of the genus *Dioscorea*, cultivated in wet tropical regions for its tubers, which are eaten like potatoes. Yams have long slender climbing stems, bearing entire or lobed leaves, and unisexual flowers in long clusters. Tubers can reach a length of 8.5 ft (2.6 m) and a weight of 100 lb (45 kg); species commonly cultivated are *D. alata* (white yam), *D. rotundata* (white guinea yam), *D. batatas* (Chinese yam), and *D. cayenensis* (yellow yam). Family: *Dioscoreaceae*.

Yamagata, Aritomo (1838–1922) Japanese soldier and statesman. As commander of the Imperial Guard, he created a modern conscript army and while home minister (1885–89) he shaped Japan's modern local government. He twice served as prime minister (1890–91, 1898–1900) and played an important role in Japan's victories over China (1894–95) and Russia (1904–05).

Yamasee War (1715–16) A war between British settlers and the Yamasee Indians living in South Carolina and Georgia. The Yamasee were driven southward and eventually absorbed by the Seminoles of Florida.

Yamato The ruling dynasty of Japan under which the country was united in the 4th century AD. All subsequent Japanese emperors have claimed descent from the Yamato, under whom Buddhism was introduced in the 6th century.

Yang, Chen Ning (1922–) US physicist, born in China, who shared the 1957 Nobel Prize with his countryman Tsung-Dao *Lee for their theoretical work suggesting that parity would not be conserved in the *weak interaction. Their hypothesis was quickly confirmed by observations of beta decay.

Yangon 16 47N 96 10E Formerly named Rangoon, the capital of Myanmar (formerly Burma), a port in the S on the Yangon River. Industry increased greatly after independence in 1948. Its university was founded in 1920. *History*: a settlement grew up in very early times around the Shwe Dagon Pagoda, which is the focal point of Burmese religious life. King Alaungpaya made it his capital in the 18th century. Twice captured by the British in the 19th century, it became the capital of all Burma in 1886. It was badly damaged in World War II during the Japanese occupation (1942–45). Population (1983): 2,513,023.

YANGON *A complex of pagodas and temples surround the Shwe Dagon Pagoda, one of the great Buddhist pilgrimage centers.*

Yangtze River (Chinese name: Chang Jiang *or* Ch'ang Chiang) The longest river in China and the third longest in the world. Rising in a remote mountain range on the borders of Tibet and Qinghai province, it flows roughly E to enter the East China Sea via an extensive delta. A Chinese survey (late 1970s), which finally established the true source of the river, estimated its total power potential to be 230,000 MW (greater than that of all the rivers in the US). The Yangtze is one of China's main transport routes and its densely populated basin is China's most productive agricultural region. Length: 3964 mi (6380 km).

Yaoundé (*or* Yaunde) 3 51N 11 31E The capital of Cameroon. Founded under the German protectorate of Kamerun in 1888, it was capital of Cameroun from 1922 until independence in 1960 (except during World War II). The Federal University of Cameroon was founded in 1962. Population (1987): 649,000.

yard A basic unit of length in the English system originally defined as the distance between two gold plugs on a bronze bar. In 1959 this definition was replaced, and the yard is now defined as exactly 0.9144 meter (*see* metric system).

Yaroslavl 57 34N 39 52E A city in Russia, on the Volga River. It has been a textile center since the 18th century. Population (1991 est): 631,000.

yarrow A perennial herb, *Achillea millefolium*, also called milfoil, native to pastures of Europe and W Asia. Up to 18 in (45 cm) high, it has feathery strongly scented leaves and small white daisylike flowers borne in flat-topped clusters. Family: *Compositae*.

Yawata. *See* Kitakyushu.

yawl A □sailing vessel with two masts, a tall one set approximately one-third of the boat's length from the bow and a very short one just behind the rudder post. Yawls, like ketches, are a favored rig for yachts, for the split rig reduces the area of each sail, making handling easier. Yawls do not sail as well toward the wind as sloops do. *See also* ketch; sloop.

yaws A chronic tropical disease caused by a *spirochete bacterium, *Treponema pertenue*. It occurs mostly among poor children and is spread by skin contact. After an incubation period of three to four weeks a growth appears on the thighs or buttocks; later, multiple growths that look like squashed raspberries appear all over the skin. Bones may also be affected and if not treated the disease can be very disfiguring. Treatment with penicillin is highly effective.

Yazd (*or* Yezd) 31 55N 54 22E A city in central Iran. It has several mosques, some built in the 11th century, and produces silk fabrics. Population (1986): 231,000.

year The time taken by the earth to complete one revolution around the sun. This is equal to the period of the sun's apparent motion around the *ecliptic. The **tropical year**, of 365.2422 days, is the interval between two successive passages of the sun through the vernal *equinox. The **sidereal year**, of 365.2564 days, refers to successive passages of the sun through a point relative to the background stars. These periods differ because of the *precession of the equinoxes. *See also* calendar.

yeast A single-celled fungus that is capable of fermenting carbohydrates and that reproduces asexually by budding new cells from its surface. Typical yeasts belong to the family *Saccharomycetaceae*. Strains of *Saccharomyces cerevisiae*, the cells of which are 0.0001–0.0078 in (0.004–0.02 mm) in diameter, are widely used to cause *fermentation in baking, brewing, and the manufacture of wines and spirits. Yeast extracts are used as a food for their high vitamin B content. Class: *Ascomycetes*.

Yeats, William Butler (1865–1939) Irish poet and dramatist. In London in the 1890s he helped found the Rhymer's Club, pursued his lifelong interest in the occult, and published several volumes of symbolist verse. His best-known poems, many of which appeared in *The Tower* (1928) and *The Winding Stair* (1929), included tragic meditations on personal and political themes. Among them are "Easter, 1916," "The Second Coming," and "Sailing to Byzantium." He was an admirer of Maud Gonne (1866–1953), Irish actress and nationalist, and with Lady *Gregory in 1904 he founded the Abbey Theatre, Dublin, for which he wrote many plays. He was a senator of the Irish Free State (1922–28) and won the Nobel Prize in 1923. His brother **Jack Butler Yeats** (1831–1957) was a noted Irish painter, born in London. After a childhood in Ireland he returned to London to study, but his paintings were essentially Irish, depicting life in bars, music halls, and racetracks in dark colors, often shot with bright explosions of color applied with a palette knife.

W. B. YEATS

Yellow-Dog Contract A contract between employer and employee, usually as a condition of employment, in which the employee agrees not to join a union or assist a union by joining in a strike. The name was applied by labor unionists who claimed only a "yellow dog," or coward, would allow such coercion. The contracts were declared unenforceable in 1932 by the Norris-LaGuardia Act.

yellow fever An acute viral infection transmitted by female mosquitoes of the genus *Aëdes*, which occur in areas of tropical rain forest. After an incubation period of 3–14 days the patient develops a fever with aching muscles. In severe cases the virus affects the liver causing jaundice (hence the name), the kidneys, and the heart; death may result from liver or heart failure. There is no specific treatment but two kinds of vaccine are available for prevention.

yellowfin tuna A large tuna fish, *Thunnus albacares*, distinguished by yellow fins and a golden stripe along its sides. It is found worldwide and is a valued food and game fish.

yellow-green algae *Algae of the division *Chrysophyta* (about 6000 species), which are yellow-green to brown in color depending on the proportion of green chlorophyll masked by the pigments fucoxanthin or diadinoxanthin. Most are unicellular or colonial and they form a major constituent of plankton (*see also* diatoms). Most reproduce asexually by spores.

yellowhammer A Eurasian *bunting, *Emberiza citrinella*, that occurs on farmland and roadsides, where it feeds on grain and seeds. It is about 6 in (16 cm) long and has a distinctive yellow plumage. The male has a bright-yellow head and underparts, chestnut rump, and a brown-streaked back; females are less colorful.

Yellowknife 62 30N 114 29W A city in N Canada, the capital of the Northwest Territories. Founded in 1935, it is the commercial and administrative center of the territory, with an airport and gold mines. Population (1984): 11,000.

Yellow River (Chinese name: Huang He *or* Huang Ho) A river in China, rising in the W and flowing roughly E to enter the Gulf of Chihli via a fertile delta. Its summer floods have resulted in frequent disasters and changes of course. Its diversion as a measure against the Japanese invasion (1938) resulted in the death of 900,000 people. Length: about 2700 mi (4350 km).

Yellow Sea (Chinese name: Huang Hai) A large shallow inlet of the W Pacific Ocean, bordered by China and Korea. It is so called because of the yellowish silt deposited by the Chinese rivers. It is rich in fish.

Yellowstone National Park The largest US national park, chiefly in NW Wyoming but extending into S Montana and E Idaho. Established in 1872, it consists mainly of forested volcanic plateaus. Its many active geysers include Old Faithful, which erupts regularly at approximately hourly intervals. Area: 3458 sq mi (8956 sq km).

Yellowstone River A river, rising in NW Wyoming and flowing N through the *Yellowstone National Park then E to join the Missouri River in North Dakota. Length: 671 mi (1080 km).

yellowwood An evergreen coniferous tree or shrub of the genus *Podocarpus* (over 100 species), mostly of warm temperate and tropical regions of the S hemisphere. The hard leathery leaves are strap-shaped and the green berrylike fruits are borne on fleshy stalks. Yellowwoods are important timber trees; the light elastic nonresinous wood is used for building, furniture, carving, and ships. A few species are grown in the S US; others are popular as houseplants. Family: *Podocarpaceae*.

Yeltsin, Boris Nikolayevich (1931–   ) Soviet and Russian political leader. He first achieved prominence in the Communist party from 1985, when he arrived to head the party organization in Moscow. Originally a close associate and supporter of Pres. Mikhail *Gorbachev, Yeltsin soon called for faster and more liberal reforms. Although dismissed by Gorbachev in 1987, Yeltsin gradually became the leader of the Soviet liberal reformers. In 1990 he was elected to head the Russian republic's parliament, and in 1991 he outmaneuvered Gorbachev politically. By December 1991, Yeltsin had eclipsed Gorbachev and had taken the lead in organizing a new system, the Commonwealth of Independent States (CIS). Following Gorbachev's resignation later in December, Yeltsin became the leader of now-independent Russia. He had to confront a deteriorating economy and to attempt to shore up Russia's weakened international image, while also trying to unify the CIS. Opposition to economic reforms forced Yeltsin to make political and economic concessions in 1992–93, but his goals were also supported in 1993 in a national referendum and in December elections. A new constitution was approved, but a strong showing by ultra-nationalists posed a new threat to Yeltsin.

Yemen, People's Democratic Republic of (*or* South Yemen; name from 1970 until 1990: People's Republic of Southern Yemen) *See* Yemen, Republic of.

Yemen, Republic of A country in the Middle East in SW *Arabia, that was formed from the unification in May 1990 of the People's Democratic Republic of Yemen (South Yemen) and the Yemen Arab Republic (North Yemen), bordering on the W Red Sea, N Saudi Arabia, E Oman, and S Gulf of Aden, including the islands of Kamaran, *Perim Island, *Socotra, and the *Kuria Maria Islands. Mountains (the wettest and most fertile in Arabia) dissected by wadis—chiefly Wadi Hadhramaut—rise from the narrow coastal plain on the S and W; the N and E are desert. There are no rivers but many wadis, oases, and springs. The mainly Arab population is largely Sunnite or Zaidi Muslim. There are nomadic tribes in the N. *Economy*: (South Yemen) mainly agricultural, although little land is cultivated. Cotton is the main crop, others include cereals, coffee, tobacco, fruit, and vegetables. Sardine fishing is important; mineral deposits are not yet exploited. Industry consists chiefly of an oil refinery and a little light industry in Aden. The economy suffered badly from the closure of the Suez Canal (1967–75). Refined oil, cotton, fish products, hides, and incense are exported and food, textiles, and crude oil are imported. (North Yemen) Mainly agricultural; cotton, coffee, cereals, vegetables, fruit, and the narcotic qat are the chief crops and livestock are kept. Industry includes textile, soft-drink, and cigarette factories; salt is mined and handicrafts are important. Machinery, oil, and textiles are imported. North Yemen received money from Yemeni workers aboard (over one-sixth of the population worked in Saudi Arabia) and relied on foreign aid. *History*: (South Yemen) ruled by the imams (priest-kings) of Yemen, the area (excluding Aden) was nominally part of the Ottoman Empire from the 16th century to 1918. Aden was captured from the Turks in 1839 and occupied by the British East India Company. The British made protectorate treaties with other local rulers (1886–1914) to safeguard Aden and its trade routes; these 24 sultanates, emirates, and sheikdoms were called the Aden Protectorate (1937). In 1963 Aden and 10 others formed the Federation of South Arabia. This collapsed in 1967, when anti-British nationalist groups in Aden took control (although the British had already agreed to withdraw), and South Yemen then became independent. Its history was marked chiefly by border disputes with Oman (until 1976) and with North Yemen, despite an agreement to unite North and South Yemen (1972). In 1983 diplomatic progess toward unification advanced. Yemen established diplomatic relations with Oman for the first time in a decade. In 1986, Marxist rebels succeeded in overthrowing the government, which was also Marxist. (North Yemen) Rule by a Muslim imam originated in the 9th century and lasted until 1962, although from 1520 until 1918 the area was nominally part of the Ottoman Empire. North Yemen's boundaries were fixed in 1934 by treaty with Saudi Arabia and the UK, although clashes with the British over the control of Aden continued. It joined the Arab League (1945) and the UN (1947) and was loosely allied with Egypt and Syria (1958–61) in the United Arab Republic. Internal disorders, during which the imam was assassinated (1948), culminated in civil war (1962–70), which ended with the recognition of a republican regime. Another coup took place in 1974 and successive heads of state were assassinated in 1977 and 1978. Relations with South Yemen were strained. Although moves were made toward uniting the two Yemens following the border clashes of 1967–72, continual conflict and distrust between the two countries prevented union. Allegations of South Yemeni involvement in the 1978 assassination were followed by increased border fighting. *Since unification*: a constitution was approved in 1991. The government hoped that increased production from the oil fields discovered in the 1980s would bolster a sagging economy. When Iraq annexed Kuwait in 1990, Yemen objected to the buildup of the UN coalition forces on Saudi Arabian soil. Thousands of Yemeni workers in Saudi Arabia were then expelled by Saudi Arabia and returned home, inflicting yet another burden on Yemen's economy. President: Saleh, Lt. Gen. Ali Abdullah. Area: about 207,000 sq mi (536,000 sq km). Population (1990 est): 11,000,000. Political capital: San'a. Economic capital: Aden.

Yemen Arab Republic (*or* North Yemen) *See* Yemen, Republic of.

Yenisei River A river in Russia, rising in the Sayan Mountains and flowing N to **Yenisei Bay** on the Kara Sea. There is a hydroelectric power station at Krasnoyarsk. Length: about 2485 mi (4000 km).

Yerevan (Russian name: Erivan) 40 10N 44 31E The capital city of Armenia. A commercial center, it has chemical, textile, and food-processing industries. *History*: it occupies the site of an ancient fortress, the city itself dating from at least the 7th century AD. Long disputed by Persia and Turkey, it was ceded to Russia in 1828. Population (1991 est): 1,283,000.

Yerwa. *See* Maiduguri.

Yesenin, Sergei Aleksandrovich (1895–1925) Russian poet. He emerged from a peasant background into Moscow literary society during a period of hectic revolutionary activity. He traveled in the US and Europe, was briefly married to the US dancer Isadora Duncan, suffered from alcoholism and drug addiction, and finally committed suicide. His volumes include *Confessions of a Hooligan* (1924).

Yeti. *See* Abominable Snowman.

Yevtushenko, Yevgenii (1933–) Russian poet. His implicit criticism of the Soviet authorities in such poems as *Babi Yar* (1961) gained him wide popularity among both Soviet and Western readers. He has given many poetry readings in Europe and the US.

yew A coniferous tree or shrub of the genus *Taxus* (10 species), native to the N hemisphere. Yews have dark-green leathery bladelike leaves, 0.04–0.16 in (1–4 cm) long and arranged in two rows along the stems, and the male and female flowers grow on separate trees. The female flowers produce bright-red cup-shaped berrylike fruits, each containing a single seed. The berries are sweet-tasting and attractive to birds, but the seeds and leaves are poisonous. The most widespread species is the common yew (*T. baccata*), of Europe, SW Asia, and N Africa; it grows to a height of 80 ft (25 m) but cultivated forms—grown for shelter, ornament, and topiary work—are often smaller. Family: *Taxaceae*.

Yezd. *See* Yazd.

Yezidis The name of a Kurd tribe of Iraq and their tribal religion. The sect, the center of which is in Mosul, is a synthetic religion that combines Islamic, Christian, Judaic, and other ancient elements.

Yezo. *See* Hokkaido.

Yggdrasill In Norse mythology, an evergreen ash tree embracing the whole universe. Its three roots join the underworld, the land of giants, and the home of the gods (Asgard). Demons threaten its existence; the serpent Nidhögg constantly chews at one of its roots, while four stags eat its buds. However, it is preserved by the *Norns (the Fates), who water it from one of the three fountains at its base. The maypole and the Christmas tree are possibly symbolic derivatives of Yggdrasill.

Yibin (*or* I-pin) 28 50N 104 35E A port in S central China, in Sichuan province at the confluence of the Yangtze and Min rivers. A commercial center, salt is mined there and chemicals and paper are manufactured. Population (1990): 241,019.

Yichang (*or* I-ch'ang) 30 43N 111 22E A port in E central China, in Hubei province on the Yangtze River. An old commercial center, it marked the limit of the Japanese advance during the Sino-Japanese War (1937–45). Population (1990): 371,601.

Yiddish A language used by *Ashkenazim (East European) Jews and based on a dialect of High German. It emerged during the 9th century and has absorbed many Slavonic and other influences. It is written in the *Hebrew alphabet. Yiddish literature flourished in the 19th and early 20th centuries, but after the *Holocaust it yielded its place as the principal literary language of the Jews to Hebrew.

yield point The point at which a body becomes permanently deformed when subjected to a sufficiently large stress. Below the yield point the body is elastic, above the yield point it becomes plastic. *See also* elasticity; plasticity.

yin and yang Contrasting but complementary principles at the root of traditional Chinese cosmology. Yin is the negative feminine mode, associated with the earth, darkness, and passivity. Yang is the positive dynamic principle of masculine energy associated with heaven and light. The principles antedate *Confucius and are particularly important in *Taoism, serving, for example, to explain the cycle of the seasons.

YIN AND YANG *The symbols are interlocked and each contains a tiny portion of the other.*

ylang-ylang A slender evergreen tropical Asian tree, *Cananga adorata*, also called perfume tree. It has pointed oval leaves, up to 8 in (20 cm) long, and bears drooping clusters of fragrant stalked greenish-yellow flowers throughout the year. An oil distilled from the flowers is used in perfumery, cosmetics, and soaps. Family: *Annonaceae*.

YMCA. *See* Young Men's Christian Association.

yoga The principles and practice of self-training that permeates all Indian philosophical traditions. Traces of it exist from the *Indus Valley civilization before the Aryan invasion (1500 BC). The methods used are generally austere and ascetic and include physical control and meditative techniques. Physical control is stressed in Hindu yoga; in the Buddhist practice contemplative methods predominate; in Jainism asceticism is emphasized. Usually the aim is a state of release and liberation from the material world. The yoga so fashionable in the

West frequently takes the form of hatha-yoga, which involves physical exercises to bring peace and insight.

yogurt. *See* dairy products.

Yokohama 35 28N 139 28E A port and second largest city of Japan, in SE Honshu on Tokyo Bay. Together with Tokyo it forms Japan's greatest urban and industrial area and handles 30% of foreign trade. Its industries include ship building, oil refining, chemicals, steel, and textiles. Its two universities were both established in 1949. *History*: it grew rapidly after 1859 as a second port for Tokyo, with which it was linked by Japan's first railroad (1872). It was almost destroyed by the 1923 earthquake and extensively bombed during World War II. Population (1991): 3,220,331.

Yokosuka 35 18N 139 39E A port in Japan, in SE Honshu on Tokyo Bay. William Adams (d. 1620), the first Englishman to visit Japan (1600), is buried there. It has a major naval base and its chief industry is ship building. Population (1991): 433,358.

Yom Kippur (Hebrew: Day of Atonement) A Jewish holy day, falling nine days after *Rosh Hashanah. It is a day of penitence and cleansing from sin and is marked by 24 hours' total fast. *See also* Holy of Holies.

Yong Le (*or* Yung-lo; 1360–1424) The title of Ch'eng-tsu, Chinese emperor (1402–24); after usurping the throne. He was a vigorous builder and expander of the *Ming dynasty, dispatching fleets to SE Asia and personally leading military expeditions. He transferred the capital to Peking from Nanjing.

Yonkers 40 56N 73 54W A city in S New York state on the Hudson River. Industries include elevators, carpets, chemicals, and clothing. Population (1990): 188,082.

York (Latin name: Eboracum) 53 58N 1 05W A city in N England, on the River Ouse. It was the principal Roman garrison in Britain and was long regarded as the northern capital. The cathedral, seat of the archbishop of York, was begun in 1154 and dominates the city. The medieval walls and four city gateways remain. Industries include chocolate manufacturing, sugar, glass, and railroad engineering. York is a major tourist center as well as an important market town and educational center. Population (1985): 102,000.

York A ruling dynasty of England descended from Edmund, duke of York (1342–1402), the fourth son of Edward III. Richard Plantaganet, duke of *York, led the Yorkist opposition to Henry VI's Lancastrian government in the Wars of the □Roses (1455–85), in which the Yorkist emblem was the white rose. His son Edward IV established the royal dynasty. After the brief rule of his son Edward V and the overthrow of Richard III (1485) the crown passed to Henry VII, the first *Tudor monarch, who married Edward IV's daughter Elizabeth.

York, archbishop of The second of the two archbishops of England and head of the northern province of the Church of England. York became an archiepiscopal see in 735 AD. Controversy between Canterbury and York regarding primacy was settled by Pope Innocent II (1352–62), with precedence given to the archbishop of *Canterbury.

York, Richard Plantagenet, 3rd Duke of (1411–60) English magnate, who was descended from the third son of Edward III. His claim to the throne against Henry VI (who was descended from Edward III's fourth son) resulted in the outbreak of the Wars of the *Roses in 1455. He was killed in a skirmish at Wakefield. His sons became Edward IV (1461) and Richard III (1483).

York mystery plays A cycle of 48 plays originating in the 14th century and performed by the trade guilds of York, England, on the feast of Corpus Christi.

The most extensive cycle of medieval plays in England, the York cycle covered the whole of history from a Christian viewpoint, from the creation of the angels to the last judgment, concentrating on the fall of man and his redemption by Christ. They were all performed in chronological order in the course of one day. The series of 14 plays devoted to Christ's Passion were revised into alliterative verse at one stage and are notable for their sometimes disturbing realism.

Yorkshire A former county in NE England, bordering on the North Sea. From the late Middle Ages onward it was an important center of the wool industry.

Yorkshire terrier A breed of toy ☐dog developed from several terrier breeds in N England during the 19th century. It is small and compact with a very long straight coat that trails on the ground. This is black at birth but matures to steel-blue with tan on the head and chest. Height: 8–9 in (20–23 cm).

Yorktown 37 14N 76 32W A village in Virginia on the York River. The last important battle of the American Revolution was fought here in 1781.

Yorktown Campaign (1781) The final decisive action of the American Rev-olution. In 1781, *Washington and French General Rochambeau moved their troops south to Virginia, where Britain's Cornwallis had entrenched his troops in the peninsular town of Yorktown, at the mouth of the York River. Washington had ordered the Marquis de *Lafayette to block Cornwallis by land, and the Chesapeake Bay was occupied by the French admiral De Grass, who success-fully repulsed British ships. Washington and Rochambeau joined Lafayette and opened the battle on Oct 6; on Oct 19, 1781, Cornwallis surrendered.

Yosemite National Park A national park in central California. The scenic Yosemite Valley, which lies within the park, contains the world's three largest monoliths of exposed granite. There are also many lakes, rivers, and waterfalls including the Yosemite Falls, which are the highest in North America with a drop in two segments of 2425 ft (739 m). Area: 1182 sq mi (3061 sq km).

Yoshkar-Ola 56 38N 47 52E A city in Russia, the capital of the Mari au-tonomous republic. Founded in 1578, it has manufacturing and food-processing industries. Population (1991 est): 275,000.

Young, Andrew (1932–   ) US politician and diplomat. As a Congregational Church minister in the Southern Christian Leadership Conference, Young was an associate of the civil-rights leader Martin Luther *King. A Democrat in the House of Representatives (1973–77), Young was US Ambassador to the UN from 1977 until 1979, when he resigned following criticism of his meeting, in contradiction of official US policy, with a representative of the Palestine Libera-tion Organization. He also served as mayor of Atlanta, Ga. (1981–89).

Young, Brigham (1801–77) US religious leader. After being converted to the *Mormon faith by Joseph *Smith in 1832, Young quickly became one of the leading members of the church. He served briefly as head of the Mormon Mis-sion in England and became Smith's successor after the latter's violent death at the hands of a mob in Carthage, Ill., in 1844. Two years later, Young led Mor-mon settlers on a mass migration westward to establish the colony of Deseret in the Valley of the Great Salt Lake (1846–47). In addition to being president of the Mormon Church, he also served as governor of the Utah Territory (1850–57), but was removed from that post by federal authorities because of government objections to the observance of polygamy among the Mormons. Young himself had 19 wives and 56 children. Retaining his leadership of the church until his death, Young established the administrative organization still used by the Mor-mon church in its activities throughout the world.

BRIGHAM YOUNG *Religious leader who succeeded Joseph Smith as head of the Mormons and who led them to Utah.*

Young, Denton Tru ("Cy"; 1867–1955) US baseball pitcher. Active from 1890 to 1911, he set the record for most games won (511). He was elected to the Baseball Hall of Fame in 1937, and annual awards for baseball's best pitcher are named in his honor.

Young, Whitney M., Jr. (1921–71) US social worker, educator, and civil rights leader. After military service in World War II, he worked with the National Urban League (1947–54), became dean of the Graduate School of Social Work at Atlanta University (1954), and joined the Urban League again in 1961 as executive director. He urged the improvement of African-American employment opportunities through job-training programs and favored cooperation rather than militant confrontation. Young wrote *To Be Equal* (1964).

Young Ireland An Irish nationalist movement formed by young Protestant radicals in the 1840s. Its uprising in 1848 under William Smith *O'Brien was a humiliating failure.

Young Italy A movement, founded by Giuseppe *Mazzini in 1831, that sought to establish a united republican Italy. After the failure of Mazzini's invasion of Savoy and other uprisings in the 1830s and 1840s its influence declined. *See also* Risorgimento.

Young Men's Christian Association (YMCA) A Christian organization for young men and, since 1971, for young women, founded in 1844 by George Williams (1821–1905), in England. Its aim is to encourage Christian morality and qualities of leadership. The World Alliance of YMCAs, formed in 1855 in Geneva, consists of 20 million members in 84 countries.

Young's modulus. *See* elastic modulus.

Youngstown 41 05N 80 40W A city in E Ohio. It is a center of an extensive iron and steel industry and produces aluminum, office furniture, and aircraft. Youngstown State University was established in 1908. Population (1990): 95,732.

Youngstown Sheet and Tube Company v. Sawyer (1952) US Supreme Court decision that held that the principle of separation of powers had been violated by Pres. Harry Truman's order to his secretary of commerce Charles Sawyer to seize and operate steel mills during a strike. Truman had feared the strike's impact on the Korean War effort.

Young Turks A Turkish revolutionary group. In 1908 the Young Turks, officially named the Committee of Union and Progress, led the revolution that resulted in Sultan *Abdülhamid's abdication. Under *Enver Pasha and Talaat Pasha (1872–1921), they were the dominant force in Turkish politics until 1918.

Young Women's Christian Association (YWCA) A Christian organization for women (to which men may now also belong). Founded in 1855 in England to promote unity among Christians and understanding between those of different faiths, it provides social welfare, education, and recreational facilities, as well as accommodation in hostels. It is a member of the world movement of the YWCA, formed in 1894 and having branches in over 80 countries.

Ypsilanti A Greek family prominent in Balkan revolts against the Ottoman Empire. Alexander Ypsilanti (c. 1725–c. 1807), governor of Walachia (1774–82, 1796–97) and of Moldavia (1786–88), was executed for allegedly conspiring against the sultan. His son Constantine Ypsilanti (1760–1816), governor of Walachia (1802–06, 1807), participated in a Serbian revolt against the Turks. His elder son Alexander Ypsilanti (1792–1828) led an uprising in Moldavia and proclaimed Greek independence (1821). Defeated, he fled to Austria, where he was imprisoned (1821–27). Alexander's brother Demetrios Ypsilanti (1793–1832) played a prominent part in the War of *Greek Independence.

Ysselmeer *See* IJsselmeer.

ytterbium (Yb) A *lanthanide element, named, like yttrium, erbium, and terbium, after the village of Ytterby in Sweden. It forms trivalent compounds, including the oxide (Yb_2O_3) and trihalides (for example $YbCl_3$). At no 70; at wt 173.04; mp 1508°F (819°C); bp 2182°F (1194°C).

yttrium (Y) A *lanthanide element, discovered in 1794 by J. Gadolin (1760–1852). It is widely used as the oxide (Y_2O_3) to make red television-tube phosphors. At no 39; at wt 88.906; mp 2773°F (1523°C); bp 6039°F (3337°C).

Yuan (1279–1368) A Mongol dynasty that ruled China after overthrowing the *Song dynasty. The first and strongest Mongol ruler was *Kublai Khan, who held the empire together by military force. Later, revolts broke out and the Mongols were eventually driven out of their capital, Peking, following 27 years of fighting.

Yuan Shi Kai (*or* Yüan Shih-k'ai; 1859–1916) Chinese general, who became president of the new Chinese republic in 1912 after the downfall of the *Qing dynasty. His attempts to rule dictatorially and to found a new dynasty brought about civil war with the followers of *Sun Yat-sen. Yuan died suddenly, leaving China in chaos.

Yucatán A peninsula of Central America, chiefly in SE Mexico but extending into Belize and Guatemala, separating the Gulf of Mexico from the Caribbean Sea. It was a center of the civilization of the □Maya; many relics remain, notably at Uxmal and Chichén Itzá. Area: about 70,000 sq mi (181,300 sq km).

Yucca A genus of succulent plants (about 40 species), native to S North America and varying in height from small shrubs to trees 50 ft (15 m) high. Most are stemless and have a rosette of stiff sword-shaped leaves crowded on a stout trunk. The waxy white bell-shaped flowers are borne in a dense terminal cluster and are pollinated by female yucca moths (genus *Pronuba*) when they lay their eggs inside the flowers. Several species are cultivated as ornamentals, including Adam's needle (*Y. filamentosa*) and Spanish dagger (*Y. gloriosa*). Family: *Agarsceae. See also* Joshua tree.

Yugoslavia, Federal Republic of (Serbo-Croat name: Jugoslavija) A country in SE Europe, bounded by the Adriatic Sea (W), Bosnia-Herzegovina, Croatia, and Hungary (NW and NE), Rumania, and Bulgaria (E), and Macedonia and Albania (S). The country erupted into civil war in 1991, and four of its six provinces became independent, leaving a primarily Serbian population. The fertile plains of the Danube-Sava basin in the NE rise to mountains in the S and W, reaching heights of almost 10,000 ft (3000 m). The Serbs and the Croats made up the majority of the population, with minorities of Slovenes, Macedonians, Albanians, and others. In the early 1980s political tension between the minorities resulted in violence and repression. *Economy*: agriculture, mainly organized in cooperatives, is important although the numbers employed in this sector have decreased dramatically in recent years. Mechanization has improved agricultural output and the country is now self-sufficient in chemical fertilizers. Livestock is especially important and the principal crops are wheat, corn, sugar beet, sunflowers, and potatoes. There is a thriving wine industry and forestry and fishing are important sources of revenue. Rich mineral resources include coal, iron ore, copper, and lead, and some oil is produced. Over half the country's power comes from hydroelectric sources. Development of heavy and light industry has been rapid since World War II, and there is a growing tourist industry. Exports include meat, machinery, nonferrous metals, timber, textiles, and ships. *History*: Yugoslavia was so named in 1927 but was formed in 1918 as the kingdom of the Serbs, Croats, and Slovenes by the federation of Serbia, Montenegro, Croatia, Slovenia, and Bosnia-Herzegovina. Alexander I assumed absolute power in 1929 and was assassinated by Croatian nationalists in 1934. In World War II Yugoslavia was occupied by the Germans and Peter II fled to London. Internal resistance to the Germans became divided between the *Chetniks and the Partisans, the latter gaining Allied support in 1943. After the war the Partisans' leader *Tito became head of a communist government. In 1948 relations with the Soviet Union were broken off and, although they became closer again after the death of Stalin, Yugoslavia preserved a policy of nonalignment in foreign affairs and a decentralized form of socialism that aimed to give more direct power to the workers. The mid-1980s witnessed severe economic crises, high unemployment, and political repression. The collapse of communism and of the Soviet Union also contributed to unrest, and in 1991 the Yugoslav confederation began to fall apart. A devastating civil war erupted as the states of Slovenia and Croatia declared their independence. Bosnia and Hercegovina and Macedonia followed in 1992. The two republics, Serbia and Montenegro, and the autonomous regions of Vojvodina and Kosovo formed a smaller Yugoslav confederation and promised, through a new constitution, that it would be a democracy with a market economy and respect for human rights. An acting government composed of leaders from the four areas was installed. Fighting continued from 1992, as local Serbian guerrillas, especially in Croatia and in Bosnia and Herce-govina, backed by Yugoslav government troops, battled over boundaries and spheres of influence. Only intense international pressure, including UN peace-keeping forces, prevented Yugoslavia from taking more aggressive action. Offi-cial currency: dinar of 100 para. Area: 98,725 sq mi (255,804 sq km). Popula-tion: (1991): 10,337,504. Capital: Belgrade.

Yukawa, Hideki (1907–81) Japanese physicist, who, while working at Kyoto University, postulated (1935) that the *strong interaction could be accounted for by the exchange of *virtual particles. He calculated the mass of the particle in-volved, but at that time no such particle was known. *Anderson's discovery of the muon was thought to have confirmed Yukawa's prediction. But in fact the confirmation did not come until 1947, when Cecil *Powell discovered the pion. Yukawa was awarded a Nobel Prize in 1949 for his work.

Yukon A territory of NW Canada, on the Beaufort Sea. Mostly high mountains and plateaus of the Cordillera, it is covered by tundra in the N. Poor soils and low precipitation produce only sparse vegetation, except in S valleys. The popu-lation is concentrated on the central plateau, where silver, lead, zinc, copper and asbestos are mined. There is some lumbering, and tourism is expanding rapidly. The Yukon is a frontier region that was first opened up by the *Klondike gold rush (1897–99) and military projects (since 1939). Area: 205,345 sq mi (531,844 sq km). Population (1991): 27,797. Capital: Whitehorse.

Yukon River A river in NW North America. Rising in NW Canada on the bor-der between the Yukon and British Columbia, it flows N through Alaska, then SW into the Bering Sea. Its great potential as a source of hydroelectricity has yet to be fully exploited. Length: 1979 mi (3185 km).

Yunnan A mountainous province in S China, bordering on Myanmar, Laos, and Vietnam. The ethnically varied population includes aboriginal groups in the mountains. It is China's greatest tin-producing area and rice and timber are grown. *History*: part of China since the 13th century, it was for long rebellious and little developed. It became industrialized during the Sino-Japanese War (1937–45), when many industries moved there from the coast. Area: 168,400 sq mi (436,200 sq km). Population (1990): 36,972,610. Capital: Kunming.

YWCA. *See* Young Women's Christian Association.

Z

Zabrze (German name: Hindenburg) 50 18N 18 47E A city in SW Poland. It is a coal-mining center; industries include steel processing, engineering, and chemicals. Population (1992 est): 206,000.

Zacynthus (*or* Zante; Modern Greek name: Zákinthos) A Greek island in the SE Ionian Sea, the southernmost of the Ionian Islands. Most of the island is fertile and currants are the main product. Area: 157 sq mi (406 sq km).

Zadar (Italian name: Zara) 44 07N 15 14E A port in Croatia on the Adriatic Sea. It has a natural deepwater harbor and was the most heavily fortified Adriatic town until the late 19th century. There are many old churches and a Roman forum. Local industries produce maraschino liqueur, cigarettes, rope, and glass. Population (1981): 116,000.

Zadkine, Ossip (1890–1967) French sculptor of Russian birth. He settled in Paris (1909), where he developed a cubist style in his monumental figure sculptures. His best-known work is the war memorial in Rotterdam, entitled *The Destroyed City* (1954).

Zagazig (*or* az-Zaqazig) 30 36N 31 30E A city in N Egypt, on the Nile Delta. The ruins of the ancient city of *Bubastis are nearby. It has a major trade in cotton and cereals. Population (1986): 245,496.

Zaghlul, Saad (1857–1927) Egyptian nationalist politician; prime minister (1924). In 1918 he helped to found the nationalist Wafd party. He was arrested by the British, but after limited independence was granted in 1922 he became prime minister. He was forced by the British to resign shortly afterward but was active behind the scenes until his death.

Zagorsk (name until 1930: Sergiyev) 56 20N 38 10E A city in Russia, 45 mi (72 km) NE of Moscow. It grew around the famous Trinity-St Sergius monastery (1337–40), the buildings within which, notably the Trinity Cathedral (1422–23) and the Cathedral of the Assumption (1559–85), may still be seen. Population (1991 est): 116,000.

Zagreb 45 48N 15 58E The largest city and capital of Croatia, on the Sava River. A cultural center of the Croats since the 16th century, it possesses a university (1669) and a gothic cathedral. Industries include textiles, machinery, and paper manufacture. Population (1991 est): 931,000.

Zagros Mountains A mountain system in W Iran, extending 1000 mi (1600 km) NW–SE between the Turkish, Armenian, and Azerbaijani borders and the Strait of Hormuz. It consists of many parallel ranges and rises to 15,784 ft (4811 m) in the N at Sabalan.

Zaïre, Republic of (name from 1960 until 1971: Congo) A large country in central equatorial Africa, with a short coastline on the Atlantic Ocean, bounded by Central African Republic, Sudan, Uganda, Rwanda, Burundi, Tanzania, Zambia, Angola, and Congo. The central part of the country is dominated by a vast plateau, rising to the Ruwenzori Mountains in the SE. It is drained by the Zaïre River and its many tributaries and fringed along its E border by a chain of lakes, including Lake Tanganyika, comprising part of the *Great Rift Valley. Most of the population is African, the largest groups being Luba, Mongo, and Kongo. *Economy*: efforts are being made to increase agricultural production, which has fallen in recent years through droughts and political unrest. The chief cash crops are coffee, cotton, palm oil, and rubber; corn, rice, and cassava are grown extensively as the staple food crops. Zaïre has rich and varied mineral resources, principally copper (the chief export) from the Shaba mines, and is the world's chief producer of industrial diamonds and cobalt. Other minerals include manganese, zinc, and uranium and oil has been found offshore (exploited since 1975). Hydroelectricity is a valuable source of power and Zaïre is estimated to have about 50% of Africa's total potential hydroelectric capacity. The rivers, especially the Zaïre River, are also important for transport. *History*: when the Portuguese penetrated the region in the late 15th century it was dominated by the kingdom of the Kongo. In the late 19th century it was explored by David *Livingstone and, under Belgian auspices, by H. M. Stanley. Leopold II of the Belgians established personal rule over the Congo Free State, which was recognized by the European powers at the Conference of Berlin (1884–85). In 1908 it was annexed by Belgium, becoming the colony of the Belgian Congo. Independence was obtained in 1960 with Kasavubu as president and Patrice Lumumba as prime minister of the newly named Republic of the Congo. The almost immediate secession of Katanga province under Tshombe resulted in civil war in which the UN intervened (an international force remained in the country until 1964). In 1965 Mobutu Sese Seko seized power and in 1971 the Congo was renamed Zaïre. In 1977 and again in 1978 an invasion force entered *Shaba (formerly Katanga) province from Angola, in unsuccessful attempts to topple Mobutu, and on the second occasion the massacre of Europeans in Kolwezi brought French and Belgian forces to Zaïre. In 1978 a constitution was ratified making Zaïre a one-party nation; in 1982 a group challenging Mobutu's government on charges of financial corruption was imprisoned for founding a new political party. The early 1980s witnessed a major slump in Zaïre's economy, border disputes, and a continuation of political repression. Economic reforms were instituted twice in the 1980s. By 1990 Mobutu allowed opposition parties to exist, but unrest continued. A national conference on planning for democracy met in 1991 and briefly in 1992 before it was suspended by the government, which claimed that the conference was contributing to the unrest. Civil disturbances increased in 1993, but Mobutu continued to resist demands for reform. Official language: French. Official currency, since 1967: zaïre of 100 makuta. Area: 2,345,409 sq mi (895,348 sq km). Population (1990 est): 35,330,000. Capital: Kinshasa. Main port: Matadi.

Zaïre River (former name: Congo R.) The second longest river in Africa. Its true source is disputed, one headstream being the *Lualaba River and the other the Chambezi River (later the Luvua River), which rises in a high plateau between Lakes Malawi and Tanganyika. Below the confluence of the two headstreams it flows N, being known as the Lualaba until the Boyoma Falls, where it becomes the Zaïre River. It flows generally W then SW, through Malebo Pool, to enter the Atlantic Ocean via a delta at Boma. The Zaïre River became an important potential source of hydroelectric power with the construction of dams in the 1970s. Length: 3000 mi (4820 km).

zaltys A green snake that was a symbol of wealth and fertility in the Baltic region in ancient times. Households often kept a zaltys and it was believed that misfortune would befall anyone who killed one.

Zambezi River A river in S Africa. Rising in NW Zambia, it flows generally S through E Angola before reentering Zambia and curving E along the Caprivi Strip frontier of Namibia. It then forms the Zambian-Zimbabwe border, the *Victoria Falls and Kariba Dam (*see* Kariba, Lake) being located along this course, before flowing SE through Mozambique to enter the Indian Ocean via an extensive delta. It has the fourth largest drainage area in Africa with an area of about 520,000 sq mi (1,347,000 sq km). Length: 1700 mi (2740 km).

Zambia, Republic of (name until 1974: Northern Rhodesia) A landlocked country in S central Africa bordered by Zaïre, Tanzania, Malawi, Mozambique, Zimbabwe, South West Africa/Namibia, and Angola. It consists chiefly of low undulating plateaus and is drained along its southern border by the Zambezi River; other main rivers are the Kafue and Luangwa. The swampy Lake Bangweulu lies in the N. The population is virtually all African, largely Bantu, with small minorities of Europeans, Asians, and Chinese. *Economy*: the mining sector is responsible for producing most of Zambia's wealth from the rich mineral resources. Copper accounts for about 96% of the total mineral production and comes mainly from the *Copperbelt. Lead and zinc from Kabwe are also important, some coal is mined, and there are extensive iron-ore deposits, as yet unexploited. Agriculture is a major occupation; the chief subsistence crop is corn. Cash crops include tobacco, groundnuts, cotton, and sugar but commercial agriculture declined during the 1970s. Livestock and forestry are also important. Communications, which were hampered by the closing of the Rhodesian border (1973) and by unrest in Mozambique, were aided by the opening (1975) of the Chinese-built Tanzam Railway to Dar es Salaam (Tanzania). *History*: the area had already been occupied by Bantu peoples when it was raided by Arab slave traders in the 18th century. In the 19th century British missionaries, notably David *Livingstone, paved the way for Cecil *Rhodes, who incorporated the region into a territory named Rhodesia in his honor and administered by the British South Africa Company. Constituted as Northern Rhodesia in 1911, it became a British protectorate in 1924. It formed part of the Federation of Rhodesia and Nyasaland (1953–63), obtaining internal self-government and, shortly afterward, full independence within the British Commonwealth as the Republic of Zambia (1964). Kenneth *Kaunda, in 1988 elected to his sixth term of office, was president from independence. In 1972 a new constitution led to one-party (the United National Independence party) rule. Zambia supported the Zimbabwe nationalist movement, providing a base for Nkomo's arm of the Patriotic Front, and its border with Rhodesia (now Zimbabwe) was closed from 1973 until 1980. Economic crises of the early 1980s resulted in the presentation of a harsh budget and currency devaluation. In 1990, one-party rule ended. Kaunda was defeated by Frederick Chiluba in 1991 multiparty elections. Record drought in southern Africa made it necessary to increase Zambia's imports of food, further burdening its sagging economy. Official language: English. Official currency, since 1968: kwacha of 100 ngwee. Area: 290,586 sq mi (752,262 sq km). Population (1990 est): 8,119,000. Capital: Lusaka.

Zamboanga 6 55N 122 05E A port in the S Philippines, in SW Mindanao. A resort, it is noted for its picturesque setting and tropical flowers and has a 17th-century Spanish fort. Brass and bronzeware are produced and it exports copra, hardwoods, and hemp. Population (1990 est): 440,000.

Zamoyski A prominent Polish family, which became powerful under **Jan Zamoyski** (1542–1605), who was adviser to Sigismund II Augustus (*see* Jagiellons) and to *Stephen Báthory. **Andrzej Zamoyski** (1716–92) worked for parliamentary reform and the abolition of serfdom, freeing his own serfs. Andrzej's son **Stanisław Zamoyski** (1775–1856) played an important role in the November Insurrection against Russian dominance, as did Stanisław's son **Andrzej Zamoyski** (1800–74), who also participated in the January Insurrection, for which he was exiled (*see* Congress Kingdom of Poland).

Zamyatin, Yevgenii Ivanovich (1884–1937) Russian novelist. His works include vivid satirical studies of life in provincial Russia and England, where he worked during World War I. He was severely criticized after the European publication of his novel *We* (1924), a bleak prophecy of a totalitarian future, and from 1931 he lived in Paris.

Zante. *See* Zacynthus.

Zanzibar An island in Tanzania, off the NE coast of the mainland. It came under Arab influence early on in its history and was, together with *Pemba, a sultanate from 1856 to 1964. It was under British rule from 1890 until it became independent within the British Commonwealth in 1963. In 1964 the Sultan was exiled and Zanzibar united with Tanganyika to form Tanzania. It exports mainly cloves and copra. Area: 640 sq mi (1658 sq km). Population (1988): 157,634. Chief town: Zanzibar.

Zao Zhan. *See* Cao Chan.

Zapata, Emiliano (?1877–1919) Mexican revolutionary, who championed the cause of agrarian reform against Porfirio *Díaz and succeeding governments. By late 1911 he controlled the state of Morelos, where he carried out land reforms, chasing out the estate owners and dividing their land among the peasants. In 1919 he was tricked into an ambush and assassinated.

Zaporozhye (name until 1921: Aleksandrovsk) 47 50N 35 10E A city in Ukraine, on the Dnepr River. A large hydroelectric station, built there between 1927 and 1932, was destroyed in World War II but subsequently rebuilt. There is an important iron and steel industry and a variety of engineering activities. Population (1991 est): 897,000.

Zapotecs An American Indian people of the Oaxaca valleys (S Mexico). Their traditional culture, emerging about 300 AD, developed into one of the classic Mesoamerican Indian civilizations. Monte Alban, their chief city, declined under pressure from the *Mixtecs (c. 900–50).

Zaragoza (English name: Saragossa) 41 39N 0 54W A city in NE Spain, in Aragon on the Ebro River. During the Peninsular War it heroically resisted a French siege until about 50,000 of its defenders had died (1808–09). It has two cathedrals and a university (founded 1533). An industrial center, it produces paper and wine. Population (1991): 586,219.

Zarathustra. *See* Zoroaster.

Zaria 11 01N 7 44E A city in Nigeria. Founded in the 16th century, it became the capital of the emirate of Zaria. It has textile, cosmetics, and cigarette industries. Nearby is the Ahmadu Bello University (1962). Population (1992 est): 345,000.

Zátopek, Emil (1922–) Czech long-distance runner. In 1948 he won his first Olympic gold medal, for the 10,000 m. At the Helsinki Olympics (1952) he won gold medals for the 5000 m, 10,000 m, and the marathon.

Zealand. *See* Sjælland.

Zealots A Jewish political party of the 1st century AD. They were bitterly opposed to Roman rule in Judea, and played a leading part in the revolt of 66 AD. Their last stronghold, *Masada, fell in 73. After the war their influence in Judea was minimal but they may have been responsible for the further revolts in Egypt, Libya, and Cyprus in 115 AD.

Zeami Motokiyo (1363–c. 1443) Japanese playwright, son of the dramatist Kanami Kiyotsugu (1333–84). He achieved fame first as an actor but later became a leading theorist of No drama, his best-known treatise being *Kadensho*. He wrote over 150 plays.

zebra An African wild horse having characteristic black-and-white stripes covering part or all of the body. There are three races of the plains zebra (*Equus burchelli*), distinguished by the extent and nature of their stripes. The mountain zebra (*E. zebra*) has very bold stripes and a dewlap on the throat, while Grévy's zebra (*E. grevyi*) is the largest species, standing over 5 ft (1.5 m) at the shoulder, with narrow stripes.

EMILIANO ZAPATA *This photograph shows the Mexican revolutionary in a formal, but aggressive pose.*

zebra finch An Australian *grassfinch, *Taeniopyga castanotis*, occurring in large flocks in the interior grasslands. It has a red bill and the males are gray above with white underparts, reddish flanks, red-brown ear patches, and black-and-white barred throat, breast, and tail. Zebra finches are popular cagebirds and have been selectively bred to produce a white form with the black-and-white barring.

zebra fish A tropical freshwater fish, *Brachydanio rerio*, also called zebra danio, found in E India and popular in aquaria. It has a shiny blue body, up to 1.8 in (4.5 cm) long, with four longitudinal yellowish gold stripes along its sides. *See also* scorpion fish; tigerfish.

zebra wood Any of several tropical trees that yield hard striped timber, used in furniture, especially *Connarus guianensis*, of Guyana. It has compound leaves with paired oval leaflets and clusters of five-petaled flowers. Family: *Connaraceae*.

zebu The domestic *cattle of Asia and Africa, *Bos indicus*, also called Brahmin (*or* Brahman). Larger and leaner than Western cattle, zebus have a distinctive hump over the shoulders, a large dewlap under the throat, and long horns. They are generally gray or red, but a number of other color varieties exist. Zebus are no longer found in the wild state and have been exported to many hot countries to confer their qualities of heat tolerance and insect resistance in crosses with beef breeds.

Zebulun, tribe of One of the 12 *tribes of Israel. It claimed descent from Zebulun, the son of Jacob and Leah. Its people lived to the W and SW of the Sea of Galilee.

Zechariah An Old Testament prophet of Judah, who delivered his prophecies about 520 BC. **The Book of Zechariah** relates a series of eight visions calculated to inspire the people to rebuild the Temple at Jerusalem. The book also deals with questions concerning fasting and predicts the coming of a kingly messiah and the end of the Diaspora.

Zedekiah The last king of Judah (597–586 BC). Having rebelled against *Nebuchadnezzar, Zedekiah was forced to witness his sons' execution and was then blinded and removed to *Babylon. The prophet Jeremiah, an eyewitness, vividly describes these events.

Zeeland A province in the SW Netherlands, on the Scheldt delta. It consists mainly of islands, including Walcheren. Severe flooding in 1953 necessitated the Delta Plan, under which several major dams were constructed and dikes strengthened. The important mussel and oyster fisheries of the Oosterschelde estuary have been preserved. Agricultural produce includes wheat, sugar beet, fruit, and dairy products. Area: 1060 sq mi (2746 sq km). Population (1990 est): 356,000. Capital: Middelburg.

Zeeman, Pieter (1865–1943) Dutch physicist, who, while working at Leiden University, discovered (1886) the splitting of the spectral lines of a substance when placed in a magnetic field (**Zeeman effect**). It is caused by changes in the energy levels of the electrons of the emitting atoms as a result of interaction between the magnetic moment of the orbit and the external field. For this discovery he shared the 1902 Nobel Prize with Hendrik *Lorentz, who had predicted the existence of such an effect.

Zeffirelli, G. Franco (1923–) Italian director and stage designer. Having started as an actor under the direction of *Visconti, he went on to direct film versions of *The Taming of the Shrew* (1966) and *Romeo and Juliet* (1968). He has worked on numerous operas in England, New York, and in Italy. His many stage productions include *Othello* (1961) and *Hamlet* (1964) and he made film versions of *La Traviata* (1983), *Otello* (1986), and *Hamlet* (1991).

Zeiss, Carl (1816–88) German industrialist and manufacturer of optical instruments. Zeiss opened his first workshop in Jena (1846) and later employed Ernst Abbe (1840–1905) to advise him on theoretical advances in optics.

Zen Buddhism (Japanese *Zen*, meditation) In China and Japan, a Buddhist school emphasizing the transmission of enlightenment from master to disciple without reliance on the scriptures. It derives from the teaching of *Bodhidharma, who came to China in 520 AD. The two major sects, *Soto and Rinzai, stress meditation and the use of logical paradoxes (*koans*) respectively, in order to confound the rational mind so that transcendental wisdom can arise and the disciple can realize his own Buddha-nature. Much of Japanese and Chinese art, music, and literature, as well as calligraphy, the tea ceremony (*see* cha-no-yu), the martial arts, etc., express the spontaneous Zen attitude to life. Recently Zen has gained followers in the West, where its opposition to rationalism has popular appeal.

Zener diode. *See* semiconductor diode.

Zenger, John Peter (1697–1746) German-born American printer. He immigrated to New York City in 1710 and was apprenticed to the colony's official printer, William Bradford, until 1719. In 1726 he established his own printing shop and became the publisher and printer of the *New York Weekly Journal*, which sharply criticized the incompetent governor, Col. William Crosby. Zenger was imprisoned for 9 months in 1734–35 on the charge of seditious libel and was finally brought to trial with noted Philadelphia attorney Andrew Hamilton defending him. Hamilton took a new approach by arguing that Zenger had published truth, not libel, and Zenger was acquitted. The trial set a precedent for the establishment of freedom of the press in America.

zenith The point in the sky lying directly above an observer and 90° from all points on his horizon. The (unobservable) point diametrically opposite the zenith is the **nadir**. □celestial sphere.

Zenobia (3rd century AD) The wife of Odaenathus of Palmyra, whom she may have murdered (267) and whom she succeeded as regent for their son. Zenobia occupied Syria, Egypt, and much of Asia Minor before *Aurelian defeated and captured her in 272. She enjoyed a reputation for beauty and intelligence.

Zeno of Citium (c. 335–262 BC) Greek philosopher, who was born in Cyprus of Phoenician stock, came to Athens in 313 BC, and attended lectures at *Plato's Academy. He was influenced by various philosophical schools, including the *Cynics, before evolving his own doctrine of *Stoicism.

Zeno of Elea (born c. 490 BC) Greek philosopher. Zeno's paradoxes, supporting *Parmenides' doctrines that reality is indivisible and reason is at variance with the senses, are the first dialectic arguments, eliciting contradictory conclusions from an opponent's hypotheses. These paradoxes include: Achilles and the tortoise—if space is infinitely divisible, once Achilles has given the tortoise a start he cannot overtake it, for whenever he arrives where the tortoise was it has already moved on; the flying arrow—if space is divisible into finite parts, a moving arrow at each moment of its flight is opposite a particular piece of ground and therefore stationary.

zeolites A group of complex silicate minerals containing loosely held water. They are divided into three groups: fibrous (natrolite, mesolite, scolecite), platy (heulandite, stilbite), and equant (harmatome, chabazite). Most occur in cavities in basic volcanic rocks. They are usually colorless or white and are relatively soft. Because of their property of base exchange they were used as water softeners before the introduction of artificial substitutes. They are also used as molecular sieves in the petroleum industry and as drying agents.

Zephaniah (late 7th century BC) An Old Testament prophet of Judah. **The Book of Zephaniah** records his condemnation of those who continued as idolaters despite the reforms carried out by Josiah (d. 608 BC) and predicts universal judgment from which few will escape.

Zeppelins. *See* airships.

Zermatt 46 01N 7 45E A village in S Switzerland, at the foot of the Matterhorn. A popular resort, it is also a famous mountaineering and winter sports center, at a height of 5315 ft (1620 m). Population (1985): 3700.

Zernicke, Frits (1888–1966) Dutch physicist, who was awarded the 1953 Nobel Prize for his invention of the phase-contrast microscope (1934). This invention enabled the parts of a cell to be seen without staining.

Zetkin, Clara (1857–1933) German communist and feminist leader. Zetkin founded the International Socialist Women's Congress in 1907 and joined the German Communist party in 1919. She was a leader of the pro-Soviet wing of the party and spent much time in the Soviet Union.

Zetland. *See* Shetland Islands.

Zeus The Greek sky and weather god, the supreme deity, identified with the Roman *Jupiter. He was the son of Cronus and Rhea, and brother of Poseidon and Hades. His defeat of Cronus and the *Titans represents the triumph of the Olympian deities over their predecessors. His offspring included *Athena, *Apollo, and *Dionysus and from his many love affairs, which excited the jealousy of his wife, *Hera, were produced numerous other divine and semidivine children. He was usually portrayed as a bearded man, with thunderbolts and the eagle as his attributes.

Zeus, statue of The chryselephantine statue designed by the Greek sculptor *Phidias in about 430 BC for the temple of Zeus at Olympia. One of the *Seven Wonders of the World, it was 40 ft (12 m) high and covered with jewels and gold. It was destroyed in the 5th century AD.

Zeuxis (late 5th century BC) Greek painter, born at Heracleia (S Italy). Zeuxis improved the contemporary use of perspective, shading, and mixed colors. His *trompe l'oeil* effect, it is said, induced birds to peck at grapes painted by him. He specialized in mythological subjects.

Zhangjiakou (*or* Chang-chia-k'ou; Mongolian name: Kalgan) 40 51N 114 59E A city in NE China, in Hebei province near the *Great Wall. It was historically important for defense against and trade with the Mongols and is the site of two forts (1429, 1613). Industries include textiles and machinery. Population (1990): 529,136.

Zhao Guang Yin. *See* Song.

Zhdanov (name until 1948: Mariupol) 47 05N 37 34E A port in Ukraine, on an estuary leading into the Sea of Azov. A railroad (1882) connects it with the Donets Basin and it exports coal. It has a variety of industries and supports a fishing fleet. Population (1991 est): 522,000.

Zhejiang (Che-chiang *or* Chekiang) A mountainous province in E China, on the East China Sea. Densely populated, it has been a cultural center since the Southern *Song dynasty was centered there (12th–13th centuries). It is a highly productive agricultural area and silk and fishing are important. Area: 39,780 sq mi (102,000 sq km). Population (1990): 41,445,930. Capital: Hangzhou.

Zheng Cheng Gong (*or* Cheng Ch'eng-kung; 1624–62) Chinese pirate also known as Koxinga, who controlled most of the Fujian coast from his base in Amoy. He led the Ming resistance to the new Qing rulers and attempted to recapture Nanjing. This failed but he seized Formosa (now Taiwan) from the Dutch in 1661, which became the last Ming stronghold.

Zheng He (*or* Cheng Ho; died c. 1433) A Chinese eunuch of the Ming dynasty, who in 1405 built a fleet and set out on a famous mission to Indochina. Further expeditions to Indochina and the Middle East reestablished trade links that had been severed on the collapse of Yuan rule in 1368.

Zhengzhou (*or* Cheng-chou) 34 35N 113 38E A city in E China, the capital of Henan province. An old administrative center, it has many industries developed since 1949. Population (1990): 1,159,679.

Zhitomir 50 18N 28 40E A city in the central Ukraine. Dating from at least the 13th century, it was subsequently held by Lithuanian and then Poland before being restored to Russia in 1793. A communications center, it processes the produce of the surrounding agricultural region. Population (1991 est): 298,000.

Zhivkov, Todor (1911–) Bulgarian statesman noted, as head of state (1954–89), for encouraging friendly relations with other Balkan countries. A partisan leader in World War II, Zhivkov led the Communist overthrow of the monarchy in 1944. He became first secretary of the Bulgarian Communist party in 1954 and was prime minister (1962–71) before becoming president (1971). He was removed from office during the 1989 revolution against the Communist regime.

Zhou (?1027–221 BC) The earliest Chinese dynasty of which there is accurate knowledge. The dynasty was founded in the area now called Shenxi after the Zhou ruler, Wu Wang, had annihilated the armies of the preceding Shang dynasty and set up a system of government under feudal rulers. These undermined Zhou authority in the so-called Warring States period (481–221), after which the *Qin emerged to unite China. Under the Zhou human sacrifice was abolished and the Chinese idea of *ancestor worship came into being. The late Zhou was also the great period of Chinese philosophy, when Taoist and Confucian thought (*see* Taoism; Confucianism) first emerged.

Zhuangzi (*or* Chuang-tzu; c. 369–286 BC) Chinese philosopher. He is known only through the book to which he gave his name, a work of Taoist philosophy containing allegories, anecdotes, and satires on Confucius. The book, which greatly influenced the development of Chinese Buddhism, advocated spiritual harmony with Tao, the essential principle of the universe, through liberation from all worldly circumstances.

Zhu De (*or* Chu Teh; 1886–1976) Chinese marshal. He joined the Chinese Communist party while a student in Germany and after his return helped organize the Nanchang Communist uprising against the *Guomindang (Nationalists; 1927). He joined Mao Tse-tung in 1928 and became commander of the Fourth Red Army (later the People's Liberation Army), a post he retained until 1954. He served with Mao throughout the period leading to the establishment of the People's Republic of *China (1949), during which his kindness to his troops became legendary.

Zhu Jiang (*or* Chu Chiang; English name: Pearl River) A river in S China, formed by the confluence of the *Xi Jiang and Bei (*or* Pei) rivers near Canton and flowing into an estuary that is used by oceangoing ships. Length: 110 mi (177 km).

Zhukov, Georgi Konstantinovich (1896–1974) Soviet marshal. An armored-warfare expert, he became chief of the army general staff (1941). He planned or commanded almost every major Soviet military operation in World War II, including the Soviet occupation force in Germany. Under Khrushchev he became defense minister and then a member of the presidium of the Communist party.

Zia ul-Haq, Gen. Mohammad (1924–88) Pakistani statesman; president (1978–88). In 1976 he was appointed chief of the army staff and in the following year led the coup that overthrew *Bhutto, becoming chief martial law administrator (1977). In 1979 Zia refused worldwide appeals to commute Bhutto's sentence of death for conspiracy to murder. He died in a mid-air plane explosion.

Ziaur Rahman (1936–81) Bangladesh statesman and army officer; president (1977–81). He fought in the war against Pakistan in 1971 and became chief of staff of the armed forces in 1975. He became chief martial law administrator in

1976, during the period of political instability that followed *Mujibur Rahman's assassination (1975), and president but was himself assassinated during an unsuccessful insurrection.

Zibo (*or* Tzu-po) 36 32N 117 47E A city in E China, in Shandong province, formed by the amalgamation of Zi-cheng (*or* Tzu-ch'eng) and Bo-shan (*or* Po-shan). It has coal-mining, chemical, electrical, and machine-building industries. Population (1990): 1,138,074.

Ziegfeld, Florenz (1867–1932) US theatrical producer. His lavish revues were modeled on the *Folies-Bergère. The Ziegfeld Follies, billed as "An American Institution," appeared annually from 1907 until his death. Using the slogan "Glorifying the American Girl," he created such hits as *Sally* (1920), *Show Boat* (1927), and *Bitter Sweet* (1929). He also launched Will Rogers, W. C. Fields, Eddie Cantor, and others on their careers.

Ziegler, Karl (1898–1973) German chemist, who shared the 1963 Nobel Prize with Giulio Natta (1903–   ) for their work on plastics and polymers. Ziegler showed that certain organometallic compounds (**Ziegler catalysts**) would catalyze the *polymerization of ethylene giving unbranched polymers that were tougher and had a higher melting point than those previously obtainable.

ziggurat An ancient Mesopotamian brick-built temple tower. Ziggurats were constructed of rectangular terraces of diminishing size, generally with the god's shrine on top. They existed in major Sumerian, Babylonian, and Assyrian centers, the one at Babylon being the probable original of the Tower of *Babel.

Zimbabwe, State of (name until 1979: Rhodesia) A landlocked country in SE Africa. It is bounded by Zambia, Mozambique, South Africa and Botswana, and geographically in the N by the Zambezi River and in the S by the Limpopo River. Much of the land consists of plateau, generally over 3300 ft (1000 m), with extensive areas of savanna. The majority of the population is Bantu, with small minorities of Europeans, Asians, and others. *Economy*: agriculture is important, but the imposition of economic sanctions (1965–79) changed its emphasis. The production of tobacco declined and a diversification to cotton and cattle took place; other cash crops include sugar, tea, and citrus fruit. The chief subsistence crops are corn, millet, and groundnuts. Forestry and fishing are important with fish farming on Lake Kariba. Zimbabwe has rich mineral resources including copper, asbestos, gold, chrome, and nickel, but it has no oil reserves. Industry is expanding and includes food processing, metal processing, engineering, and textiles. The main exports are tobacco, nickel, copper, asbestos, and sugar. *History*: ruins at *Great Zimbabwe attest the existence of a medieval Bantu civilization in the region. In 1837 its Mashona inhabitants were conquered by the Matabele and later in the 19th century it was explored by European missionaries, notably David *Livingstone. In 1889 Cecil *Rhodes obtained a charter for the British South Africa Company, which conquered the Matabele and their territory, named Rhodesia (1895) in Rhodes's honor. In 1911 it was divided into Northern Rhodesia (now *Zambia) and Southern Rhodesia, the latter becoming a self-governing British colony in 1922. In 1953 the two parts of Rhodesia were reunited in the Federation of *Rhodesia and Nyasaland, and after its dissolution in 1963 the whites demanded independence from Southern Rhodesia (Rhodesia from 1964). The UK's refusal to permit independence without a guarantee of majority rule within a specific period led the Rhodesian prime minister Ian *Smith to issue a unilateral declaration of independence (UDI) in 1965. Both the UK and the UN imposed economic sanctions on Rhodesia but these and further talks in 1966 and 1968 proved fruitless. In 1970 Rhodesia declared itself a republic. In 1974 the Rhodesian government opened negotiations with the leaders of the Zimbabwe African People's Union (ZAPU) and the Zimbabwe African

National Union (ZANU), which had pursued guerrilla activities since the 1960s. Smith failed to negotiate an agreement with the black nationalists, who remained seriously divided under the nominal umbrella of the African National Council (ANC). In 1978, following the intervention of the US secretary of state Henry Kissinger (1976) and the UK (1977), agreement was reached between Smith and the ANC on a transitional government leading to black majority rule. However, the failure of the subsequent government under Muzorewa to obtain the support of the Patriotic Front led to agreement at the 1979 Commonwealth Conference to hold an all-party conference in an attempt to achieve internal unity. Following the conference, held in London (1979–80), Britain's Lord *Soames was appointed governor to oversee the disarming of guerrillas, the holding of elections (which brought Robert *Mugabe, leader of ZANU, to power), and the granting of independence to Zimbabwe as a member of the Commonwealth (1980). Mugabe formed an uneasy coalition government with Joshua Nkomo, head of the Zimbabwe African People's Union, which was shattered in 1982 when Nkomo was dismissed from the cabinet. Mugabe supported an increasingly socialist plan of government and sought one-party rule. Economic problems including inflation, fuel shortages, and severe drought plagued Zimbabwe in the early and mid-1980s. Large numbers of whites left Zimbabwe. Despite a policy of hostility to South Africa, Zimbabwe retained a preferential trade agreement that made South Africa its principal trading partner. Elections in 1985 confirmed Mugabe's hold on the country. He was reelected in 1990. The drought in southern Africa, perhaps the worst of the century, affected Zimbabwe so severely that a national disaster was declared in 1992. Once again, the country called upon South Africa, which arranged for the transportation of food by rail and by truck. Official language: English; the most important African languages are Ndebele and Shona. Official currency: Zimbabwe dollar of 100 cents. Area: 150,820 sq mi (390,622 sq km). Population (1990): 10,200,000. Capital: Harare.

zinc (Zn) A bluish-white metal known in antiquity in India and the Middle East and rediscovered in Europe in 1846 by A. S. Marggraf (1709–82). It occurs in nature principally in the ores calamine ($ZnCO_3$), zincite (ZnO), and zinc blende (ZuS). It is extracted by reduction of the oxide (ZnO) with carbon. The metal is more electropositive than iron and is widely used to make *galvanized steel. Zinc forms a number of useful low-melting alloys, including *brass and type metal, and is also used to make castings. The sulfide (ZnS) is a phosphor and is used in making television screens and fluorescent tubes. Zinc oxide (ZnO) is widely used as a paint pigment and in medicines, batteries, cosmetics, plastics, and other products. Trace amounts of zinc are also important for growth in animals, including human beings. At no 30; at wt 65.37; mp 788°F (419.58°C); bp 1666°F (907°C).

zinc blende. *See* sphalerite.

zincite A minor ore of zinc, consisting of zinc oxide. It is often found in association with *sphalerite and probably results from the alteration of sphalerite. It usually contains some manganese.

zinc yellow A greenish yellow pigment, usually made by reaction of zinc oxide, potassium dichromate, and sulfuric acid. It is light fast, inhibits rusting, and is resistant to sulfides.

Zinjanthropus. *See* Australopithecus.

Zinnia A genus of herbs and shrubs (about 15 species), mostly native to North America. They have stiff hairy stems, oval to heart-shaped leaves, and daisy-like flower heads with yellow or brownish central disk florets and variously colored ray florets. Cultivated zinnias are hybrids derived from the Mexican species *Z. elegans*. They have double flowers, about 4.3 in (11 cm) across, and most are half-hardy annuals. Family: **Compositae*.

Zinoviev, Grigori Yevseevich (1883–1936) Soviet politician. Zinoviev became a member of the politburo (1918) and chairman of the Comintern (1919) but was expelled from the Communist party in 1927. In 1935 he was accused of complicity in the murder of *Kirov and was executed.

Zinzendorf, Nikolaus Ludwig, Graf von (1700–60) German nobleman and churchman, who re-formed the *Moravian Brethren by settling Hussite refugees from Moravia on his estate in Saxony. Exiled from Saxony (1736–47), he became a bishop of the Moravian Church in 1737, spreading its beliefs in England, America, and elsewhere.

Zion (*or* Sion) A stronghold (II Samuel 5.6–7) on the SE hill of Jerusalem, captured by David, who made it the center of his capital (Jerusalem). Another name for Jerusalem, it is also described throughout the Old Testament as the place in which God dwells and reigns. In the New Testament and in later Christian writings, it symbolizes heaven.

Zionism A Jewish nationalist movement. It emerged during the 19th century on a tide of European nationalism, and was formally established (against considerable Jewish opposition) at the First Zionist Congress (Basle, 1897). The Congress defined its political aim as the establishment of a Jewish national home in Palestine; the World Zionist Organization was set up, with Theodor *Herzl as its first president. Jewish immigration into Palestine (*aliyah*) was encouraged, especially through the Jewish National Fund (founded 1901) and the Jewish Agency for Palestine (1929). Among other breakaway groups, the Territorialists sought a land outside Palestine, and the Revisionists opposed collectivism and collaboration with the British. Since the establishment of *Israel in 1948 the Zionist movement has continued to foster *aliyah* and support for and interest in Israel. *See also* Ahad Ha'am; Balfour Declaration.

Zion National Park A national park in SW Utah. The main feature of the park is Zion Canyon, a gorge 8 mi (13 km) long and 0.5 mi (0.8 km) deep, carved by the Virgin River. Its sandstone walls exhibit many different shades of red and other colors. Sentinel Mountain rises to 7157 ft (2182 m). Discovered in 1858, the canyon was given its name by Mormon settlers in 1861; a national park was established in 1919 and expanded in 1956. Area: 230 sq mi (595 sq km).

zircon A mineral consisting of zirconium silicate, found as an accessory mineral in intermediate and acid igneous rocks. It is usually colorless or yellowish. Gem varieties include hyacinth (red) and jargoon (colorless or smoky gray). It is the chief ore of zirconium and is used as a refractory material.

zirconium (Zr) A gray high-melting-point transition metal, isolated by J. J. Berzelius in 1824. It occurs in nature as zircon (zirconium silicate; $ZrSiO_4$), which is used as a gemstone. The dioxide (zirconia; ZrO_2) has a high melting point (2715°C) and is used as a refractory and crucible material. The metal is used in cladding fuel elements in nuclear reactors. At no 40; at wt 91.22; mp 3365°F (1852°C); bp 7910°F (4377°C).

zither A plucked stringed instrument of ancient origin, consisting of a flat resonating box fitted with 30 to 40 strings, approximately 5 of which lie across a fretted fingerboard for playing the melody. The rest are used for playing accompanying chords. It is particularly popular in Bavaria and the Tyrol.

Zi Xi (*or* Tz'u-hsi; 1835–1908) Chinese empress. The daughter of a middle-class Manchu family, she became an imperial concubine. She was made empress on the birth of her son *Tong Zhi, becoming his regent and, after his death, regent for her young nephew *Guang Xu. She thus wielded enormous power over state affairs, her reactionary policies being largely responsible for the fall of imperial China.

Žižka, Jan, Count (c. 1370–1424) Bohemian military leader, who was head of the *Hussite military community at Tabar. He was victorious against the Holy Roman Emperor Sigismund, using armored farm wagons and tactics that anticipated modern tank warfare.

Ziatoust 55 10N 59 38E A city in W Russia. It has been the largest metallurgical center in the Urals since the 18th century. Population (1991 est): 211,000.

zodiac A zone of the heavens extending about 8° on either side of the *ecliptic. Within it lies the apparent annual path of the sun, as seen from the earth, and the orbits of the moon, and major planets, apart from Pluto. The 12 constellations in the zodiac are known as "signs" or "houses" to astrologers, who believe them capable of stamping their individual dispositions upon those born under their influence (*see* astrology). The 12 signs and their astrologically effective dates (different from their astronomical periods on account of *precession) are: Aries, the Ram, Mar 21–Apr 19; Taurus, the Bull, Apr 20–May 20; Gemini, the Twins, May 21–June 21; Cancer, the Crab, June 22–July 22; Leo, the Lion, July 23–Aug 22; Virgo, the Virgin, Aug 23–Sept 22; Libra, the Scales, Sept 23–Oct 23; Scorpio, the Scorpion, Oct 24–Nov 21; Sagittarius, the Archer, Nov 22–Dec 21; Capricorn, the Goat, Dec 22–Jan 19; Aquarius, the Water-carrier, Jan 20–Feb 18; and Pisces, the Fish, Feb 19–Mar 20.

zodiacal light A faint glow that is visible in the western sky just after sunset and the eastern sky just before sunrise, especially in the tropics. It can be seen along the direction of the *ecliptic, tapering upward from the horizon to an altitude of perhaps 20°. It is sunlight reflected from interplanetary dust particles.

Zog I (1895–1961) King of Albania (1928–39). Zog was proclaimed king after serving as prime minister (1922–24) and president (1925–28). He let Albania fall under Italian economic domination and when Mussolini invaded Albania (1939), he fled into exile.

Zohar (Hebrew: splendor) The classical text of the *kabbalah. Written in Aramaic, it purports to be a mystical commentary on the *Torah and a collection of theosophical discussions dating from the time of the *Mishnah. It was actually written about 1280 by the Spanish kabbalist Moses de Leon, although it contains some later additions.

Zola, Émile (1840–1902) French novelist. He went to Paris in 1858 and lived in poverty, working as a journalist and as a clerk in a publishing firm until the success of his first major novel, *Thérèse Raquin* (1867). He then dedicated himself to a literary career, conceiving the plan for the series of 20 novels entitled *Les Rougon-Macquart* (1871–93), which concern a family during the Second Empire (1852–70). Despite the pseudoscientific theory of naturalism that first motivated his fiction, his talent for detailed realism produced powerful exposés of social problems. *L'Assommoir* (1877) describes the effects of drink on the disintegration of a working-class family. *Nana* (1880), concerning a girl from the slums, *Germinal* (1885), about a mining community, and *La Terre* (1887), concerning the life of peasants, are among his outstanding novels. He fled to England after defending *Dreyfus in an open letter, *J'accuse* (1898), but was welcomed back as a hero after Dreyfus had been cleared of the charges against him.

Zollverein A customs union of 18 German states formed under Prussian dominance in 1834. By 1867 all German states except Hamburg and Bremen had joined. This commercial union helped pave the way for German unification under Prussian leadership (1871).

ZODIAC *The signs of the zodiac from* De astrorum scientia *by Leopold of Austria (Augsburg, 1489).*

Zomba 15 23S 35 19E A city in Malawi, in the Shire Highlands. It was the capital of Malawi until 1975 and has the University of Malawi (1964). It is the center of a tobacco-growing and dairy-farming area. Population (1987): 43,250.

zoogeography The study of the geographical distribution of animals. It is based mainly on the work of A. R. *Wallace (with later modifications), who divided the world into a number of zoogeographical regions, each with a distinctive fauna. The present-day distribution of animals reflects both their evolutionary history and the movements of the land masses in past geological ages (*see* continental drift). Thus the concentration of marsupials in the Australasian region is explained by the fact that the separation of Australia from the Asian mainland coincided with the evolutionary radiation of this group. The Australian marsupials therefore avoided competing with the more efficient placental mammals, which subsequently evolved on the mainland.

zoological gardens Places in which wild animals are housed in captivity for scientific study or display. Private zoos were maintained by many rulers in the past, probably including King Solomon and Emperor Charlemagne. Zoos have contributed to knowledge of animals and in many cases have helped save endangered species through establishing breeding colonies. Among the world's outstanding zoos are those in San Diego, the Bronx (N.Y.), Chicago, Philadelphia, London, Berlin, Tokyo, Amsterdam, Sydney, and Paris.

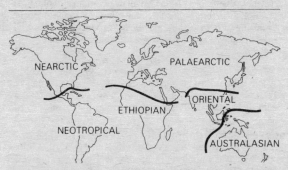

ZOOGEOGRAPHY *The world can be divided into six regions according to the distribution of its animals. Since some animals are less fixed in their habitats than others and may be found in more than one region, the divisions between the regions are somewhat arbitrary. For example, Wallace's line, separating the Oriental and Australasian regions, has been modified since Wallace proposed it.*

zoology The branch of *biological sciences specializing in the scientific study of animals. This includes their classification, anatomy, physiology, ecology, behavior, evolution, etc. The importance of animals as food producers, pests, etc., in relation to man makes many aspects of zoology economically significant. *See also* entomology; ichthyology; ornithology.

zorilla An African carnivorous mammal, *Ictonyx striatus*, also called striped weasel. It is 20–27.5 in (50–70 cm) long including the tail (8–12 in; 20–30 cm) with distinct longitudinal black-and-white stripes. It hunts at night, preying on small reptiles and birds. When attacked, it ejects a vile-smelling fluid from anal glands. Family: *Mustelidae*.

Zorn, Anders (Leonard) (1860–1920) Swedish artist, best known as an etcher. Traveling in Europe and the US until 1896, he then returned to his native Mora in Sweden. He is noted for his impressionist landscapes and scenes of peasant girls bathing. He also produced portraits and some sculpture.

Zoroaster (*or* Zarathustra; c. 628–c. 551 BC) Iranian prophet, founder of *Zoroastrianism. Probably born near Tehran, he is believed to have been a priest in the ancient polytheistic religion when he received a vision of *Ahura Mazda, who exhorted him to preach a new faith based on his worship. Zoroaster introduced reforms, abolishing orgiastic rituals, although animal sacrifice and the ancient fire cult continued to be practiced. The teachings attributed to him are preserved in the Gathas (hymns) in the *Avesta.

Zoroastrianism The pre-Islamic dualistic religion of Persia founded by *Zoroaster, surviving in Iran in some areas and in India among the Parsees (*see* Parseeism). It recognizes two principles, good and evil, as personified by *Ahura Mazda and *Ahriman. Life is the struggle between these forces. The dualism is not equal, for good will eventually outweigh evil and Ahura Mazda will triumph, resurrecting the dead and creating a paradise on earth, presaged by the return of Zoroaster. Man's irreversible free choice of good or evil renders him responsible for his fate after death in heaven or hell. Procreation and life are extolled, but death defiles—hence the custom of exposing corpses to be devoured by vultures.

Zorrilla y Moral, José (1817–93) Spanish poet and dramatist. In *Cantos del trovador* (1840–41), *Granada* (1852), and other volumes of poetry he evoked the history and legends of Spain. His best-known play is *Don Juan Tenorio* (1844), a verson of the *Don Juan story with a happy ending.

Zoser. *See* Djoser.

Zouaves Members of a French infantry corps, originally recruited from the Algerian Zwawa tribe following the French conquest of Algeria (1830). The Algerians were replaced after 1840 with French soldiers. The Zouaves' colorful uniforms, with their baggy red trousers, inspired other armies to form similarly dressed units.

Zsigmondy, Richard Adolph (1865–1929) Austrian chemist, whose interest in colloids led him to use the Tyndall effect to devise the *ultramicroscope (1902). In 1908 he was appointed professor at Göttingen University and was awarded the Nobel Prize in chemistry in 1925.

Zuccarelli, Francesco (1702–88) Italian painter. He worked chiefly in Venice (after 1732) and in England (1752–62, 1765–71). A founding member of Britain's Royal Academy, he specialized in picturesque landscapes.

Zuccari Two Italian painters, born at Sant' Angelo in Vado. Both leading figures in Roman *mannerism, **Taddeo Zuccari** (1529–66) is known for his frescoes, while his brother and pupil **Federico Zuccari** (c. 1540–1609) was also an art theorist. Federico painted Elizabeth I in England (1575) and decorated the dome of the Duomo, Florence, and the high altar in the *Escorial.

zucchini. *See* squash.

Zugspitze 47 25N 11 00E The highest mountain in Germany, in the S on the Austrian border. Height: 9721 ft (2963 m).

Zuider Zee A former inlet of the SE North Sea, within the Netherlands. The N part, the *Waddenzee, is separated from the S part (now the *IJsselmeer) by a huge dam (completed 1932).

Zululand An area of South Africa, in NE Natal. The home of the *Zulu people, it became a powerful state during the 1820s under their king *Shaka. Following conflict with the Boers the Zulus, under *Cetshwayo, were defeated by the British (1879) and Zululand was incorporated into Natal in 1897. It comprises part of the *Bantu Homeland of KwaZulu.

Zulus A Bantu people of Natal (South Africa). They are traditionally cattle herders and cattle are still a prestige possession. Polygyny is practiced by important men. In the 19th century under *Shaka, the Zulus conquered an extensive empire until eventually defeated in wars with the Europeans. Their highly efficient military organization was based on the age-set system; warriors could not marry until they attained a certain grade. *Ancestor worship and witchcraft were prominent in their religious beliefs and the king had important ritual functions. Today, many Zulus are migrant laborers.

Zurbarán, Francisco de (1598–1664) Spanish painter. Working chiefly in Seville, where he was appointed the city painter, and for religious orders, he specialized in scenes from the lives of the saints, in the manner of *Caravaggio, portraits, and still lifes. In Madrid (1634) he painted historical and mythological subjects for the Buen Retiro Palace and settled there permanently in 1658. The paintings of the last few years of his life are characterized by a sentimental piety and lack the austere realism of his greatest works.

Zürich 47 23N 8 33E The largest city in Switzerland, on Lake Zürich. It is the commercial and industrial center of Switzerland; heavy engineering and machine production are the chief industries; banking and insurance are of international importance. Zürich's Alpine setting has contributed to the rise of its tourist industry. It has a notable romanesque cathedral, a university (1833), and the Federal Institute of Technology (1854). *History*: the Romans occupied the site in the 1st century BC. During the Middle Ages it became the most important Swiss town and joined the Swiss confederation in 1351. A leading center of the Reformation under Ulrich Zwingli, Zürich became a refuge for those persecuted in the Counter-Reformation. Population (1991 est): 341,000.

Zweig, Arnold (1887–1968) East German Jewish novelist. After exile in Palestine, he returned to Germany in 1948. His pacifism and social criticism are reflected in such novels as *The Case of Sergeant Grischa* (1927).

Zweig, Stefan (1881–1942) Austrian Jewish writer. After studying in Austria, France, and Germany, he settled in Salzburg. Exiled in 1934, he later committed suicide with his wife in Brazil. His interest in Freud is reflected in acute historical and biographical analyses of a number of great European writers. *The Tide of Fortune* (1927) deals with European culture in crisis. He also produced poetry, novels, stories, and translations.

Zwickau 50 42N 12 25E A city in S Germany, on the Zwickauer Mulde River. The birthplace of Robert Schumann, it has fine medieval and Renaissance buildings. Its industries include coal mining and the manufacture of automobiles, chemicals, and machinery. Population (1991 est): 119,000.

Zwingli, Ulrich (1484–1531) Swiss Protestant reformer. A Roman Catholic priest and a chaplain to Swiss mercenaries, he became people's vicar at the Grossmünster in Zürich in 1518. There he emerged as a reformer, welcoming the writings of *Luther and preaching the doctrine of salvation by faith. He opposed his bishop, supported by the civil authorities, and by 1525 had established a reformed church. He separated from Luther over the theology of the Eucharist, regarding Luther's views as a persistence of Roman doctrine. Zwingli was killed during fighting between Roman Catholic and Protestant cantons.

zwitterion An *ion that has both positive and negative charges on the same group of atoms. Zwitterions can be formed under suitable conditions from molecules that have both basic and acidic groups attached. *Amino acids, for instance, can form zwitterions by transfer of a proton from the carboxyl group to the amino group.

Zwolle 52 31N 6 06E A city in the central Netherlands, the capital of Overijssel province. Thomas à Kempis lived at a nearby monastery. A trading center, its industries include chemicals and ship building. Population (1988 est): 91,000.

Zworykin, Vladimir Kosma (1889–1982) US physicist, born in Russia, who went to the US in 1919 and eventually became a vice president of the Radio Corporation of America. Working with cathode-ray tubes, he invented the form of television camera called the iconoscope (1938) and a year later produced the first *electron microscope.

Picture Credits

The names of the agencies appear first, followed by the relevant page numbers. Where applicable, the photographers' names follow immediately after the page number.

Heather Angel: 563, 615, 791, 1972, 2264, 2348, 2394; Ardea London: 1/P. Morris, 1164/J.B. and S. Bottomley, 1243/Dennis Avon and Tony Tilford, 1258/ 2705/K. Fink, 1697/B.N. Douetil, 1741/Pat Morris, 2097/David and Katie Urry, 2593/Acans Weaving; Ashmolean Museum, Oxford: 132, 2608; Australian Information Service, London: 156 (bottom), 505, 1730, 1844, 1850, 2468; Clive Barda: 250; Barnaby's Picture Library: 153 (top left, bottom), 156 (center), 217, 246, 406, 440, 478, 1151, 1229 (bottom right), 1367, 2545, 2551, 2725; BBC Hulton Picture Library: 575, 606, 682, 740, 768, 799, 833, 1016, 1211, 1396, 1491, 1544, 1637, 1775, 1886, 2118, 2168, 2198, 2272, 2362, 2529, 2683, 2770; Courtesy of the British Library: 1906; Courtesy of the Trustees, The British Museum: 1184, 2460; Courtesy of the British Tourist Authority: 5, 1538, 2234, 2520 (bottom right), 2717; Camera Press: 70 (bottom), 75, 89, 139, 167, 191, 219, 270, 291, 298, 344, 379, 381, 396, 485, 496, 529, 531, 567, 669, 705, 760, 771, 817, 919, 939, 979, 1018, 1058, 1136, 1247, 1351, 1361, 1392, 1401, 1439, 1497, 1574, 1578, 1618, 1641, 1655, 1659, 1674, 1733, 1740, 1757, 1917, 1944, 1963, 1977, 1990, 2006, 2216, 2237, 2343, 2394, 2466, 2479, 2518, 2547, 2555, 2628, 2647, 2680, 2704; Bruce Coleman Ltd.: 24/Peter Jackson, 98/John Markham, 214/Udo Hirsh, 586/Bill Wood, 1052, 1566/Graham Pizzey, 1707/Jane Burton; The Danish Tourist Board: 102; Mary Evans Picture Library: 223, 452, 536, 748, 990/Sigmund Freud Collection, 1100, 1232/Harry Price Collection, University of London, 1347, 1356, 1548, 1840, 2126, 2491, 2520 (top left and top right), 2785, 2794; Eric and David Hosking: 55, 264, 353, 458, 520, 656, 926, 1041, 1158, 1261, 1274, 1518, 1822, 1934, 2114, 2137, 2269, 2328, 2729, 2747; Courtesy of the Imperial War Museum: 551, 1529; Reproduced by permission of the Director of the India Office Library and Records: 2667; Courtesy of the Italian State Tourist Office: 2250, 2334/Japan National Tourist Organization: 527; Crown Copyright, Reproduced with the permission of the Controller of Her Majesty's Stationery Office and of the Director, Royal Botanic Gardens, Kew: 11; Keystone: 850, 947, 1070, 1459, 1544, 1703, 2431; Frank W. Lane: 524/Yves Temple: 804/Arthur Christiansen: 1881/R. van Nostrand; Mansell Collection: 57, 64, 70 (top), 190, 203, 205, 274, 279, 285, 343, 490, 501, 539, 593, 695, 718, 806, 850, 1024, 1058, 1103, 1269, 1287, 1291, 1378, 1433, 1436, 1527, 1614, 1788, 1835, 1889, 1909, 1917, 1929, 2162, 2181, 2195, 2282, 2414, 2441, 2559, 2615, 2623, 2678, 2711, 2713; Merseyside County Museums, Liverpool: 510; Tony and Marion Morrison: 412, 1463; Courtesy of the Trustees, The National Gallery, London: 1008, 1668, 2060, 2154, 2211; The National Portrait Gallery, London: 399, 424, 431, 641, 757, 1477, 1803, 2172, 2309, 2656, 2692, 2750; The Natural History Photographic Agency: 369, 811 (top and bottom)/ Stephen Dalton, Courtesy of the High Commissioner for New Zealand: 1052, 2387; Popperfoto: 107, 366, 733, 764, 811, 902, 1228 (bottom center), 1385, 1412, 1487, 1611, 1778, 1862, 2005, 2071, 2342, 2405, 2412, 2634; Reproduced by gracious permission of Her Majesty the Queen: 532, 783, 1495, 2650; Royal Greenwich Observatory: 621, 1800, 2371, 2454; The Salvation Army: 2242; SATOUR photograph: 467; The Scottish National Portrait Gallery: 2050; Smith Collection: 37, 435 (top and bottom), 725, 1224, 1283, 2357; Sperry New Holland: 610; Sport and General Press Agency: 1372, 1387, 1429; Sporting Pictures (UK) Ltd.: 359, 1829, 1964/The Tate Gallery, London: 1207, 2598; Thomas Photos, Oxford: 412; John Topham Picture Library: 241, 322, 428, 471, 556, 849, 1116, 1228 (bottom left), 1483, 1634, 1766, 1894, 1953, 2134; U.S. Army: 1569, 2584; U.S. Library of Congress: 21, 488, 787, 799, 834, 909, 962, 978, 1047, 1078, 1185, 1223, 1333, 1398, 1484, 1514, 1516, 1840, 1890, 2349, 2437, 2531, 2602, 2691, 2726, 2736, 2777; U.S. Military Academy Archives: 1092; U.S. National Portrait Gallery: 427; U.S. Office of the Vice President: 427; U.S. Office of War Information, National Archives: 355, 1179; U.S. The White House: 1363, 2139; Victoria and Albert Museum, Crown Copyright: 302, 330, 411, 561, 1271, 1319, 1342, 1446, 1463, 1472, 1592, 1720, 1760, 1782, 2143, 2520 (bottom left); Vision International: 153; Angelo Hornak: (top right), 156/Paolo Koch: (top), 1229/Elizabeth Weiland (top: left, center, right), Reproduced by permission of the Trustees; The Wallace Collection, London: 972, 1119; Peter Warren: 150 (top, center, bottom); Windsor Safari Park: 1410; The Zoological Society of London: 317, 2637.

COMPUTER TERMS

Adapter Any printed circuit board that plugs into one of the slots in a computer system board.

Algorithm Sets of instructions sent to the CPU expressed in a programming or human language.

Application Pre-programmed software bought off the shelf, used to operate a computer.

ASCII (American National Standard Code for Information Interchange) A system of common coding of characters to permit communication of data between different operating systems.

Backup An extra copy of computer data, created as a defense against corruption or destruction of the original data.

Basic A general purpose programming language. Basic is easily learned and easily used to write computer programs.

Baud A unit that defines the number of times a data signal changes state each second.

BIT (BInary digiT) The smallest unit of information that the computer can recognize. It is represented by 0 or 1.

Bit Mapped Graphic images formed by dots.

Boot To start up the computer. A "cold" boot occurs when the computer is first turned on; a "warm" boot clears the data currently in active memory.

Byte A group of bits that stand for a single letter or number. Each byte is stored in an assigned location or address in the computer's memory.

CAD/CAM (Computer-Aided-Design/Computer-Aided/Manufacturing) A program that contains almost every computer-related design used in manufacturing and other industries.

Cassette A way to store information when the computer is off.

Chip A tiny piece of silicon that is etched to create impurities on the pattern of its surface, creating computer circuitry.

COBOL (Common Business Oriented Language) A language for business application.

Commands Numerous computer- level instructions to the CPU indicating the steps to be taken by the computer to perform a function.

CPI (Characters Per Inch) A measurement of individual letters, characters and numbers.

CPU (Central Processing Unit) The "brain" of the computer. It follows program instructions to tell the computer how to act upon data.

Crash The sudden termination of a program due to a hardware or software problem.

CRT (Cathode Ray Tube) Another name for the monitor or video display terminal of a computer.

Cursor The blinking indicator on the computer screen used to indicate location.

Cylinder The set of tracks, two per disk, on a hard disk system, that are all of the same diameter.

Data Base Software geared to manipulating information in similar records.

Default A feature setting that is used each time the computer is turned on.

Disk Drive The machinery that reads and writes data onto disks.

DOS (Disk/Diskette Operating System) A specific set of programs that are required to support the basic operations of the computer, relying upon the specialized wording of a "command" language.

Downloading The process of transferring the soft fonts stored in a computer memory to the printer memory.

DPI (Dots Per Inch) A measure of printer or monitor resolution.

E-mail Software that allows users to send and receive messages between their computers.

Enable To set up a condition that permits a future action to be taken.

Error Message A phrase that is displayed on the screen when an error occurs, usually in the software.

File A unit of records in the computer.

Floppy Disk Term for a 5 1/4" flexible magnetic diskette or a 3 1/2" diskette encased in plastic.

Font A collection of type characters with a distinctive and consistent graphics style.

Format To prepare the surface of a diskette or fixed disk to receive information.

Graphics Software used to create and manipulate pictures and other images.

Hard Disk Drive The permanently installed storage device in a computer.

Hardware The physical machinery of a computer system.

Icon A small graphic image that represents a computer function.

Install To physically add a device to the computer, and configure the computer system as required.

Interface The method used by the computer to communicate with its user or other parts of a computer.

Internal fonts Also called resident fonts, these fonts are programmed into the computer at the factory.

I/O (Input/Output) Refers to a printer's parallel or serial connection.

Kilobytes Represents 210 or 1,024 bytes. 64Kb is 65,536 bytes.

Kerning Adjusting the space between letters.

Kilo The abbreviation, lower case k, for 1,000 exactly.

Computer terms

Landscape Orientation Printing so the widest edge of the paper is the top edge.

Languages Programming languages such as Basic, COBOL, Fortran, and Pascal that usually reduce characters to ASCII.

LASER (Light Amplification by Stimulated Emission of Radiation) A monochromatic light source that is highly focused to scan images to a high resolution.

LED (Light Emitting Diode) A special purpose semiconductor device used as an indicator lamp. Usually used for power on, device in use indicators.

Macro A command that combines two or more other commands to run a miniature program within an application.

Megabyte (MB) A measurement of computer storage capacity.

Memory Measured in kilobytes, it is the space available to manipulate data in the computer.

Modem (MOdulator/DEModulator) A device to translate computer data from digital information to analog information for transmission over telephone lines.

Mouse A special computer device used for entering information and performing a variety of tasks.

Network A group of computers or other hardware devices that are linked by communications lines, permitting them to share information.

Off Line The status in which the printer will not accept data.

Operating System The process of accepting data and/or compiling instructions.

Page Orientation Determines whether a page will print in portrait or landscape orientation.

Peripheral Any hardware other than the main housing of the computer, including printers, monitors, and other accessories.

Pixel The smallest screen area that can be controlled for color and intensity.

Port The place in the computer to plug peripherals into.

Portrait Orientation Printing so the shortest edge of the paper is the top edge.

Power A measure of the electrical energy used by a device, measured in watts (W).

Primary Display The video display that is automatically displayed when the system is turned on.

Prompt The screen display of a current drive letter followed by the "greater than"(>) symbol and a blinking cursor.

Program A series of commands, written in computer language, that instructs the computer to perform certain tasks.

RAM (Random- Access Memory) The memory space available for manipulation of data by a computer user. Its contents disappear when the computer is turned off.

ROM (Read-Only Memory) Memory space that stores key operating information in the computer.

Software The electronic instructions used to enter and manipulate data.

Tape Drive Computer hardware that stores data on a magnetic tape, for relatively massive data storage.

Track A single concentric circle of magnetic data on a storage system, divided into sectors.

Utility Software that makes an application easier.

Virus A hidden program that later destroys computer data.

Word Processing Software designed for the writing and manipulation of data.

Write To record data on a disk, diskette or random-access memory.

PRESIDENTS OF THE UNITED STATES

Name (and party)	State of Birth	Born	Term	Died
George Washington (F)	VA	1732	1789-97	1799
John Adams (F)	MA	1735	1797-1801	1826
Thomas Jefferson (D-R)	VA	1743	1801-09	1826
James Madison (D-R)	VA	1751	1809-17	1836
James Monroe (D-R)	VA	1758	1817-25	1831
John Q. Adams (D-R)	MA	1767	1825-29	1848
Andrew Jackson (D)	SC	1767	1829-37	1845
Martin Van Buren (D)	NY	1782	1837-41	1862
William H. Harrison (W)	VA	1773	1841	1841
John Tyler (W)	VA	1790	1841-45	1862
James K. Polk (D)	NC	1795	1845-49	1849
Zachary Taylor (W)	VA	1784	1849-50	1850
Millard Fillmore (W)	NY	1800	1850-53	1874
Franklin Pierce (D)	NH	1804	1853-57	1869
James Buchanan (D)	PA	1791	1857-61	1868
Abraham Lincoln (R)	KY	1809	1861-65	1865
Andrew Johnson (R)	NC	1808	1865-69	1875
Ulysses S. Grant (R)	OH	1822	1869-77	1885
Rutherford B. Hayes (R)	OH	1822	1877-81	1893
James A. Garfield (R)	OH	1831	1881	1881
Chester A. Arthur (R)	VT	1830	1881-85	1886
Grover Cleveland (D)	NJ	1837	1885-89	1908
Benjamin Harrison (R)	OH	1833	1889-93	1901
Grover Cleveland (D)	NJ	1837	1893-97	1908
William McKinley (R)	OH	1843	1897-1901	1901
Theodore Roosevelt (R)	NY	1858	1901-1909	1919
William H. Taft (R)	OH	1857	1909-13	1930
Woodrow Wilson (D)	VA	1856	1913-21	1924
Warren G. Harding (R)	OH	1865	1921-23	1923
Calvin Coolidge (R)	VT	1872	1923-29	1933
Herbert C. Hoover (R)	IA	1874	1929-33	1964
Franklin D. Roosevelt (D)	NY	1882	1933-45	1945
Harry S. Truman (D)	MO	1884	1945-53	1972
Dwight D. Eisenhower (R)	TX	1890	1953-61	1969
John F. Kennedy (D)	MA	1917	1961-63	1963
Lyndon B. Johnson (D)	TX	1908	1963-69	1973
Richard M. Nixon (R)	CA	1913	1969-74 (r)	1994
Gerald R. Ford (R)	NE	1913	1974-77	
James E. Carter, Jr. (D)	GA	1924	1977-81	
Ronald W. Reagan (R)	IL	1911	1981-89	
George Bush (R)	MA	1924	1989-93	
William J. Clinton (D)	AR	1946	1993-	

F-Federalist; D-Democratic; R-Republican; W-Whig; (r)-resigned

VICE-PRESIDENTS OF THE UNITED STATES

Name (and party)	State of Birth	Born	Term	Died
John Adams (F)	MA	1735	1789-97	1826
Thomas Jefferson (D-R)	VA	1743	1797-1801	1826
Aaron Burr (R)	NJ	1756	1801-05	1836
George Clinton (R)	NY	1739	1805-12	1812
Elbridge Gerry (R)	MA	1744	1813-14	1814
Daniel D. Tompkins (R)	NY	1774	1817-25	1825
John C. Calhoun (R)	SC	1782	1825-32	1850
Martin Van Buren (D)	NY	1782	1833-37	1862
Richard M. Johnson (D)	KY	1780	1837-41	1850
John Tyler (W)	VA	1790	1841	1862
George M. Dallas (D)	PA	1792	1845-49	1864
Millard Fillmore (W)	NY	1800	1849-50	1874
William R. King (D)	NC	1786	1853	1853
John C. Breckinridge (D)	KY	1821	1857-61	1875
Hannibal Hamlin (R)	ME	1809	1861-65	1891
Andrew Johnson (R)	NC	1808	1865	1875
Schuyler Colfax (R)	NY	1823	1869-73	1885
Henry Wilson (R)	NH	1812	1873-75	1875
William A. Wheeler (R)	NY	1819	1877-81	1887
Chester A. Arthur (R)	VT	1830	1881	1886
Thomas A. Hendricks (D)	OH	1819	1885	1885
Levi P. Morton (R)	VT	1824	1889-93	1920
Adlai E. Stevenson (D)	KY	1835	1893-97	1914
Garrett A. Hobart (R)	NJ	1844	1897-99	1899
Theodore Roosevelt (R)	NY	1858	1901	1919
Charles W. Fairbanks (R)	OH	1852	1905-09	1918
James S. Sherman (R)	NY	1855	1909-12	1912
Thomas R. Marshall (D)	IN	1854	1913-21	1925
Calvin Coolidge (R)	VT	1872	1921-23	1933
Charles G. Dawes (R)	OH	1865	1925-29	1951
Charles Curtis (R)	KS	1860	1929-33	1936
John N. Garner (D)	TX	1869	1933-41	1967
Henry A. Wallace (D)	IA	1888	1941-45	1965
Harry S. Truman (D)	MO	1884	1945	1972
Alben W. Barkley (D)	KY	1877	1949-53	1956
Richard M. Nixon (R)	CA	1913	1953-61	1994
Lyndon B. Johnson (D)	TX	1906	1961-63	1973
Hubert H. Humphrey (D)	SD	1911	1965-69	
Spiro T. Agnew (R)	MD	1918	1969-73 (r)	
Gerald R. Ford (R)	NE	1913	1973-74	
Nelson A. Rockefeller (R)	ME	1906	1974-77	
Walter F. Mondale (D)	MN	1928	1977-81	
George Bush (R)	MA	1924	1981-89	
Dan Quayle (R)	MA	1947	1989-93	
Albert Gore, Jr. (D)	DC	1948	1993-	

F-Federalist; D-Democratic; R-Republican; W-Whig; (r)-resigned

U.S. DECLARATION OF INDEPENDENCE

Adopted by the Continental Congress in Philadelphia on July 4, 1776.

IN CONGRESS, July 4, 1776,
A DECLARATION
By the REPRESENTATIVES of the
UNITED STATES OF AMERICA,
in GENERAL CONGRESS assembled

When in the course of human Events, it becomes necessary for one People to dissolve the Political Bands which have connected them with another, and to assume among the Powers of the Earth, the separate and equal Station to which the Laws of Nature and of Nature's God entitle them, a decent Respect to the Opinions of Mankind requires that they should declare the causes which impel them to the Separation.

We hold these Truths to be self-evident, that all Men are created equal, that they are endowed by their Creator with certain unalienable Rights, that among these are Life, Liberty, and the Pursuit of Happiness—That to secure these Rights, Governments are instituted among Men, deriving their just Powers from the Consent of the Governed, that whenever any Form of Government becomes destructive of these Ends, it is the Right of the People to alter or to abolish it, and to institute new Government, laying its Foundation on such Principles, and organizing its Powers in such Form, as to them shall seem most likely to effect their Safety and Happiness. Prudence, indeed, will dictate that Governments long established should not be changed for light and transient Causes; and accordingly all Experience hath shewn, that Mankind are more disposed to suffer, while Evils are sufferable, than to right themselves by abolishing the Forms to which they are accustomed. But when a long Train of Abuses and Usurpations, pursuing invariably the same Object, evinces a Design to reduce them under absolute Despotism, it is their Right, it is their Duty, to throw off such Government, and to provide new Guards for their future Security. Such has been the patient Sufferance of these Colonies; and such is now the Necessity which constrains them to alter their former Systems of Government. The History of the present King of Great-Britain is a History of repeated injuries and Usurpations, all having in direct Object the Establishment of an absolute Tyranny over these States. To prove this, let Facts be submitted to a candid World.

He has refused his Assent to laws, the most wholesome and necessary for the public Good.

He has forbidden his Governors to pass Laws of immediate and pressing importance, unless suspended in their Operation till his Assent should be obtained; and when so suspended, he has utterly neglected to attend to them.

He has refused to pass other Laws for the Accommodation of large Districts of People, unless those People would relinquish the Right of Representation in the Legislature, a Right inestimable to them, and formidable to Tyrants only.

He has called together Legislative Bodies at Places unusual, uncomfortable, and distant from the Depository of their Public Records, for the sole Purpose of fatiguing them into Compliance with his Measures.

He has dissolved Representative Houses repeatedly, for opposing with manly Firmness his invasions on the Rights of the People.

He has refused for a long Time, after such Dissolutions, to cause others to be elected; whereby the Legislative Powers, incapable of Annihilation, have returned to the People at large for their exercise; the State remaining in the meantime exposed to all the Dangers of Invasion from without, and Convulsions within.

He has endeavoured to prevent the Population of these States; for that Purpose obstructing the laws for Naturalization of Foreigners; refusing to pass others to encourage their Migrations hither, and raising the Conditions of new Appropriations of Lands.

He has obstructed the Administration of Justice, by refusing his Assent to Laws for establishing Judiciary Powers.

He has made Judges dependent on his Will alone, for the Tenure of their Offices, and the Amount and payment of their Salaries.

He has erected a Multitude of new Offices, and sent hither Swarms of Officers to harness our People, and eat out their Substance.

He has kept among us, in Times of Peace, Standing Armies, without the consent of our Legislatures.

He has affected to render the Military independent of, and superior to the Chief Power.

He has combined with others to subject us to a Jurisdiction foreign to our Constitution, and unacknowledged by our Laws; giving his Assent to their Acts of pretended Legislation:

For quartering large Bodies of Armed Troops among us:

For protecting them, by a mock trial, from Punishment for any Murders which they should commit on the inhabitants of these States:

For cutting off our Trade with all Parts of the World:

For imposing Taxes on us without our Consent:

For depriving us, in many Cases, of the Benefits of Trial by Jury:

For transporting us beyond Seas to be tried for pretended Offences:

For abolishing the free System of English Laws in a neighbouring Province, establishing therein an arbitrary Government, and enlarging its Boundaries, so as to render it at once an Example and fit instrument for introducing the same absolute Rule into these Colonies:

For taking away our Charters, abolishing our most valuable Laws, and altering fundamentally the Forms of our Governments:

For suspending our own Legislatures, and declaring themselves invested with Power to legislate for us in all Cases whatsoever.

He has abdicated Government here, by declaring us out of his Protection and waging War against us.

He has plundered our Seas, ravaged our Coasts, burnt our towns, and destroyed the Lives of our People.

He is, at this Time, transporting large Armies of foreign Mercenaries to compleat the works of Death, Desolation, and Tyranny, already begun with circumstances of Cruelty and Perfidy, scarcely paralleled in the most barbarous Ages, and totally unworthy the Head of a civilized Nation.

He has constrained our fellow Citizens taken Captive on the high Seas to bear Arms against their Country, to become the Executioners of their Friends and Brethren, or to fall themselves by their Hands.

He has excited domestic insurrections amongst us, and has endeavoured to bring on the Inhabitants of our Frontiers, the merciless Indian Savages, whose known Rule of Warfare, is an undistinguished Destruction of all Ages, Sexes and Conditions.

In every stage of these Oppressions we have Petitioned for Redress in the most humble Terms: Our repeated Petitions have been answered only by repeated injury. A Prince, whose Character is thus marked by every act which may define a Tyrant, is unfit to be the Ruler of a free People.

Nor have we been wanting in Attention to our British Brethren. We have warned them from Time to Time of Attempts by their Legislature to extend an unwarrantable Jurisdiction over us. We have reminded them of the Circumstances of our Emigration and Settlement here. We have appealed to their native Justice and Magnanimity, and we have conjured them by the Ties of our common Kindred to disavow these Usurpations, which would inevitably interrupt our Connections and Correspondence. They too have been deaf to the Voice of Justice and of Consanguinity. We must, therefore, acquiesce in the Necessity, which denounces our Separation, and hold them as we hold the rest of Mankind, Enemies in War, in Peace, Friends.

Declaration of Independence

We, therefore, the Representatives of the UNITED STATES OF AMERICA, in General Congress, Assembled, appealing to the Supreme Judge of the World for the Rectitude of our Intentions, do, in the Name, and by Authority of the good People of these Colonies, solemnly Publish and Declare, That these United Colonies are, and of Right ought to be, Free and Independent States; that they are absolved from all Allegiance to the British Crown, and that all political Connection between them and the State of Great-Britain, is and ought to be totally dissolved; and that as Free and Independent States, they have full Power to levy War, conclude Peace, contract Alliances, establish Commerce, and to do all other Acts and Things which Independent States may of right do. And for the support of this declaration, with a firm Reliance on the Protection of divine Providence, we mutually pledge to each other our lives, our Fortunes, and our sacred honor.

JOHN HANCOCK, President

Attest.

CHARLES THOMSON, Secretary

Signers of the Declaration of Independence

Delegate and State	Vocation	Birthplace	Born	Died
Adams, John (Mass.)	Lawyer	Braintree (Quincy), Mass.	Oct. 30, 1735	July 4, 1826
Adams, Samuel (Mass.)	Political leader	Boston, Mass.	Sept. 27, 1722	Oct. 2, 1803
Bartlett, Josiah (N.H.)	Physician, judge	Amesbury, Mass.	Nov. 21, 1729	May 19, 1795
Braxton, Carter (Va.)	Farmer	Newington Plantation, Va.	Sept. 10, 1736	Oct. 10, 1797
Carroll, Chas. of Carrollton (Md.)	Lawyer	Annapolis, Md.	Sept. 19, 1737	Nov. 14, 1832
Chase, Samuel (Md.)	Judge	Princess Anne, Md.	Apr. 17, 1741	June 19, 1811
Clark, Abraham (N.J.)	Surveyor	Roselle, N.J.	Feb. 15, 1726	Sept. 15, 1794
Clymer, George (Pa.)	Merchant	Philadelphia, Pa.	Mar. 16, 1739	Jan. 23, 1813
Ellery, William (R.I.)	Lawyer	Newport, R.I.	Dec. 22, 1727	Feb. 15, 1820
Floyd, William (N.Y.)	Soldier	Brookhaven, N.Y.	Dec. 17, 1734	Aug. 4, 1821
Franklin, Benjamin (Pa.)	Printer, publisher	Boston, Mass.	Jan. 17, 1706	Apr. 17, 1790
Gerry, Elbridge (Mass.)	Merchant	Marblehead, Mass.	July 17, 1744	Nov. 23, 1814
Gwinnett, Button (Ga.)	Merchant	Down Hatherly, England	c. 1735	May 19, 1977
Hall, Lyman (Ga.)	Physician	Wallingford, Conn.	Apr. 12, 1724	Oct. 19, 1790
Hancock, John (Mass.)	Merchant	Braintree (Quincy), Mass.	Jan. 12, 1737	Oct. 8, 1793
Harrison, Benjamin (Va.)	Farmer	Berkeley, Va.	Apr. 5, 1726	Apr. 24, 1791
Hart, John (N.J.)	Farmer	Stonington, Conn.	c. 1711	May 11, 1779
Hewes, Joseph (N.C.)	Merchant	Princeton, N.J.	Jan. 23, 1730	Nov. 10, 1779
Heyward, Thos. Jr. (S.C.)	Lawyer, farmer	St. Luke's Parish, S.C.	July 28, 1746	Mar. 6, 1809
Hooper, William (N.C.)	Lawyer	Boston, Mass.	June 28, 1742	Oct. 14, 1790
Hopkins, Stephen (R.I.)	Judge, educator	Providence, R.I.	Mar. 7, 1707	July 13, 1785
Hopkinson, Francis (N.J.)	Judge, author	Philadelphia, Pa.	Sept. 21, 1737	May 9, 1791
Huntington, Samuel (Conn.)	Judge	Windham County, Conn.	July 3, 1731	Jan. 5, 1796
Jefferson, Thomas (Va.)	Lawyer	Shadwell, Va.	Apr. 13, 1743	July 4, 1826
Lee, Francis Lightfoot (Va.)	Farmer	Westmoreland County, Va.	Oct. 14, 1734	Jan. 11, 1797
Lee, Richard Henry (Va.)	Farmer	Westmoreland County, Va.	Jan. 20, 1732	June 19, 1794
Lewis, Francis (N.Y.)	Merchant	Llandaff, Wales	Mar., 1713	Dec. 31, 1802
Livingston, Philip (N.Y.)	Merchant	Albany, N.Y.	Jan. 15, 1716	June 12, 1778
Lynch, Thomas Jr. (S.C.)	Farmer	Winyah, S.C.	Aug. 5, 1749	(at sea) 1779
McKean, Thomas (Del.)	Lawyer	New London, Pa.	Mar. 19, 1734	June 24, 1817
Middleton, Arthur (S.C.)	Farmer	Charleston, S.C.	June 26, 1742	Jan. 1, 1787
Morris, Lewis (N.Y.)	Farmer	Morrisania (Bronx County), N.Y.	Apr. 8, 1726	Jan. 22, 1798
Morris, Robert (Pa.)	Merchant	Liverpool, England	Jan. 20, 1734	May 9, 1806
Morton, John (Pa.)	Judge	Ridley, Pa.	1724	Apr., 1777
Nelson, Thos. Jr. (Va.)	Farmer	Yorktown, Va.	Dec. 26, 1738	Jan. 4, 1789
Paca, William (Md.)	Judge	Abingdon, Md.	Oct. 31, 1740	Oct. 23, 1799
Paine, Robert Treat (Mass.)	Judge	Boston, Mass.	Mar. 11, 1731	May 12, 1814
Penn, John (N.C.)	Lawyer	Near Port Royal, Va.	May 17, 1741	Sept. 14, 1788
Read, George (Del.)	Judge	Near North East, Md.	Sept. 18, 1733	Sept. 21, 1798
Rodney, Caesar (Del.)	Judge	Dover, Del.	Oct. 7, 1728	June 29, 1784
Ross, George (Pa.)	Judge	New Castle, Del.	May 10, 1730	July 14, 1779
Rush, Benjamin (Pa.)	Physician	Byberry, Pa. (Philadelphia)	Dec. 24, 1745	Apr. 19, 1813
Rutledge, Edward (S.C.)	Lawyer	Charleston, S.C.	Nov. 23, 1749	Jan. 23, 1800
Sherman, Roger (Conn.)	Lawyer	Newton, Mass.	Apr. 19, 1721	July 23, 1793
Smith, James (Pa.)	Lawyer	Dublin, Ireland	c. 1719	July 11, 1806
Stockton, Richard (N.J.)	Lawyer	Near Princeton, N.J.	Oct. 1, 1730	Feb. 28, 1781
Stone, Thomas (Md.)	Lawyer	Charles County, Md.	1743	Oct. 5, 1787
Taylor, George (Pa.)	Ironmaster	Ireland	1716	Feb. 23, 1781
Thornton, Matthew (N.H.)	Physician	Ireland	1714	June 24, 1803
Walton, George (Ga.)	Judge	Prince Edward County, Va.	1741	Feb. 2, 1804
Whipple, William (N.H.)	Merchant, Judge	Kittery, Me.	Jan. 14, 1730	Nov. 28, 1785
Williams, William (Conn.)	Merchant	Lebanon, Conn.	Apr. 23, 1731	Aug. 2, 1811
Wilson, James (Pa.)	Judge	Carskerdo, Scotland	Sept. 14, 1742	Aug. 28, 1798
Witherspoon, John (N.J.)	Educator	Gifford, Scotland	Feb. 5, 1723	Nov. 15, 1794
Wolcott, Oliver (Conn.)	Judge	Windsor, Conn.	Dec. 1, 1726	Dec. 1, 1797
Wythe, George (Va.)	Lawyer	Elizabeth City Co. (Hampton), Va.	1726	June 8, 1806

Constitution of the United States
The Original 7 Articles

PREAMBLE

We, the people of the United States, in order to form a more perfect Union, establish justice, insure domestic tranquility, provide for the common defense, promote the general welfare, and secure the blessings of liberty to ourselves and our posterity do ordain and establish this Constitution for the United States of America.

ARTICLE I.

Section 1—Legislative powers; in whom vested:

All legislative powers herein granted shall be vested in a Congress of the United States, which shall consist of a Senate and House of Representatives.

Section 2—House of Representatives, how and by whom chosen. Qualifications of a Representative. Representatives and direct taxes, how apportioned. Enumeration. Vacancies to be filled. Power of choosing officers, and of impeachment.

1. The House of Representatives shall be composed of members chosen every second year by the people of the several States, and the electors in each State shall have the qualifications requisite for electors of the most numerous branch of the State Legislature.

2. No person shall be a Representative who shall not have attained to the age of twenty-five years, and been seven years a citizen of the United States, and who shall not, when elected, be an inhabitant of that State in which he shall be chosen.

3. *(Representatives and direct taxes shall be apportioned among the several States which may be included within this Union, according to their respective numbers, which shall be determined by adding to the whole number of free persons, including those bound to service for a term of years, and excluding Indians not taxed, three-fifths of all other persons.) (The previous sentence was superseded by Amendment XIV, section 2.)* The actual enumeration shall be made within three years after the first meeting of the Congress of the United States, and within every subsequent term of ten years, in such manner as they shall by law direct. The number of Representatives shall not exceed one for every thirty thousand, but each State shall have at least one Representative; and until such enumeration shall be made, the State of New Hampshire shall be entitled to choose three, Massachusetts eight, Rhode Island and Providence Plantations one, Connecticut five, New York six, New Jersey four, Pennsylvania eight, Delaware one, Maryland six, Virginia ten, North Carolina five, South Carolina five, and Georgia three.

4. When vacancies happen in the representation from any State, the Executive Authority thereof shall issue writs of election to fill such vacancies.

5. The House of Representatives shall choose their Speaker and other officers; and shall have the sole power of impeachment.

Section 3—Senators, how and by whom chosen. How classified. Qualifications of a Senator. President of the Senate, his right to vote. President pro tem., and other officers of the Senate, how chosen. Power to try impeachments. When President is tried, Chief Justice to provide. Sentence.

1. The Senate of the United States shall be composed of two Senators from each State, *(chosen by the Legislature thereof). (The preceding five words were superseded by Amendment XVII, section 1.)* for six years; and each Senator shall have one vote.

2. Immediately after they shall be assembled in consequence of the first election, they shall be divided as equally as may be into three classes. The seats of the Senators of the first class shall be vacated at the expiration of the second year, of the second class at the expiration of the fourth year, and of the third class at the expiration of the sixth year, so that one-third may be chosen every second year; *(and if vacancies happen by resignation, or otherwise, during the recess of the Legislature of any State, the Executive thereof may make temporary appointments until the next meeting of the Legislature, which shall then fill such vacancies.) (The words in parentheses were superseded by Amendment XVII, section 2.)*

3. No person shall be a Senator who shall not have attained to the age of thirty years, and been nine years a citizen of the United States, and who shall not, when elected, be an inhabitant of that State for which he shall be chosen.

4. The Vice President of the United States shall be President of the Senate, but shall have no vote, unless they be equally divided.

5. The Senate shall choose their other officers, and also a President pro tempore, in the absence of the Vice President, or when he shall exercise the office of President of the United States.

6. The Senate shall have the sole power to try all impeachments. When sitting for that purpose, they shall be on oath or affirmation. When the President of the United States is tried, the Chief Justice shall preside: and no person shall be convicted without the concurrence of two-thirds of the members present.

7. Judgment in cases of impeachment shall not extend further than to removal from office, and disqualification to hold and enjoy any office of honor, trust or profit under the United States: but the party convicted shall nevertheless be liable and subject to indictment, trial, judgment and punishment, according to law.

Section 4—Times, etc., of holding elections, how prescribed. One session each year.

1. The times, places and manner of holding elections for Senators and Representatives, shall be prescribed in each State by the Legislature thereof; but the Congress may at any time by law make or alter such regulations, except as to the places of choosing Senators.

2. The Congress shall assemble at least once in every year, and such meeting shall *(be on the first Monday in December.) (The words in parentheses were superseded by Amendment XX, section 2),* unless they shall by law appoint a different day.

Section 5—Membership, quorum, adjournments, rules. Power to punish or expel. Journal. Time of adjournments, how limited, etc.

1. Each House shall be the judge of the elections, returns and qualifications of its own members, and a majority of each shall constitute a quorum to do business, but a smaller number may adjourn from day to day, and may be authorized to compel the attendance of absent members, in such manner, and under such penalties as each House may provide.

2. Each House may determine the rules of its proceedings, punish its members for disorderly behavior, and, with the concurrence of two-thirds, expel a member.

3. Each House shall keep a journal of its proceedings, and from time to time publish the same, excepting such parts as may in their judgment require secrecy; and the yeas and nays of the members of either House on any question shall, at the desire of one-fifth of those present, be entered on the journal.

4. Neither House, during the session of Congress shall, without the consent of the other, adjourn for more than three days, nor to any other place than that in which the two Houses shall be sitting.

Section 6—Compensation, privileges, disqualifications in certain cases.

1. The Senators and Representatives shall receive a compensation for their services, to be ascertained by law, and paid out of the Treasury of the United States. They shall in all cases, except treason, felony and breach of the peace, be privileged from arrest during their attendance at the session of their respective Houses, and in going to and returning from the same; and for any speech or debate in either House, they shall not be questioned in any other place.

2. No Senator or Representative shall, during the time for which he was elected, be appointed to any civil office under the authority of the United States, which shall have been created, or the emoluments whereof shall have been increased during such time; and no person holding any office under the United States, shall be a member of either House during his continuance in office.

Section 7—House to originate all revenue bills. Veto. Bill may be passed by two-thirds of each House, notwithstanding, etc. Bill, not returned in ten days, to become a law. Provisions as to orders, concurrent resolutions, etc.

1. All bills for raising revenue shall originate in the House of Representatives; but the Senate may propose or concur with amendments as on other bills.

2. Every bill which shall have passed the House of Representatives and the Senate, shall, before it becomes a law, be presented to the President of the United States; if he approves he shall sign it, but if not he shall return it, with his objections to that House in which it shall have originated, who shall enter the objections at large on their journal, and proceed to reconsider it. If after such reconsideration two-thirds of that House shall agree to pass the

Constitution of the United States

bill, it shall be sent, together with the objections, to the other House, by which it shall likewise be reconsidered, and if approved by two-thirds of that House, it shall become a law. But in all such cases the votes of both Houses shall be determined by yeas and nays, and the names of the persons voting for and against the bill shall be entered on the journal of each House respectively, if any bill shall not be returned by the President within ten days (Sundays excepted) after it shall have been presented to him, the same shall be a law, in like manner as if he had signed it, unless the Congress by their adjournment prevent its return, in which case it shall not be a law.

3. Every order, resolution, or vote to which the concurrence of the Senate and House of Representatives may be necessary (except on a question of adjournment) shall be presented to the President of the United States; and before the same shall take effect, shall be approved by him, or being disapproved by him, shall be repassed by two-thirds of the Senate and House of Representatives, according to the rules and limitations prescribed in the case of a bill.

Section 8—Powers of Congress.

The Congress shall have power

1. To lay and collect taxes, duties, imposts and excises, to pay the debts and provide for the common defense and general welfare of the United States; but all duties, imposts and excises shall be uniform throughout the United States;

2. To borrow money on the credit of the United States;

3. To regulate commerce with foreign nations, and among the several States, and with the Indian tribes;

4. To establish a uniform rule of naturalization, and uniform laws on the subject of bankruptcies throughout the United States;

5. To coin money, regulate the value thereof, and of foreign coin, and fix the standard of weights and measures.

6. To provide for the punishment of counterfeiting the securities and current coin of the United States;

7. To establish post-offices and post-roads;

8. To promote the progress of science and useful arts, by securing for limited times to authors and inventors the exclusive right to their respective writings and discoveries;

9. To constitute tribunals inferior to the Supreme Court;

10. To define and punish piracies and felonies committed on the high seas, and offenses against the law of nations;

11. To declare war, grant letters of marque and reprisal, and make rules concerning captures on land and water;

12. To raise and support armies, but no appropriation of money to that use shall be for a longer term than two years.

13. To provide and maintain a navy;

14. To make rules for the government and regulation of the land and naval forces;

15. To provide for calling forth the militia to execute the laws of the Union, suppress insurrections and repel invasions;

16. To provide for organizing, arming, and disciplining the militia, and for governing such part of them as may be employed in the service of the United States, reserving to the States respectively, the appointment of the officers, and the authority of training the militia according to the discipline prescribed by Congress;

17. To exercise exclusive legislation in all cases whatsoever, over such district (not exceeding ten miles square) as may, by cession of particular States, and the acceptance of Congress, become the seat of the Government of the United States, and to exercise like authority over all places purchased by the consent of the Legislature of the State in which the same shall be, for the erection of forts, magazines, arsenals, dockyards, and other needful buildings;-And

18. To make all laws which shall be necessary and proper for carrying into execution the foregoing powers, and all other powers vested by this Constitution in the Government of the United States, or in any department or officer thereof.

Section 9—Provision as to migration or importation of certain persons. Habeas corpus, bills of attainder, etc. Taxes, how apportioned. No export duty. No commercial preference. Money, how drawn from Treasury, etc. No titular nobility. Officers not to receive presents, etc.

1. The migration or importation of such persons as any of the States now existing shall think proper to admit, shall not be prohibited by the Congress prior to the year one thousand eight hundred and eight, but a tax or duty may be imposed on such imporation, not exceeding ten dollars for each person.

2. The privilege of the writ of habeas corpus shall not be suspended, unless when in cases of rebellion or invasion the public safety may require it.

3. No bill of attainder or ex post facto law shall be passed.

4. No capitation, or other direct, tax shall be laid, unless in proportion to the census or enumeration herein before directed to be taken. (Modified by Amendment XVI.)

5. No tax or duty shall be laid on articles exported from any State.

6. No preference shall be given by any regulation of commerce or revenue to the ports of one State over those of another: nor shall vessels bound to, or from, one State, be obliged to enter, clear, or pay duties in another.

7. No money shall be drawn from the Treasury, but in consequence of appropriations made by law; and a regular statement and account of the receipts and expenditures of all public money shall be published from time to time.

8. No title of nobility shall be granted by the United States; and no person holding any office of profit or trust under them, shall, without the consent of the Congress, accept of any present, emolument, office, or title, of any kind whatever, from any king, prince, or foreign state.

Section 10—States prohibited from the exercise of certain powers.

1. No State shall enter into any treaty, alliance, or confederation; grant letters of marque and reprisal; coin money; emit bills of credit; make anything but gold and silver coin a tender in payment of debts, pass any bill of attainder, ex post facto law, or law impairing the obligation of contracts, or grant any title of nobility.

2. No State shall, without the consent of the Congress, lay any imposts or duties on imports or exports, except what may be absolutely necessary for executing its inspection laws: and the net produce of all duties and imposts, laid by any State on imports or exports, shall be for the use of the Treasury of the United States; and all such laws shall be subject to the revision and control of the Congress.

3. No State shall, without the consent of Congress, lay any duty of tonnage, keep troops, or ships of war in time of peace, enter into any agreement or compact with another State, or with a foreign power, or engage in war, unless actually invaded, or in such imminent danger as will not admit of delay.

ARTICLE II.

Section 1—President; his term of office. Electors of President; number and how appointed. Electors to vote on same day. Qualification of President. On whom his duties devolve in case of his removal, death, etc. President's compensation. His oath of office.

1. The Executive power shall be vested in a President of the United States of America. He shall hold his office during the term of four years, and together with the Vice President, chosen for the same term, be elected as follows

2. Each State shall appoint, in such manner as the Legislature thereof may direct, a number of electors, equal to the whole number of Senators and Representatives to which the State may be entitled in the Congress: but no Senator or Representative, or person holding an office of trust or profit under the United States, shall be an elector.

(The electors shall meet in their respective States, and vote by ballot for two persons, of whom one at least shall not be an inhabitant of the same State with themselves. And they shall make a list of all the persons voted for, and of the number of votes for each; which list they shall sign and certify, and transmit sealed to the seat of the Government of the United States, directed to the President of the Senate. The President of the Senate shall, in the presence of the Senate and House of Representatives, open all the certificates, and the votes shall then be counted. The person having the greatest number of votes shall be the President, if such number be a majority of the whole number of electors appointed; and if there be more than one who have such majority, and have an equal number of votes, then the House of Representatives shall immediately choose by ballot one of them for President; and if no person have a majority, then from the five highest on the list the said House shall in like manner choose the President. But in choosing the President, the votes shall be taken by States, the representation from each State having one vote; a quorum for this purpose shall consist of a member or members from two-thirds of the States, and a majority of all the States shall be necessary to a choice. In every case, after the choice of the President, the person having the greatest number of votes of the electors shall be the Vice President. But if there should remain

Constitution of the United States

two or more who have equal votes, the Senate shall choose from them by ballot the Vice President.)

(This clause was superseded by Amendment XII.)

3. The Congress may determine the time of choosing the electors, and the day on which they shall give their votes; which day shall be the same throughout the United States.

4. No person except a natural born citizen, or a citizen of the United States, at the time of the adoption of this Constitution, shall be eligible to the office of President, neither shall any person be eligible to that office who shall not have attained to the age of thirty-five years, and been fourteen years a resident within the United States.

(For qualification of the Vice President, see Amendment XII.)

5. In cases of the removal of the President from office, or of his death, resignation, or inability to discharge the powers and duties of the said office, the same shall devolve on the Vice President, and the Congress may by law provide for the case of removal, death, resignation or inability, both of the President and Vice President, declaring what officer shall then act as President, and such officer shall act accordingly, until the disability be removed, or a President shall be elected.

(This clause has been modified by Amendments XX and XXV.)

6. The President shall, at stated times, receive for his services, a compensation, which shall neither be increased nor diminished during the period for which he shall have been elected, and he shall not receive within that period any other emolument from the United States, or any of them.

7. Before he enter on the execution of his office, he shall take the following oath or affirmation:

"I do solemnly swear (or affirm) that I will faithfully execute the office of President of the United States, and will to the best of my ability, preserve, protect and defend the Constitution of the United States."

Section 2—President to be Commander-in-Chief. He may require opinions of cabinet officers, etc., may pardon. Treaty-making power. Nomination of certain officers. When President may fill vacancies.

1. The President shall be Commander-in-Chief of the Army and Navy of the United States, and of the militia of the several States, when called into the actual service of the United States; he may require the opinion, in writing, of the principal officer in each of the executive departments, upon any subject relating to the duties of their respective offices, and he shall have power to grant reprieves and pardons for offenses against the United States, except in cases of impeachment.

2. He shall have power, by and with the advice and consent of the Senate, to make treaties, provided two-thirds of the Senators present concur; and he shall nominate, and by and with the advice and consent of the Senate, shall appoint ambassadors, other public ministers and consuls, judges of the Supreme Court, and all other officers of the United States, whose appointments are not herein otherwise provided for, and which shall be established by law: but the Congress may by law vest the appointment of such inferior officers, as they think proper, in the President alone, in the courts of law, or in the heads of departments.

3. The President shall have power to fill up all vacancies that may happen during the recess of the Senate, by granting commissions, which shall expire at the end of their next session.

Section 3—President shall communicate to Congress. He may convene and adjourn Congress, in case of disagreement, etc. Shall receive ambassadors, execute laws, and commission officers.

He shall from time to time give to the Congress information of the state of the Union, and recommend to their consideration such measures as he shall judge necessary and expedient; he may, on extraordinary occasions, convene both Houses, or either of them, and in case of disagreement between them, with respect to the time of adjournment, he may adjourn them to such time as he shall think proper; he shall receive ambassadors and other public ministers; he shall take care that the laws be faithfully executed, and shall commission all the officers of the United States.

Section 4—All civil offices forfeited for certain crimes.

The President, Vice President, and all civil officers of the United States, shall be removed from office on impeachment for, and conviction of, treason, bribery, or other high crimes and misdemeanors.

ARTICLE III.

Section 1—Judicial powers, Tenure, Compensation.

The judicial power of the United States, shall be vested in one Supreme Court, and in such inferior courts as the Congress may from time to time ordain and establish. The judges, both of the Supreme and inferior courts, shall hold their offices during good behavior, and shall at stated times, receive for their services, a compensation, which shall not be diminished during their continuance in office.

Section 2—Judicial power; to what cases it extends. Original jurisdiction of Supreme Court; appellate jurisdiction. Trial by jury, etc. Trial, where.

1. The judicial power shall extend to all cases, in law and equity, arising under this Constitution, the laws of the United States, and treaties made, or which shall be made, under their authority; to all cases affecting ambassadors, other public ministers and consuls; to all cases of admiralty and maritime jurisdiction; to controversies to which the United States shall be a party; to controversies between two or more States; between a State and citizens of another State; between citizens of different States, between citizens of the same State claiming lands under grants of different States, and between a State, or the citizens thereof, and foreign states, citizens or subjects.

(This section is modified by Amendment XI.)

2. In all cases affecting ambassadors, other public ministers and consuls, and those in which a State shall be party, the Supreme Court shall have original jurisdiction. In all the other cases before mentioned, the Supreme Court shall have appellate jurisdiction, both as to law and fact, with such exceptions, and under such regulations as the Congress shall make.

3. The trial of all crimes, except in cases of impeachment, shall be by jury; and such trial shall be held in the State where the said crimes shall have been committed; but when not committed within any State, the trial shall be at such place or places as the Congress may by law have directed.

Section 3—Treason Defined, Proof of, Punishment of.

1. Treason against the United States, shall consist only in levying war against them, or in adhering to their enemies, giving them aid and comfort. No person shall be convicted of treason unless on the testimony of two witnesses to the same overt act, or on confession in open court.

2. The Congress shall have power to declare the punishment of treason, but no attainder of treason shall work corruption of blood, or forfeiture except during the life of the person attainted.

ARTICLE IV.

Section 1—Each State to give credit to the public acts, etc., of every other State.

Full faith and credit shall be given in each State to the public acts, records, and judicial proceedings of every other State. And the Congress may by general laws prescribe the manner in which such acts, records and proceedings shall be proved, and the effect thereof.

Section 2—Privileges of citizens of each State. Fugitives from justice to be delivered up. Persons held to service having escaped, to be delivered up.

1. The citizens of each State shall be entitled to all privileges and immunities of citizens in the several States.

2. A person charged in any State with treason, felony, or other crime, who shall flee from justice, and be found in another State, shall on demand of the Executive authority of the State from which he fled, be delivered up, to be removed to the State having jurisdiction of the crime.

(3. No person held to service or labor in one State, under the laws thereof, escaping into another, shall in consequence of any law or regulation therein, be discharged from such service or labor, but shall be delivered up on claim of the party to whom such service or labor may be due.)
(This clause is superseded by Amendment XIII.)

Section 3—Admission of new States. Power of Congress over territory and other property.

1. New States may be admitted by the Congress into this Union; but no new State shall be formed or erected within the jurisdiction of any other State; nor any State be formed by the junction of two or more States, or parts of States, without the consent of the Legislature of the States concerned as well as of the Congress.

Constitution of the United States

2. The Congress shall have power to dispose of and make all needful rules and regulations respecting the territory or other property belonging to the United States; and nothing in this Constitution shall be so construed as to prejudice any claims of the United States, or of any particular State.

Section 4—Republican form of government guaranteed. Each state to be protected.

The United States shall guarantee to every State in this Union a Republican form of government, and shall protect each of them against invasion; and on application of the Legislature, or of the Executive (when the Legislature cannot be convened) against domestic violence.

ARTICLE V.

Constitution: how amended; proviso.

The Congress, whenever two-thirds of both Houses shall deem it necessary, shall propose amendments to the Constitution, or, on the application of the Legislatures of two-thirds of the several States, shall call a convention for proposing amendments, which, in either case, shall be valid to all intents and purposes, as part of this Constitution, when ratified by the Legislatures of three-fourths of the several States, or by conventions in three-fourths thereof, as the one or the other mode of ratification may be proposed by the Congress; provided that no amendment which may be made prior to the year one thousand eight hundred and eight shall in any manner affect the first and fourth clauses in the Ninth Section of the First Article; and that no State, without its consent, shall be deprived of its equal suffrage in the Senate.

ARTICLE VI.

Certain debts, etc., declared valid. Supremacy of Constitution, treaties, and laws of the United States. Oath to support Constitution, by whom taken. No religious test.

1. All debts contracted and engagements entered into, before the adoption of this Constitution, shall be as valid against the United States under this Constitution, as under the Confederation.

2. This Constitution, and the laws of the United States which shall be made in pursuance thereof; and all treaties made, or which shall be made, under the authority of the United States, shall be the supreme law of the land, and the judges in every State shall be bound thereby, any thing in the Constitution or laws of any State to the contrary notwithstanding.

3. The Senators and Representatives before mentioned, and the members of the several State Legislatures, and all executive and judicial officers, both of the United States and of the several States, shall be bound by oath of affirmation, to support this Constitution, but no religious test shall ever be required as a qualification to any office or public trust under the United States.

ARTICLE VII.

What ratification shall establish Constitution.

The ratification of the Conventions of nine States, shall be sufficient for the establishment of the Constitution between the States so ratifying the same.

Done in convention by the unanimous consent of the States present the Seventeenth day of September in the year of our Lord one thousand seven hundred and eighty seven, and of the independence of the United States of America the Twelfth. In witness whereof we have hereunto subscribed our names.

George Washington, President and deputy from Virginia.
New Hampshire—John Langdon, Nicholas Gilman.
Massachusetts—Nathaniel Gorham, Rufus King.
Connecticut—Wm. Saml. Johnson, Roger Sherman.
New York—Alexander Hamilton.
New Jersey—Wil Livingston, David Brearley, Wm. Paterson, Jonas Dayton.
Pennsylvania—B. Franklin, Thomas Mifflin, Robt. Morris, Geo. Clymer, Thos. FitzSimmons, Jared Ingersoll, James Wilson, Gouv. Morris.
Delaware—Geo. Read, Gunning Bedford Jun., John Dickinson, Richard Bassett, Jaco Broom.
Maryland—James McHenry, Daniel of Saint Thomas' Jenifer, Danl. Carroll.
Virginia—John Blair, James Madison, Jr.
North Carolina—Wm. Blount, Rich'd. Dobbs Spaight, Hugh Williamson.

South Carolina—J. Rutledge, Charles Colesworth Pinckney, Charles Pinckney, Pierce Butler.
Georgia—William Few, Abr. Baldwin.
Attest: William Jackson, Secretary.

Ten Original Amendments: The Bill of Rights
In force Dec. 15, 1791

(The First Congress, at its first session in the City of New York, Sept. 25, 1789, submitted to the states 12 amendments to clarify certain individual and state rights not named in the Constitution. They are generally called the Bill of Rights.

(Influential in framing these amendments was the Declaration of Rights of Virginia, written by George Mason (1725-1792) in 1776. Mason, a Virgin'a delegate to the Constitutional Convention, did not sign the Constitution and opposed its ratification on the ground that it did not sufficiently oppose slavery or safeguard individual rights.

(In the preamble to the resolution offering the proposed amendments, Congress said: "The conventions of a number of the States having at the time of their adopting the Constitution, expressed a desire, in order to prevent misconstruction or abuse of its powers, that further declaratory and restrictive clauses should be added, and as extending the ground of public confidence in the government will best insure the beneficient ends of its institution, be it resolved," etc.

(Ten of these amendments now commonly known as one to 10 inclusive, but originally 3 to 12 inclusive, were ratified by the states as follows: New Jersey, Nov. 20, 1789; Maryland, Dec. 19, 1789; North Carolina, Dec. 22, 1789; South Carolina, Jan. 19, 1790; New Hampshire, Jan. 25, 1790; Delaware, Jan. 28, 1790; New York, Feb. 24, 1790; Pennsylvania, Mar. 10, 1790; Rhode Island, June 7, 1790; Vermont, Nov. 3, 1791; Virginia, Dec. 15, 1791; Massachusetts, Mar. 2, 1939; Georgia, Mar. 18, 1939; Connecticut, Apr. 19, 1939. These original 10 ratified amendments follow as Amendments I to X inclusive.

(Of the two original proposed amendments which were not ratified by the necessary number of states, the first related to apportionment of Representatives; the second, to compensation of members.)

AMENDMENT I.

Religious establishment prohibited. Freedom of speech, of the press, and right to petition.

Congress shall make no law respecting an establishment of religion, or prohibiting the free exercise thereof; or abridging the freedom of speech, or of the press; or the right of the people peaceably to assemble, and to petition the Government for a redress of grievances.

AMENDMENT II.

Right to keep and bear arms.

A well-regulated militia, being necessary to the security of a free State, the right of the people to keep and bear arms, shall not be infringed.

AMENDMENT III.

Conditions for quarters for soldiers.

No soldier shall, in time of peace be quartered in any house, without the consent of the owner, nor in time of war, but in a manner to be prescribed by law.

AMENDMENT IV.

Right of search and seizure regulated.

The right of the people to be secure in their persons, houses, papers, and effects, against unreasonable searches and seizures, shall not be violated, and no warrants shall issue, but upon probable cause, supported by oath or affirmation, and particularly describing the place to be searched, and the persons or things to be seized.

AMENDMENT V.

Provisions concerning prosecution. Trial and punishment—private property not to be taken for public use without compensation.

No person shall be held to answer for a capital, or otherwise infamous crime, unless on a presentment or indictment of a Grand Jury, except in cases arising in the land or naval forces, or in the militia, when in actual service in time of war or public danger; nor shall any person be subject for the same offense to be twice put in jeopardy of life or limb; nor shall be

Constitution of the United States

compelled in any criminal case to be a witness against himself, nor be deprived of life, liberty, or property, without due process of law; nor shall private property be taken for public use without just compensation.

AMENDMENT VI.
Right to speedy trial, witnesses, etc.

In all criminal prosecutions, the accused shall enjoy the right to a speedy and public trial, by an impartial jury of the State and district wherein the crime shall have been committed, which district shall have been previously ascertained by law, and to be informed of the nature and cause of the accusation; to be confronted with the witnesses against him; to have compulsory process for obtaining witnesses in his favor, and to have the assistance of counsel for his defense.

AMENDMENT VII.
Right of trial by jury.

In suits at common law, where the value in controversy shall exceed twenty dollars, the right of trial by jury shall be preserved, and no fact tried by a jury shall be otherwise reexamined in any court of the United States, than according to the rules of the common law.

AMENDMENT VIII.
Excessive bail or fines and cruel punishment prohibited.

Excessive bail shall not be required, nor excessive fines imposed, nor cruel and unusual punishments inflicted.

AMENDMENT IX.
Rule of construction of Constitution.

The enumeration in the Constitution, of certain rights, shall not be construed to deny or disparage others retained by the people.

AMENDMENT X.
Rights of States under Constitution.

The powers not delegated to the United States by the Constitution, nor prohibited by it to the States, are reserved to the States respectively, or to the people.

Amendments Since the Bill of Rights

AMENDMENT XI.
Judicial powers construed.

The judicial power of the United States shall not be construed to extend to any suit in law or equity, commenced or prosecuted against one of the United States by citizens of another State, or by citizens or subjects of any foreign state.

(This amendment was proposed to the Legislatures of the several States by the Third Congress on March 4, 1794, and was declared to have been ratified in a message from the President to Congress, dated Jan. 8, 1798.

(It was on Jan. 5, 1798, that Secretary of State Pickering received from 12 of the States authenticated ratifications, and informed President John Adams of that fact.

(As a result of later research in the Department of State, it is now established that Amendment XI became part of the Constitution on Feb. 7, 1795, for on that date it had been ratified by 12 States as follows:

(1. New York, Mar. 27, 1794. 2. Rhode Island, Mar. 31, 1794. 3. Connecticut, May 8, 1794. 4. New Hampshire, June 16, 1794. 5. Massachusetts, June 26, 1794. 6. Vermont, between Oct. 9, 1794, and Nov. 9, 1794. 7. Virginia, Nov. 18, 1794. 8. Georgia, Nov. 29, 1794. 9. Kentucky, Dec. 7, 1794. 10. Maryland, Dec. 26, 1794. 11. Delaware, Jan. 23, 1795. 12. North Carolina, Feb. 7, 1795.

(On June 1, 1796, more than a year after Amendment XI had become a part of the Constitution (but before anyone was officially aware of this), Tennessee had been admitted as a State; but not until Oct. 16, 1797, was a certified copy of the resolution of Congress proposing the amendment sent to the Governor of Tennessee (John Sevier) by Secretary of State Pickering, whose office was then at Trenton, New Jersey, because of the epidemic of yellow fever at Philadelphia; it seems, however, that the Legislature of Tennessee took no action on Amendment XI, owing doubtless to the fact that public announcement of its adoption was made soon thereafter.

(Besides the necessary 12 States, one other, South Carolina, ratified Amendment XI, but this action was not taken until Dec. 4, 1797; the two remaining States, New Jersey and Pennsylvania, failed to ratify.)

AMENDMENT XII.
Manner of choosing President and Vice-President

(Proposed by Congress Dec. 9, 1803; ratification completed June 15, 1804.)

The Electors shall meet in their respective States and vote by ballot for President and Vice-President, one of whom, at least, shall not be an inhabitant of the same State with themselves; they shall name in their ballots the person voted for as President, and in distinct ballots the person voted for as Vice-President, and they shall make distinct lists of all persons voted for as President, and of all persons voted for as Vice-President, and of the number of votes for each, which lists they shall sign and certify, and transmit sealed to the seat of the government of the United States, directed to the President of the Senate; the President of the Senate shall, in the presence of the Senate and House of Representatives, open all the certificates and the votes shall then be counted;—The person having the greatest number of votes for President, shall be the President, if such number be a majority of the whole number of Electors appointed; and if no person have such majority, then from the persons having the highest numbers not exceeding three on the list of those voted for as President, the House of Representatives shall choose immediately, by ballot, the President. But in choosing the President, the votes shall be taken by States, the representation from each State having one vote; a quorum for this purpose shall consist of a member or members from two-thirds of the States, and a majority of all the States shall be necessary to a choice. *(And if the House of Representatives shall not choose a President whenever the right of choice shall devolve upon them, before the fourth day of March next following, then the Vice-President shall act as President, as in the case of the death or other constitutional disability of the President.) (The words in parentheses were superseded by Amendment XX, section 3.)* The person having the greatest number of votes as Vice-President, shall be the Vice-President, if such number be a majority of the whole number of Electors appointed, and if no person have a majority, then from the two highest numbers on the list, the Senate shall choose the Vice-President; a quorum for the purpose shall consist of two-thirds of the whole number of Senators, and a majority of the whole number shall be necessary to a choice. But no person constitutionally ineligible to the office of President shall be eligible to that of Vice-President of the United States.

THE RECONSTRUCTION AMENDMENTS

(Amendments XIII, XIV, and XV are commonly known as the Reconstruction Amendments, inasmuch as they followed the Civil War, and were drafted by Republicans who were bent on imposing their own policy of reconstruction on the South. Post-bellum legislatures there—Mississippi, South Carolina, Georgia, for example—had set up laws which, it was charged, were contrived to perpetuate Negro slavery under other names.)

AMENDMENT XIII.
Slavery abolished.

(Proposed by Congress Jan. 31, 1865; ratification completed Dec. 18, 1865. The amendment, when first proposed by a resolution in Congress, was passed by the Senate, 38 to 6, on Apr. 8, 1864, but was defeated in the House, 95 to 66 on June 15, 1864. On reconsideration by the House, on Jan. 31, 1865, the resolution passed, 119 to 56. It was approved by President Lincoln on Feb. 1, 1865, although the Supreme Court had decided in 1798 that the President has nothing to do with the proposing of amendments to the Constitution, or their adoption.)

1. Neither slavery nor involuntary servitude, except as a punishment for crime whereof the party shall have been duly convicted, shall exist within the United States or any place subject to their jurisdiction.

2. Congress shall have power to enforce this article by appropriate legislation.

AMENDMENT XIV.
Citizenship rights not to be abridged.

(The following amendment was proposed to the Legislatures of the several states by the 39th Congress, June 13, 1866, and was declared to have been ratified in a proclamation by the Secretary of State, July 28, 1868.)

Constitution of the United States

(The 14th amendment was adopted only by virtue of ratification subsequent to earlier rejections. Newly constituted legislatures in both North Carolina and South Carolina (respectively July 4 and 9, 1868), ratified the proposed amendment, although earlier legislatures had rejected the proposal. The Secretary of State issued a proclamation, which, though doubtful as to the effect of attempted withdrawals by Ohio and New Jersey, entertained no doubt as to the validity of the ratification by North and South Carolina. The following day (July 21, 1868), Congress passed a resolution which declared the 14th amendment to be a part of the Constitution and directed the Secretary of State so to promulgate it. The Secretary waited, however, until the newly constituted Legislature of Georgia had ratified the amendment, subsequent to an earlier rejection, before the promulgation of the ratification of the new amendment.)

1. All persons born or naturalized in the United States, and subject to the jurisdiction thereof, are citizens of the United States and of the State wherein they reside. No State shall make or enforce any law which shall abridge the privileges or immunities of citizens of the United States; nor shall any State deprive any person of life, liberty, or property, without due process of law; nor deny to any person within its jurisdiction the equal protection of the laws.

2. Representatives shall be apportioned among the several States according to their respective numbers, counting the whole number of persons in each State, excluding Indians not taxed. But when the right to vote at any election for the choice of Electors for President and Vice-President of the United States, Representatives in Congress, the executive and judicial officers of a State, or the members of the Legislature thereof, is denied to any of the male inhabitants of such State, being twenty-one years of age, and, citizens of the United States, or in any way abridged, except for participation in rebellion, or other crime, the basis of representation therein shall be reduced in the proportion which the number of such male citizens shall bear to the whole number of male citizens twenty-one years of age in such State.

3. No person shall be a Senator or Representative in Congress, or Elector of President and Vice-President, or hold any office, civil or military, under the United States, or under any State, who, having previously taken an oath, as a member of Congress, or as an officer of the United States, or as a member of any State Legislature, or as an executive or judicial officer of any State, to support the Constitution of the United States, shall have engaged in insurrection or rebellion against the same, or given aid or comfort to the enemies thereof. But Congress may by a vote of two-thirds of each House, remove such disability.

4. The validity of the public debt of the United States, authorized by law, including debts incurred for payment of pensions and bounties for services in suppressing insurrection or rebellion, shall not be questioned. But neither the United States nor any State shall assume or pay any debt or obligation incurred in aid of insurrection or rebellion against the United States, or any claim for the loss or emancipation of any slave; but all such debts, obligations and claims, shall be held illegal and void.

5. The Congress shall have power to enforce, by appropriate legislation, the provisions of this article.

AMENDMENT XV.

Race no bar to voting rights.

(The following amendment was proposed to the legislatures of the several States by the 40th Congress, Feb. 26, 1869, and was declared to have been ratified in a proclamation of the Secretary of State, Mar. 30, 1870.)

1. The right of citizens of the United States to vote shall not be denied or abridged by the United States or by any State on account of race, color, or previous condition of servitude.

2. The Congress shall have power to enforce this article by appropriate legislation.

AMENDMENT XVI.

Income taxes authorized.

(Proposed by Congress July 12, 1909; ratification declared by the Secretary of State Feb. 25, 1913.)

The Congress shall have power to lay and collect taxes on incomes, from whatever source derived, without apportionment among the several States, and without regard to any census or enumeration.

AMENDMENT XVII.

United States Senators to be elected by direct popular vote.

(Proposed by Congress May 13, 1912; ratification declared by the Secretary of State May 31, 1933.)

1. The Senate of the United States shall be composed of two Senators from each State, elected by the people thereof, for six years; and each Senator shall have one vote. The electors in each State shall have the qualifications requisite for electors of the most numerous branch of the State legislatures.

2. When vacancies happen in the representation of any State in the Senate, the executive authority of such State shall issue writs of election to fill such vacancies: Provided, That the Legislature of any State may empower the Executive thereof to make temporary appointments until the people fill the vacancies by election as the Legislature may direct.

3. This amendment shall not be so construed as to affect the election or term of any Senator chosen before it becomes valid as part of the Constitution.

AMENDMENT XVIII.

Liquor prohibition amendment.

(Proposed by Congress Dec. 18, 1917; ratification completed Jan. 16, 1919. Repealed by Amendment XXI, effective Dec. 5, 1933.)

(1. After one year from the ratification of this article the manufacture, sale, or transportation of intoxicating liquors within, the importation thereof into, or the exportation thereof from the United States and all territory subject to the jurisdiction thereof for beverage purposes is hereby prohibited.

(2. The Congress and the several States shall have concurrent power to enforce this article by appropriate legislation.

(3. This article shall be inoperative unless it shall have been ratified as an amendment to the Constitution by the Legislatures of the several States, as provided in the Constitution, within seven years from the date of the submission hereof to the States by the Congress.)

(The total vote in the Senates of the various States was 1,310 for, 237 against—84.6% dry. In the lower houses of the States the vote was 3,782 for, 1,035 against—78.5% dry.)

(The amendment ultimately was adopted by all the States except Connecticut and Rhode Island.)

AMENDMENT XIX.

Giving nationwide suffrage to women.

(Proposed by Congress June 4, 1919; ratification certified by Secretary of State Aug. 26, 1920.)

1. The right of citizens of the United States to vote shall not be denied or abridged by the United States or by any State on account of sex.

2. Congress shall have power to enforce this article by appropriate legislation.

AMENDMENT XX.

Terms of President and Vice President to begin on Jan. 20; those of Senators, Representatives, Jan. 3.

(Proposed by Congress Mar. 2, 1932; ratification completed Jan. 23, 1933.)

1. The terms of the President and Vice President shall end at noon on the 20th day of January, and the terms of Senators and representatives at noon on the 3rd day of January, of the years in which such terms would have ended if this article had not been ratified; and the terms of their successors shall then begin.

2. The Congress shall assemble at least once in every year, and such meeting shall begin at noon on the 3rd day of January, unless they shall by law appoint a different day.

3. If, at the time fixed for the beginning of the term of the President, the President elect shall have died, the Vice President elect shall become President. If a President shall not have been chosen before the time fixed for the beginning of his term, or if the President elect shall have failed to qualify, then the Vice President elect shall act as President until a President shall have qualified; and the Congress may by law provide for the case wherein neither a President elect nor a Vice President elect shall haved qualified,

Constitution of the United States

declaring who shall then act as President, or the manner in which one who is to act shall be selected, and such person shall act accordingly until a President or Vice President shall have qualified.

4. The Congress may by law provide for the case of the death of any of the persons for whom the House of Representatives may choose a President whenever the right of choice shall have devolved upon them, and for the case of the death of any of the persons from whom the Senate may choose a Vice President whenever the right of choice shall have devolved upon them.

5. Sections 1 and 2 shall take effect on the 15th day of October following the ratification of this article (Oct., 1933).

6. This article shall be inoperative unless it shall have been ratified as an amendment to the Constitution by the Legislatures of three-fourths of the several States within seven years from the date of its submission.

AMENDMENT XXI.

Repeal of Amendment XVIII.

(Proposed by Congress Feb. 20, 1933; ratification completed Dec. 5, 1933.)

1. The eighteenth article of amendment to the Constitution of the United States is hereby repealed.

2. The transportation or importation into any State, Territory, or Possession of the United States for delivery or use therein of intoxicating liquors, in violation of the laws thereof, is hereby prohibited.

3. This article shall be inoperative unless it shall have been ratified as an amendment to the Constitution by conventions in the several States, as provided in the Constitution, within seven years from the date of the submission hereof to the States by the Congress.

AMENDMENT XXII.

Limiting Presidential terms of office.

(Proposed by Congress May 24, 1947; ratification completed Feb. 27, 1951.)

1. No person shall be elected to the office of the President more than twice, and no person who has held the office of President, or acted as President, for more than two years of a term to which some other person was elected President shall be elected to the office of President more than once. But this article shall not apply to any person holding the office of President when this article was proposed by the Congress, and shall not prevent any person who may be holding the office of President, or acting as President, during the term within which this article becomes operative from holding the office of President or acting as President during the remainder of such term.

2. This article shall be inoperative unless it shall have been ratified as an amendment to the Constitution by the Legislatures of three-fourths of the several States within seven years from the date of its submission to the States by the Congress.

AMENDMENT XXIII.

Presidential vote for District of Columbia.

(Proposed by Congress June 16, 1960; ratification completed Mar. 29, 1961.)

1. The District constituting the seat of Government of the United States shall appoint in such manner as the Congress may direct:

A number of electors of President and Vice President equal to the whole number of Senators and Representatives in Congress to which the District would be entitled if it were a State, but in no event more than the least populous State; they shall be in addition to those appointed by the States, but they shall be considered, for the purposes of the election of President and Vice President, to be electors appointed by a State; and they shall meet in the District and perform such duties as provided by the twelfth article of amendment.

2. The Congress shall have power to enforce this article by appropriate legislation.

AMENDMENT XXIV.

Barring poll tax in federal elections.

(Proposed by Congress Aug. 27, 1962; ratification completed Jan. 23, 1964.)

1. The right of citizens of the United States to vote in any primary or other election for President or Vice President, for electors for President or Vice President, or for Senator or Representative in Congress, shall not be denied or abridged by the United States or any State by reason of failure to pay any poll tax or other tax.

2. The Congress shall have power to enforce this article by appropriate legislation.

AMENDMENT XXV.

Presidential disability and succession.

(Proposed by Congress July 6, 1965; ratification completed Feb. 10, 1967.)

1. In case of the removal of the President from office or of his death or resignation, the Vice President shall become President.

2. Whenever there is a vacancy in the office of the Vice President, the President shall nominate a Vice President who shall take office upon confirmation by a majority vote of both houses of Congress.

3. Whenever the President transmits to the President pro tempore of the Senate and the Speaker of the House of Representatives his written declaration that he is unable to discharge the powers and duties of his office, and until he transmits to them a written declaration to the contrary, such powers and duties shall be discharged by the Vice President as Acting President.

4. Whenever the Vice President and a majority of either the principal officers of the executive departments or of such other body as Congress may by law provide, transmit to the President pro tempore of the Senate and the Speaker of the House of Representatives their written declaration that the President is unable to discharge the powers and duties of his office, the Vice President shall immediately assume the powers and duties of the office as Acting President.

Thereafter, when the President transmits to the President pro tempore of the Senate and the Speaker of the House of Representatives his written declaration that no inability exists, he shall resume the powers and duties of his office unless the Vice President and a majority of either the principal officers of the executive department or of such other body as Congress may by law provide, transmit within four days to the President pro tempore of the Senate and the Speaker of the House of Representatives their written declaration that the President is unable to discharge the powers and duties of his office. Thereupon Congress shall decide the issue, assembling within forty-eight hours for that purpose if not in session. If the Congress, within twenty-one days after receipt of the latter written declaration, or, if Congress is not in session, within twenty-one days after Congress is required to assemble, determines by two-thirds vote of both houses that the President is unable to discharge the powers and duties of his office, the Vice President shall continue to discharge the same as Acting President; otherwise, the President shall resume the powers and duties of his office.

AMENDMENT XXVI.

Lowering voting age to 18 years.

(Proposed by Congress Mar. 8, 1971; ratification completed July 1, 1971.)

1. The right of citizens of the United States, who are 18 years of age or older, to vote shall not be denied or abridged by the United States or any state on account of age.

2. The Congress shall have the power to enforce this article by appropriate legislation.

WEIGHTS AND MEASURES

Troy Weight

Used for weighing gold, silver and jewels.
3.086 grains = 1 carat.   20 pwts. = 1 ounce.
24 grains = 1 pwt.   12 ounces = 1 pound.

Apothecaries' Weight

The ounce and pound in this are the same as in troy weight.
20 grains = 1 scruple.   8 drams = 1 ounce.
3 scruples = 1 dram.   12 ounces = 1 pound.

Avoirdupois Weight

27¹¹⁄₃₂ grains = 1 dram. 4 quarters = 1 cwt.
16 drams = 1 ounce.   2,000 lbs. = 1 short ton.
16 ounces = 1 pound.   2,240 lbs. = 1 long ton.
25 pounds = 1 quarter.

Dry Measure

2 pints = 1 quart.   4 pecks = 1 bushel.
8 quarts = 1 peck.   36 bushels = 1 chaldron.

Liquid Measure

4 ounces = 1 gill.   4 quarts = 1 gallon.
4 gills = 1 pint.   31½ gallons = 1 barrel.
2 pints = 1 quart.   2 barrels = 1 hogshead.

Time Measure

60 seconds = 1 minute. 24 hours = 1 day.
60 minutes = 1 hour.   7 days = 1 week.
28, 29, 30 or 31 days = 1 calendar month.
365 days = 1 year.   366 days = 1 leap year.

Linear Measure

12 inches = 1 foot.   40 rods = 1 furlong.
3 feet = 1 yard.   8 furlongs = 1 sta. mile.
5½ yards = 1 rod.   3 miles = 1 league.

Cloth Measure

2¼ inches = 1 nail.   4 quarters = 1 yard.
4 nails = 1 quarter.

Square Measure

144 sq. inches = 1 sq. ft.   40 sq. rds. = 1 rood.
9 sq. ft. = 1 sq. yard.   4 roods = 1 acre.
30¼ sq. yds. = 1 sq. rd.   640 acres = 1 sq. mile.

Surveyors' Measure

7.92 inches = 1 link.   4 rds. = 1 chain.
25 links = 1 rod.
10 sq. chains or 160 sq. rods = 1 acre.
640 acres = 1 sq. mile.
36 sq. miles (6 smiles sq.) = 1 township.

Cubic Measure

1,728 cu. in. = 1 cu. ft.128 c. f. = 1 cord (wood)
27 cubic ft. = 1 cu. yd.   40 c. f. ¼ 1 ton (shpg.)
2,150.42 cubic inches = 1 standard bushel.
231 cubic inches = 1 standard gallon.
1 cubic ft. = about ⅘ of a bushel.

pwt = pennyweight.   cwt = hundredweight.   sta = statute.

METRIC EQUIVALENTS

Linear Measure

1 centimeter = 0.3937 in.   1 kilometer = 0.62137 mile.
1 decimeter = 3,937 in. = 0.328 feet.   1 in. = 2.54 centimeters.
1 ft. = 3.048 decimeters.
1 meter = 39.37 inches = 1.0936 yards.   1 yd. = 0.9144 meter.
1 rod = 0.5029 dekameter.
1 dekameter = 1.9844 rods.   1 mile = 1.6093 kilometers.

Square Measure

1 sq. centimeter = 0.1550 sq. in.   1 sq. inch = 6.452 sq. centimeters.
1 sq. decimeter = 0.1076 sq. ft.   1 sq. ft. = 9.2903 sq. decimeters.
1 sq. meter = 1.196 sq. yds.   1 sq. yd. = 0.8361 sq. meter.
1 are = 3.954 sq. rds.   1 sq. rd. = 0.2529 are.

1 hectare = 2.47 acres.   1 acre = 0.4047 hectare.
1 sq. kilometer = 0.386 sq. m.   1 sq. m. = 2.59 square kilometers.

Weights

1 gram = 0.03527 oz.   1 oz. = 28.35 grams.
1 kilogram = 2.2046 lbs.   1 lb. = 0.4536 kilogram.
1 metric ton = 1.1023 English ton.   1 English ton = 0.9072 metric ton.

Approximate Metric Equivalents

1 decimeter = 4 inches. 1 liter = 1.06 qts. liquid, 0.9 qt. dry.
1 meter = 1.1 yards.
1 kilometer = ⅝ of a mile.   1 hektoiler = 2½ bushels.
1 hectare = 2½ acres.   1 kilogram = 2⅕ lbs.
1 stere. or cu. meter = ¼ of a cord.   1 metric ton = 2,200 lbs.

KITCHEN WEIGHTS, MEASURES

Usual Weights and Measures

1 tablespoonful = 1 fl. ounce
4 large tablespoonsful = ½ gill
1 teacup = 1 gill
1 common sized tumbler = ½ pint
2 cups = 1 pint
2 pints = 1 quart
1 tablespoonful = ½ ounce
1 large wine glass = 2 ounces
8 quarts = 1 peck
4 cups flour = 1 pound
2 cups solid butter = 1 pound
4 quarts = 1 gallon
2 cups granulated sugar = 1 pound
3 cups cornmeal = 1 pound
2⅔ cups brown sugar = 1 pound
2 cups solid meat = 1 pound
2⅔ cups powdered sugar = 1 pound
16 ounces = 1 pound
2 tablespoons butter, sugar, salt = 1 ounce
4 tablespoons flour = 1 ounce
16 tablespoonsful = 1 cupful
60 drops = 1 teaspoonful
8 saltspoonsful = 1 teaspoonful
3 teaspoonsful = 1 tablespoonful
4 tablespoonsful = ¼ cupful
1 cup shelled almonds = ¼ pound
¼ pound cornstarch = 1 cupful

Approximate Cup Measures

1 cup granulated sugar = ½ pound
1 cup butter = ½ pound
1 cup lard = ½ pound
1 cup flour = ¼ pound
1 cup rice = ½ pound
1 cup cornmeal = 5 ounces
1 cup raisins (stemmed) = 6 ounces
1 cup currants (cleaned) = 6 ounces
1 cup bread crumbs (stale) = 2 ounces
1 cup chopped meat = ½ pound
3 teaspoons = 1 tablespoon
½ fluid ounce = 1 tablespoon
16 tablespoons = 1 cup
2 gills = 1 cup
½ liquid pint = 1 cup
8 fluid ounces = 1 cup
1 liquid pint = 2 cups
16 fluid ounces = 2 cups

CHEMICAL TABLE OF ELEMENTS

Chemical element	Symbol	Atomic number	Relative atomic mass	Year discov.	Discoverer
Actinium	Ac	89	227	1899	Debierne
Aluminum	Al	13	26.9815	1825	Oersted
Americium	Am	95	243	1944	Seaborg, et al.
Antimony	Sb	51	121.75	1450	Valentine
Argon	Ar	18	39.948	1894	Rayleigh, Ramsay
Arsenic	As	33	74.9216	13th c.	Albertus Magnus
Astatine	At	85	210	1940	Corson, et al.
Barium	Ba	56	137.34	1808	Davy
Berkelium	Bk	97	249	1949	Thompson, Ghiorso, Seaborg
Beryllium	Be	4	9.0122	1798	Vauquelin
Bismuth	Bi	83	108.980	15th c.	Valentine
Boron	B	5	10.811	1808	Gay-Lussac, Thenard
Bromine	Br	35	79.904	1826	Balard
Cadmium	Cd	48	112.40	1817	Stromeyer
Calcium	Ca	20	40.08	1808	Davy
Californium	Cf	98	251	1950	Thompson, et al.
Carbon	C	6	12.01115	B.C.	
Cerium	Ce	58	140.12	1803	Klaproth
Cesium	Cs	55	132.905	1860	Bunsen, Kirchhoff
Chlorine	Cl	17	35.453	1774	Scheele
Chromium	Cr	24	51.996	1797	Vauquelin
Cobalt	Co	27	58.9332	1735	Brandt
Copper	Cu	29	63.546	B.C.	
Curium	Cm	96	247	1944	Seaborg, James, Ghiorso
Dysprosium	Dy	66	162.50	1886	Boisbaudran
Einsteinium	Es	99	254	1952	Ghiorso, et al.
Erbium	Er	68	167.26	1843	Mosander
Europium	Eu	63	151.96	1901	Demarcay
Fermium	Fm	100	257	1953	Ghiorso, et al.
Fluorine	F	9	18.9984	1771	Scheele
Francium	Fr	87	223	1939	Perey
Gadolinium	Gd	64	157.25	1886	Marignac
Gallium	Ga	31	69.72	1875	Boisbaudran
Germanium	Ge	32	72.59	1886	Winkler
Gold	Au	79	196.967	B.C.	
Hafnium	Hf	72	178.49	1923	Coster, Hevesy
Hahnium	Ha	105	262	1970	Ghiorso, et al.
Helium	He	2	4.0026	1868	Janssen, Lockyer
Holmium	Ho	67	164.930	1878	Soret, Delafontaine
Hydrogen	H	1	1.00797	1766	Cavendish
Indium	In	49	114.82	1863	Reich, Richter
Iodine	I	53	126.9044	1811	Courtois
Iridium	Ir	77	192.2	1804	Tennant
Iron	Fe	26	55.847	B.C.	
Krypton	Kr	36	83.80	1898	Ramsay, Travers
Lanthanum	La	57	138.91	1839	Mosander
Lawrencium	Lr	103	260	1961	Ghiorso, T. Sikkeland, A.E. Larsh, and R.M. Latimer

Chemical Table

Chemical element	Symbol	Atomic number	Relative atomic mass	Year discov.	Discoverer
Lead	Pb	82	207.19	B.C.	
Lithium	Li	3	6.939	1817	Arfvedson
Lutetium	Lu	71	174.97	1907	Welsbach, Urbain
Magnesium	Mg	12	24.312	1829	Bussy
Manganese	Mn	25	54.9380	1774	Gahn
Mendelevium	Md	101	258	1955	Ghiorso, et al.
Mercury	Hg	80	200.59	B.C.	
Molybdenum	Mo	42	95.94	1782	Hjelm
Neodymium	Nd	60	144.24	1885	Welsbach
Neon	Ne	10	20.183	1898	Ramsay, Travers
Neptunium	Np	93	237	1940	McMillan, Abelson
Nickel	Ni	28	58.71	1751	Cronstedt
Niobium	Nb	41	92.906	1801	Hatchett
Nitrogen	N	7	14.0067	1772	Rutherford
Nobelium	No	102	258	1958	Ghiorso, et al.
Osmium	Os	76	190.2	1804	Tennant
Oxygen	O	8	15.9994	1774	Priestley, Scheele
Palladium	Pd	46	106.4	1803	Wollaston
Phosphorus	P	15	30.9738	1669	Brand
Platinum	Pt	78	195.09	1735	Ulloa
Plutonium	Pu	94	242	1940	Seaborg, et al.
Polonium	Po	84	210	1898	P. and M. Curie
Potassium	K	19	39.102	1807	Davy
Praseodymium	Pr	59	140.907	1885	Welsbach
Promethium	Pm	61	147	1945	Glendenin, Marinsky, Coryell
Protactinium	Pa	91	231	1917	Hahn, Meitner
Radium	Ra	88	226	1898	P. & M. Curie, Bermont
Radon	Rn	86	222	1900	Dorn
Rhenium	Re	75	186.2	1925	Noddack, Tacke, Berg
Rhodium	Rh	45	102.905	1803	Wollaston
Rubidium	Rb	37	85.47	1861	Bunsen, Kirchhoff
Ruthenium	Ru	44	101.07	1845	Klaus
Rutherfordium	Rf	104	261	1969	Ghiorso, et al.
Samarium	Sm	62	150.35	1879	Boisbaudran
Scandium	Sc	21	44.956	1879	Nilson
Selenium	Se	34	78.96	1817	Berzelius
Silicon	Si	14	28.086	1823	Berzelius
Silver	Ag	47	107.868	B.C.	
Sodium	Na	11	22.9898	1807	Davy
Strontium	Sr	38	87.62	1790	Crawford
Sulfur	S	16	32.064	B.C.	
Tantalum	Ta	73	180.948	1802	Ekeberg
Technetium	Tc	43	99	1937	Perrier and Segre
Tellurium	Te	52	127.60	1782	Von Reichenstein
Terbium	Tb	65	158.924	1843	Mosander
Thallium	Tl	81	204.37	1861	Crookes
Thorium	Th	90	232.038	1828	Berzelius
Thulium	Tm	69	168.934	1879	Cleve
Tin	Sn	50	118.69	B.C.	
Titanium	Ti	22	47.90	1791	Gregor
Tungsten (Wolfram)	W	74	183.85	1783	d'Elhujar
Uranium	U	92	238.03	1789	Klaproth

Chemical Table

Chemical element	Symbol	Atomic number	Relative atomic mass	Year discov.	Discoverer
Vanadium	V	23	50.942	1830	Sefstrom
Xenon	Xe	54	131.30	1898	Ramsey, Travers
Ytterbium	Yb	70	173.40	1878	Marignac
Yttrium	Y	39	88.905	1794	Gadolin
Zinc	Zn	30	65.37	B.C.	
Zirconium	Zr	40	91.22	1789	Klaproth